Cases to Accompany *Contemporary Strategy Analysis*, Fifth Edition

Robert M. Grant

Georgetown University

Blackwell Publishing

BLACKWELL PUBLISHING
350 Main Street, Malden, MA 02148-5020, USA
108 Cowley Road, Oxford OX4 1JF, UK
550 Swanston Street, Carlton, Victoria 3053, Australia

First published as *Cases in Contemporary Strategy Analysis*, 1996 by Blackwell Publishers Ltd
Second edition published 1999
Third edition published 2003
First published as *Cases to Accompany* Contemporary Strategy Analysis, *Fifth Edition* in 2005
by Blackwell Publishing Ltd

Library of Congress Cataloging-in-Publication Data

Grant, Robert M., 1948–
Cases to accompany Contemporary strategy analysis fifth edition / Robert M. Grant.
p.   cm.
Written to accompany the 5th ed. of Contemporary strategy analysis, published in 2005.
Includes bibliographical references
ISBN 1-4051-2408-3 (pbk. : alk. paper)
1. Strategic planning—Case studies.   2. Decision making—Case studies.
I. Grant, Robert M., 1948– Contemporary strategy analysis.
II. Title.

HD30.28.G716 2004
658.4′012—dc22
2004012923

A catalogue record for this title is available from the British Library.

Set in 10/12 Photina
by SNP Best-set Typesetter Ltd, Hong Kong
Printed and bound in the United Kingdom
by TJ International, Padstow, Cornwall

The publisher's policy is to use permanent paper from mills that operate a sustainable
forestry policy, and which has been manufactured from pulp processed using acid-free and
elementary chlorine-free practices. Furthermore, the publisher ensures that the text paper
and cover board used have met acceptable environmental accreditation standards.

For further information on
Blackwell Publishing, visit our website:
www.blackwellpublishing.com

Contents

Madonna Ciccone has been one of the world's leading female entertainers for more than two decades. Madonna shows an inexhaustible capacity to defy changes in style and her own aging by continually reinventing herself. What can we learn from Madonna's remarkable career about the nature of strategy and the foundations of success?

In February 1999 Ng Kwan Cheong took over as the seventh CEO of Laura Ashley Holdings since the death of its founder in 1985. During this period, the company's performance had been mostly downhill. Cheong faces a critical situation: despite several years of cost cutting and restructuring, sales were declining and operating losses were mounting. Cheong must determine the sources of Laura Ashley's problems, and determine what can be done to stem the losses and protect the interests of Laura Ashley's long-suffering shareholders.

Having survived the aftermath of the terrorist hijackings of September 11, 2001, the US airline industry spent 2002 and 2003 struggling with the problem of excess capacity. As the airlines return to greater normalcy, their attention shifts to the longer term problems of the industry. Since deregulation in 1978, the airlines have been the least profitable of any major industry sector in the US. Given the structure of the industry, the characteristics of the product, and the success of the low-cost carriers, is the airline doomed to price wars and low profits, or are there strategies that offer the airline companies opportunities for improving their dismal financial performance?

was to maintain its superior performance against powerful rivals such as Honda and BMW, it would need to carefully examine the sources of its competitive advantage and implement strategies that would broaden and deepen these competitive advantages in order to meet the challenges of a changing market and competitive environment.

13 Birds Eye and the UK Frozen Food Industry *(Robert M. Grant)* 266

During the 1950s and 1960s, Unilever subsidiary, Birds Eye Foods, used a strategy of vertical integration to develop and dominate the British frozen foods industry. Birds Eye invested heavily in a national network of cold stores and refrigerated trucks, while securing supplies of fresh produce through contracts with growers and fishing boats. As the industry developed, Birds Eye lost market share to competitors that concentrated on a few stages of the value chain, outsourcing most other activities. As the industry evolved, the competitive advantages that Birds Eye had derived from vertical integration were transformed into disadvantages.

14 Euro Disney: From Dream to Nightmare, 1987–94 *(Robert M. Grant)* 279

Walt Disney's decision to build a European theme park was its biggest and riskiest project since the Epcot Center a decade earlier. What considerations explained the complex mode of entry that Disney adopted for Euro Disney? Unlike Tokyo Disneyland in which Disney held no equity stake and the US parks that were wholly owned, Disney held minority ownership in Euro Disney as well as licensing and management contracts. However, despite the careful planning of the project, huge losses at Euro Disney were forcing Disney to reassess its strategy.

15 Richard Branson and the Virgin Group of Companies in 2004 *(Robert M. Grant)* 308

Between 1998 and 2004, Richard Branson's Virgin group of companies had diversified into an ever-widening set of industries – wireless telephony, financial services, an Australian airline, soft drinks, and Internet sales of cars, motorcycles, and wine. At the same time, many of his larger business were making losses, and cash flow was strongly negative. Branson needs to consider the strategy of his loose-knit corporate empire. What is the logic, if any, that links together this motley collection of business ventures? Should any of the businesses be divested? What criteria should be used to guide future diversification? Are changes needed in the financial and management structure of the group?

16 General Electric: Life After Jack *(Robert M. Grant)* 336

In summer 2001, Jeffrey Immelt succeeded Jack Welch as chairman and CEO of General Electric. Following "the greatest CEO of the twentieth century" at the "world's most admired company" was a difficult act to follow, and during his first ten months in the job GE's shares fell by almost half their value. During two decades as CEO of GE, Welch had transformed GE's portfolio of businesses, and created the organizational structure, management systems, and corporate culture that could mesh the benefits of massive size and diversity with the agility and entrepreneurial drive of much small enterprises. Where was Immelt to go from here?

AES was like no other company in the electricity-generation industry. It was committed to social responsibility and providing fun for employees. Its management system had been described as "empowerment gone mad." During the 1990s it had enjoyed phenomenal growth and startling shareholder returns. By early 2002, it was reeling from the effects of Enron, the California power crisis, and overseas difficulties – notably in Venezuela, Brazil, Argentina, and Pakistan. Should AES maintain its commitment to social responsibility, fun, and employee empowerment, or is a more conventional approach to management needed?

Preface

This new edition of *Cases in Contemporary Strategy Analysis* has been retitled *Cases to Accompany* Contemporary Strategy Analysis, *Fifth Edition* to more clearly indicate that the cases have been written and selected to complement the new edition of the textbook (Robert M. Grant, *Contemporary Strategy Analysis*, 5th edn, also recently published by Blackwell Publishing).

This casebook embodies a continuing commitment to examining the concepts and techniques of business strategy analysis in the context of real business situations. Thus, each of the cases presents issues that illuminate the ideas, concepts, and analytical techniques covered in one or more chapters of the textbook. For example: Cases Three and Four ("The US Airline Industry in 2004" and "Ford and the World Automobile Industry") are industry cases that allow readers to apply the tools of industry and competitive analysis discussed in chapters 3 and 4 of the textbook; Cases Five and Six ("Wal-Mart Stores Inc., March 2004" and "Eastman Kodak: Meeting the Digital Challenge") are primarily cases in the analysis of resources and capabilities that apply the tools of textbook chapter 5.

The cases in this collection represent the challenges faced by managers at the beginning of a new century. Most of the cases relate to company situations from 2001 to 2004, though a few discuss situations further back in time. However, no matter how up to date at the time of writing, by the time the book reaches the market, the business environment of 2005 will be different from that which existed between 2001 and 2004. This use of teaching cases that refer to recent history rather than the immediate present is not an impediment. The challenge for students, and their instructors, is to address the business situation as it existed at the time of the case. The only danger here is that hindsight does not necessarily yield wisdom. We now know that Vodafone and other wireless telecom companies overpaid for their 3G licenses. However, the critical strategic issue is this: going back to 1999, look at the information available at the time and ask, "How much should the companies pay for these licenses?"

The cases outline situations where decision making is required: How can Laura Ashley avoid disaster? What can Wal-Mart do to sustain its competitive advantage into the future? How can Microsoft supplant Sony as leader of the worldwide market for video game consoles? Other cases focus more on gaining understanding of strategy formulation and the determinants of competitive advantage: How has a niche player like Harley-Davidson become one of the most profitable motorcycle companies in the world? What lessons can we learn from Kodak's difficulties in adjusting to the digital revolution in photography? By being more focused than the typical strategy cases, the cases are typically shorter than is normal for business strategy teaching cases. Brevity means also limits on the amount of information that is supplied to students. Does this mean that students should seek out additional information? Preferably not – the cases provide all the data needed to identify and analyze the key issues. More data permits more detailed analysis, but at the cost of slowing and overloading the decision process. For most companies strategic decisions must be taken with only a fraction of the relevant information available – events are moving too quickly to allow the luxury of extensive, in-depth research.

I hope you will find the cases instructive and enjoyable. I intend to continue updating the casebook regularly and I would appreciate any comments and suggestions that you have. I would also appreciate any suggestions for new cases that you might have.

Rob Grant
Washington, DC
grant@georgetown.edu

Acknowledgments

The editor and publishers gratefully acknowledge the following for permission to reproduce copyright material:

Stern Stewart & Co. for table 4.1 "Economic Value Added of major automobile producers," *Best of Times, Worst of Times*, Stern Stewart & Co., December 2000.

Wal-Mart for extracts from www.walmartstores.com, "Sam Walton's Three Basic Beliefs," "Exceeding Customer Expectation," "Helping People Make Difference," "Sam's Rules for Building a Business," "Sundown Rule." Reprinted by permission of Wal-Mart.

A. Bakhru and A. Brown for *On-line broking strategies: Merrill Lynch, Charles Schwab, and E*Trade*. London: City University Business School, 2002. Copyright © 2002 A. Bakhru and A. Brown. Reprinted by permission of the authors.

Christopher A. Bartlett for *EMI and the CT Scanner [A] and [B]*. Copyright © 1993 President and Fellows of Harvard College. Reprinted by permission of Harvard Business School Publishing.

C. Baden Fuller for table 12.4 "Shares of UK packaged grocery sales by type of retailer." From C. Baden Fuller, *Rising Concentration: The UK Grocery Trade 1970–82*, London Business School, 1984. Reprinted by permission of C. Baden Fuller.

Virgin Group of Companies for figure 15.1 and Virgin's Vision taken from Virgin Management Company. Reprinted by permission of The Virgin Group.

Noel Tichy and Ram Charan for extracts from interview with Jack Welch in *Harvard Business Review*. "Speed, simplicity, and self confidence: an interview with Jack Welch," *Harvard Business Review*, September/October 1989. Reprinted by permission of Harvard Business School Publishing.

The publishers apologize for any errors or omissions in the above list and would be grateful to be notified of any corrections that should be incorporated in the next edition or reprint of this book.

case one

Madonna

Robert M. Grant

■ THE STRUGGLE ■

In July 1978, shortly before her 20th birthday, Madonna Louise Ciccone arrived in New York City with $35 in her pocket. She had left Ann Arbor where she was majoring in dance at the University of Michigan. Madonna was raised in the suburbs of Detroit. The third of eight children, her mother had died when she was 6 years old. Her prospects in the world of show business looked poor. Apart from her training in dance, she had little musical background and no contacts.

Life in New York was a struggle. "I worked at Dunkin' Donuts, I worked at Burger King, I worked at Amy's. I had a lot of jobs that lasted one day. I always talked back to people and they'd fire me. I was a coat-check girl at the Russian Tea Room. I worked at a health club once a week."[1] She spent a few months training with the Alvin Ailey Dance Theater and had a succession of modeling engagements for photographers and artists. During 1979, Madonna explored a wider range of opportunities. With new boyfriend Dan Gilroy, his brother Ed, and bassist Angie Smit, "Breakfast Club" was formed, with Madonna sharing vocals and drums with Dan. For 6 months Madonna was dancer and backup singer to French singing star Patrick Hernandez, during which time she performed in Paris and around Europe and North Africa. In August 1979, Madonna was offered the lead role in underground movie director Stephen Lewicki's low-budget film *A Certain Sacrifice*.

After breaking up with Dan Gilmore, Madonna was nomadic, sleeping on the couches of various friends and acquaintances before finding a commercial loft in the garment district. "There was no hot water. There wasn't even a fucking shower."[2] "At one point I was living in a New York flophouse and eating out of garbage cans."[3]

In a new effort to form a band, Madonna invited her former Michigan boyfriend, Steve Bray, to New York. They moved into the Music Building – a converted 12-story building crammed with studios, rehearsal rooms, and striving, impoverished young bands. Together they worked on writing songs and developing their sound. The resulting rock band, "Emmy," made little impression, but Madonna maintained a continuous stream of calls to managers, agents, record companies, and club owners. Camille Barbone offered a management contract – but only for Madonna. However, Barbone was unable to deliver success fast enough for Madonna and after 18 months Madonna fired her.

Finding a Sound, Finding a Style

During 1981, Madonna's music and image moved in a new direction. Influenced by the emerging dance scene in New York, Madonna moved increasingly from Pretenders/ Pat Benatar rock to the dance music that was sweeping New York clubs. In addition to working with Steve Bray to develop songs and mix demo tapes, she worked on her image – a form of glam-grunge that featured multilayered, multicolored combinations of thrift-store clothing together with scarves and junk jewelry. She adopted "Boy Toy" as her "tag name" and prominently displayed it on her belt buckle. It was a look that she would continue to develop with the help of jewelry designer Maripole. Her trademark look of messy, badly dyed hair, neon rubber bracelets, black lace bras, white lace gloves, and chunky belt buckles would soon be seen on teenage girls throughout the world.

Madonna was quick to recognize the commercial implications of the new musical wave – it was the dance clubs that were key inroads and the DJs who were the key gate-keepers. Armed with her demo tapes, Madonna and her friends increasingly frequented the hottest dance clubs where they would make a splash with their flamboyant clothing and provocative dancing. At Danceteria, one of the staff referred to her as a "heat-seeking missile targeting the hottest DJs." There she attracted the attention of DJ Mark Kamins who introduced her to Mike Rosenblatt and Seymour Stein of Sire Records. A recording contract and $5,000 were soon hers.

The first release was a 12-inch single with different versions of *Everybody* on each side. The record gained extensive dance-club play. Madonna began working on her first album. Although she had promised both longtime friend and music collaborator Steve Bray and DJ Mark Kamins the job of producer, she dumped both in favor of Warner Records' house producer, Reggie Lucas. Together with Warner Records' national dance promoter, Bobby Shaw, Madonna began a relentless round of courting DJs and pushing her record for play time. Central to the promotion plan was New York's hottest DJ, John "Jellybean" Benitez, who Madonna began dating in November 1982.

Her second single, *Burning Up*, with *Physical Attraction* (written by Reggie Lewis) on the B-side, was released in March 1983. It too was a dance-club hit and bounded up the dance charts to number three. With full attention and full resources of Warner Brothers and a network of DJs, Madonna had most of the pieces she needed in place – but not quite. Early in 1983 she flew to Los Angeles to visit Freddie DeMann, then manager of megastar Michael Jackson. DeMann remembers the meeting vividly: "I was knocked off my feet. I've never met a more physical human being in my life." In a short time DeMann dropped Michael Jackson in favor of managing Madonna.

Breakthrough

The record album *Madonna* was released in July 1983. By the end of 1983, the record was climbing the US album charts supported by the success of single release *Holiday*. In April 1984, another single release from the album, *Borderline*, became Madonna's first top-10 hit. At Madonna's national TV debut on *American Bandstand*, presenter Dick Clark asked Madonna "What do you really want to do when you grow up?" "Rule the world," she replied.

Within little more than a year Madonna was partway there. The fall of 1984 saw Madonna filming in *Desperately Seeking Susan*. Although initially hired as support for the movie's star, Rosanna Arquette, Madonna soon turned the movie into a vehicle for herself. By the time the shooting was complete, it was essentially a movie about Madonna playing herself, wearing her own style of clothes, and featuring her own music. The release of the movie coincided with a surge of Madonna-mania. Her second album, *Like a Virgin*, had gone triple-platinum in February 1985, while the singles charts featured a succession of individual tracks from the album. Madonna's first concert tour was a sell-out. Her marriage to bad-boy actor Sean Penn on August 16, 1985 further reinforced her celebrity status. When Madonna took up residence in Los Angeles during 1985, she was already a star and seldom far from the popular press headlines.

■ FAME, FORTUNE, NOTORIETY ■

During the next two decades, little would come between Madonna and her quest for fame. Between 1986 and 1990, she released six record albums. The 16 single releases from these albums gave her a near-continuous presence in the charts including a remarkable seven number one hits.[4] In the process, Madonna rejected the industry's conventional wisdom of "Find a winning formula and stick to it." Madonna's career was a continuous experimentation with new musical ideas and new images, and a constant quest for new heights of fame and acclaim. Having established herself as the queen of popular music, Madonna did not stop there. By the end of the 1980s she was destined to be "the most famous woman on the planet."

Madonna in Charge

Behind Madonna's rags-to-riches story is her own drive, determination, and appetite for hard work. "I'm tough, I'm ambitious, and I know exactly what I want – and if that makes me a bitch, that's okay," she told the London *News of the World* newspaper in 1985. On the set of *Desperately Seeking Susan* she maintained a blistering pace. "During the shoot we'd often get home at 11:00 or 12:00 at night and have to be back at 6:00 or 7:00 the next morning. Half the time the driver would pick up Madonna at her health club. She'd get up at 4:30 in the morning to work out first."[5]

There was never any doubt as to who was in charge of managing and developing Madonna's career. While Madonna relied upon some of the best minds and strongest companies in the entertainment business, there was never any ambiguity as to who was calling the shots. In addition to Freddie DeMann as manager, Madonna hired top lawyer Paul Schindler to represent her business deals. Her swift exit from her marriage with Sean Penn further emphasized her unwillingness to allow messy personal relationships to compromise her career goals. When it came to her third album – *True Blue* – released in June 1986 – Madonna insisted on being co-producer.

The best evidence of her hands-on management style is the documentary of her 1990 "Blonde Ambition" tour, *Truth or Dare*. The tour itself was a masterpiece of the pop concert as multimedia show embracing music, dance, and theater. The tour's planning began in September 1989. Madonna was involved in every aspect of the show's design and planning, including auditioning dancers and musicians, planning, costume design, and choice of themes. For example, Madonna worked closely with Jean-Paul Gaultier on the metallic, cone-breasted costumes that became one of the tour's most vivid images. On the tour itself, the *Truth or Dare* movie revealed Madonna as both creative director and operations supremo. In addition to her obsessive attention to every detail of the show's production, she was the undisputed organizational leader responsible for building team spirit among the diverse group of dancers, musicians, choreographers, and technicians, motivating the troupe when times were tough; resolving disputes between her fractious and highly strung male dancers; and establishing the highest standards of commitment and effort.

The summer of 1990 marked new heights of international obsession with Madonna. The "Blonde Ambition" tour was the must-see concert of that summer in North America, Europe and Japan. The tour coincided with the release of *Dick Tracy*, the Disney movie that was a vehicle for the high-profile lovers – Madonna and Warren Beatty. The film did much to rectify a string of Hollywood flops and scathing reviews of Madonna's own acting capabilities. Madonna's portrayal of Breathless Mahoney exuded her natural talents for style and seductiveness and became her biggest box office hit to date, and allowed her to indulge in her seductiveness. In the September 4, MTV annual music awards, Madonna yet again stole the show with a version of her *Vogue* single in which she portrayed French queen, Marie Antoinette.

Fame and Controversy

From her initial launch into stardom, Madonna's fame was tinged with notoriety. From the early days of her singing career, her overt sexuality was reinforced by her "Boy Toy" moniker. This combined with her sexually audacious, expletive-laced talk and use of crucifixes as items of jewelry raised disquiet within conservative and religious circles. Madonna's explanation only added fuel to the fire: "Crucifixes are sexy because there's a naked man on them." With every video and interview, Madonna was pushing a little harder against the boundaries of acceptable language, behavior, and imagery. Her *Like a Prayer* album, released in March 1989 proved to be a landmark in this process.

Pepsi Cola saw the opportunity to piggy-back on the surge of Madonna-mania by making an advertising video based upon the album's title track *Like a Prayer*. Madonna received $5 million for appearing in the video. What Pepsi had not taken into account was that Madonna was making her own music video of *Like a Prayer* to accompany the launch of the record. The day after the first broadcast of the Pepsi commercial, Madonna's own *Like a Prayer* video appeared on MTV. The video was a stunning mixture of sex and religion that featured Madonna dancing in front of burning crosses, making love on an altar, and revealing stigmata on her hands. The video outraged many Christian groups and the American Family Association threatened to boycott Pepsi products. Pepsi pulled its Madonna commercial, leaving Madonna with $5 million in the bank.

The explicit sexuality of the "Blonde Ambition" tour and its mixing of sexual and religious imagery resulted in Madonna achieving new heights of controversy – and public awareness. In Toronto, city authorities threatened to cancel the show. The Vatican condemned the show as "blasphemous." Her *Justify My Love* video released in November 1990 set a new record for Madonna – it was banned by MTV on the basis of its inclusion of homosexuality, voyeurism, nudity, sado-masochism, and oral sex. Again, Madonna was quick to turn controversy into profit: as soon as MTV refused to air *Justify My Love*, the video was rush released for retail sale. The publicity generated helped the *Justify My Love* single to the top of the charts.

During the early 1990s, Madonna continued to break new ground in sexual explicitness. Her photographic "art" book *Sex* featured Madonna in an array of sexual poses. The book itself introduced several marketing and design innovations from its unusual size (14 by 11 inches), its stainless steel covers and spiral binding, its sale in sealed wrapping, and its inclusion of Madonna's latest CD, *Erotica*. And it was a smash hit. Despite its high price ($49.95 for 120 pages) the book sold half a million copies in its first week. The record too went beyond any of Madonna's prior albums in terms of the sexually explicit content of its lyrics and supporting videos.

■ EVITA ■

While Madonna has been compared to previous superstars and goddesses of sex and glamour – Greta Garbo, Marilyn Monroe, Mae West, Brigitte Bardot – she has gone further in creating a persona that transcends her work as an entertainer. All the prior-mentioned female superstars were defined by their movie roles. The same is true of the big names in popular music, from Lena Horne to Janet Jackson. Madonna achieved a status that was no longer defined by her work. By the 1990s, Madonna was no longer famous as a rock singer or an actress – she was famous for being Madonna. For the next decade she worked to reinforce this status. Strategically, superstar status has much to commend it. Joining the pantheon of superstars acts as insulation from comparison with lesser mortals. As her website proclaims, she is "icon, artist, provocateur, diva, and mogul."

In her acting roles the key has been to take roles which are primarily vehicles for Madonna to be Madonna. Her successes in *Desperately Seeking Susan* and *Dick Tracy* were the result of roles where Madonna could be herself. However, both these roles were to be eclipsed by Madonna's portrayal of Eva Peron in the movie version of the Andrew Lloyd Webber musical *Evita*. Madonna had coveted the role for years and mounted a vigorous campaign to gain the support of director Alan Parker and Argentine

President Carlos Menem. While in previous roles Madonna had been able to use her talents as a singer, a poser, a sharp talker, and a seductress, in *Evita* Madonna could present her own life. Like Madonna, Evita had working class origins, a burning ambition, and had used sex and shrewd judgement to become a legend in her time. The film, released in December 1996, was a huge commercial and critical success. As *Q* magazine's Paul Du Noyer remarked, "If ever there was an ideal vehicle for Madonna's dream of transcendent stardom, this must be it."[6]

■ MOTHERHOOD, AND MORE ■

During most of the filming of *Evita*, Madonna was coping with her pregnancy. On October 14, 1996, she gave birth to Lourdes Maria Ciccone Leon at the Good Samaritan Hospital in Los Angeles. The baby's father was Carlos Leon, Madonna's personal trainer.

In terms of her life, image, and career, motherhood was a major discontinuity for Madonna. The press began reporting a host of life style changes: Madonna abandoned pumping iron in favor of yoga, she had begun to study Kabbalah ("A mystical interpretation of the Old Testament," she explained), she developed a closer circle of women friends, she spent increasing amounts of time writing music, she became less available to the media. Her interviews were amazingly devoid of sex, expletives, and shock value. "I think [motherhood] made me face up to my more feminine side. I had a much more masculine view of the world. What I missed and longed for was that unconditional love that a mother gives you. And so, having my daughter is the same kind of thing. It's like that first, true, pure, unconditional love."[7]

The clearest revelation of these changes was in Madonna's new album, *Ray of Light*, which was unlike any previous Madonna album. Working with William Orbit, the album incorporated a host of new influences: electronic music; traditional Indian music; Madonna's thoughts about the troubles of the world and the hollowness of fame; Madonna's own emotional development and her reflection on her unhappy childhood. In performing tracks from the album both on TV and on video, Madonna revealed a series of entirely new looks including Madonna as Goth-Girl (black hair, black clothes, black nail polish), Madonna as Shiva (multi-armed with henna tattoos on her hands), Madonna as geisha (straight black hair, kimono, and white makeup).

The new persona was the most ambitious and risky reinvention of Madonna's career, insofar as it was the first that was not founded upon sexuality and sexual aggression. Yet this transformation was met with no loss of popularity or worldwide acclaim. *Ray of Light* hit number two on the album charts and went triple platinum (over 3 million copies) on the basis of US sales alone, and at the MTV Music Video Awards she walked away with a total of six awards followed by three Grammy Awards.

■ MADONNA AS INVESTOR AND BUSINESS MANAGER ■

Not only did Madonna maintain control over her own content; she increasingly wanted a cut in distribution too. In April 1992 she signed a $60 million deal with Time Warner,

Inc. The joint venture, Maverick Records, was a music production company (together with TV, video, and music publishing wings) that was to provide a vehicle for Madonna's creative and promotional talent. Warner Records provided distribution. Although Madonna remained contracted to Warner Records for her own recordings, Maverick offered an avenue for her to develop and promote other singers and musicians.

During the late 1990s her efforts became increasingly focused towards identifying and nurturing emerging young singers and musicians, relying upon her creative and promotional intuition and experience, the wealth of talented specialists and media moguls who were part of her personal networks, and, above all, her ability to open any door in the business. Among Maverick's early signings was Canadian singer/songwriter Alanis Morissette, whose *Jagged Little Pill* album sold over 30 million copies. Through Madonna's links with director Mike Myers, Maverick released the soundtrack for the Austin Powers movie *The Spy Who Shagged Me*. Other Maverick artists included William Orbit, Prodigy, Ben Jelen, Muse, the Deftones, Erasure, Tantric, and Michelle Branch. Madonna also teamed up with British comedian-rapper Ali G, and helped him to launch himself on to the US market.

Madonna's interest in new musicians and in developing and producing their music was linked closely to her own widening musical interests. Her involvement with William Orbit on *Ray of Light* was followed by increased interest both in electronic and world music, including collaboration with the French electro-boffin, Mirwais. But Madonna's interests also embraced more standard popular music. In February 2000, Madonna's recording of the 1971 hit *American Pie* became an international best-seller.

Madonna's business interests extended beyond records. Through a series of collaborative ventures, Madonna became involved in a series of movie, TV, and pop video productions. With her Maverick Records partner, Guy Oseary, Madonna set up Madguy Films. Among the Madguy projects were several television films based on music history and culture, including *The Dusty Springfield Story*. In collaboration with New Line Films, Madguy also produced the 2002 movie *Turn It Up* featuring the Fugee's Pras.

■ THE NEW DECADE ■

During the new millennium, neither Madonna's career nor her popularity showed much sign of flagging. In 2000 Madonna set up home in London with a new partner, the actor and director Guy Ritchie. In August, shortly before her 42nd birthday, Madonna gave birth to her second child, Rocco. In the following month, her new album, *Music*, was released. The album was an immediate hit, topping the album charts within two weeks. In October, the *Music* single from the album became her 12th number one single in the US. On December 22, Madonna and Ritchie were married at Dornoch Castle in Scotland.

After an 8-year lapse, 2001 marked Madonna's return to concert touring. The "Drowned World" tour opened in Europe with shows in Barcelona and Milan followed by a run of shows at London's Earls Court before moving on to its US leg. Like prior Madonna concert tours, the show was a sophisticated and meticulously planned multimedia event embracing music, light, video projection, elaborate dance scenes, and pure theater – including Madonna riding a mechanical bull. Observations of

Madonna's audience for the shows suggested that the adoring fans who bought tickets for Madonna's "Drowned World" concerts were not the same people who had attended her earlier tours – they were, for the most part, simply too young. Unlike the aging fans of aging rock stars from Bob Dylan to Tom Jones, Madonna's successive reinventions had been successful not just in renewing her appeal to existing fans, but in creating new audiences in entirely new generations, some of whom had not been born when she recorded her debut album.

With the 20th anniversary of Madonna's first album release, she celebrated the occasion by topping the album charts in March 2003 with her new release *American Life*. Outside of music her artistic efforts met less success. Her 2002 London stage performance in the leading role of the comedy *Up for Grabs* and her *Swept Away* movie co-starring with Guy Ritchie were both panned by the critics. These set-backs do little to dent Madonna's entry into new fields. During 2003 she published the first two in a series of children's books. The first, *The English Roses*, was printed in 42 languages and launched in 100 countries. As part of a deal with The Gap in which Madonna promoted Gap clothing, the book was distributed through Gap stores.

APPENDIX
Madonna's Biographical Timeline

1958: Born August 16 in Bay City, Michigan to Sylvio Ciccone (design engineer for Chrysler and General Motors) and Madonna Ciccone.

1964: Mother dies of breast cancer.

1973: Starts at Rochester Adams High School.

1976: Freshman at University of Michigan, Ann Arbor; majoring in drama.

1977: July: arrives in New York City with $35.
September: begins training with Alvin Ailey Dance Theater.

1979: Flies to Paris, becomes back-up singer for Patrick Hernandez.
Joins Dan and Ed Gilroy to form "Breakfast Club."
Lands part of Bruna in underground movie *A Certain Sacrifice*.

1980: Forms rock band "Emmy" with Steve Bray.

1982: Establishes friendship with DJ Mark Kamins.
Signs recording contract with Sire Records (division of Warner Brothers).
First record release, *Everybody*, goes to #3 in the dance charts.
Begins dating DJ John "Jellybean" Benitez.

1983: Second single, *Burning Up/Physical Attraction*, reaches #3 in dance charts.
Release of first record album, *Madonna*; first top ten hit, *Borderline*.
Persuades Freddie DeMann (Michael Jackson's manager) to become her manager.
Appears in the movie *Vision Quest*.

1984: TV appearance on *American Bandstand*.
Appears and performs on annual MTV Awards.
Release of second record album *Like A Virgin* (produced by Niles Rodgers); sells 7 million copies worldwide.
Begins work on major studio movie *Desperately Seeking Susan*.

1985: "Virgin" tour opens April 10 in Seattle.
Signs merchandising deal for official Madonna Boy-Toy clothing designs sold under the Wazoo label.
Appears in *Live Aid* charity concert (London/Philadelphia, July 13).
Marries Sean Penn.

1986: Releases *True Blue* album.
Shoots *Shanghai Surprise* with Sean Penn.
Establishes her own film production company, Siren Productions, backed by Universal Studios.

1987: "Who's That Girl" tour opens Osaka, Japan on June 14; closes in Turin, Italy. *Who's That Girl* album and film also released.

1989: Divorce with Sean Penn (January 10).
Signs contract with Pepsi to produce video commercial based upon *Like A Prayer*.
Pepsi pays Madonna $5 million.
Madonna's own video *Like A Prayer* creates storm of protest from Christian groups. Pepsi pulls its commercial after just one showing.
Releases *Like A Prayer* album.
Plays Breathless Mahoney in *Dick Tracy*, co-starring with Warren Beatty.
Begins affair with Warren Beatty.

1990: Album releases: *I'm Breathless* and *The Immaculate Collection*.
"Blonde Ambition" world concert tour kicks off in Tokyo, April 13. Shows in Toronto and Italy threatened with closure because of their explicit sexual content.
MTV refuses to screen Madonna's *Justify My Love* video.

1991: *Truth Or Dare* documentary of "Blonde Ambition" tour is released.
Appears in Woody Allen's *Shadows and Fog*.

1992: Grammy Award: Best Music Video (Long Form), *Madonna: Blonde Ambition World Tour Live*; award shared with Dave Mallet, Mark "Aldo" Miceli and Tony Eaton.
Release of photographic book *Sex*: sells 500,000 copies in first week; tops *New York Times* best-seller list.
Release of feature movie, *A League of Their Own*.
Madonna signs deal with Time Warner to create Maverick, her own record label.

1993: Movie releases: *Body Of Evidence* and *Dangerous Game*.

1994: *Bedtime Stories* album released.

1995: Releases *Something to Remember* album.
Movie releases include *Blue In The Face* and *Four Rooms*.

1996: Release of *Evita* in which Madonna plays Eva Peron. Wins Golden Globe Award for Best Actress in a Motion Picture (Musical or Comedy).
Also release of the movie *Girl 6*.
Gives birth to Lourdes Maria Ciccone Leon, October 14; father is Carlos Leon.

1997: Release of *Ray of Light* album, which in 1998 wins three Grammy Awards in the categories Dance Recording, Pop Album, and Music Video, and two MTV Video Music Awards.

1999: Grammy Award for *Beautiful Stranger* – best song written for a motion picture, television or other visual media (shared with William Orbit).
Release of movie *The Next Best Thing*.

2000: Son, Rocco Ritchie born August 11, 2000; father is actor/director Guy Ritchie.
Release of new album, *Music*.
Wins WIPO arbitration to gain control of Madonna.com domain name.
Marries Guy Ritchie at Dornoch Castle, Scotland.

2001: July–Sept. "Drowned World" concert tour kicks off in London prior to US.

2002: US release of movie *Swept Away* – goes direct to video in UK.

Lead role in London stage comedy *Up for Grabs*.

2003: Release of *American Life* album.

Publication of children's books *The English Roses* and *Mr Peabody's Apples*.

NOTES

1. Mark Bego, *Madonna: Blonde Ambition*, Cooper Square, New York, 2000, p. 46.
2. Bill Zehme, "Madonna: Candid about music, movies, and marriage," *Rolling Stone*, March 23, 1989.
3. Scott Cohen, "Confessions of Madonna," *Spin*, May 1985.
4. Her Billboard number ones during 1986–90 were: *Live to Tell* (1986), *Papa Don't Preach* (1986), *Open Your Heart* (1986), *Who's that Girl* (1987), *Like a Prayer* (1988), *Vogue* (1990), *Justify my Love* (1990).
5. Carl Arrington, "Madonna," *People*, March 11, 1985.
6. "Commanding" (Review of Evita), *Q*, December 1996.
7. Mary Murphy, "Madonna Confidential," *TV Guide*, April 11–17, 1998.

case two

Laura Ashley Holdings plc: The Battle for Survival

Robert M. Grant

On February 1, 1999 Ng Kwan Cheong took over as chief executive of Laura Ashley Holdings. Cheong was the company's seventh CEO since the death of Laura Ashley in 1985. Indeed, the life expectancy of Laura Ashley CEOs was shortening. John James was CEO from 1976 to 1990, Jim Maxmin from 1991 to 1993, A. Schouten from 1993 to 1995, Ann Iverson from 1995 to 1997, David Hoare from 1997 to 1998, while Cheong's immediate predecessor, Victoria Egan, had held the job a mere 5 months.

The top management turmoil coincided with a downward spiral for the company. In the financial year ended January 31 1999, sales were down 17 percent on the previous year, and the bottom line showed a net loss of £33 million. Ng Kwan Cheong was one of the senior management team of MUI Asia Group – a diversified Malaysian corporation that acquired 40 percent of Laura Ashley's equity in May 1998. He had been chief executive of MUI's retailing arm, Metrojaya Berhad, as well as holding board positions with several other Malaysian companies. However, despite a considerable senior management experience as well as familiarity with the UK (Cheong was a graduate of Middlesex University), little in his prior career could have prepared him for the situation at Laura Ashley. Despite a succession of restructurings and strategy redirections since 1990, the company continued on its downhill trajectory. Laura Ashley continued to bleed cash – cash outflow from operations was £11.4 million during the most recent financial year and MUI's cash injection of £43.5 million had been absorbed by debt repayment and covering operating losses. Many outside observers wondered whether there was any future for this icon of the 1970s, or whether Laura Ashley Holdings would follow its founder to the grave.

■ THE HISTORY ■

Development of the Business, 1953–1985

Bernard and Laura Ashley began designing and printing scarves and tablemats in their flat in Pimlico, London in 1953.[1] The products combined Laura's interest in color and design with Bernard's expertise in printing and dyeing. The product range was extended to include Victorian-styled aprons and linen kitchen towels. Laura's designs drew upon British traditional country styles, patterns, and colors. The designs were mainly floral, and the colors predominantly pastel. They sold mainly to department stores such as John Lewis, Heals, and Peter Jones. In 1957 the Ashleys opened a showroom in London, and in 1961 they transferred their production operations to a disused railway station at Carno, Wales, and used a flatbed printing process designed by Bernard.

The popularity of Laura's first dress designs encouraged the Ashleys to open a London retail store in Pelham Street, South Kensington in 1968. Although sales were initially slow, advertisements on the London Underground stimulated a surge of interest in Laura Ashley's dresses and fabrics. Throughout the early 1970s, the reaction against modernism, pop art, and other trends of the 1960s rekindled a strong interest in the rural English styles and traditions of the Victorian and Edwardian eras. Laura Ashley's positioning between English bourgeois tradition and hippie abandon, and her ability to evoke nostalgia for the comfort and simplicity of pre-industrial Britain placed her styles in the vanguard of contemporary fashion. During the early 1970s Laura Ashley expanded the company's product range from furnishing fabrics, clothes, and housewares into wallpaper and house paints. What Laura Ashley offered was a coordinated approach to home décor and clothing with a perfect matching of designs and colors across fabrics, wallpapers, paints, and ceramic tiles.

The company expanded internationally too, with shops in Geneva, Paris, Amsterdam, and Düsseldorf. In Canada, Australia, and Japan licenses were sold to local companies to open Laura Ashley stores. In 1974 Laura Ashley entered the US, initially by licensing McCall's Patterns of New York to distribute its fabrics, and then with an office and retail store in San Francisco.

The business was highly vertically integrated. By the beginning of the 1980s, almost all products were designed by a design team led by Laura and her son Nick (who became design director in 1982) and 85 percent of all products were manufactured either in the company's own plants or by subcontractors. The majority of sales were through Laura Ashley retail stores. The company became expert in the fast, flexible production of quality fabrics manufactured in small runs. By the early 1980s there were eight garment making-up plants close to Carno in Wales, a fabric plant in Dublin, and two plants in England making home furnishing products and made-to-measure curtains and blinds. Distribution from plants and warehouses to retail stores was done by the company's own transport division. Products for the North American stores were airfreighted weekly; others were manufactured under contract at a plant in Kentucky.

The distinctive design of Laura Ashley products was extended to the retail stores. The dark-green Laura Ashley storefronts were clearly recognizable in the high street, and the interiors with their wooden fittings projected an image of quality and homeli-

Classic & preppy ⇒ like Polo

ness. The company was an early adopter of electronic point-of-sale systems, which linked retail sales to inventory planning, distribution, and production planning. Laura Ashley also offered mail order sales.

The family ownership and management of the group was reflected in relationships with employees. There was a cooperative, non-hierarchical working environment with a high level of job security and generous employee benefits.

Continued growth encouraged the adoption of a divisional structure: in addition to design and production divisions, retailing was organized around separate divisions for the UK, Continental Europe, North America, and Asia-Pacific.

In November 1985, the company went public. The offer for 23 percent of Laura Ashley Holdings plc was oversubscribed 34 times. Just 1 month before the public offering, Laura Ashley died after a fall in her home. *The Economist* wrote:

> Her popularity lay in the taste she stamped on her international empire, not so much for the elegance and smartness as for the prettiness and comfort. Nobody was intimidated by the look or price of a Laura Ashley design. Her home furnishings offered a cheap and feminine alternative to the drab, the posh, and the sternly post-war Habitat Scandinavian. She made it possible to look smart without paying Liberty prices. Her company's success has been the acceptable face of British capitalism in the past two decades. She was deputy chairman to her husband and her power has been considerable. She prized the loyalty of her staff and cared for their welfare.

Expansion 1986–1989

Fueled with capital from the public offering, Laura Ashley Holdings launched a new phase of its growth. Between 1986 and 1989 a series of acquisitions extended the product range and geographical scope of the company. These included Sandringham Leather Goods Ltd, Bryant of Scotland (a knitwear company), Willis and Geiger (a US outdoor clothing company with both production facilities and retail outlets), and Penhaligons (an old-established producer of perfumes and toiletries).

The company also continued its internal expansion. In 1985 a 135,000 square foot textile factory in Wales was completed. This increased the company's production capacity by 50 percent. The new capacity was supported by heavy investment in a new computer-aided design system, computerized fabric-cutting equipment, and a computerized material-handling system.

Emerging Problems 1990–1991

The expansion of the late 1980s was followed by a deteriorating bottom line as the UK recession of 1989–92 coincided with a series of internal difficulties. Problems included:

- massive overproduction of Laura Ashley catalogs in 1989;
- losses at the Willis and Geiger subsidiary;
- delivery of the 1989 autumn range to the retail stores was 3 months late;
- manufacturing costs rose with the appreciation of the pound sterling;

Table 2.1 Laura Ashley Holdings plc: summary of selected financial data, 1989–1999 (£ million)

	Financial year to January 31										
	1999	1998	1997	1996	1995	1994	1993	1992	1991	1990	1989
Turnover	288.3	344.9	327.6	336.6	322.6	300.4	247.8	262.8	328.1	296.6	252.4
Operating (loss)/profit before exceptional items	(15.2)	(23.6)	14.8	9.1	4.1	2.3	1.1	(0.6)	3.4	n.a.	n.a.
Exceptional operating costs	(2.9)	(12.4)	(0.4)	0.1	(33.4)	–	–	–	–	–	–
Operating (loss)/profit	(16.6)	(36.0)	14.4	9.2	(29.3)	2.3	1.1	(0.6)	3.4	6.1	23.6
Income from associated cos.	(0.2)	0.5	2.1	2.0	1.5	1.8	1.5	1.9	0.1	(0.2)	42.0
Exceptional items	(13.8)	(11.4)	0.4	–	(1.0)	–	–	(8.1)	(2.6)	(3.1)	–
Net interest payable	(1.3)	(2.4)	(0.7)	(0.9)	(1.8)	(1.1)	(0.8)	(2.3)	(12.4)	(8.6)	(5.0)
(Loss)/profit before taxation	(31.9)	(49.3)	16.2	10.3	(30.6)	3.0	1.8	(9.1)	(11.5)	(4.7)	20.3
Taxation	(1.1)	–	(6.1)	(3.3)	(0.9)	(1.9)	(1.0)	–	2.5	(2.1)	(7.1)
(Loss)/profit after taxation	(33.0)	(49.3)	10.1	7.0	(31.5)	1.1	0.8	(9.1)	(9.0)	(6.8)	13.1
Dividends	–	–	(2.4)	(1.2)	–	(0.2)	(0.1)	(0.1)	(0.1)	(1.7)	(4.7)
Retained (loss)/profit	(33.0)	(49.3)	7.7	5.8	(31.5)	0.9	0.7	(9.2)	(9.1)	(9.8)	8.4
Fixed assets	22.0	42.2	49.5	45.2	48.3	71.7	66.3	60.5	67.1	81.5	80.2
Net current assets	36.7	27.6	49.7	27.0	43.7	50.2	53.9	52.8	66.9	n.a.	n.a.
Long-term creditors	(0.9)	(30.4)	(21.8)	(0.9)	(15.0)	(35.1)	(34.4)	(28.0)	(41.4)	3.5	44.7
Provisions for liabilities/charges	(27.4)	(19.7)	(7.3)	(8.3)	(21.3)	(0.7)	(0.3)	(0.5)	(0.4)	2.9	2.2
Net assets	30.4	19.7	70.1	63.0	55.7	86.1	85.5	84.8	92.2	72.9	79.8
Share capital	19.9	11.9	11.9	11.8	11.7	11.7	11.7	11.7	11.7	10.0	10.0
Reserves	10.5	7.8	58.2	51.2	44.0	74.4	73.8	73.1	80.5	n.a.	n.a.
Equity shareholders' funds	30.4	19.7	70.1	63.0	55.7	86.1	85.5	84.8	92.2	72.9	79.8
Employees											
Total	3,634	3,657	4,104	4,173	4,430	n.a.	n.a.	n.a.	7,800	8,350	8,100
Manufacturing	582	617	859	1,019	1,010	n.a.	n.a.	n.a.	n.a.	n.a.	n.a.
Retail	2,452	2,415	2,592	2,459	2,639	n.a.	n.a.	n.a.	n.a.	n.a.	n.a.
Administrative	600	625	653	695	781	n.a.	n.a.	n.a.	n.a.	n.a.	n.a.

n.a. = not available.
Source: Laura Ashley Holdings plc, Annual Reports.

- rising interest rates boosted borrowing costs;
- exceptional charges were incurred from the sale or closure of non-core businesses including Penhaligons, Bryant of Scotland, Sandringham Leather Goods, and the Units chain of stores;
- the closure or sale of several production plants.

As the company shifted from expansion to retrenchment, it simultaneously searched for a new design look that would be faithful to Laura Ashley values while appealing more to the 1990s consumer. Table 2.1 shows financial performance during the 1990s.

■ THE IVERSON ERA ■

In June 1995, Ann Iverson was appointed Laura Ashley's chief executive. Iverson was one of the most sought-after executives in the retail sector after a successful retailing career on both sides of the Atlantic. She had been a vice president at Bloomingdale's, the US department store, a senior vice president at Bonwit Teller, CEO of Kay-Bee Toys, and had led the turnaround of Mothercare, the British mother and baby chain. With an annual salary of £883,000, Iverson became one of the highest paid retail executives in Britain.

Iverson moved quickly to restructure Laura Ashley's manufacturing, purchasing, and merchandising. Processes were redesigned, decision-making was centralized, international procedures were standardized, unprofitable businesses sold, smaller shops closed, and cost controls tightened. In March 1996, Iverson outlined her strategy for the future (see exhibit 2.1).

Exhibit 2.1 Ann Iverson's Strategy

I was delighted to become Group Chief Executive in June 1995 because I saw a retail business that could be fixed and also a brilliant brand with great potential. However, it was a time of great unrest for the organization, as it was showing no signs of improvement or turnaround.

The restructuring program announced last year was needed for the business. With that said, there were many business issues this program did not address. It only looked at overhead costs, it had no retail focus, it identified no change to our business processes and nothing was mentioned about sales growth and improving gross margins. All of these elements are vital to the turnaround of this business and if not addressed could allow history to repeat itself.

When I joined the business I had many impressions that needed validation. I reacted from three different points of reference: as a customer, as a non-executive and finally as the new Group Chief Executive. I saw a business not led by a single point of view; we had multi-design, multi-buying, multi-merchandising and even multi-catalogues.

In other words, each market or business category was defining what they thought the Laura Ashley brand was all about. As you and I know, every successful brand has a single message consistently delivered to their customer. That was not the case at Laura Ashley.

I also found serious supply chain inefficiencies and, most importantly, shops that were too small to show the extensive range in garments and home furnishings. There were also no clear lines of accountability, which is an unproductive and demotivating culture to have. It doesn't allow hardworking people to really know what their job is, how they are going to be measured and where to go for answers.

So in my first three months we set about making things right. We consolidated design, buying and merchandising, the pivotal areas of our business, into our Fulham office.

We began the necessary changes in the buying process, reducing the width of the product ranges by 25% and also developing a common catalogue worldwide. We delivered the head count reduction that was identified in the restructuring program, changed and eliminated tasks and put the right structure in place. Simply said, we set about establishing a retail culture.

Additionally, I identified six key initiatives which were critical to the consolidation and turn-around of the Group. They have proved to be exactly the right priorities to have aggressively focused on for the second half of the financial year.

These initiatives are ongoing and I would like to describe them:

- *Product ranges and gross margins.* Improvement of product ranges and gross margins are the most important for topline growth. The key to this is modernizing the fashion offer in garments and expanding our strengths in home furnishings. The improved product offer in fashion will increase sales and reduce mark-downs and is absolutely essential for repositioning this international lifestyle brand. The home furnishings ranges are already very strong and offer the greatest opportunity for growth. They must be expanded, however, to reflect the developments in the market sector and realize the strength of the Laura Ashley brand.
- *Supply chain.* Development of efficient product sourcing is critical in achieving supply chain improvement. This will be accomplished by developing and working closely with our suppliers so they are more reactive to the needs of the business.
- *Manufacturing review.* A total review of manufacturing continues, within the context of the overall supply chain, focusing primarily on home furnishings where we produce 80% of our own product. It is essential that we ensure our factories are competitive as a supplier to a worldwide retailer.
- *Distribution.* In the area of distribution, our costs are well above industry standards. Work is being done to reduce these costs and we will begin to see these reductions coming through in the next financial year. We will strive to achieve best practice industry standards in this important supply chain category.
- *Shop portfolio.* The assessment of our shop portfolio with regard to both location and shop size is underway. Increasing the size of our shops is absolutely necessary to remain competitive in today's retail environment.
- *The US market.* And lastly, determining the potential of the US market. This market should be our greatest vehicle for topline growth and profit improvement. Our brand values, reaffirmed through customer research, show a potential audience of over 19 million female shoppers. But our shops are too small to even begin presenting the width of the range that supports customer perception and demand. We have started to change this and have already opened the first of our new shops, much larger in format, positioned in premier locations.

The strategy of the Laura Ashley brand is already clearly defined. We are the quintessential English company with a timelessness and spirit understood and embraced worldwide. Our research supports the brand values our customer identifies with: love of flowers, family, romanticism, freedom and simplicity and the tradition which directly relates to the enduring brand qualities and its uniqueness.

In the past the business has talked too much about strategy and not about results. It is time we delivered to our customers and shareholders. As a retailer I see clearly what needs to be done and how to do it.

The way forward continues to be about focus and implementation of the key initiatives which are fundamental to the Company's turnaround. Additionally, we have identified two new initiatives, namely: to establish an appropriate infrastructure for licensing, franchising and wholesaling and to build a new mail order business.

Source: "Chief Executive's Statement," *Laura Ashley Holdings plc Annual Report 1996*, London 1996.

Table 2.2 Laura Ashley Holdings plc: retail stores and floor space

Financial year to January 31:	Number of stores				Square footage (000s)			
	1999	1998	1997	1996	1999	1998	1997	1996
UK	234	237	189	174	587	561.5	441.8	394.1
North America	106	132	155	168	301	379.3	349.6	276.8
Continental Europe	69	72	74	76	112	114.1	115.9	117.7
Total	409	441	418	418	1000	1055.2	907.3	788.6

Source: Laura Ashley Holdings plc, Annual Reports 1996–9.

Iverson's first year at Laura Ashley was hailed by investors and industry observers as the long-awaited turnaround in the fortunes of the beleaguered group. *Business Week* enthused:

> Since becoming CEO of Laura Ashley Holdings, plc last July, Ann Iverson has replaced most of top management, cut the payroll, slashed costs, and unveiled an aggressive expansion plan in the US. "I'm the kind of person who has a steamroller behind her back," says Iverson, 52, who was recruited when shareholders were getting fed up. Now the market's applauding. On April 18, the company reported pretax income of $15.6 million for 1995, compared with a $46.5 million loss a year before. Since Iverson's appointment, Laura Ashley's stock has more than doubled . . . [but] no one knows yet if Iverson can solve the biggest problem: the apparel line with its signature floral prints and long, girlish dresses, is deeply unfashionable in the minimalist 1990s. . . . Iverson acknowledges that the company's Victorian look is dated, but cites recent research showing that the brand could appeal to 19 million women in America and Britain. She hopes the new designer she lured from Carole Little, Basha Cohen, will help freshen the line, but still keep the flowing romantic look. More important, she is betting that home furnishings will boost sales. The company's wallpaper, bedspreads, linens and curtains have proven much more resistant to fashion's whims than the frocks have.[2]

Even long-serving Laura Ashley executives were heartened by Iverson's clarity of vision and effective leadership. Visiting the first of the new-style, large-format Laura Ashley stores in the US (in North Carolina), Sir Bernard Ashley commented, "I almost cried, it was so marvelous."

During 1996, the company's capital expenditures increased as the number of stores and their average size increased. (Table 2.2 shows the expansion in US retail floor space.) However, any prospects of the new strategy delivering improved sale profit performance soon evaporated. Despite the emphasis on expansion in the US, North American sales fell during 1996. Then, in the spring of 1997, problems of poor coordination caused losses to mount. Overoptimistic sales projections for garments resulted in excessive inventories, while in home furnishings demand was also weak. Clearance sales during spring and early summer devastated margins. Table 2.3 shows sales by region.

In April 1996, John Thornton, a senior partner at Goldman Sachs, succeeded Lord Hooson as Chairman of the Board, and in November 1996, Ann Iverson was replaced as CEO by David Hoare, formerly a partner with Bain & Company and chief executive of the conglomerate Cope Allman plc.

Table 2.3   Laura Ashley Holdings plc: sales by product group and by region (£ million)

	UK and Ireland	North America	Continental Europe
Year to 1.31.99			
Garments	70.0	37.1	19.4
Furnishings	85.4	25.9	21.1
Year to 1.31.98			
Garments	85.9	57.0	23.0
Furnishings	90.0	34.5	24.7
Year to 1.31.97			
Garments	82.3	49.7	21.7
Furnishings	76.9	34.5	24.1
Year to 1.31.96			
Garments	80.8	60.1	28.6
Furnishings	67.4	35.9	31.9
Year to 1.31.95			
Garments	78.3	61.8	27.2
Furnishings	59.9	36.6	30.1

Source: Laura Ashley Holdings plc, Annual Reports 1996–9.

■ RETRENCHMENT: NOVEMBER 1996–APRIL 1998 ■

Almost immediately, David Hoare began undoing much of the previous strategy. Plans for new stores were pruned and several existing stores were closed. Attention was focused on cost reduction, particularly on reducing inventory. To staunch losses and raise finance, several manufacturing plants were sold, and a 13 percent stake in Laura Ashley Japan Ltd. was sold to Laura Ashley's Japanese partner Jusco, for £9.5 million.

In March 1998, David Hoare reported on his progress since September 1997 and on his plans for the future (see exhibit 2.2).

Exhibit 2.2   David Hoare's Three-Phase Strategy

I am pleased to have joined Laura Ashley in September 1997. I am well aware that over the past 12 years, since flotation, Laura Ashley's financial performance has been most disappointing. A number of serious problems face our business and need to be addressed. However, we have an opportunity to build a successful business on the back of a strong international brand.

■ KEY PROBLEMS FACING LAURA ASHLEY ■

- *Complexity of the Business*. Laura Ashley is too complex for a business of its size. We attempt to be experts in design, manufacturing, distribution, retailing in 13 countries, franchising, licensing and mail order. Our management information systems are outdated and our cost base is too high. We have not been sufficiently focused on our core competencies of brand management and retailing.

- *Garment Design*. Over the past three years, the garment range has been repositioned towards the High Street and a younger market. However, it has been taken too quickly and too far in this most competitive sector of the market. We have confused our loyal customers and not attracted sufficient new ones.
- *North American Expansion*. In 1996, we operated 168 stores in North America, with an average size of 1,600 sq. ft. This small-store format was not profitable. Over the past two years our North American store portfolio was restructured by closing 68 smaller stores and opening 32 larger stores (5,000 sq. ft.) in prestige mall locations. Store merchandising was centralized in London. This program was implemented rapidly without sufficient planning and knowledge of market conditions and with an inadequate supply chain. Costs, particularly rents, have increased whilst sales have not grown significantly.

Overall, these problems led to a shortfall in sales against expectations and excess stocks in both garments and home furnishings, across all markets, which was cleared throughout the year with heavy discounting. As a result, gross profit margins reduced by 10% from 48% to 38% on sales of £345 million, a £34 million adverse gross profit variance. In addition, operating costs rose by 8% or £11.5 million, principally due to a 16% increase in floor space in North America and the UK. As a result, we have reported an operating loss before exceptional items and tax of £25.5 million for 1997/98 against £16.2 million profit last year. In addition, exceptional charges of £23.8 million have been taken mainly to restructure our North American and manufacturing business.

■ **RECOVERY PROGRAM** ■

Whilst it is clear that we have had a number of significant problems at Laura Ashley, and that it will take time to fix them, it is also clear that there are great opportunities for our business. Laura Ashley is one of the best known international brand names, representing the quintessential English country lifestyle. We trade in 34 countries, in over 550 owned and franchised stores. We have a base of loyal customers who, though disappointed in the recent past, will return provided we can develop products and services that meet their aspirations.

In order to tackle our current problems and take advantage of the significant opportunities, we have put in place a three-phase recovery plan to be implemented over the next five years.

- *Phase I. Stabilize the Business*
  - stop significant new store development
  - rebuild the senior management team
  - generate cash by reducing stocks and selling non-core assets
  - raise additional finance
- *Phase II. Improve the Profitability of the Business*
  - return to full price retailing
  - redesign the product to meet the wishes of our core customers
  - fix the North American retail business
  - reduce business complexity and costs
  - invest in systems
- *Phase III. Grow the Business*
  - focus on core competence of brand management
  - build our brand internationally with new products, new distribution channels and new partners

■ **PHASE I** ■

In late 1997 and into 1998 good progress was made to stabilize the business. Store expansion was stopped, and we refocused on managing the existing business. Our worsening trading position in the autumn of 1997 required us to renegotiate with our banks. They supported us with a 15 month £170m bank facility through to April 1999. Cash outflow was minimized by reducing year end stock by 32% from £93 million to £63 million. In addition, following the year end, we announced the sale of part of our shareholding in our Japanese licensee, Laura Ashley Japan, to Jusco, the majority owner . . . in a transaction which realized aggregate gross proceeds of 9.5 million pounds. The transaction included a revision of the terms of the license agreement between us.

■ PHASE II ■

Progress has also been made in improving the profits of the existing business. Following our January 1998 end of year sale, we returned to more normal full price retailing with occasional marketing promotions. We recognize that our garment range has moved too far towards the High Street and a younger market and has lost an element of its Laura Ashley signature. We are redesigning our product range, which, because of lead times, will be only partly evident in our Autumn/Winter 1998 collection. More substantial change will be seen in Spring/Summer 1999.

North America remains a major challenge. Our business there has suffered disproportionately from the problems affecting the Group. The product range was not right, the large-stores format did not work and the complexity of the business led to severe supply problems. Significant losses were incurred. However, research shows that there is a major opportunity in North America for lifestyle brands aimed at discerning 30–50 year old customers, and we believe that our quintessential English country brand can succeed in this market.

In order to fix our North American business . . . a decisive program of restructuring, cost reduction, store closures and carefully targeted new investment will be required. As part of this program, we intend to close a number of larger stores while investing in information systems, store refurbishment and brand development.

Throughout the Group, our overheads are too high, partly as a result of the complexity of the business and partly due to the weakness of our systems which require significant investment. Some steps have been taken to reduce costs but greater progress will need to be made in 1998.

As a first step to simplifying our business we announced, in January 1998, our intention to sell our manufacturing operations with a continuing supply agreement.

■ PHASE III ■

We have significant opportunities to expand our franchise, license and wholesale activities internationally. In 1997/98 we opened 22 new franchised stores. In addition, we continue to expand our range of licensed products. However, we will pursue this expansion program only once we are satisfied that we have the right product, service and infrastructure to give the required levels of support.

■ EQUITY ■

In the light of last year's results, the investment need in North America, the opportunities in the rest of the business and the current levels of debt, we have added additional equity capital essential to improve the financial stability and operational health of the Group. On 17 April 1998 we announced that we intend to raise new equity of £43.7 million net in a subscription by the Malayan United Industries Group. The Board believes that raising this new equity is essential in order to implement the recovery plan.

Source: Extracts from the "Chief Executive's Statement," *Laura Ashley Holdings plc Annual Report 1998*, London 1998

By the end of 1997, Laura Ashley's need for new financing became increasingly evident. Debt had more than doubled to £30.6 million and renegotiation of the company's bank facility had resulted in an agreement that Laura Ashley could use within the business the £9.5 million received from the sale of shares in Laura Ashley Japan, but could not draw further on its banking facility, nor could it use funds from outside of North America to fund continued losses within North America.

■ MUI TO THE RESCUE: APRIL 1998 ■

In April 1998, the Board agreed to increase the issued equity of Laura Ashley Holdings and to sell the new equity to the MUI Group, a diversified Malaysian group with interests in retailing, hotels and resorts, food and confectionery, cement and building materials, real estate, and financial services. After the equity sale, MUI would own 40 percent of Laura Ashley's equity and would appoint four board members. Mrs Victoria Egan, president of MUI's retail subsidiary in the Philippines, would become chief executive and Mr Paul Ng Tuand an Tee, executive director of Metrojaya, would become President of Laura Ashley North America.

The £43.5 million that the equity sale would raise (net of expenses) put Laura Ashley on a sounder financial footing. Extensive restructuring and repositioning were needed, especially in North America. (Tables 2.4 and 2.5 show the deteriorating financial performance of the North American business, while table 2.6 shows performance by business segment.) The North America recovery program would require about £20 million (mainly for store closures) and £6.5 million was needed to upgrade its logistics and information systems. The Board agreed with its banks to reduce its existing £50 million revolving credit facility to £35 million pounds by the end of 1998.

Victoria Egan's approach was to continue with the three-phase strategy developed by the previous CEO with a particular emphasis on reducing losses, restructuring the North American business, and disposing of assets. In August 1998, a reorganization plan was announced, involving the creation of three profit centers: Europe, North America, and Franchising. A £2.5 million provision was made to cover the redundancy costs associated with this reorganization. However, during 1998, the business continued to deteriorate – especially in the US. (Tables 2.4 to 2.6 show financial performance by region.) Although inventories were reduced and the costs of closing US large-format stores remained within budget, sales were sharply lower than the year-ago period. The half-yearly results (to August 1, 1998) were greeted with a fall in Laura Ashley's share price to 17 pence – an all-time low.

■ FEBRUARY 1999 ■

As he prepared for his first board meeting as group chief executive of Laura Ashley Holdings, Ng Kwan Cheong reviewed the company's financial statements for the financial year ended January 31, 1999 (see Appendix). His immediate concerns were for Laura Ashley's cash position. MUI had pumped £43.5 million into Laura Ashley in order to underpin its recovery program. This sum, plus the £7.9 million raised from the

Table 2.4 Laura Ashley Holdings plc: retail sales and contribution by geographical segment (£ million)

	UK and Ireland	North America	Continental Europe	Total retail
Turnover				
Year to Jan. 31, 1999	155.4	63.0	40.5	258.9
Year to Jan. 31, 1998	175.9	91.5	47.7	315.1
Year to Jan. 31, 1997	159.2	84.2	45.8	289.2
Contribution				
Year to Jan. 31, 1999	15.0	(7.1)	6.9	14.8
Year to Jan. 31, 1998	14.9	(12.9)	7.3	9.3
Year to Jan. 31, 1997	24.5	7.6	10.7	42.8

Source: Laura Ashley Holdings plc, Annual Reports 1999 and 1998.

Table 2.5 Laura Ashley Holdings plc: sales, profit, and net assets by geographical segment (£ million)

	Year to 1.31.99	Year to 1.31.98	Year to 1.31.97	Year to 1.31.96	Year to 1.31.95
Sales:					
UK and Ireland	176.1	197.2	175.1	160.0	145.2
North America	68.2	96.4	92.7	104.6	107.0
Continental Europe	42.5	50.2	57.7	65.8	57.4
Other	1.5	1.1	1.1	1.3	0.9
Profit before tax (after exceptionals):					
UK and Ireland	(21.7)	(12.6)	8.6	(0.5)	(29.5)
North America	(20.0)	(29.4)	3.3	1.7	(1.2)
Continental Europe	10.7	(7.8)	1.4	5.6	(0.8)
Other	(0.9)	0.5	3.2	3.5	1.6
Net assets:					
UK and Ireland	(3.6)	16.0	25.7	15.4	14.1
North America	(5.6)	(18.6)	11.4	13.3	14.3
Continental Europe	38.0	19.9	29.2	32.5	26.4
Other	1.6	2.4	2.3	1.8	0.9

Source: Laura Ashley Holdings plc, Annual Reports 1996–9.

sale of 13 percent of Laura Ashley Japan, had been eaten up by debt repayment, restructuring and closure costs, and continuing operating losses. With continuing operating losses together with the need to close unprofitable stores, and refurbish profitable stores, Laura Ashley would need to find new sources of finance during the coming financial year. Given the weakness of Laura Ashley's balance sheet in relation to the continuing cash drain, it was unlikely that the banks would be willing to lend. It seemed as though the parent company, MUI, was the only possible source of additional funding. With Chairman John Thornton stepping down to become president and chief operat-

Table 2.6 Laura Ashley Holdings plc: sales, contribution, and net assets by business segment (£ million)

	Year to 1.31.99	Year to 1.31.98	Year to 1.31.97
Turnover:			
Retail	258.9	315.1	289.2
Non-retail	29.4	29.8	22.9
Contribution:			
Retail	14.8	9.3	42.8
Non-retail	7.8	7.6	12.1
Net assets:			
Retail	14.6	(0.6)	40.7
Non-retail	15.8	20.3	27.9

Retail includes Laura Ashley managed retail stores and mail order. Non-retail includes wholesale, licensing, franchising, and manufacturing.
Source: Laura Ashley Holdings plc, Annual Reports 1998 and 1999.

ing officer of Goldman Sachs, and MUI's Khoo Kay Peng taking over his position and chairmanship of Laura Ashley, this might be an opportune moment to press MUI for additional funding.

But did it make sense for MUI to continue to invest in Laura Ashley? Despite an improvement in margins, sales had continued to decline. Did a profitable market exist for Laura Ashley products? If so, was this market primarily within Britain, or did it extend overseas? And how could Laura Ashley best access and develop this market?

APPENDIX

Table 2.A1 Laura Ashley Holdings plc: profit and loss statement (£ million)

	Year to 1.31.99	Year to 1.31.98	Year to 1.31.97
Turnover	288.3	344.9	327.6
Cost of sales	(159.9)	(214.0)	(168.9)
Gross profit	128.4	130.9	158.7
Operating expenses	(146.5)	(166.9)	(144.3)
Other operating income	1.5	–	–
Operating profit/(loss)	(16.6)	(36.0)	(14.4)
Share of operating (loss)/profit of associate cos.	(0.2)	0.5	2.1
Profit on sale of investment in associate	7.5	–	–
Profit on sale of freehold property	2.0	–	–
Amounts written-off investment	–	(2.4)	–
Provision for disposal of businesses	(23.3)	(9.0)	–

Table 2.A1 *continued*

	Year to 1.31.99	Year to 1.31.98	Year to 1.31.97
(Loss)/profit on ordinary activities before interest	(30.6)	(46.9)	16.9
Net interest payable	(1.3)	2.4	0.7
(Loss)/profit on ordinary activities before taxation	(31.9)	(49.3)	16.2
Taxation on (loss)/profit on ordinary activities	(1.1)	–	6.1
(Loss)/profit on ordinary activities after tax	(33.0)	(49.3)	16.2
Dividend		–	(2.4)
Retained (loss)/profit for the period	(33.0)	(49.3)	7.7

Source: Laura Ashley Holdings plc, Annual Reports 1997–9.

Table 2.A2 Laura Ashley Holdings plc: balance sheet (£ million)

	At 1.31.99	At 1.31.98	At 1.31.97
Fixed assets			
Tangible fixed assets	19.5	38.9	44.0
Investment in associated undertaking	1.7	2.5	2.2
Own shares	0.8	0.8	3.3
Total	22.0	42.2	49.5
Current assets			
Stocks (inventories)	56.4	63.2	93.1
Debtors	19.7	21.2	24.4
Short-term deposits and cash	8.4	10.2	6.2
Total	84.5	94.6	123.7
Creditors: amounts due within one year			
Borrowings	0.1	9.9	–
Trade and other creditors	47.7	57.1	72.6
Total	47.8	67.0	74.0
Net current assets	36.7	27.6	49.7
Total assets less current liabilities	58.7	69.8	99.2
Creditors: amounts due after 1 year			
Borrowings	–	29.2	21.0
Trade and other creditors	0.9	1.2	0.8
Total	0.9	30.4	21.8
Provisions for liabilities and charges	27.4	19.7	7.3
Net assets	30.4	19.7	70.1
Capital and reserves			
Share capital	19.9	11.9	11.9
Share premium account	87.1	51.6	51.5
Profit and loss account	(76.6)	(43.8)	6.7
Equity shareholders' funds	30.4	19.7	70.1
Ordinary shares issued (millions)	398	236	236

Source: Laura Ashley Holdings plc, Annual Reports 1997–9.

Table 2.A3 Laura Ashley Holdings plc: cash flow statement (£ million)

	Year to 1.31.99	Year to 1.31.98	Year to 1.31.97
Net cash flow from operating activities	(11.4)	5.2	(0.7)
Returns on investments and servicing of finance:			
Interest received	0.5	1.2	0.8
Interest paid	(1.6)	(3.3)	(1.2)
Interest element of lease payments	(0.2)	(0.3)	(0.3)
Dividends received from associates	0.1	0.2	0.1
Net cash outflow for returns on investments and the servicing of finance	(1.3)	(2.2)	(0.6)
Tax paid	(1.6)	(5.5)	(1.6)
Capital expenditure and financial investment:			
Acquisition of tangible fixed assets	(3.9)	(9.6)	(14.2)
Disposal of tangible fixed assets	4.6	0.1	0.2
Net cash flow for capital investment	0.7	(9.5)	(14.0)
Acquisitions and disposals	7.9	–	–
Equity dividends paid	–	(1.4)	(2.1)
Net cash outflow before financing	(5.6)	(13.4)	(18.8)
Financing:			
Issue of ordinary share capital	44.6	0.1	1.4
Expenses of share issue	(1.1)	–	–
Settlement of currency swaps	–	0.5	4.0
Loans taken out	–	18.1	21.0
Repayment of loans	(39.0)	–	(5.0)
Capital element of lease payments	(0.8)	(0.9)	(1.2)
Net cash inflow from financing	3.7	17.8	20.2
Increase in cash	(1.9)	4.4	1.4

Source: Laura Ashley Holdings plc, Annual Reports 1997–9.

Table 2.A4 Financial ratios: Laura Ashley compared with other clothing retailers

	Laura Ashley	Talbots	Next plc	Ann Taylor Stores	The Limited	Monsoon plc
Sales ($, m.)	478	1,142	2,041	912	9,347	212
Gross profit margin (%)	44.4	34.4	30.1	48.8	32.1	61.0
SGA/Sales (%)	50.8	28.5	17.6	38.4	24.6	45.0
Operating margin (%)	(5.8)	5.9	12.7	10.4	7.5	15.1
Net profit margin (%)	(11.5)	3.2	10.0	14.3	22.0	9.9
Inventory turns*	5.1	6.6	8.7	6.6	7.6	10.2
Total asset turns*	2.7	1.7	1.5	1.2	2.8	2.5
Current ratio*	1.8	2.4	1.8	2.3	1.0	1.3
ROE (%)*	(108.6)	9.1	22.8	7.9	72.0	47.5

*Based upon balance sheet values.
Source: Laura Ashley Holdings plc, Annual Reports 1997–9.

NOTES

1. This section draws upon "Laura Ashley: History," Laura Ashley Holdings plc; and J. L. Heath, *Laura Ashley Holdings PLC (A) and (B)*, European Case Clearing House, 1991.
2. "Giving Laura Ashley a Yank," *Business Week*, May 27, 1997, p. 147.

case three

The US Airline Industry in 2004

Robert M. Grant

Here's a list of 129 airlines that in the past 20 years filed for bank-ruptcy. Continental was smart enough to make that list twice. As of 1992, in fact – though the picture would have improved since then – the money that had been made since the dawn of aviation by all of this country's airline companies was zero. Absolutely zero.

Sizing all this up, I like to think that if I'd been at Kitty Hawk in 1903 when Orville Wright took off, I would have been farsighted enough, and public-spirited enough – I owed this to future capitalists – to shoot him down. I mean, Karl Marx couldn't have done as much damage to capitalists as Orville did.

Warren Buffett, chairman, Berkshire Hathaway

The December 17, 2003 centenary of Orville Wright's first powered flight passed with subdued celebration. Most of America's airlines were too preoccupied with short-term survival to think much about the achievements of the previous hundred years.

During 2003 the airlines were coping with the aftermath of September 11, 2001, the war in Iraq, a depressed world economy, high fuel prices, and increased competition from low-cost carriers (LCCs). United and US Airways were in Chapter 11 bankruptcy and American had narrowly escaped the same fate. Only government support through the Air Transportation Stabilization Board had prevented more widespread airline failures. During 2003 the airlines continued the cutbacks in routes, capacity, and jobs that had begun in the last quarter of 2001. The most visible consequence of the cutbacks were the over 2,000 aircraft parked in different locations throughout the world – including close to 1,000 jets in the Mojave Desert. Table 3.1 shows the situation for the airlines between 2002 and 2003.

Table 3.1   Revenues, profits, and employment of the seven largest US airlines, 2002–2003

	Revenue		Net income		Return on assets*		Employees	
	2003 $, billion	Change from 2002 (%)	2003 $, million	2002 $, million	2003 (%)	2002 (%)	2003	Change from 2002 (%)
AMR	17.4	0.8	(1,228)	(3,511)	(2.7)	(8.7)	96,400	(12.0)
UAL	13.7	(3.9)	(2,808)	(3,212)	(6.2)	(12.0)	63,000	(12.5)
Delta	13.3	0.0	(773)	(1,272)	(1.1)	(0.7)	75,000	(1.5)
Northwest	9.5	0.2	248	(798)	(1.9)	(6.4)	39,100	(11.8)
Continental	8.9	5.6	38	(451)	2.8	(0.6)	37,680	(14.2)
US Airways Group	7.0	(15.8)	(1,646)	(2,117)	(2.6)	(20.2)	37,100	(20.4)
Southwest	5.9	7.5	442	241	4.9	4.7	32,847	(2.5)
TOTAL	75.7	(5.6)	(5,727)	(11,114)	n.a.	n.a.	381,127	n.a.

Notes: * return on assets = pre-tax operating income/total assets; n.a. = not applicable.
Sources: 10K reports.

At the beginning of 2004, the primary focus of most of the major airlines was survival in the short term: most of the major airlines were experiencing negative free cash flow and were heavily indebted – all had levels of debt in excess of 75% of their capital employed. At the same time, the companies also had to plan for the longer term – in particular, all the airlines were being courted by Airbus and Boeing for orders for the new passenger jets that they were developing: the Airbus 380 super-jumbo and the Boeing 7E7 Dreamliner. Although most projections pointed to US demand for airline travel growing at a long-term trend of 4 percent per annum, the central question was whether market growth would translate into profits for the industry. If the industry was to return to the level of profitability it had earned prior to September 2001, this would not be much to celebrate – between 1990 and 2001, the US airline industry as a whole did little better than break even and all of the major airlines were earning negative EVA during the period. In order to make some assessment of the prospects of profitability in the future, the starting point was to understand why the industry's record of profitability was so poor. Most major airline executives pointed to the economics of the industry since deregulation: intense competition, high fixed costs, and price-sensitive customers. Many industry commentators, however, pointed towards poor strategies and inept cost management by the airlines' top executives. They noted that those airlines that had kept their costs far below those of the majors – Southwest, Air Tran, and JetBlue – had shown growth and profitability that was a marked contrast to that of the major airlines. As these LCCs captured more and more of the domestic market, the major airlines were forced to reconsider both their own strategies and the implications of the industry as a whole.

■ FROM REGULATION TO COMPETITION ■

The history of the US airline industry breaks into two main phases: the period of regulation up until 1978, and the period of deregulation since then.

The Airlines Under Regulation (Pre-1978)

The US civil airline industry began in the 1920s when scheduled services began primarily for carrying mail rather than passengers. As a result, the postmaster-general exercised regulatory control over the industry and, by the early 1930s, transcontinental routes were controlled by three airlines: United Airlines in the north, American Airlines in the south, and TWA through the middle. New entry and growing competition (notably from Delta and Continental) led to the threat of instability in the industry, and in 1938 Congress established the Civil Aeronautics Board (CAB) with authority to administer the structure of the industry and competition within it. The CAB awarded interstate routes to the existing 23 airlines, established safety guidelines priorities, and strict rules for passenger fares, airmail rates, route entry and exit, mergers and acquisitions, and interfirm agreements. Fares were set by CAB on the basis of cost plus a reasonable rate of return. The result was that cost increases could be passed on to customers. The outcome was an ossification of industry structure – despite more than 80 applications from firms seeking to operate scheduled domestic flights, not a single new carrier was approved between 1938 and 1978. Instead, new entrants set up as local carriers offering intrastate routes.

Rapid expansion of the industry after World War II and a wave of technological innovations – notably the jet – led to increasing concerns over airline safety. In 1958, following an aircraft collision in 1956 that killed 128 people, the Federal Aviation Administration was created to regulate airline safety.

During the 1970s, two factors created the impetus for reform. First, the oil shock of 1974 caused a massive rise in fuel costs. Attempts were made by the CAB to protect the airlines through large fare increases, a four-year moratorium on new routes, and agreements among the airlines to limit capacity on major routes. The result was the public's growing dissatisfaction with the high cost and inefficiency of air travel. Second, a major shift was occurring in political opinion. During the 1970s, increasing support for economic liberalism resulted in demands for less government regulation and greater reliance upon market forces.

Political arguments for deregulation were supported by new developments in economics. The case for regulation had been based traditionally upon arguments about "natural monopoly" – competitive markets were impossible in industries where scale economies and network effects were important. During the early 1970s, the *theory of contestable markets* was developed. The main argument was that industries did not need to be competitively structured in order to result in competitive outcomes. So long as barriers to entry and exit were low, then the potential for "hit and run" entry would cause established firms to charge competitive prices and earn competitive rates of return.[1] The outcome was the Airline Deregulation Act which, in October 1978, abolished the CAB and inaugurated a new era of competition in the airline industry.

The Impact of Deregulation

The elimination of restrictions over domestic routes and schedules and over domestic fares resulted in a wave of new entrants and an upsurge in price competition. By 1980, 20 new carriers including People Express, Air Florida, and Midway had set up.

Table 3.2 Financial and operating data for the US airline industry, 1978–2003

	Available seat miles – domestic (billions)	Load factor (%)	Breakeven load factor (%)	Operating revenue ($, billion)	Net income ($ million)	Operating margin (%)	Net margin (%)	Rate of return on investment (%)
1978	369	61.5	57.4	22.9	1,197	6.0	5.2	13.3
1979	416	63.0	62.5	27.2	347	0.7	1.3	6.5
1980	433	59.0	59.1	33.7	17	(0.7)	0.1	5.3
1981	425	58.6	59.2	36.7	(301)	(1.2)	(0.8)	4.7
1982	440	59.0	60.0	36.4	(916)	(2.0)	(2.5)	2.1
1983	465	60.7	60.1	39.0	(188)	0.8	0.5	6.0
1984	515	59.2	56.3	43.8	825	4.9	1.9	9.9
1985	548	61.4	59.7	46.7	863	3.1	1.8	9.6
1986	607	60.3	58.7	50.5	(235)	2.6	(0.5)	4.9
1987	649	62.4	59.6	57.0	593	4.3	1.0	7.2
1988	677	62.5	58.9	64.6	1,686	5.4	2.6	10.8
1989	684	63.2	61.6	69.3	128	2.6	0.2	6.3
1990	733	62.4	64.0	76.1	(3,921)	(2.5)	(5.1)	(6.0)
1991	715	62.6	64.1	75.2	(1,940)	(2.4)	(2.6)	(0.5)
1992	753	63.6	65.6	78.1	(4,791)	(3.1)	(3.1)	(9.3)
1993	771	63.5	62.4	83.8	(2,136)	1.7	1.7	(0.4)
1994	784	66.2	66.8	88.3	(344)	3.0	(0.4)	5.2
1995	807	67.0	64.9	94.6	2,314	6.2	2.4	11.9
1996	835	69.3	66.9	101.9	2,804	6.1	2.8	11.5
1997	861	70.3	65.0	109.6	5,168	7.8	4.7	14.7
1998	874	70.7	66.7	113.5	4,903	8.2	4.3	12.0
1999	918	71.0	66.4	119.0	5,360	7.0	4.5	11.1
2000	957	71.2	70.2	130.8	2,486	5.3	2.0	6.6
2001	923	69.1	77.0	115.4	(8,275)	(5.4)	(8.9)	(9.1)
2002	893	70.3	84.1	107.0	(11,295)	(8.0)	(10.6)	n.a.
2003	894	72.4	86.0	115.9	(3,625)	(1.9)	(3.1)	n.a.

Deregulation was quickly followed by the oil shock of 1979, the onset of worldwide recession, and the air traffic controllers' strike of 1981. During 1978–82, the industry incurred massive losses (see table 3.2), causing widespread bankruptcy (between 1978 and 1988 over 150 carriers went bust) and a wave of mergers and acquisitions. By 1982, expansion had resumed and during the rest of the 1980s and into the 1990s mileage flown grew at a trend rate of 4 percent per annum. At the same time, competition and the quest for efficiency resulted in a continuous decline in real prices (see figure 3.1).

■ FIRM STRATEGY AND INDUSTRY EVOLUTION AFTER DEREGULATION ■

Changes in the structure of the airline industry during the 1980s and 1990s were primarily a result of the strategies of the airlines as they sought to adjust to the new conditions of competition in the industry and gain competitive advantage.

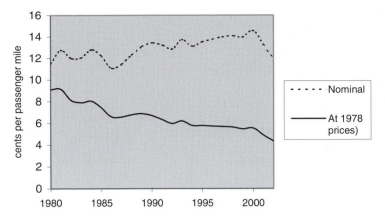

Figure 3.1 Domestic airfares: nominal and real yield per passenger mile

Route Strategies: The Hub-and-Spoke System

During the 1980s a system of predominantly point-to-point routes was replaced by one where the major airlines concentrated their routes on a few major airports linked by frequent services using large aircraft, with smaller, nearby airports connected to these hubs by shorter routes using smaller aircraft. This "hub-and-spoke" system offered two major benefits:

- It allowed greater efficiency through concentrating traveler and maintenance facilities in fewer locations, while permitting cost savings through higher levels of capacity utilization and the use of larger, more cost-efficient aircraft for interhub travel. The efficiency benefits of the hub-and-spoke system were reinforced by scheduling flights such that incoming short-haul arrivals were concentrated at particular times to allow passengers to be pooled for the longer haul flights on large aircraft. The efficiency benefits of hub-and-spoke over point-to-point in terms of economizing on routes and aircraft distance traveled are illustrated in figure 3.2.
- It allowed major carriers to establish dominance in major regional markets and on particular routes. In effect, the major airlines became more geographically differentiated in their route offerings. The ability of a single airline to dominate individual hubs was reinforced by mergers. For example, when TWA acquired Ozark in 1986, it controlled over 80 percent of flights in and out of St Louis. Northwest accounted for 65 percent of traffic in and out of Detroit Metropolitan Airport. The hub-and-spoke system also created a barrier to the entry of new carriers who often found it difficult to obtain gates and landing slots at the major hubs.

The hub-and-spoke system also allowed the major airlines to offer a more integrated, through-ticketing service by establishing alliances with local ("commuter") airlines.

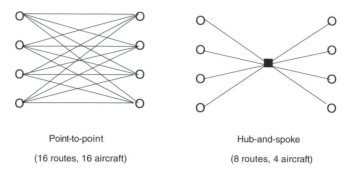

Point-to-point

(16 routes, 16 aircraft)

Hub-and-spoke

(8 routes, 4 aircraft)

Figure 3.2   The efficiency of the hub-and-spoke system

Table 3.3   Concentration in the US airline industry

Year	Four-firm concentration ratio	Year	Four-firm concentration ratio
1935	88%	1982	54.2%
1939	82%	1987	64.8%
1949	70%	1990	61.5%
1954	71%	1999	66.4%
1977	56.2%	2002	71.0%

Notes: The 4-firm concentration ratio measures the share of the industry's passenger-miles accounted for by the four largest companies. During 1935–54, the four biggest companies were United, American, TWA, and Eastern. During 1982–2002, the four biggest companies were United, American, Delta, and Northwest.
Source: US Dept. of Transport.

Thus, American Eagle, United Express, and Delta Shuttle were franchise systems established by AMR, UAL and Delta respectively whereby commuter airlines used the reservation and ticketing systems of the major airlines and coordinated their operations and marketing policies with those of their bigger partners.

Mergers

New entry during the period of deregulation had reduced seller concentration in the industry (see table 3.3). However, the desire of the leading companies to build national (and international) route networks encouraged a wave of mergers and acquisitions in the industry – many of which were facilitated by the financial troubles that beset several leading airlines. Consolidation would have gone further without government intervention on antitrust grounds – the proposed merger between United and US Airways was halted in 2001. Figure 3.3 shows some of the main mergers and acquisitions.

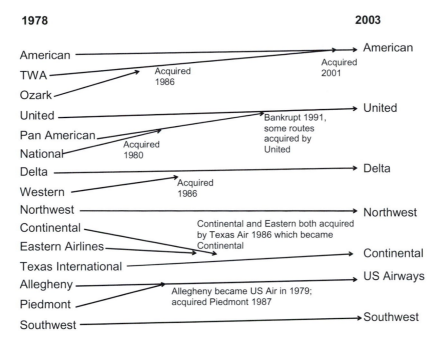

1978   **2003**

Figure 3.3 Consolidation in the US airline industry after deregulation
Source: Updated from S. Borenstein, "The evolution of US airline competition." *Journal of Economic Perspectives*, Vol. 6 No. 2, 1992, p. 48.

Prices and Costs

The growth of competition in the post-deregulation era was most apparent in the prices of air tickets. The instigators of lower prices were mainly established airlines suffering from weak revenues and excess capacity and eager for cash flow, and new entrants into the industry. The new, low-cost entrants played a critical role in stimulating the price wars that came to characterize competition after deregulation. People Express, Braniff, New York Air, and Southwest all sought aggressive expansion through rock bottom fares made possible by highly efficient cost structures and a bare-bones service (the low-cost airlines typically offered no in-flight meals or entertainment and no baggage handling). Although most of the low-cost newcomers failed during the early years of airline deregulation, new entrants continued to appear throughout the 1980s and 1990s.

In response to the price initiatives of the low-cost airlines, the major carriers sought to cut prices selectively. Fare structures became increasingly complex as airlines sought to separate price-sensitive leisure customers from price-inelastic business travelers. As a result, fare bands widened: advanced purchased economy fares with Saturday night stays were as little as 10 percent of the first-class fare for the same journey.

Price cuts were also selective by route. Typically the major airlines offered low prices on those routes where they faced competition from low-cost rivals. Southwest, the biggest and most successful of the economy carriers, complained continually of predatory price cuts by its larger rivals. However, the ability of the major airlines to compete against the budget airlines was limited by the majors' cost structures – in particular restrictive labor agreements, infrastructure, and commitment to extensive route networks. Hence, to meet the competition of low-cost newcomers, several of the majors set up new subsidiaries to imitate the strategies and cost structures of the budget airlines. Continental launched Continental Lite in 1994, and was followed the next year by UAL's "Shuttle by United." American Airlines, on the other hand, sought to compete with Southwest and other budget airlines by forging agreements with smaller airlines such as Midway and Reno Air in which it ceded some of its most price-competitive (and loss-making) routes to its smaller partners. Despite the failure of Continental Lite, the success of the LCCs provided a continuing incentive to the major airlines to open subsidiaries with similarly low-cost structures. In 2003 Delta launched Song and in February 2004, United's new airline, Ted, began flights.

The Quest for Differentiation

Under regulation, the inability to compete on price resulted in airline competition shifting to non-price dimensions – customer service and in-flight food and entertainment. Deregulation brutally exposed the myth of customer loyalty: most travelers could not distinguish major differences between the offerings of the different major airlines and were increasingly indifferent as to which airline they flew on a particular route. Increasing evidence that airline seats were fundamentally commodity products did not stop the airlines from attempting to differentiate their offerings and build customer loyalty.

For the most part, efforts to attract customers through enhanced services and facilities were directed towards business travelers. The high margins on first- and business-class tickets provided a strong incentive to attract these customers by means of spacious seats and intensive in-flight pampering. For leisure travelers it was unclear whether their choice of carrier was responsive to anything other than price, and the low margins on these tickets limited the willingness of the airlines to increase costs by providing additional services. Some airlines – notably TWA and American – experimented with cabin configurations that offered coach passengers more legroom. The most widespread and successful initiative to build customer loyalty was the introduction of frequent flyer schemes. American's frequent flyer program was introduced in 1981 and was soon followed by all the other major airlines. By offering free tickets and upgrades on the basis of number of miles flown, and building in different threshold levels for receiving benefits, the airlines encourage customer loyalty and discourage customers from switching airlines in response to small price differentials. By the end of the 1990s, these frequent flyer programs had become a major part of the airlines' operations. *The Economist* estimated that unredeemed frequent flyer miles had surged to 8 trillion miles by the end of 2001 and were worth roughly $500 billion.[2] Through involving other companies as partners – car rental companies, hotel chains, credit card issuers – frequent flyer programs had become an important source of additional revenue for the airlines worth about $10 billion in 2001.[3]

Table 3.4 The US passenger airline companies in 2003

Major airlines	Alaska, America West, American, Continental, Delta, Northwest, Southwest, United, US Airways
National airlines	Air Tran, Air Wisconsin, Aloha, Atlantic Southeast, Comair, Continental Express, Continental Micronesia, Executive, Frontier, Hawaiian, Horizon Air, JetBlue, Mesaba, Midway, Midway Express, Ryan Int'l, Skywest, Spirit Air, Sun Country, Trans States, US Airways Shuttle
Regional airlines	Air Midwest, Allegiant, Ata, Atlantic Coast, Casino Express, Chautauqua, Chicago Express, Colgan, Corporate, Falcon, Air Freedom, Florida West, Gulfstream, North American, Pan American, Pinnacle, PSA, Skyway, Sun Pacific, Trans Air Link, Trans States, Transmeridian

Source: Air Transport Association.

■ THE INDUSTRY IN 2004 ■

The Airlines

At the beginning of 2004, the US passenger airline industry comprised about 60 firms, ranging from the major airlines to small local companies (see table 3.4). The industry was dominated by seven major passenger airlines – United, American, Delta, Northwestern, Continental, US Airways, and Southwest. This dominance of the leading group was increased by their networks of alliances with smaller airlines. Thus, American, United, Delta, Northwest, and US Airways all had alliances with smaller airlines with whom they coordinated schedules and routes and allowed access to their reservations and ticketing systems. Given the perilous financial state of so many of the leading airlines, most observers expected that the trend towards consolidation in the industry would continue (see table 3.5).

Market for Air Travel

At the beginning of the twenty-first century, airlines provided the dominant mode of long-distance travel in the US. For shorter journeys, cars provided the major alternative. Alternative forms of public transportation – bus and rail – accounted for a small and diminishing proportion of journeys in excess of a hundred miles. Only on a few routes (e.g. between Washington, New York, and Boston) did trains provide a viable alternative to air.

Most forecasts pointed to continued growth in the demand for air travel – probably below the 5% annual trend rate of the past two decades, but most likely faster than the rate of population growth. The chances of any significant shift of demand to alternative modes of transport seemed slight. With Amtrak mired in financial and political difficulties, there seemed little chance that the US would develop high-speed train services similar to those of Europe and Japan. Meanwhile, the communications revolution seemed to have done little to relieve business people of the need to meet face-to-face.

Table 3.5 Operating data for the larger airlines

	Available seat miles (billions)		Load factor (%)		Operating revenue per available seat mile (cents)		Operating expense per available seat mile (cents)	
	2003	2002	2003	2002	2003	2002	2003	2002
United	136.6	148.8	76.5	73.5	9.4	9.4	10.5	11.4
American	165.2	172.2	72.8	70.7	8.7	8.4	10.2	11.1
Delta	134.4	141.7	73.4	72.0	9.9	9.4	10.5	10.3
Northwest	88.6	93.4	77.3	77.1	8.6	8.3	9.9	10.0
Continental	78.4	80.1	75.5	74.1	8.7	8.6	9.4	9.5
Southwest	71.8	68.9	66.8	65.9	8.3	8.0	7.6	7.4
US Airways	58.0	62.3	71.5	69.6	10.6	10.1	11.6	12.7
AirTran	10.0	8.3	71.1	67.6	8.9	8.6	6.5	6.6
Jet Blue	13.6	8.2	84.5	83.0	7.3	7.7	6.0	6.1
America West	27.9	27.0	76.4	73.6	9.9	9.7	7.9	8.1
Alaska	2.2	2.3	62.9	62.1	19.0	19.3	17.7	19.5

More important changes were occurring within the structure of market demand. Of particular concern to the airlines was evidence that the segmentation between business and leisure customers was breaking down. Conventional wisdom dictated that while the demand for air tickets among leisure travelers was fairly price elastic, that of business travelers was highly inelastic, allowing the airlines to subsidize leisure fares with high-margin business fares. Between 2001 and 2003, the price gap between leisure fares (restricted tickets typically requiring a Saturday night stay) and business fares (first-class tickets and flexible coach tickets without advance purchase requirements) continued to grow.[4] The primary reason was falling leisure fares as LCCs offered increasing price competition over more and more routes. However, the huge and growing premium of full-price coach and first-class fares to leisure fares was causing many companies to change their travel policies. During the 2001–03 period, the demand for first- and business-class travel slumped as business travelers traded down.[5]

Major changes were occurring within the distribution side of the industry. Historically, the primary channel of distribution of airline tickets was travel agencies – retailers that specialized in the sale of travel tickets, hotel reservations, and vacation packages. From 1996, airlines began pruning their commissions paid to travel agents with cuts from 10% to 8%, then to 5%. In 2001 Northwest led the way in withdrawing standard rates of commissions from independent travel agents altogether, and was followed by Continental, American and Delta in 2002. Sales commissions were still paid to larger travel agents, but only on a selective basis. By 2003, commissions paid by the airline companies amounted to only 1.7% of the industry's operating expenses (see table 3.7 below).

Meanwhile the companies were developing their direct sales organizations using both telephone and Internet reservations and ticketing systems. However, the airlines were slower than e-commerce start-ups in exploiting the opportunities of the Internet. Despite the launch of Orbitz (the airlines' own online reservations service) in June 2001, by June

Table 3.6 The cost structure of the US airline industry, 2002: breakdown by activity

	Percentage of total operating costs
Flying operations	30.1
Aircraft and traffic servicing	15.9
Maintenance	12.2
Promotion and sales	9.3
Transport related	10.0
Passenger services	8.3
Administrative	7.5
Depreciation and amortization	6.7
TOTAL	100.0

Source: Air Transport Association.

2002, Expedia, Travelocity, Cheap Tickets, Priceline, and a host of other "e-tailers" had established themselves as leading online sellers of air tickets. Not only did their size allow them to wield greater bargaining power than traditional travel agencies, but also they provided consumers with unparalleled transparency of prices permitting the lowest price deals to be quickly spotted. Meanwhile, the traditional travel agent sector was consolidating rapidly as small independents closed and global leaders such as American Express and Thomas Cook acquired rivals. In attempting to grow their sales through their own web sites and telephone sales services, the major airlines were again imitating the LCCs who had long focused upon direct sales in order to avoid commissions.

Airline Cost Conditions

Less than one-third of airline operating costs are accounted for by flying operations: servicing and maintenance account for almost the same proportion of costs as flying operations (see table 3.6). In terms of individual cost items, labor costs are by far the biggest, followed by fuel and the depreciation on aircraft (see table 3.7). A key feature of the industry's cost structure was the very high proportion of costs that are fixed. For example, because of union contracts, it was difficult to reduce employment and hours worked during downturns. The majors' need to maintain their route networks added to the inflexibility of costs – the desire to retain the integrity of the entire network made the airlines reluctant to shed unprofitable routes during downturns. An important implication of the industry's cost structure was that, at times of excess capacity, the marginal costs of filling empty seats on scheduled flights were extremely low.

LABOR

The industry's labor costs are boosted by the high level of employee remuneration – average pay in airlines was 45 percent higher than the average for all private industries in 2003. Labor costs were also boosted by low labor productivity that resulted from rigid

Table 3.7 Airline costs by expense item, 1991 and 2003

	Cost index (1982 = 100)		% of total operating expenses	
	1991	2003	1991	2003
Labor cost	129	210	32.5	37.1
Fuel cost	89	81	14.5	12.6
Fleet cost	187	317	8.6	10.0
Interest cost	81	52	2.4	3.1
Aircraft insurance	81	423	0.2	0.2
Non-aircraft insurance	241	591	0.5	1.1
Maintenance materials	183	92	3.4	1.5
Landing fees	153	214	1.9	2.3
Advertising and promotion	94	42	1.0	0.9
Sales commissions	76	28	6.2	1.7
Other	127	169	28.8	29.5

Source: Air Traffic Association.

working practices agreed with unions. Most airline workers belong to one of a dozen major unions, the Association of Flight Attendants, the Air Line Pilots Association, the International Association of Machinists and Aerospace Workers being the most important. These unions have a tradition of militancy and have been highly successful in negotiating pay increases far above the rate of inflation despite intense competition, falling real ticket prices, and the financial weakness of the industry. Labor relations in the industry have been historically adversarial, with work stoppages and strike threats becoming increasingly frequent as contracts come up for renewal. In summer 2000, United pilots refused to work overtime, resulting in delays and canceled flights. The outcome was a 28 percent pay rise for pilots agreed just before United announced a $600 million loss for the first half of 2001.

During 2002 and 2003, the threat and reality of bankruptcy resulted in widespread negotiation of union contracts. American avoided bankruptcy in 2003 primarily because of pay concessions by unions, while United's unions agreed wage cuts of between 4% and 18% and allowed the company the flexibility to use small regional jets on routes previously flown by larger jets.[6]

FUEL

How much a carrier spends on fuel depends on the age of its aircraft and its average flight length. Newer planes and longer flights equate to higher fuel efficiency. Also, the fuel efficiency of different aircraft varies widely, primarily dependent on the number of engines. Fuel prices represent the most volatile and unpredictable cost item for the airlines due to fluctuations in the price of crude oil. Since January 1999 crude prices have fluctuated between $14 and $40 a barrel. Although there is strong competition between different refiners in the supply of petroleum products (including jet fuel), ultimately, fuel prices depend upon the cost of crude, the level of which is determined by the OPEC cartel. As OPEC has become increasingly effective in enforcing adherence to production quotas among its members, so the price of crude has remained high.

EQUIPMENT

Aircraft were the biggest capital expenditure item for the airlines. At prices of up to $150 million apiece (the A380 will be over $200 million), the purchase of new planes represented a major source of financial strain for the airlines. While Boeing and Airbus competed fiercely for new business (especially when, as in 2002–04, they had massive spare capacity), aggressive discounts and generous financing terms for the purchase of new planes disguised the fact that a major source of profits for the aircraft manufacturers was aftermarket sales. Over the past 20 years the number of manufacturers of large jets declined from four to two. Lockheed ceased civilian jet manufacture in 1984; McDonnell Douglas was acquired by Boeing in 1997. The leading suppliers of regional jets were Bombardier of Canada and Embraer of Brazil. In 2002, the third regional jet manufacturer, Fairchild Dornier, went bankrupt and was acquired by D'Long, a Chinese investment firm.

AIRPORT FACILITIES

Airports play a critical role in the US aviation industry. They are hugely complex, expensive facilities and few in number. Only the largest cities are served by more than one airport. Despite the rapid, sustained growth in air transport over the 25 years since deregulation, only one major new airport has been built – Denver. Most airports are owned by municipalities and can generate substantial revenue flows for the cities. Landing fees are set by contracts between the airport and the airlines, and are typically based upon aircraft weight. Although airports are required to base landing fees on the basis of cost, calculations are problematic given the difficulty of determining the appropriate capital costs. In 1993, Los Angeles International airport raised its landing fees by 200 percent, and increased them again by 33 percent in 1995. Threatened with the withdrawal of their landing rights, the airlines soon fell into line. Landing fees and terminal rents increased substantially over the past decade. In 2002, the airlines paid $1.47 billion to US airports in landing fees.[7]

Four US airports – JFK and La Guardia in New York, Chicago's O'Hare, and Washington's Reagan National – are officially "congested" and takeoff and landing slots are allocated to individual airlines where the airlines assume de facto ownership. Growth of air travel is likely to increase problems of congestion and increase the value of takeoff and landing slots. At London's Heathrow airport, slots have been traded between airlines at high prices: American and United paid more than $27 million each for PanAm's takeoff/landing slots; Qantas paid BA $30 million for two slots.[8]

COST DIFFERENCES BETWEEN AIRLINES

One of the arguments for deregulation had been that there were few major economies of scale in air transport; hence large and small airlines could coexist. Subsequently, little evidence has emerged of large airlines gaining systematic cost advantages over their smaller rivals. However, there are economies associated with network density – the greater the number of routes within a region, the easier it is for an airline to gain economies of utilization of aircraft, crews, and passenger and maintenance facilities. In practice, cost differences between airlines are due more to managerial, institutional, and historical factors rather than the influence of economies of scale, scope, or density. The industry's cost leader, Southwest, built its strategy and management systems around the goal of low costs. By offering services from minor airports, with limited customer service, a single type of airplane, job-sharing among employees, and salary levels substantially less than those paid by other major carriers, Southwest achieves one of the industry's lowest costs per available seat mile (CASM) despite flying relatively short routes. Conversely, US Airways has the highest operating costs of the majors. Its high costs were partly a result of external factors – short routes, smaller planes, and routes concentrated on the eastern seaboard with its frequent adverse weather conditions – but mainly the consequence of managerial factors such as highly restrictive labor agreements, poor employee relations, and deficiencies in operational management. Both companies' cost positions are the result of history – US Airways is a product of a regulated environment where unions were allowed to gain great power and where rigidities and inefficiencies became institutionalized. Southwest was a product of deregulation where the driving forces behind the airline were customer satisfaction, entrepreneurial spirit, and stockholder return.

A critical factor determining average costs was capacity utilization. Because most costs, at least in the short run, were fixed, profitable operation depended upon achieving break-even levels of capacity operation. When airlines were operating below break-even capacity there were big incentives to cut prices in order to attract additional business. The industry's periodic price wars tended to occur during periods of slack demand and on routes where there were several competitors and considerable excess capacity.

Achieving high load factors while avoiding ruinously low prices is a major preoccupation for the airlines. During the late 1990s, all the major airlines adopted yield management systems – highly sophisticated computer models that combine capacity and purchasing data and rigorous financial analysis to provide flexible price determination. The goal is to earn as much revenue on each flight as possible. Achieving this goal has meant a proliferation of pricing categories and a plethora of special deals ranging from "weekend Internet specials" to the auctioning of tickets over Internet auction sites such as eBay.

Entry and Exit

Hopes by the deregulators that the US airline business would be a case study of competition in a contestable industry were thwarted by two factors: significant barriers to both entry and exit, and evidence that potential competition was no substitute for actual competition in lowering fares on individual routes. While the capital requirements of setting up an airline can be low (a single leased plane will suffice), offering an airline service requires setting up a whole system comprising gates, airline and aircraft certification, takeoff and landing slots, baggage handling services, and the marketing and distribution of tickets. At several airports, the dominance of gates and landing slots by a few major carriers made entry into particular routes difficult and forced start-up airlines to use secondary airports. Yet, despite the challenges of entry barriers and the dismal financial performance of the industry there seemed to be no shortage of willing entrepreneurs attracted to the apparent glamour of owning an airline. In 2004, Britain's Richard Branson announced plans to establish a new LCC, Virgin USA.[9] Looking further ahead, large-scale entry was also a possibility if a new airline agreement between the US and the EU lifted US restriction on European airlines either acquiring US airlines or offering internal services within the US.

A major reason for the chaotic competitive conditions in the industry has been the barriers to exit that prevent the orderly exit of companies and capacity from the industry. The tendency for loss-making airlines to continue in the industry for long periods of time can be attributed to two key extra barriers: first, contracts (especially with employees) give rise to large closure costs; second, Chapter 11 of the bankruptcy code allows insolvent companies to seek protection from their creditors (and from their existing contracts) and continue operation under supervision of the courts. A critical problem for otherwise financially healthy airlines was meeting competition from bankrupt airlines which had the benefit of artificially lowered costs.

■ FUTURE PROSPECTS ■

Looking to the future, any feelings of relief over surviving the turmoil of 2003 were tempered by apprehensions about the future. In the absence of any new disruptions to the industry caused by global strife or macroeconomic turbulence, demand growth of 6 percent seemed feasible in 2004. Yet, such stability seemed elusive during the first quarter of 2004. The US economic situation remained precarious – a record current account deficit and projections of a rapidly escalating federal deficit looked likely to undermine the 2004 economic recovery. Politically, the industry remained exposed to international events, the March terrorist bombing in Madrid providing a stark reminder of this vulnerability.

For the major airlines, efforts to address the severe financial problems of their companies remained focused upon cost cutting. During 2002 and 2003, American succeeded in cutting its annual costs by $4 billion, and claimed that this was just a start in what it described as "the largest consensual restructuring in the history of the airline industry." Yet, for all new-found eagerness for cost reduction, most industry commentators were skeptical over the industry's capacity for substantial and sustained cost reduction.

A study by McKinsey consultants argued that the major airlines had limited scope for radical cost cutting. New wide-body airliners cost between $80 million and $150 million each – they impose a heavy ongoing cost whether used or not. The airline unions also show little inclination to give up their hard-won privileges in relation to pay, benefits, and working conditions. The 20 percent reduction in available seat miles by the airlines following September 11 was achieved mainly by lower utilization of active aircraft – the resulting cost reductions were modest. Moreover, some costs – notably the costs of insurance, security, and fuel – increased sharply during 2002–4. Even as the airlines were cutting capacity during 2002 and 2003, their fleets were augmented by the delivery of aircraft ordered piror to September 2001.[10]

The McKinsey study also noted that the problems had not all been on the cost side. A critical determinant of profitability is passenger yield – the price paid for each passenger-kilometer flown. A key factor causing yield to deteriorate was the contraction in business travel. Although business men and women continued to travel, typically they were doing so in coach class – often at the cheapest available fare. By 2003 the proportion of passengers in the premium sections of the cabin had fallen to around 20 percent as compared to around 35 percent in 1999. As increased security increased the inconvenience of scheduled air travel, so corporate jets became an increasingly attractive alternative for top executives. The McKinsey consultants also pointed to the possibility that videoconferencing might finally take off as an alternative to face-to-face meetings, especially with the lower cost and increased convenience of web-based conferencing.[11]

The other factor depressing the yields (and overall revenues) of the established airlines was the rapid growth in competition from the budget airlines during 2002–4. Despite depressed market conditions, 2002 and 2003 saw unprecedented growth in the number and size of America's low-cost airline companies. While Southwest continued its steady expansion, its smaller imitators – JetBlu, AirTran, America West, and Frontier – grew aggressively and rapidly. Several long-established regional carriers transformed themselves into budget airlines. Atlantic Coast Airlines became Independence Air and, instead of being a feeder and partner for United Airlines, emerged as its vigorous competitor. *The Economist* estimated that between 2000 and mid-2004, the budget airline sector had grown by 44 percent.[12] This expansion looked set to continue: in June 2004, the major airlines had 150 new jets on order; the budget airlines had orders totaling 200.

The ability of the low-cost carriers to take market share from the major airlines was not simply a result of non-union labor. It was the result of a business model and set of operating practices that were not a legacy of a bygone era of regulation. According to *The Economist*: "The cost advantages enjoyed by low-cost carriers are striking. Flexible workforces mean that airlines such as Southwest need only 80 workers to fly and support each aircraft, compared with 115 or more at a traditional network carrier. For passengers, the clearest evidence of the rival cost structures is the way the cabin staff of low-cost carriers parade rubbish bags before and after each landing, performing the task assigned by the network carriers to an expensive, standby cleaning crew."[13] As a result, it was the budget airlines that were increasingly in control of pricing on a growing number of routes.

If the established network carriers follow American's lead and are successful in reducing costs, this may make them better able to compete with the low-cost carriers. But would it make much difference to industry-wide profitability? As long as competition in the industry remains strong, it seems likely that the major beneficiaries of cost reductions would be airline customers who would receive lower fares. For this reason, some industry insiders believe that the industry's best chances for improved long-run profitability lie with measures that would reduce the intensity of competition in the industry, either through mergers or through some form of regulatory intervention by government.

NOTES

1. For a review of contestability as applied to the airline industry, see S. Borenstein, "The evolution of US airline competition," *Journal of Economic Perspectives*, Vol. 6, No. 2, 1992, pp. 45–73.
2. "Fly me to the moon," *The Economist*, May 4, 2002, p. 80.
3. Ibid.
4. American Express reported that in 2003, the typical business fare (a flexible coach ticket with no advance purchase requirement) was about six times the lowest discount fare. Only six years ago, the ratio was just over two and a half times.
5. "Saturday night fever," *The Economist*, April 20, 2002, p. 72.
6. "Talking Turkey," *The Economist*, November 28, 2002, p. 74.
7. Air Transport Association, *Airline Handbook*, 2000.
8. "Special Report: Soaring Cost of Touching Down," *The Times*, London, February 24, 2004.
9. "Richard Branson's Next Big Adventure," *Business Week*, March 8, 2004.
10. Peter R. Costa, Doug S. Harned, and Jerrold T. Lundquist, "Rethinking the aviation industry," *The McKinsey Quarterly*, No. 2, 2002.
11. Ibid.
12. "Low-cost Airlines: Turbulent Skies," *The Economist*, July 8, 2004, Special Section.
13. Ibid.

case four

Ford and the World Automobile Industry

Robert M. Grant

■ FORD'S REVITALIZATION STRATEGY ■

In September 2003, Bruce Blythe took up the new position as chief strategy officer at Ford Motor Company. His appointment came in the wake of a massive upheaval of Ford's strategy, leadership, and organization.

In 2001, Ford's CEO Jacques Nasser had been ousted by the board after a three-year tenure. Nasser's goal had been to transform Ford into a flexible, customer-focused, innovative, global giant – that simultaneously paid careful attention to profitability and shareholder return. By late 2001, it was clear that the strategy was not working. Over-priced acquisitions had dissipated shareholder value, the Firestone–Ford Explorer recall severely dented Ford's reputation with consumers, and Ford was heading for its biggest loss ever. Company chairman Bill Ford assumed executive control of the company his great-grandfather had created.

In January 2002, Bill Ford announced a new strategic direction for the company. Cost cutting would eliminate 35,000 jobs worldwide, close five plants in North America, divest $1 billion of non-core assets, and take $2 billion out of operating costs in the first year. At the same time, Ford would invest heavily in new models – between 2002 and 2006, $20 billion would be spent on a new product development program that would introduce 20 new or upgraded models to the US market every year. Particular emphasis was to be placed on the Premier Automotive Group which comprised Ford's up-market brands including Aston Martin, Jaguar, Land Rover, Lincoln, and Volvo.

By the beginning of 2004, the revitalization strategy was beginning to show results. During 2003, cost reductions totaled $3.2 billion, as a result of which the company's net income was $495 million – after heavy losses during the previous two years. Yet, despite these clear signs of turnaround, Bruce Blythe was concerned over the outlook for the next five years. For all the improvements made in Ford's core automotive busi-

Table 4.1 Economic Value Added of major automobile producers during the 1990s (in $, millions)

	1991–5	1996–9
General Motors	(34,684)	(25,241)
Ford	(28,654)	(327)
DaimlerChrysler	340	8,828
Toyota	(15,374)	(6,744)
VW	(10,322)	(5,192)
Nissan	(21,353)	(9,525)
Honda	(5,477)	637
Fiat	(7,713)	(5,418)
Renault	n.a.	(8,209)
Peugeot	n.a.	(1,197)
Hyundai	n.a.	(971)
Suzuki	(774)	(369)
BMW	(2,648)	(2,220)

Source: "Economic value added of major automobile producers," *Best of Times, Worst of Times*, Stern Stewart & Co., December 2000.

ness, cars and trucks were still losing a lot of money – the automotive side made a pre-tax loss of $1,957 million in 2003, much bigger than the loss in 2002. Ford's profits derived entirely from its financial services business, which produced a pre-tax profit of $3,327 million in 2003.

However, Blythe's main concerns related to the future. During 2004, Ford's capital expenditure would amount to $7 billion, and similar levels of capital expenditure were planned for subsequent years. Could these investments be justified by the returns that they were likely to generate? Much depended upon the state of the industry. Since the beginning of the 1990s, the performance of the world automobile industry had been dismal. During the 1990s, the industry had failed to cover its cost of capital – all the world's leading automobile manufacturers (with the exception of DaimlerChrysler) earned a negative Economic Value Added (see table 4.1). And during 2000–03, industry profitability had deteriorated further. If Ford's heavy investments in new products and plant flexibility were to yield the returns necessary to deliver on Bill Ford's commitment to the superior shareholder returns then it was essential that the industry environment became more conducive to price stability and positive margins. As Blythe began examining the financial projections for 2004–06 made by CFO Allan Gilmour's staff, his thoughts focused increasingly on the future of the automobile industry. Would demand growth take up the excess capacity that has plagued the industry for most of the past six years, would mergers and acquisitions consolidate the industry to the point that destructive price competition could be consigned to history, and would consolidation both upstream (among components suppliers) and downstream (among dealers) mean that the auto manufacturers would constantly be squeezed from both ends?

■ THE MARKET ■

Trends in Market Demand

During the 1880s, the first internal combustion powered vehicles were produced in Europe – notably by Gottlieb Daimler and Karl Benz in Germany. By the turn of the century hundreds of small companies were producing automobiles both in Europe and in America. The subsequent 120 years saw the industry developing at different rates in different parts of the world. The US industry entered a period of rapid growth during 1910–28, and reached its peak of production in 1965. In the two decades up to 2004, car production was on a downward trend, but if trucks were included, output was broadly stable (see table 4.2). In Europe and Japan too, total production was showing a declining trend. The problem of market saturation was exacerbated by the tendency for cars to last longer (see table 4.3).

As a result, the automobile producers have looked increasingly to the newly industrializing countries for market opportunities. During the 1980s and 1990s countries such as Korea, Malaysia, Taiwan, Thailand, Turkey, Brazil, and Argentina offered the best growth prospects. As these markets became increasingly saturated, so China, India, and the former Soviet Union were seen as the "next wave" of attractive markets. With the opening of many of these countries to trade and direct investment, the world production of cars and trucks continued to grow (see table 4.4).

The Evolution of the Automobile

The early years of the industry were characterized by considerable uncertainty over the design and technology of the motorcar. Early "horseless carriages" were precisely that – they followed design features of existing horse-drawn carriages and buggies. Early motorcars demonstrated a bewildering variety of technologies. During the early years, the internal-combustion engine vied with the steam engine. Among internal-combustion engines there was a wide variety of cylinder configurations. Transmission systems, steering systems, and brakes all displayed a remarkable variety of technologies and designs, as well as considerable ingenuity.

Over the years technologies and designs tended to converge as competition relegated many once-promising designs to the scrapheap of history. The Ford Model T represented the first "dominant design" in automobiles – the technologies and design features of the Model T set a standard for other manufacturers to imitate. Convergence of technologies and designs was the dominant trend of the next 90 years. During the 1920s, all manufacturers adopted enclosed, all-steel bodies. During the last few decades of the twentieth century most models with distinctively different designs disappeared: the VW Beetle with its rear, air-cooled engine, the Citroen 2-CV and its idiosyncratic braking and suspension system, Daf with its "Variomatic" transmission, and the distinctive models made by Eastern European manufacturers, such as the 3-cylinder Wartburg and the 2-cycle Trabant. Engines became more similar: typically 4 or 6 cylinders

Table 4.2 US motor vehicle production

	Passenger vehicles	Trucks and buses	Total
1900	4,192	n.a.	4,192
1905	24,250	750	25,000
1910	181,000	6,000	187,000
1915	895,930	74,000	969,930
1920	1,905,560	321,789	2,227,349
1925	3,735,171	530,659	4,265,830
1930	2,787,456	575,364	3,362,820
1935	3,273,874	697,367	3,971,241
1940	3,717,385	754,901	4,472,286
1945	69,532	655,683	725,215
1950	6,665,863	1,337,193	8,003,056
1955	7,920,186	1,249,105	9,169,291
1960	6,674,796	1,194,475	7,869,271
1965	9,305,561	1,751,805	11,057,366
1967	7,436,764	1,539,462	8,976,226
1970	6,546,817	1,692,442	8,239,259
1975	6,712,852	2,272,160	8,985,012
1977	9,200,849	3,411,521	12,612,370
1980	6,400,026	1,667,283	8,067,309
1985	8,002,259	3,464,327	11,466,586
1990	6,049,749	3,718,781	9,768,530
1991	5,407,120	3,375,422	8,782,542
1992	5,684,221	4,042,486	9,726,707
1993	5,981,046	4,883,157	10,864,203
1994	6,601,223	5,648,767	12,249,990
1995	6,350,367	5,634,742	11,985,109
1996	6,083,000	5,749,000	11,832,000
1997	5,927,000	6,169,000	12,096,000
1998	5,554,390	6,451,689	12,006,079
1999	5,637,949	7,387,029	13,024,978
2000	5,542,217	7,228,497	12,770,714
2001	4,879,119	6,545,570	11,424,689
2002	5,016,306	7,258,611	12,274,917

Source: Based on *Ward's Automotive Yearbooks*.

arranged in-line, with V-6 and V-8 configurations for larger cars. Front-wheel drive and anti-lock disk brakes became standard on smaller cars; suspension and steering systems became more similar; body shapes became increasingly alike. Although the automobile continued to evolve, technological progress was incremental: innovations primarily involved new applications of electronics and new safety features. A 1950 Mercedes had about 10 meters of wiring. A 1995 SL 500 with full options had 3,000 meters of wiring and 48 different microcomputers. In terms of automotive engineering the main advances were multi-valve cylinders, traction control systems, all-wheel drive, variable

Table 4.3   Average age of passenger cars in the US (years)

	Mean	Median
2002	8.8	8.4
2000	8.8	8.3
1998	8.7	8.1
1996	8.5	7.4
1994	8.4	7.4
1992	8.1	7.0
1990	7.8	6.5
1988	7.6	6.8
1984	7.5	6.7
1980	6.6	6.0
1976	6.2	5.5
1972	5.7	5.1
1968	5.6	4.7
1962	6.0	5.7
1958	5.6	5.1
1952	6.8	4.5
1948	8.8	8.0
1941	5.5	4.9

Source: R. L. Polk & Co.

Table 4.4   World motor vehicle production (passenger cars and commercial vehicles)

	Total (mil.)	US and Canada as % of total		Total (mil.)	US and Canada as % of total
1950	10.58	79.4	1990	48.35	24.2
1955	13.63	70.9	1991	46.50	23.0
1960	16.49	50.4	1992	47.69	24.5
1965	24.27	49.4	1993	46.40	28.3
1970	29.40	32.1	1994	49.69	29.4
1975	33.00	31.4	1995	49.93	28.8
1980	38.51	24.8	1996	52.50	28.2
1985	44.81	30.3	1997	54.15	28.0
1986	45.30	29.1	1998	53.50	27.3
1987	45.90	27.4	1999	55.74	28.7
1988	48.21	27.3	2000	57.43	27.4
1989	49.10	26.2	2001	56.33	24.8
			2002	58.31	25.3

Source: OICA, American Automobile Manufacturers Association.

suspensions, and intercooled turbos. The quest for fuel economy resulted in the substitution of lighter materials (aluminum, plastics, ceramics, and composites) for iron and steel (see table 4.5). Despite continuing advances in the application of electronics – including satellite navigation systems, communications technology (telematics),

Table 4.5 Weight of material in a typical family automobile (lbs)

	1978	2003
Steel	2,128	1,814
Iron	512	328
Plastic and plastic composites	180	255
Aluminum	112	279
Copper and brass	37	50
Zinc castings	31	8
Glass	86	99
Rubber	146	149
Other	337	377
Total	3,569	3,359

Source: American Metal market.

Table 4.6 From option to standard: convergence in automobile features

Feature	Introduction	General adoption
Speedometer	1901 by Oldsmobile	Circa 1915
Automatic transmission	First installed 1904	Introduced by Packard as an option 1938. Standard on Cadillac and other luxury cars early 1950s
Electric headlamps	GM introduced 1908	Standard equipment by 1916
All-steel body	Adopted by GM 1912	Becomes standard early 1920s
Steel enclosed body	Dodge 1923	Becomes standard late 1920s
Radio	Optional extra 1923	Standard equipment 1946
Four-wheel drive	Appeared 1924	Only limited availability by 1994
Hydraulic brakes	Introduced 1924	Becomes standard 1939
Shatterproof glass	First used in cars 1927	Standard feature in Fords 1938
Power steering	Introduced 1952	Standard equipment by 1969
Anti-lock brakes	Introduced 1972	Standard on GM cars in 1991
Air bags	Introduced by GM 1974	Standard in most new cars by 1994

Source: Various reports.

emergency signaling, collision-avoidance radar, and intelligent monitoring systems – little in today's family cars was radically new (see table 4.6).

Designs and technologies also converged among manufacturers. While different categories of vehicle (family cars, sports cars, passenger minivans, sports utility vehicles) retained distinctive design features, within each category the manufacturers' product offerings became increasingly similar. By 2000, GM was using wireless telephony-based "vehicle locators" to help owners find their vehicles among the ranks of similar-looking cars. Convergence of technology and design meant a quest for new types of differentiation. All the major manufacturers developed new "concept cars," and introduced novel design features. Many of the most innovative car designs – such Ford's Ka,

Toyota's Yaris, and DaimlerChrysler's Smart car – were targeted at the European small-car market. Some manufacturers experimented with retro design features (e.g. DaimlerChrysler's PT Cruiser and the BMW Mini).

Convergence also occurred across countries. US cars downsized, Japanese and Italian cars became larger. The same market segments tended to emerge in different countries. The major differences between countries were in the *sizes* of the various segments. Thus, in the US, the "mid-size" family sedan was the largest segment, with the Ford Taurus, Honda Accord, and Toyota Camry the leading models. In Europe and Asia, small family cars ("subcompacts") formed the largest market segment. Other national differences were also apparent. In North America, pickup trucks, used as commercial vehicles in most of the world, increasingly displaced passenger cars.

The Evolution of Manufacturing Technology

At the beginning of the twentieth century, car manufacture, like carriage-making, was a craft industry. Cars were built to order according to individual customers' preferences and specifications. In Europe and North America there were hundreds of companies producing cars, few with annual production exceeding 1,000 vehicles. When Henry Ford began production in 1903, he used a similar approach. Even with fairly long runs of a single model (the first version of the Model T, for example), each car was individually built. The development of more precise machine tools permitted interchangeable parts, which ushered in mass production: batch or continuous production of components which were then assembled on moving assembly lines by semi-skilled workers. The productivity gains were enormous. In 1912 it took 23 man-hours to assemble a Model T; just 14 months later it took only four. The resulting fall in the price of cars opened up a new era of popular motoring.

If "Fordism" was the first major revolution in process technology, then Toyota's "lean production" was the second. The system was developed by Toyota in post-war Japan at a time when shortages of key materials encouraged extreme parsimony and a need to avoid inventories and waste through defects. Key elements of the system were statistical process control, just-in-time scheduling, quality circles, teamwork, and flexible production (more than one model manufactured on a single production line). Central to the new manufacturing was the transition from static concepts of efficiency optimization towards continuous improvement to which every employee contributed. During the 1980s and 1990s all the world's car manufacturers redesigned their manufacturing processes to incorporate variants of Toyota's lean production.

New manufacturing methods required heavy investments by the companies in both capital equipment and training. The 1980s were a period of unprecedented high investment expenditures. However, as GM was to learn after spending more than $10 billion in upgrading its plants, the essence of the Toyota system was not new manufacturing "hardware" in the form of robotics and computer-integrated manufacturing systems. The critical elements were the "software" – new employee skills, new methods of shop-floor organization, redefined roles for managers, and new relationships with suppliers.

The new flexible manufacturing technology together with modular designs reduced the extent of scale economies in assembly. During the 1960s and 1970s it was believed

Table 4.7 New car development costs during the 1990s and 2000s

Ford Mondeo/Contour	$6 billion
GM Saturn	$5 billion
Ford Taurus (1996 model)	$2.8 billion
Ford Escort (new model)	$2 billion
Chrysler Neon	$1.3 billion
Renault Clio (1999 model)	$1.3 billion
Honda Accord (1997 model)	$0.6 billion
BMW Mini	$0.5 billion
Rolls Royce Phantom (2003 model)	$0.3 billion

Source: Assembled from various newspaper reports.

that efficiency required giant assembly plants with outputs of at least 400,000 units a year. During the past decade, most of the new plants established had output capacities of between 150,000 and 300,000 units. The quest for flexibility was a central feature of Bill Ford's revitalization strategy. Starting in Ford's North American plants, reorganizing for flexibility would enable the manufacturing of multiple models in individual plants, which would allow capacity totaling one million units to be closed.

New Product Development

The declining importance of scale economies in assembly did little to assist smaller automobile producers. The critical scale economy was the ability to amortize the huge costs of new product development over a large enough number of vehicles.

The cost of developing new models had risen steeply as a result of increasing complexity of automobiles, the application of electronics and new materials, higher safety requirements, quality improvements, new environmental standards and the need for increased fuel efficiency. By the late 1980s the cost of creating an entirely new, mass-production passenger car from drawing board to production line was about $1.25 billion. By the early 1990s, costs had escalated substantially above this level (see table 4.7).

Smaller manufacturers could survive only by avoiding these massive product development costs. One way was to avoid new model changes: at the time of its acquisition by Ford, Jaguar's two models, the XJ6 and XJS, were almost two decades old and almost no investment had been made in developing a new model. The tiny Morgan car company has made the same model since the late 1930s. The alternative was to license designs from larger manufacturers. Thus, Tofas of Turkey built Fiat-designed cars, Proton of Malaysia built Mitsubishi-designed cars, and Maruti of India produced Suzuki-designed cars.

The cost of new product development has been the major reason for the wave of mergers and acquisitions in the industry. Economies from sharing development costs also encouraged increased collaboration and joint ventures: Renault and Peugeot established joint engine manufacturing; GM established collaborations with Suzuki, Daewoo, Toyota, and Fiat to build cars and share components. In China and India most new auto plants were joint ventures between local and overseas companies.

During the 1990s, new product development emerged as the critical organizational capability differentiating car manufacturers. Designing, developing, and putting into production a completely new automobile was a hugely complex process involving every function of the firm, up to 3,000 engineers, close collaboration with several hundred suppliers, and up to five years from drawing board to market launch. By 2004, the leading Japanese manufacturers, Toyota and Honda, were still viewed as industry leaders in new product development. Attempts to lower product development costs focused around modular designs and "virtual prototyping" – the use of 3D computer graphics to design and test prototypes.

■ THE INDUSTRY ■

The Manufacturers

The major automobile manufacturers are shown in table 4.8. The ranks of the leading producers were dominated by US, Japanese, and European companies: outside of these countries only Hyundai of Korea was among the leading manufacturers. All the major manufacturers are multinational. Thus, both GM and Ford produce more cars outside the US than within it. Similarly, Honda produces more Accords in the US than in Japan. As a result some countries – notably Canada, Spain, and the UK – are significant auto producing countries without having any significant domestic auto companies. Over the past two decades the industry has consolidated through mergers and acquisitions (see table 4.9). The financial problems of Japanese and Korean auto companies during the late 1990s accelerated this process. As a result, US and European carmakers had acquired significant proportions of the Japanese and Korean auto industries by 2004. At the same time, a number of small producers continued to survive, especially in protected markets. Trade liberalization represented a threat to these companies – it seemed likely that few of China's 30-odd motor vehicle manufacturers would survive China's accession to the World Trade Organization.

Outsourcing and the Role of Suppliers

Henry Ford's system of mass production was supported by heavy backward integration. In Ford's giant River Rouge plant, iron ore entered at one end, Model Ts emerged at the other. Ford even owned rubber plantations in the Amazon basin. The trend of the past 20 years has been towards increasing outsourcing of materials, components, and subassemblies. This has been led primarily by the desire for lower costs and increased flexibility. Again, leadership came from the Japanese: Toyota and Nissan have traditionally been much more reliant upon their supplier networks than their US or European counterparts. At the end of the 1990s GM and Ford both spun off their

Table 4.8   The world's leading auto manufacturers

		Production ('000s of autos and commercial vehicles)					
		1992	1994	1996	1998	2000	2002
GM	US	6,764	8,254	8,176	8,155	8,114	8,326
Ford	US	5,742	6,679	6,611	6,850	7,206	6,729
Toyota	Japan	4,249	4,565	4,794	4,643	5,897	6,626
DaimlerChrysler	Germany	2,782	2,764	4,082	4,562	4,666	4,456
Volkswagen	Germany	3,286	2,436	3,977	3,320	5,106	5,017
Peugeot	France	2,437	2,027	1,975	1,294	2,879	3,262
Honda	Japan	1,762	1,725	2,021	2,298	2,469	2,988
Nissan	Japan	2,963	2,702	2,712	2,610	2,698	2,719
Hyundai	S. Korea	874	1,153	1,402	889	2,488	2,642
Renault	France	1,929	1,881	1,755	2,234	2,515	2,329
Fiat	Italy	1,800	1,967	2,545	2,341	2,639	2,191
Mitsubishi	Japan	1,599	1,504	1,452	1,353	1,613	1,821
Suzuki	Japan	888	1,076	1,387	1,450	1,434	1,704
BMW	Germany	598	573	641	706	835	1,091
Mazda	Japan	1,248	1,215	984	1.030	972	1,044
AutoVAZ	Russia	674	528	562	n.a	756	703
Fuji	Japan	648	434	525	n.a.	581	542
Daihatsu	Japan	610	554	691	724	–	–
Kia	S. Korea	502	675	847	498	735	–
Isuzu	Japan	473	487	462	461	572	437
Daewoo	S. Korea	179	419	710	758	834	407
Volvo	Sweden	365	439	446	487	n.a.	161
Rover	UK	405	485	510	502	345	147

Volkswagen's production for 1996 and 1997 includes Skoda and Seat.
Sources: Ward's Automotive Yearbook; Fortune.

component manufacturing businesses as separate companies: Delphi and Visteon, respectively.

Relationships with suppliers also changed. In contrast to the US model of arm's-length relationships and written contracts, the Japanese manufacturers developed close, collaborative long-run relationships with their "first-tier" suppliers. During the 1990s, the Japanese model of close collaboration and extensive technical interchange with a smaller number of leading suppliers became the model for the entire global auto industry – all the world's manufacturers outsourced more manufacturing and technology development while greatly reducing the number of their suppliers.

As the leading component suppliers have gained increasing responsibility for technological development – especially in sophisticated subassemblies such as transmissions, braking systems, and electrical and electronic equipment – they have also grown in size and global reach. By 2004, Bosch, Johnson Controls, Denso, and Delphi were as big as some of the larger automobile companies (see table 4.10).

Table 4.9 Mergers and acquisitions among automobile manufacturers, 1986–2002

2002	GM (US)	Daewoo (S. Korea)	42% of equity acquired
2000	Renault (France)	Samsung Motors (S. Korea)	70% of equity acquired
2000	GM (US)	Fiat (Italy)	20% of equity acquired
2000	DaimlerChrysler (Germ.)	Hyundai (S. Korea)	10% of equity acquired
2000	DaimlerChrysler (Germ.)	Mitsubishi Motors (Japan)	34% of equity acquired
1999	Renault (France)	Nissan (Japan)	38.6% of equity acquired
1999	Ford (US)	Volvo (Sweden)	Car business acquired from Volvo
1999	Ford (US)	Land Rover (UK)	Acquired from BMW
1998	Daimler Benz (Germany)	Chrysler (US)	
1998	VW (Germany)	Rolls Royce Motors (UK)	
1998	Hyundai (S. Korea)	Kia (S. Korea)	
1998	Daewoo (S. Korea)	Ssangyong Motor (S. Korea)	
1998	Daewoo (S. Korea)	Samsung Motor (S. Korea)	
1997	Proton (Malaysia)	Lotus (UK)	
1997	BMW (Germany)	Rover (UK)	
1996	Daewoo (S. Korea)	FSO (Poland)	
1996	Daewoo (S. Korea)	FS Lublin (Poland)	
1995	Fiat (Italy)	FSM (Poland)	
1995	Ford (US)	Mazda (Japan)	
1994	Daewoo (S. Korea)	Oltcit/Rodae (Romania)	
1991	VW (Germany)	Skoda (Czech Republic)	
1990	GM (US)	Saab-Scandia (Sweden)	50% of equity acquired
1990	Ford (US)	Jaguar (UK)	
1987	Ford (US)	Aston Martin (UK)	
1987	Chrysler (US)	Lamborghini (Italy)	
1986	VW (Germany)	Seat (Spain)	

Table 4.10 Revenues and profitability of the biggest automotive component suppliers

	Revenues ($ billion)					ROE 2003 (%)
	1994	1996	1998	2000	2003	
Robert Bosch (Germany)	19.6	16.3	17.8	29.1	36.7	7
Delphi Automotive	–	–	–	29.1	28.1	(4)
Johnson Controls (US)	7.1	6.3	12.6	17.2	22.6	16
Denso Corp. (Japan)	11.0	13.9	11.7	18.2	19.5	8
Visteon (US)	–	–	–	19.5	17.7	(65)
Lear Corp (US)	3.1	6.2	9.0	14.1	15.7	17
Magna International (Canada)	–	–	–	10.5	15.3	12
Aisin Seiki (Japan)	7.3	7.8	6.5	8.9	11.7	7
Valeo SA (France)	3.8	5.0	5.7	8.9	11.6	13
Dana (US)	5.5	7.7	12.5	12.7	10.1	11
Eaton (US)	4.4	7.0	6.6	8.3	8.1	12

Sources: *Business Week* "Global 1000"; Hoovers Online.

The Quest for Cost Reduction

Increasing competition in the industry has intensified the quest for cost reduction among automobile manufacturers. Cost-reduction measures have included:

- *Worldwide outsourcing.* The tendency for increased outsourcing of components has been noted above. In addition, auto firms have developed original equipment manufacturer (OEM) supply arrangements amongst themselves: Daewoo supplies several of GM's models; GM supplies components to Fiat; Mitsubishi and Chrysler supply engines for the BMW Mini.
- *Just-in-time scheduling,* which has radically reduced levels of inventory and work-in-progress.
- *Shifting manufacturing to lower-cost locations:* VW's North American production is based in Mexico and it moved production from Germany to the Czech Republic, Spain, and Hungary; Japanese companies have moved more and more production to lower-cost locations in Southeast Asia; Mercedes and BMW developed greenfield plants in the deep south of the US.
- *Automation.* In high-cost locations (North America, Western Europe, and Japan), increased automation has reduced labor input.

Different companies have faced different cost issues. While European manufacturers were constrained by rigid working conditions, restrictions on layoffs, and generous benefits, US companies were hit by increased provisions for pensions and healthcare. In Japan the critical cost issue of the past decade was the strength of the yen.

The quest for economies of scale and scope in relation to product development meant that companies sought to spread rising development costs over larger production and sales volumes. Increasingly during the 1990s the auto manufacturers attempted to introduce single global products. After more than a decade of coordinating its European and US models, Ford's Mondeo/Contour was the company's first truly global model.

This desire for scale economies in development, manufacture, and purchasing also resulted in the standardization of designs and components across the different models of each manufacturer. Ford emphasized the critical importance of: "... realizing efficiencies in manufacturing, engineering and product costs for new vehicles by sharing vehicle platforms and components among various models and the re-use of those platforms and components from one generation of a vehicle model to the next."[1]

During the late 1990s, Ford synchronized platforms with Mazda, and by 2000 was building its luxury models on the same platforms used for its volume models. Thus, the Jaguar X-type used the Mondeo platform, while the Jaguar S-type and the Lincoln LS also shared the same platform. *Automotive News* explained: "Ford's platform strategy is evolving out of the company's desire to cut costs by spreading its technology across as many brands as possible. The idea is to share systems in areas that customers can't see and feel, and differentiate the brands in areas they can."

Similar standardization occurred in engines. Ford moved to just five basic engine designs whose modular structure allowed many common components and multiple

Table 4.11 Capacity utilization in motor vehicle manufacturing (%)

	2002	2000	1998	1996	1994	1992	1990
United States	80.4	83.7	79.6	78.8	85.3	71.29	66.4
Western Europe	73.8	71.8	71.5	72.0	69.8	75.8	77.8
Asia	70.3	64.5	61.2	68.5	69.8	75.1	76.7

Sources: Federal Reserve Board, *The Economist*, economagic.com.

variations. Thus, Ford's Global Inline 4-cylinder engine family, launched in 2003 in the Mazda 6, had 100 possible variations, and consolidated eight engine families into one.

Excess Capacity

A major problem for the industry was the tendency for the growth of production capacity to outstrip the growth in the demand for cars. During the 1980s and early 1990s, Japanese companies were major investors in new capacity with a number of greenfield "transplants" in North America and Europe. During the 1990s all the world's major car companies responded to the quest for globalization with new plants (many of them joint ventures) in the growth markets of Southeast Asia, China, India, South America, and Eastern Europe. During 1992–7, the Korean car companies were especially aggressive investors in new capacity. It was particularly worrying that, even in the markets where demand was growing fastest (such as China, where sales grew by over 50 percent in 2002 and 2003), growth of production capacity outstripped growth in demand. KPMG forecast that in 2005 Chinese car sales would be 2.6 million while production capacity would be 4.9 million.[2] The resulting overhang of excess capacity was a key factor exacerbating intense competition in the industry. Table 4.11 shows trends in capacity utilization.

Internationalization

The driving force behind capacity expansion was internationalization. Although multinational growth extends back to the 1920s (when Ford and General Motors established their European subsidiaries), until the 1970s the world auto industry was made up of fairly separate national markets. Each of the larger national markets was supplied primarily by domestic production, and indigenous manufacturers tended to be market leaders. For example, in 1970 the Big Three (GM, Ford, and Chrysler) held close to 85 percent of the US market, VW and Daimler Benz dominated the market in Germany, as did Fiat in Italy, British Leyland (later Rover) in the UK, Seat in Spain, and Renault, Peugeot, and Citroen in France. By 2004, the industry was global in scope – the world's leading manufacturers were competing in most of the countries of the world.

Internationalization required establishing distributors and dealership networks in overseas countries, and often building manufacturing plants. Foreign direct investment

Table 4.12 Japanese and European "transplants" in North America

Company	Parent(s)	Location	Production of cars and lt. trucks 2002
Honda of America	Honda	E. Liberty and Marysville, OH	641,109
Toyota USA	Toyota	Georgetown, KY	667,648
NUMMI	Toyota and GM	Fremont, CA	205,306
CAMI Automotive	Suzuki and GM	Ontario	62,746
Toyota Canada	Toyota	Ontario	218,010
Honda of Canada	Honda	Ontario	391,100
Diamond-Star Motors	Mitsubishi/Chrysler	Normal, IL	202,352
Subaru-Isuzu Auto	Fuji and Isuzu	Lafayette, IN	97,643
Nissan Motor USA	Nissan	Sryrna, TN	409,673
BMW	BMW	Spartanburg, NC	163,188
AutoAlliance International	Mazda/Ford	Flat Rock, MI	47,603
Volkswagen	Volkswagen	Puebla, Mexico	332,876

Source: *Ward's Automotive Yearbook.*

in manufacturing plants had been encouraged by trade restrictions. Restrictions on Japanese automobile imports into North America and Europe encouraged the Japanese auto makers to build plants in these regions. Table 4.12 shows some of the North American auto plants established by overseas (mainly Japanese) companies. Similarly, the high tariffs protecting the motor vehicle markets of most Asian and Latin American countries obliged the major auto makers to set up local assembly.

Different companies pursued different internationalization strategies:

- Toyota and Honda had expanded throughout the world by establishing wholly owned greenfield plants.
- Ford, which had initially internationalized by creating wholly owned subsidiaries throughout the world, extended its global reach during 1987–99 by acquiring Mazda, Jaguar, Aston Martin, Land Rover, and Volvo.
- GM extended its global reach through a series of alliances and minority equity stakes: notably with Fiat, Suzuki, Saab, and Daewoo.
- DaimlerChrysler was created through a transatlantic merger in 1998, and established a position in Asia by acquiring equity in Mitsubishi Motors and Hyundai.
- Volkswagen made a series of acquisitions in Europe (Seat, Skoda, and Rolls Royce) and had focused heavily on investing in manufacturing capacity outside the advanced industrial countries, notably in Eastern Europe, Latin America, and China.

Although the logic of maximizing volume in order to spread the costs of developing new models and new technologies pushed companies into expanding into all three of the world's major markets – North America, Europe, and Asia (Japan in particular) – many sizable companies remained regional players. Renault had effectively merged with Nissan and Samsung Motors, but lacked any presence in North America, while Fiat and Peugeot were essentially European manufacturers.

Despite the tremendous internationalization of the auto industry, it was the home market that remained the most important market for every car maker: that was where they typically exercised market leadership. For example, Fiat was market leader in Italy, VW in Germany, Renault and PSA in France, Hyundai and Daewoo in Korea (see table 4.13). This was partly a legacy of earlier import protection, partly due to national preferences of domestic consumers, and partly a result of well-developed local dealership networks and intimate local knowledge.

Industry Location

Given the shift in demand to the emerging market countries and the auto makers' quest for lower production costs, it might be expected that the geographical distribution of the industry would have changed substantially over recent decades (in the same way that other manufacturing industries – consumer electronics, small appliances, textiles, and semiconductors – have relocated in newly industrializing countries). Yet, in automobiles, such shifts have been surprisingly small. The main feature of 1950–80 was the rise of production in Japan, but since 1980, changes have been small, with the three major manufacturing regions – western Europe, North America, and Japan – each accounting for close to 30 percent of world production. The continuing dominance of this triad is despite the attempts of newly industrializing countries to develop their domestic industries, either by protecting domestic manufacturers or by encouraging inward investment. (Tables 4.14 and 4.15 show production by different regions and countries in recent years.)

The advantages of these countries lie primarily in labor costs, which were often a fraction of those in the older industrialized countries (see table 4.16). Nevertheless, with the exception of Korea, none of the new auto-manufacturing countries has emerged as a major world center for motor vehicle production. The ability of the established auto-manufacturing countries to sustain their leadership points to the importance of factors other than wage rates in driving international competitiveness in the auto industry. Table 4.17 shows that, although wage costs were much lower in Mexico than in the US, this cost advantage was outweighed by other factors.

Market Segments and Market Positioning

As already noted, despite the globalization of the leading auto makers, the world market by 2004 was still composed of many national markets due to differences in national regulations and customer preferences, differences in affluence and infrastructure, trade restrictions, and the need for each manufacturer to build a dealership network in each market it served. The world market was also segmented by types of product. The market for passenger vehicles was traditionally segmented by size of automobile. At the top end

Table 4.13 Automobile market shares in individual countries (%)

	2002	2000	1997	1994	1988
Japan					
Toyota	29.8	28.5	30.6	33.7	43.9
Honda	18.8	16.2	10.1	8.5	10.8
Nissan	12.2	11.8	14.0	18.0	23.2
Suzuki	10.3	10.0	8.6	n.a.	n.a.
Mitsubishi	5.8	6.9	7.9	9.2	4.9
Mazda	4.9	6.0	4.3	6.3	6.7
*Korea**					
Hyundai	52.0	50.3	46.6	46.5	55.9
Kia	18.7	19.7	23.0	26.5	25.0
Daewoo	11.9	24.8	30.2	16.0	19.1
Australia					
GM-Holden	26.3	22.0	17.7	21.3	20.9
Toyota	16.9	16.8	13.4	19.0	15.3
Ford	13.5	15.9	19.6	24.4	28.1
Mitsubishi	8.5	9.6	11.9	10.1	12.2
Hyundai	5.6	8.1	11.1	8.9	n.a.
France					
Renault	27.0	28.2	27.4	30.0	29.1
Peugeot	33.6	30.9	28.8	31.1	34.2
VW	10.7	11.2	11.4	8.0	9.2
Ford	5.5	6.2	8.0	8.1	7.1
Italy					
Fiat	30.3	35.5	43.0	46.0	59.9
VW	12.4	11.8	9.9	10.4	11.7
Ford	9.3	8.8	9.3	9.6	3.7
Peugeot	9.9	7.6	6.3	n.a.	n.a.
Renault	6.9	7.0	6.8	7.0	7.1
UK					
Ford	15.6	20.7	18.7	22.2	26.3
GM	13.0	14.2	14.3	16.9	13.7
Peugeot	13.2	12.3	11.4	12.1	8.7
VW	12.1	11.1	7.9	n.a.	n.a.
BMW/Rover	8.6	7.7	12.9	12.8	15.0
Germany					
VW/Audi	26.0	27.8	25.0	20.9	28.3
GM	10.4	12.5	15.6	16.5	16.1
Ford	8.1	7.6	11.0	9.9	10.1
Mercedes	11.9	12.8	8.5	8.2	9.2
Japanese	10.6	10.8	12.3	12.5	15.2
US					
GM	25.5	28.6	325	34.3	36.3
Ford	16.4	19.1	20.8	22.6	21.7
Chrysler**	8.6	10.5	9.0	9.8	11.3
Toyota	12.2	11.0	9.9	8.5	6.9
Honda	10.3	10.0	10.0	8.5	6.2

* Domestic producers only (excludes imports).
** DaimlerChrysler from 1990.
Source: *Ward's Automotive Yearbooks.*

Table 4.14 World motor vehicle production by countries and regions (% of world total)

	1960	1989	1992	1994	1997	1998	2000	2002
United States	52.0	23.8	20.6	24.5	22.0	23.0	22.2	20.9
Western Europe	38.0	31.7	32.5	31.2	32.6	32.6	29.9	28.8
Central and E. Europe	2.0	4.8	–	4.3	5.6	4.3	4.6	4.4
Japan	1.0	18.2	26.7	21.2	20.5	19.2	17.7	17.4
Korea	–	1.8	3.7	4.6	4.8	3.4	5.0	5.3
Other	7.0	19.7	16.4	14.4	14.5	17.5	20.6	23.2
Total units (millions)	12.8	49.5	47.5	50.0	55.0	53.3	57.4	58.8

Products for E. Europe and USSR included in "Other" for 1991 and 1992.
Sources: AAMA, *Automotive News*.

Table 4.15 Automobile production by country (thousands of cars)

	2002	2000	1998	1997	1995	1994	1992	1990	1987
US	5,016	5,542	5,554	5,884	6,338	6,601	5,664	6,077	7,099
Canada	1,396	1,551	1,481	1,374	1,339	1,215	1,020	1,072	810
Mexico	961	1,130	958	833	710	840	778	346	266
Total N. America	7,373	8,223	7,993	8,091	8,387	8,657	7,463	7,496	8,176
Germany	5,123	5,132	5,348	4,678	4,360	4,040	4,864	4,805	4,604
France	3,284	2,883	2,582	3,326	3,051	3,175	3,320	3,295	3,052
Italy	1,126	1,442	1,378	1,580	1,422	1,341	1,477	1,874	1,701
UK	1,628	1,641	1,748	1,868	1,532	1,467	1,292	1,296	1,143
Spain	2,267	2,445	2,216	1,961	1,959	1,822	1,799	1,679	1,403
Sweden	238	260	368	373	390	353	294	336	432
Total W. Europe	14,435	14,853	14,790	14,687	14,350	13,844	13,520	13,672	13,471
Japan	8,619	8,363	8,055	8,494	7,664	7,801	9,379	9,948	7,891
Korea	2,651	1,881	1,434	2,088	1,893	1,805	1,307	987	793
Australia	307	324	349	323	284	286	270	361	225
China	1,091	620	543	543	356	313	208	n.a.	n.a.
India	706	541	406	380	n.a.	n.a.	n.a.	n.a.	n.a.
Taiwan	245	265	285	258	271	263	283	277	175
Former USSR	981	967	836	1,066	834	798	1,050	1,260	1,329
Poland	287	533	574	426	260	250	212	256	301
Brazil	1,521	1,348	1,223	1,680	1,312	1,249	816	663	789

Sources: Japan Automobile Manufacturers Association, Korean Automobile Manufacturers Association, *Marketing Systems*.

of the market were "luxury cars" distinguished primarily by their price. There were also specific types of vehicle: sports cars, sports utility vehicles (SUVs), small passenger vans ("minivans"), and pickup trucks. Although industry statistics distinguish between automobiles and trucks – the latter being for commercial use – in practice, the distinction was less clear. In the US small pickup trucks were a popular alternative to automobiles; SUVs were also classed as trucks.

Table 4.16 Hourly compensation for motor vehicle workers (US$ per hour including benefits)

	1975	1981	1984	1986	1990	1994	1998	2002
US	9.55	17.03	19.02	20.09	22.48	26.56	27.49	29.15
Mexico	2.94	5.27	2.55	2.03	2.79	4.05	2.94	5.44
Japan	3.56	7.61	7.90	11.80	15.77	26.36	23.38	25.88
Korea	0.45	1.33	1.74	1.84	5.78	8.83	7.75	10.85
Taiwan	0.64	1.86	2.09	2.23	5.72	6.76	6.68	7.00
France	5.10	9.11	8.20	11.06	15.94	17.66	19.32	17.25
Germany	7.89	3.34	11.92	16.96	27.58	36.10	36.70	31.41
Italy	5.16	8.21	8.00	11.03	17.97	16.74	18.56	15.02
Spain	–	7.03	5.35	7.74	15.00	15.17	14.72	13.68
UK	4.12	8.10	7.44	9.22	13.87	15.07	19.63	19.40

Source: US Dept. of Labor, Bureau of Labor Statistics.

Table 4.17 The cost of producing a compact automobile, US and Mexico, 1992 ($)

	US	Mexico
Parts and components	7,750	8,000
Labor	700	140
Shipping costs	300	1,000
Inventory	20	40
Total	8,770	9,180

Source: US Office of Technology Assessment, October 1992.

Margins varied considerably between product segments. Chrysler's position as one of the world's most profitable auto manufacturers for much of the 1990s was primarily a result of its strong position in SUVs (through Jeep) and minivans (through its Dodge Caravan and Plymouth Voyager models). The luxury car segment, too, was traditionally associated with high margins. By contrast, small and medium sized family cars have typically lost money. However, mobility barriers between segments tend to be low. Modular product designs and common platforms and components have facilitated the entry of the major manufacturers into specialty segments. As the pressure of competition has increased across all market segments, manufacturers have sought differentiation advantage through introducing models that combine design features from different segments. During 2000–03, an increasing number of "crossover" vehicles were introduced into the US market, notably: SUVs that adopted the integrated body and frame of the typical automobile, such as the BMW X5, Honda Pilot, and Saturn Vue; minivan–SUV hybrids such as the Chrysler Pacifica and Pontiac Aztec; sports utility station wagons such as the Cadillac SRX; four-wheel drive minivans; luxury SUVs; and smaller SUVs based on small-car platforms such as the Honda CR-X and Toyota RAV4.

Vertical segmentation was also an issue for the industry. Profitability varied across the different stages of the auto industry's value chain. The prevailing wisdom was that downstream activities offered better profit potential than manufacturing activities – certainly financial services (mainly customer and dealer credit) were far more profitable than vehicle manufacturing. It was this logic that had encouraged the auto companies to outsource and spin off most of their production of components. It also motivated Ford's previous CEO, Jacques Nasser, to acquire downstream companies such as the repair and parts supplier Kwik Fit and Hertz car rental.

■ THE OUTLOOK ■

In February 2004, Bruce Blythe reviewed the presentation that the Ford Treasurer, Malcolm MacDonald, would be making on the roadshow that would take him to London, Singapore, and Tokyo. The milestones set for the current year, which predicted pretax profits in automotive operations to reach $0.9–$1.1 billion on volumes that would be similar to 2003, looked achievable, especially given the robust state of the US economy in terms of GDP growth. His concerns related to the longer term. The roadshow presentation forecast that Ford's pretax profit would reach $7 billion by "the middle of the decade." Certainly Ford was determined to maintain its cost cutting momentum. However, cost cutting alone would not be sufficient to achieve this target. Ford's ability to earn a satisfactory margin on its cars would depend critically upon a more favorable industry environment than that which had existed for the past three years. With the world economy still sluggish and dependent primarily on the continuing consumer boom in the US and sustainability of China's booming industrial production, it was not apparent that the excess capacity that had plagued the industry in recent years would be eliminated any time soon. One of the things that Blythe had learned from his years with Ford of Europe was that, even when faced with vast over-capacity, closing car plants was not easy. The presence of powerful unions was one problem, the other was the desire for national governments to provide subsidies to keep uneconomic plants in business in order to avoid localized unemployment.

The most hopeful current trend was the increasing concentration that had resulted from mergers and acquisitions. The ability of the industry to control excess capacity and avoid aggressive price competition (including generous discounts and credit terms) depended critically upon continued consolidation around a dominant group of global producers. The spate of mergers and acquisitions had reduced the number of independent automobile manufacturers producing over 400,000 units a year from 23 in 1995 to 13 in 2002. Most industry experts believed that this consolidation would continue: as early as 1999 *Business Week* had forecast that only manufacturers with annual production of five million vehicles or over would survive, leading to the emergence of a global "Big Six": GM, Ford, DaimlerChrysler, Toyota, VW, and Honda.[3] Others disagreed: Peugeot and BMW were adamant that the benefits of huge volume and broad scope were offset by advantages of flexibility, innovation, and brand strength that placed medium-sized players at a competitive advantage to lumbering giants such as GM, Ford, and DaimlerChrysler.

Looking longer term, there was disagreement over whether the industry would mature through steady, gradual evolution, or would be subject to more radical change. The auto makers had adapted to electronics, new materials, and other technological changes without any major impact on basic automotive design. The prospects for more radical technological change were linked closely with environmental issues. Fears for the demise of the internal combustion engine had proved groundless and most of the investments by the companies in electrical propulsion had been viewed as wasted money. Yet, the threat of global warming was growing, and in several cities of the world problems of pollution were already encouraging government measures to substitute electrical propulsion for gasoline propulsion.

Important developments were also occurring within the value chain. The transfer of manufacturing and technology development from the auto makers to component suppliers seemed likely to continue. Many manufacturers seemed to be unconcerned about losing control over production and technology so long as they could control marketing and distribution. But here, too, some disturbing developments were occurring. The auto companies' control over their distribution networks was threatened by the emergence of new automobile "megastores" (such as Auto Nation and CarMax) and the growth of Internet sales. As *Business Week* observed, "Retailers have historically been the apparatus auto makers use to find homes for all the new cars they crank out. Powerful new buyers could be a threat, the relationship could change to one where the retailer tells the auto maker what to do and what price to sell at."[4]

Changes in the industry's structure over time would influence not just the overall intensity of competition and the prospects of industry profitability, but also how that profit was shared among the different companies. As the companies had converged in terms of technology, design and even quality levels, so cost had emerged as the critical success factor. This in turn had created the drive to exploit economies of scale and scope. Now that all manufacturers were following similar strategies to exploit economies of scale and scope through common vehicle platforms, common components, global models, and global sourcing, what factors would emerge as the critical determinants of competitive advantage during the remainder of the decade?

APPENDIX
The World's Major Automobile Producers, Sales, and Profitability 1980–2003

Table 4.A1 Sales ($ billion)

	2003	2002	2001	2000	1999	1998	1997	1996	1995	1990–4	1985–9	1980–4
GM	186	187	177	185	167	161	178	168	169	128	110	68
Ford	164	163	162	170	163	144	154	147	137	96	77	42
DaimlerChrysler	172	157	136	152	151	142	–	–	–	–	–	–
Chrysler	–	–	–	–	–	–	61	61	53	39	28	13
Daimler Benz	–	–	–	–	–	–	70	72	72	59	34	12
Toyota	129	107	106	121	120	113	84	109	111	82	42	18
VW	109	91	78	79	70	60	64	67	61	48	28	16
Honda	67	55	52	58	57	60	43	47	44	35	18	8
Fiat	61	55	58	53	45	56	51	51	46	42	27	18
Nissan	57	47	49	55	61	54	47	59	63	51	26	16
Peugeot	68	57	46	41	38	39	31	34	33	28	19	13
Renault	47	38	32	37	35	43	35	36	37	31	31	15
BMW	52	44	34	33	33	35	34	35	32	21	10	5
Mitsubishi	32	24	26	30	32	27	n.a	33	37	25	14	12
Hyundai Motor	21	40	30	29	21	15	n.a.	n.a.	n.a.	n.a.	n.a.	n.a.
Mazda	20	16	16	16	20	17	15	17	19	21	12	n.a.

Table 4.A2 Return on equity (%)

	2003	2002	2001	2000	1999	1998	1997	1996	1995	1990–4	1985–9	1980–4
GM	15.1	25.6	3.0	14.8	29.9	19.7	37.1	21.2	29.5	3.2	11.8	11.4
Ford	4.2	(17.5)	(70.0)	18.6	26.3	94.3	22.9	16.6	16.9	5.9	21.8	0.4
DaimlerChrysler	1.3	13.5	(1.7)	18.3	15.9	15.9	–	–	–	–	–	–
Chrysler	–	–	–	–	–	–	24.6	30.5	18.5	2.0	20.8	66.5
Daimler Benz	–	–	–	–	–	–	12.0	10.5	43.8	6.9	18.3	24.3
Toyota	10.5	7.7	9.5	7.5	6.5	6.8	8.0	7.5	5.4	6.1	10.6	12.6
VW	4.4	–	10.5	12.1	18.0	13.2	6.2	14.6	3.4	(0.4)	6.3	1.6
Honda	16.1	14.0	10.6	11.8	14.9	17.3	18.8	17.5	6.8	5.3	11.8	18.1
Fiat	(51.3)	(3.7)	5.0	4.9	3.4	4.8	10.6	9.7	9.7	6.8	18.7	10.9
Nissan	27.2	23.0	36.4	39.2	(3.8)	(2.2)	(8.0)	6.3	7.2	3.6	4.68	10.3
Peugeot	12.1	14.6	15.3	13.8	9.5	5.7	(4.7)	1.3	3.1	12.5	36.7	(15.2)
Renault	17.6	16.4	10.1	11.0	6.5	17.0	12.6	14.2	4.8	9.1	51.1	(152.4)
BMW	11.8	14.5	17.3	20.6	11.3	(63.2)	14.1	9.4	8.5	9.7	10.4	14.8
Mitsubishi	12.5	3.9	n.a.	(123.2)	(26.8)	0.2	n.a.	2.6	2.9	4.8	7.9	10.0
Hyundai Motor	n.a.	10.7	10.0	8.9	7.7	1.0	n.a.	n.a.	n.a.	n.a.	n.a.	n.a.
Mazda	12.0	4.9	(93.2)	(110.7)	11.6	10.9	(1.0)	5.6	4.3	5.0	4.8	n.a.

NOTES

1. Ford Motor Company, 10K Report, 2003.
2. "Survey of China," *The Economist*, March 20, 2004, p. 6.
3. "Autos: The Global Six," *Business Week*, January 25, 1999, pp. 68–72.
4. *Business Week*, February 24, 1997, p. 89.

case five

Wal-Mart Stores Inc., March 2004

Robert M. Grant

How did a peddler of cheap shirts and fishing rods become the mightiest corporation in America?

Fortune, **April 12, 2002**

Wal-Mart's financial results for the year ended January 31, 2004 set new records for the company: compared with the previous year, sales were up by 2 percent and net income had increased by 13 percent. For the second year running, Wal-Mart would top the *Fortune* Global 500 as the world's largest company and the world's biggest private sector employer, with 1.4 million employees.

Wal-Mart's transformation from a small chain of discount stores in Arkansas, Missouri, and Oklahoma in 1970 to the world's largest retailer was one of the most remarkable corporate success stories of the twentieth century. Its founder, Sam Walton, had combined folksy charm and homespun business wisdom with cutting-edge information technology and supply chain management to create the world's most efficient retail organization.

Lee Scott was Wal-Mart's third CEO. Like his predecessors Sam Walton and David Glass, he had remained firmly committed to Wal-Mart's long-term goals of growth and continual adaptation. His main contributions to these goals were, first, his emphasis on overseas growth, and, second, his pioneering of new retail formats, notably the building of "Supercenters" (100,000–200,000 sq ft stores that combined a discount store with a supermarket). By early 2004, there were more Supercenters than traditional Wal-Mart discount stores in the US. During 2004, expansion would continue with 270 new stores in the US and some 140 new stores overseas – an 8 percent increase in Wal-Mart's retail square footage. In March 2004, the company added to its growing list of overseas acquisitions with the purchase of the Bompreco chain of supermarkets in Brazil from Ahold, the Dutch retail giant. Yet, despite Wal-Mart's proven ability to grow its sales and profits irrespective of the state of the national or international economy, Scott remained concerned about the future. He recognized that in the fast-moving, hyper-competitive retail sector, size offered no guarantee of continued success. Previous decades had witnessed the decline of many of America's greatest retailing empires – Sears Roebuck, Montgomery Ward, A&P, and Federated Department Stores, to mention just a few. Wal-Mart's success had been built upon a unique culture founded by Sam Walton and forged in rural Arkansas. But Sam Walton has been dead for ten years and Wal-Mart had far outgrown its Arkansas home base. By 2004, Wal-Mart was a global retailing colossus that was still closely linked to its small-town, Arkansas origins. Wal-Mart's success rested upon its ability to offer its customers "Always low prices. Always." Wal-Mart's success at keeping its costs below those of its competitors rested upon its culture of frugality and the continual striving of its employees to find new ways to reduce costs and better serve customers. How far would size and success blunt Wal-Mart's drive for efficiency, responsiveness, and innovation? As Wal-Mart grew it increasingly became a target for antiglobalization activists, pro-labor groups, small businesses, and conservationists. In response to these threats, Wal-Mart was continually adding to its headquarters staff. Would existing competitors imitate Wal-Mart's strategy and systems? In discount stores, Target had successfully adopted many of Wal-Mart's retailing and supply chain practices while Costco was seen by many as outflanking Wal-Mart's Sam's Club warehouses by combining down-market prices with up-market appeal. And would new competitors emerge with new and superior approaches to retailing? Despite the collapse of the dot.com boom, online retailers were capturing more and more of the retail market across a broad range of products from computers to pharmaceuticals.

■ HISTORY ■

Sam Walton opened his first store – a franchised Ben Franklin variety store – in 1945. Over the next 15 years, Sam together with his brother, Bud, developed a chain of 15 Ben Franklin stores throughout rural Arkansas. During this period, Sam Walton became aware of the increasing price competition from discount retailers – large format stores that offered a broad range of products that included apparel, appliances, toiletries, household goods, and sometimes groceries as well. This new category of retailer emerged in the US following World War II. Discount stores were located within large towns – it was generally believed that a minimum population of 100,000 was necessary for a discount store to be viable. Sam Walton believed that discount stores could be viable in smaller communities: if the prices were right, the stores would attract customers from a wide area: "Our strategy was to put good-sized stores into little one-horse towns that everyone else was ignoring."[1] Walton opened his first Wal-Mart in 1962 and within eight years had 30 discount stores in small and medium-sized towns in Arkansas, Oklahoma, and Missouri.

Distribution was a problem for Wal-Mart:

> Here we were in the boondocks, so we didn't have distributors falling over themselves to serve us like our competitors in larger towns. Our only alternative was to build our own distribution centers so that we could buy in volume at attractive prices and store the merchandise.[2]

In 1970, Walton built his first distribution center, and in the same year took the company public in order to finance the heavy investment involved. With this structure of large distribution hubs serving a group of 15 to 20 discount stores, Wal-Mart began its rapid expansion across the country. At the end of 1980, Wal-Mart had 330 stores in 11 states (Arkansas, Oklahoma, Missouri, Texas, Kansas, Kentucky, Tennessee, Mississippi, Louisiana, Alabama, and Illinois). By the end of 1985, there were 859 stores in 22 southern and mid-western states. At the beginning of 1994, there were 1,953 stores operating in every state except Vermont, Alaska, and Hawaii. Wal-Mart's geographical expansion was incremental. It moved into a new area, first, by building a few stores that were served by extending Wal-Mart's distribution lines from a nearby cluster; eventually, when a critical mass of stores had been established in the new area, Wal-Mart would build a distribution center to serve the new cluster. Expansion brought Wal-Mart into closer competition with other discount chains. In the small towns of the southwest and south, Wal-Mart faced few major competitors. As Wal-Mart became a national retail chain it entered more developed retailing areas, including larger cities. By 1993, 55 percent of Wal-Mart stores faced direct competition from Kmart and 23 percent from Target.[3]

strategy

Diversification

During the 1980s, Sam Walton began experimenting with alternative retail formats. These included Sam's Club (1983), Helen's Arts and Crafts (1995), and Dot Deep Discount Drugstores. In addition, very large retail outlets, Wal-Mart Supercenters and Hypermart USA, were introduced. Helen's Arts and Crafts, Dot Drugstores, and Hypermart USA were sold off, but the other two store types – the Sam's warehouse clubs and the Supercenters – grew rapidly to become important components of Wal-Mart's business.

Sam's Clubs imitated a distribution concept established by Price Club. The warehouse clubs were not retailers since they were not open to the public. They were clubs where access was through membership. They carried a small number of lines and most items were available in multipacks and catering-size packs. The clubs were literally warehouses with products available on pallets and minimal customer service. The rationale was to maximize economies in purchasing, minimize operating costs, and pass the savings on to members through very low prices. Competition among warehouse clubs was ferocious, resulting in rapid consolidation of the sector. Wal-Mart acquired The Wholesale Company in 1991 and Kmart's PACE clubs in 1993, while Costco Wholesale and PriceCo merged in 1993.

Supercenters were Wal-Mart stores with larger floor space – typically 120,000 to 180,000 square feet, about double the size of the average Wal-Mart discount store. Supercenters were modeled on the European concept of the "hypermarket" that had been pioneered by the French retailer Carrefour. A Supercenter combined a discount store with a grocery supermarket; in addition, a Supercenter incorporated a number of specialty units such as an eyeglass store, hair salon, dry cleaners, and photo lab. The Supercenters were open for 24 hours a day, seven days a week. The Supercenter stores and Sam's Clubs were supplied through a separate distribution network from the Wal-Mart discount stores. In 1990, Wal-Mart acquired McLane, a Texas-based wholesale distributor, that became the basis for Wal-Mart's distribution to Supercenters and Sam's Clubs throughout the US.

International Expansion

By the end of the 1980s, Wal-Mart was concerned that it might be running out of new territory and began looking for opportunities abroad. In 1992, Wal-Mart established a joint venture with Mexico's largest retailer, Cifra S.A., and began opening Wal-Mart discount stores and Sam's Clubs in several Mexican cities. Within seven years the two companies had opened 416 stores in Mexico, and Wal-Mart had established a dominant position in the venture through acquiring 51 percent of Cifra.

In 1994, Wal-Mart entered the Canadian market by acquiring 120 Woolco stores from Woolworth and converting them to its own discount stores format. Wal-Mart boosted the sales per square foot of the Woolco stores from $98 in 1994 to $287 in 1999, taking 40 percent of total discount store sales, and establishing Wal-Mart as Canada's largest retailer.

In Argentina, Wal-Mart entered by establishing a number of Sam's Club outlets, while in Brazil it concentrated upon opening stores in the Sao Paulo area.

In Europe, Wal-Mart established itself through acquisition. In Germany, Wal-Mart acquired the 21-store Wertkauf chain, and followed this with the purchase of 21 Interspar stores. In the UK, the third largest supermarket chain, Asda Stores, with its 232 retail outlets was purchased for $10.8 billion in 1999.

In Asia, Wal-Mart proceeded more cautiously – aware of the huge market potential but wary of the risks. In South Korea, Wal-Mart acquired four stores, previously operated by the Dutch retailer Makro, from H. S. Chang, a Korean businessman. In China, Wal-Mart initially proposed to enter through an alliance with CP, the Thailand-based conglomerate. Disagreements between CP and Wal-Mart eventually resulted in Wal-Mart going it alone with Sam's Club and Supercenter stores initially in the Shenzhen Economic Zone of southern China.

Wal-Mart's performance in overseas markets was mixed. Its strongest performance was in adjacent countries – Mexico and Canada – and also in Britain, where its Asda supermarket chain enthusiastically adopted Wal-Mart's systems and its culture. In Argentina and Germany it encountered major difficulties in adjusting to local conditions, while in Indonesia, a joint venture with PT Multipolar collapsed amidst acrimony and lawsuits.

Table 5.1 lists major events in Wal-Mart's development.

Table 5.1   Wal-Mart – Key Historical Facts

1962	Wal-Mart's founder, Sam Walton, opens the first Wal-Mart in Rogers, Arkansas
1970	Wal-Mart opens its first distribution center, Bentonville, Ark.
1970	Wal-Mart goes public
1971	Continued expansion results in Wal-Mart stores in five states: Arkansas, Kansas, Louisiana, Missouri and Oklahoma
1972	Wal-Mart listed on NYSE
1975	After visit to Korea, Walton introduces the "Wal-Mart Cheer"
1977	Acquires 16 Mohr-Value stores in Michigan and Illinois
1981	Acquires 92 Kuhn's Big K stores
1983	First Sam's Club opens, Midwest City, Oklahoma
1983	Woolco's US stores acquired
1985	Sam Walton becomes the wealthiest person in the US
1987	Wal-Mart Satellite Network completed
1988	David Glass takes over from Sam Walton as CEO
1988	First Supercenter opens, Washington, Missouri
1990	Wal-Mart becomes largest retailer in the US
1991	Begins international expansion with store in Mexico City
1992	Death of Sam Walton. S. Robson Walton becomes Chairman
1992	Enters Puerto Rico
1993	91 Pace Warehouse clubs acquired
1994	Enters Canada with acquisition of 122 Woolco stores
1995	Wal-Mart enters its 50th state – Vermont
1995	Enters Argentina and Brazil
1996	Expands into Asia with first Wal-Mart in China
1998	Enters Germany and Korea
1999	Acquires Asda Stores, a major UK discount retailer
2000	H. Lee Scott named president and CEO
2001	Wal-Mart named by *Fortune* as the third most admired company in America
2002	*Fortune* Global 500 identifies Wal-Mart as the world's largest company
2003	Wal-Mart named by *Fortune* as the most admired company in America

Sam Walton

Wal-Mart's strategy and management style was inseparable from the philosophy and values of its founder. Until his death in 1992, Sam Walton was the embodiment of Wal-Mart's unique approach to retailing. After his death, Sam Walton's beliefs and business principles continued to be the beacon that guided Wal-Mart from success to success. As Harry Cunningham, founder of Kmart Stores, observed: "Sam's establishment of the Walton culture throughout the company was the key to the whole thing. It's just incomparable. He is the greatest businessman of this century."[4]

For Sam Walton, thrift and value for money was a religion. Undercutting competitors' prices was an obsession, as was the never-ending quest for cost economies that would permit continuing price cutting. Walton established a culture in which every item of expenditure was questioned – was it necessary? Could it be done cheaper? He set an example that few of his senior colleagues could match: he walked rather than took taxis, shared rooms at budget motels while on business trips, and avoided any corporate trappings or manifestations of opulence or success. For Walton, wealth was a threat and an embarrassment, rather than a reward and a privilege. His own lifestyle gave little indication that he was America's richest person (before being eclipsed by Bill Gates). He also felt uncomfortable about the wealth of his associates: "We've had lots of millionaires in our ranks. And it drives me crazy when they flaunt it. Every now and then somebody will do something especially showy, and I don't hesitate to rant and rave about it at the Saturday morning meeting. I don't think that big mansions and flashy cars is what the Wal-Mart culture is supposed to be about."[5]

His attention to detail was legendary. As chairman and chief executive, he was quite clear that his priorities lay with his employees ("associates"), customers, and the operational details through which the former created value for the latter. He shunned offices in favor of spending time in his stores. Most of his life was spent on the road (or, in his case, in the air flying between stores piloting his own plane), making impromptu visits to stores and distribution centers. He collected information on which products were selling well in Tuscaloosa; why margins were down in Santa Maria; how a new display system for children's clothing in Carbondale had boosted sales by 15 percent. His passion for detail extended to competitors' stores as well as his own: not only did he regularly visit competitors' stores; he was known to count cars in their parking lots.

Central to his leadership role at Wal-Mart was his relationship with his employees – the Wal-Mart associates. In an industry known for low pay and hard working conditions, Walton created a unique feeling of motivation and involvement. He believed fervently in giving people responsibility, trusting them, but also continually monitoring their performance.

Since his death, Sam Walton's habits and utterances have become hallowed principles guiding the values of the company and the behavior of its employees. For example, Wal-Mart's "10-foot attitude" pledge is based upon Sam Walton's request to a store employee that: "I want you to promise that whenever you come within 10 feet of a customer, you will look him in the eye, greet him and ask if you can help him."[6]

Sam Walton's ability to attract the affection and loyalty of both employees and customers owes much to his ability to generate fun and excitement within the otherwise sterile world of discount retailing. Sam Walton brought a sense of unpredictability and fun to the business. He engendered a positive attitude among Wal-Mart employees and he reveled in his role as company cheerleader.

Sam Walton's contribution to the management systems and management style of Wal-Mart is reflected in Wal-Mart's web site's description of "The Wal-Mart Culture" (see the Appendix).

■ WAL-MART IN 2004 ■

The Businesses

During the early months of 2004, Wal-Mart's 4,900 stores and 1.4 million employees were selling at the rate of $260 billion annually to the 100 million customers who visited Wal-Mart stores each week. These sales occurred through four major areas of business:

- *Wal-Mart stores*. Wal-Mart's core area of business in 2004 was US retail stores. These comprised Wal-Mart's traditional discount stores – large, self-service stores offering a broad range of non-food products that included apparel, shoes, household textiles (bedding, towels, fabrics), appliances, toys and games, sporting goods, electronic products, recorded music, pharmaceuticals, health and beauty products, stationery, auto supplies, jewelry, and candy. However, the most rapidly growing part of the business was the Wal-Mart Supercenters, much larger stores that combined a discount store with a super-market. Superstores were based upon the European "hypermarket" concept. By 2004, Wal-Mart was the nation's No. 1 food retailer with $60 billion of grocery sales a year – roughly 11 percent of the US grocery market. The ratio-nale for entry into food was simple: whereas the average shopper might come to Wal-Mart only once or twice a month, people buy groceries, on average, more than twice a week. Some Supercenters employed over 500 associates and generated over $100 million in sales each year. Most of Wal-Mart's super-stores were the result of converting existing Wal-Mart stores. By 2004, Super-stores were generating substantially more sales than the traditional Wal-Mart discount stores.
- *Sam's Clubs*. Wal-Mart's entry into warehouse clubs in the mid-1980s demonstrated its ability to transfer its retailing capabilities to a very different retail format. These wholesale outlets offered a narrower range of products – typically around 4,000 stock-keeping units (SKUs) as compared with the 50,000 SKUs for most Wal-Mart discount stores – at prices significantly below those of discount stores. The development of Sam's Club also demon-strated Wal-Mart's capacity for continuous improvement and innovation. From the stark, austere warehouses of the 1980s, Wal-Mart had created a unique wholesale distribution experience. During 2002–04, Wal-Mart upgraded many of its Sam's Clubs to include a members' restaurant, a section featuring premium wines and gourmet foods, a gas station, and an optical department.
- *Wal-Mart's international operations*. These comprised a number of separate national subsidiaries, each attempting to interpret the basic Wal-Mart business principles and underlying approach to retailing within a distinctive economic structure and national culture. Wal-Mart's differentiated approach to different countries reflected the different retailing environments of these countries and the different entry opportunities that had presented themselves. Wal-Mart's joint ventures in Mexico and South America reflected its desire to access local knowledge and utilize the resources and capabilities of strong local players. Its acquisition of Asda in the UK was the result of the strong affinities that the two retailers felt for one another. (Asda had long modeled its strategy and management style upon Wal-Mart.) Wal-Mart's inter-national expansion had been a process of learning and adaptation where senior executives openly acknowledged the difficulties: "Cultural transi-

Table 5.2 Wal-Mart stores by types and location, January 2004

	Discount stores	Supercenters	Sam's Clubs	Neighborhood markets
USA	1,478	1,471	538	64
Argentina	0	11	0	0
Brazil	0	13	10	2[a]
Canada	231	0	4	0
China	0	28	4	2
Germany	0	92	0	0
South Korea	0	15	0	0
Mexico	487[b]	83	53	0
Puerto Rico	9	3	9	32
United Kingdom	255[c]	12	0	0
TOTAL	2,460	1,728	618	100

[a] Includes *To do Dia* stores.
[b] Includes Bodegas, Suburbia, Superamas, and VIP stores.
[c] Includes 253 Asda stores and 2 George stores.
Source: www.wal-mart.com.

tions haven't always been this smooth for Wal-Mart International. In Argentina, for example, Wal-Mart initially faced challenges in adapting its US-based retail mix and store layouts to the local culture."[7] John Menzer, head of the international division, observed: "It wasn't such a good idea to stick so closely to the domestic Wal-Mart blueprint in Argentina or in some other international markets we have entered. In Mexico City we sold tennis balls that wouldn't bounce right in the high altitude. We built large parking lots at some of our Mexican stores only to realize that many of our customers there rode the bus to the store, then trudged across these large parking lots carrying bags of merchandise . . . We're now working smarter internationally to avoid cultural and regional problems on the front end."[8]

- *McLane Company Inc.* This company distributes to Sam's Clubs and Supercenters. It is the main component of the business segment denoted "other" in Wal-Mart's accounts (see table 5.3).

Table 5.2 lists Wal-Mart stores by types and location. Table 5.3 shows sales and profits for the different business segments.

Performance

Table 5.4 summarizes some key financial data for Wal-Mart during the period 1994 to 2004. Table 5.5 shows Wal-Mart's recent performance compared with other discount retailers.

Table 5.3 Wal-Mart: performance by segment

	Wal-Mart stores	Sam's Clubs	International	Other
Sales ($, bill.)				
2004	174.2	34.5	47.6	0
2003	157.1	31.7	40.8	0
2002	139.1	29.4	35.5	13.8
2001	121.9	26.8	32.1	10.5
2000	108.7	24.8	22.7	8.8
Sales increase				
2004	10.9%	8.9%	16.6%	0%
2003	12.9%	7.8%	15.0%	0%
2002	14.1%	9.7%	10.5%	30.8%
2001	12.1%	8.1%	41.2%	20.3%
2000	14.0%	8.4%	85.6%	23.2%
Operating income ($, mill.)				
2004	12.9	1.13	2.4	(1.39)
2003	11.8	1.02	2.0	(1.57)
2002	10.3	1.03	1.46	(0.71)
2001	9.70	0.94	1.11	(0.29)
2000	8.70	0.85	0.82	(0.26)
Op. income/Sales				
2004	7.4%	3.3%	5.0%	–
2003	7.5%	3.2%	4.9%	–
2002	7.4%	3.5%	4.1%	(5.2)%
2001	8.0%	3.5%	3.5%	(2.7)%
2000	8.0%	3.4%	3.6%	(3.0)%

Source: Wal-Mart annual financial statements.

■ WAL-MART STORES' OPERATIONS AND ACTIVITIES[9] ■

Purchasing and Vendor Relationships

The size of Wal-Mart's purchases and its negotiating ability meant that Wal-Mart was both desired and feared by manufacturers. Being accepted as a Wal-Mart vendor offered access to a huge share of the US retail market. At the same time, Wal-Mart buyers were well aware of their ability to take full advantage of economies of scale available to their suppliers and to squeeze their margins to razor-thin level. Purchasing was centralized. All dealing with buyers took place at Wal-Mart's Bentonville headquarters. Here vendors were escorted to interview rooms equipped only with a table and four chairs. Suppliers regarded the experience of selling to Wal-Mart as intimidating and grueling: "Once you are ushered into one of the spartan little buyer's rooms, expect a steely eye across the table and be prepared to cut your

Table 5.4 Wal-Mart Stores Inc.: financial summary 1994–2004

	2004	2003	2002	2001	2000	1999	1998	1997	1996	1995	1994
Income											
Net sales	256.3	229.6	217.8	191.3	165.0	137.6	118.0	104.9	93.6	82.5	67.3
Net sales increase	12%	5%	4%	16%	20%	17%	12%	12%	13%	22%	21%
Same-store sales increase	4%	6%	6%	5%	8%	9%	6%	5%	4%	7%	6%
Other income – net	2.4	2.0	2.0	2.0	1.8	1.6	1.3	1.3	1.1	0.9	0.6
Cost of sales	198.7	178.3	171.6	150.3	129.7	108.7	93.4	83.5	74.5	65.6	53.4
SGA administrative expenses	44.9	40.0	36.2	31.6	27.0	22.4	19.4	16.9	15.0	12.9	10.3
Interest costs:											
Debt	0.7	0.8	1.1	1.1	0.8	0.5	0.6	0.6	0.7	0.5	0.3
Capital leases	0.3	0.3	0.3	0.3	0.3	0.3	0.2	0.2	0.2	0.2	0.2
Provision for income taxes	5.1	4.4	3.9	3.7	3.3	2.7	2.1	1.8	1.6	1.6	1.4
Minority interests	1.4	1.2	(183)	(129)	(170)	(153)	(78)	(27)	(13)	(4)	(4)
Net income	9.1	8.0	6.7	6.3	5.4	4.4	3.5	3.1	2.7	2.7	2.3
Financial Position											
Current assets	34.5	30.7	28.2	26.6	24.4	21.1	19.4	18.0	17.3	15.3	12.1
Inventories (replacement cost)	26.6	24.4	22.7	21.6	20.2	17.5	16.8	16.2	16.3	14.4	11.5
Net property, plant, equipment, and capital leases	58.5	51.4	45.8	40.9	36.0	26.0	23.6	20.3	18.9	15.9	13.2

Total assets	104.9	94.8	83.5	78.1	70.3	50.0	45.4	39.6	37.5	32.8	26.4
Current liabilities	37.4	32.5	27.3	28.9	25.8	16.8	14.5	11.0	11.5	10.0	7.4
Long-term debt	17.1	16.6	15.7	12.5	13.7	6.9	7.2	7.7	8.5	7.9	6.2
Long-term lease obligations	3.0	3.0	3.0	3.2	3.0	2.7	2.5	2.3	2.1	1.8	1.8
Shareholders' equity	43.6	39.5	35.1	31.3	25.8	21.1	18.5	17.1	14.8	12.7	10.8
Financial Ratios											
Current ratio	0.9	0.9	1.0	0.9	0.9	1.3	1.3	1.6	1.5	1.5	1.6
Return on assets*	9.0%	9.0%	8.5%	8.7%	9.5%	9.6%	8.5%	7.9%	7.8%	9.0%	9.9%
Return on equity**	21.0%	21.0%	20.1%	22.0%	22.9%	22.4%	19.8%	19.2%	19.9%	22.8%	23.9%
Other Year-End Data											
No. of US discount stores	1,478	1,568	1,647	1,736	1,801	1,869	1,921	1,960	1,995	1,985	1,950
No. of U.S. Supercenters	1,471	1,258	1,066	888	721	564	441	344	239	147	72
No. of U.S. Sam's Clubs	538	525	500	475	463	451	443	436	433	426	417
No. of U.S. Neighborhood Mkts.	64	49	31	19	7	4	–	–	–	–	–
International units	1,355	1,272	1,170	1,071	1,004	715	601	314	276	226	24
Number of Associates ('000s)	1,400	1,400	1,383	1,244	1,140	910	825	728	675	622	528

*Net income before minority interest, equity in unconsolidated subsidiaries and cumulative effect of accounting change/Average assets.

**Net income/average shareholders' equity.

Source: Wal-Mart annual financial statements.

Table 5.5 Wal-Mart and its competitors: Performance comparisons

	Wal-Mart	Target	Kmart	Costco	Dollar General
Sales revenue ($, bill.)					
2004	256.3	48.2	–	–	6.9
2003	244.5	43.9	30.8	42.5	6.1
2002	217.8	39.9	36.2	38.8	5.3
2001	191.3	36.9	37.0	32.2	4.6
Cost of goods sold ($, bill.)					
2004	194.9	31.8	–	–	4.7
2003	188.4	29.3	26.3	36.8	4.2
2002	168.3	27.2	29.1	33.6	3.7
2001	147.4	25.3	28.9	28.1	3.2
Gross profit ($, bill.)					
2004	61.4	16.4	–	–	2.2
2003	56.1	14.7	4.5	5.7	1.9
2002	49.5	12.6	7.0	5.1	1.6
2001	43.9	11.6	8.1	4.1	1.4
Gross margin (%)					
2004	24.0	34.0	–	–	31.6
2003	22.9	33.4	14.6	13.4	30.5
2002	22.7	31.7	19.5	13.2	30.7
2001	23.0	31.5	22.0	12.7	29.9
SG&A expense ($, bill.)					
2004	44.9	11.5	–	–	1.5
2003	41.0	10.2	7.2	4.2	1.3
2002	36.2	8.9	7.6	3.6	1.1
2001	31.6	8.2	6.7	2.8	0.9
Depreciation & amortization ($, bill.)					
2004	3.9	1.3	–	–	0.2
2003	3.4	1.2	–	0.4	0.1
2002	3.3	1.1	0.8	0.3	0.1
2001	2.9	0.9	0.8	0.3	0.1
Operating income ($, bill.)					
2004	12.7	3.5	–	–	0.5
2003	11.6	3.3	(2.7)	1.2	0.4
2002	10.1	2.7	(1.4)	1.1	0.4
2001	9.5	2.5	0.7	1.0	0.3
Operating margin (%)					
2004	4.9	7.3	–	–	7.6
2003	4.8	7.4	(8.8)	2.7	7.0
2002	4.6	6.7	(3.9)	2.9	7.0
2001	5.0	6.7	1.8	3.2	6.9
Net income ($, bill.)					
2004	9.1	1.8	–	–	0.3
2003	8.0	1.7	(3.3)	0.7	0.3
2002	6.7	1.4	(2.4)	0.7	0.2
2001	6.3	1.3	(0.2)	0.6	0.1
Net profit margin (%)					
2004	3.5	3.8	–	–	4.4
2003	3.3	3.8	(10.4)	1.7	4.3
2002	3.1	3.4	(6.6)	1.8	3.9
2001	3.3	3.4	(0.5)	2.0	1.6
Cash ($, bil.)					
2004	5.2	0.7	–	–	0.4

Table 5.5 *continued*

	Wal-Mart	Target	Kmart	Costco	Dollar General
2003	2.8	0.8	0.6	1.5	0.1
2002	2.2	0.5	1.2	0.8	0.3
2001	2.1	0.4	0.4	0.5	0.2
Net receivables ($, bill.)					
2004	1.3	5.8	–	–	0.0
2003	2.1	5.6	0.0	0.6	0.0
2002	2.0	3.8	0.0	0.5	0.0
2001	1.8	1.9	0.0	0.2	0.0
Inventories ($, bill.)					
2004	26.6	5.3	–	–	1.2
2003	24.9	4.8	4.8	3.3	1.1
2002	22.6	4.5	5.8	3.1	1.1
2001	21.4	4.3	6.4	2.7	0.9
Total current assets ($, bill.)					
2004	34.4	12.9	–	–	1.7
2003	30.5	11.9	6.1	5.7	1.3
2002	28.2	9.6	7.9	4.6	1.6
2001	26.6	7.3	7.6	3.9	1.1
Total assets ($, bill.)					
2004	104.9	31.4	–	–	2.7
2003	94.7	28.6	11.2	13.2	2.3
2002	83.5	24.2	14.3	11.6	2.6
2001	78.1	19.5	14.6	8.6	2.3
Short-term debt ($, bill.)					
2004	6.4	0.9	–	–	0.0
2003	5.8	1.0	0.0	0.0	0.0
2002	3.1	0.9	0.0	0.1	0.4
2001	6.7	0.9	0.1	0.0	0.0
Total current liabilities ($, bill.)					
2004	37.4	8.3	–	–	0.7
2003	32.6	7.5	2.1	5.0	0.7
2002	27.3	7.1	0.6	4.4	1.1
2001	28.9	6.3	3.8	3.4	0.5
Long-term debt ($, bill.)					
2004	20.1	10.2	–	–	0.3
2003	19.6	10.2	0.6	1.3	0.3
2002	18.7	8.1	1.2	1.2	0.3
2001	15.7	5.6	3.0	0.8	0.7
Total liabilities ($, bill.)					
2004	61.3	20.3	–	–	1.1
2003	55.3	19.2	10.9	6.6	1.0
2002	48.3	16.3	10.8	5.9	1.5
2001	46.8	13.0	8.5	4.4	1.4
Shareholders' equity ($, bill.)					
2004	43.6	11.1	–	–	1.6
2003	39.3	9.4	0.3	6.6	1.3
2002	35.1	7.9	3.5	5.7	1.0
2001	31.3	6.5	6.1	4.9	0.9

Source: Hoovers.com.

price."[10] Another vendor commented: "all normal mating rituals are verboten. Their highest priority is making sure everybody at all times in all cases knows who's in charge . . . They talk softly, but they have piranha hearts, and if you aren't totally prepared when you go in there, you're in deep trouble."[11] The requirements that Wal-Mart imposed on its suppliers extended well beyond low prices. Increasingly Wal-Mart involved itself in its suppliers' employment policies, including workplace safety, working hours, and absence of child labor.

All negotiations were directly between manufacturers and Wal-Mart: from 1992 onwards Wal-Mart refused to do business with manufacturers' representatives and agents. To avoid dependence on any one supplier, Wal-Mart did not allow any single manufacturer to supply more than 2.5 percent of its total purchases.

During the past ten years, Wal-Mart established closer collaborative arrangements with its biggest suppliers. Wal-Mart's cooperation with Procter & Gamble provided a model for these relationships. P&G was Wal-Mart's biggest supplier accounting for about 2 percent of Wal-Mart's purchases, but nearly 10 percent of P&G's sales. The companies began electronic data interchange (EDI) at the beginning of the 1990s, and by 1993 there were 70 P&G employees working at Bentonville to manage sales and deliveries to Wal-Mart.

By the mid-1990s, Wal-Mart had extended EDI to cover about 70 percent of its vendors. Through Wal-Mart's "Retail Link" system of supply-chain management, data interchange included point-of-sale data, levels of inventory, Wal-Mart's sales forecasts, vendors' production and delivery schedules, and electronic funds transfer.

Through collaboration with Cisco Systems, Retail Link was moved to the Internet during the mid-1990s allowing suppliers to log onto the Wal-Mart database for real-time store-by-store information on sales and inventory for their products. This allowed suppliers to work with Wal-Mart company's buyers to manage inventory in the stores – forecasting, planning, producing, and shipping products as needed. The result was faster replenishment, a product mix tuned to the needs of local customers, and lower inventory costs for Wal-Mart. "We transformed it from a traditional dial-in network to an internet application," says Flanagan. "Now it's easier for our vendors to use, because they just need a web browser. More of our international suppliers can get access, because it's on the internet. And it's easier and less expensive for us to maintain."

Warehousing and Distribution

Wal-Mart distributed a higher proportion of goods to its own stores than any other discount retailer. While most discount retailers relied heavily upon their suppliers to undertake distribution to individual stores, over 80 percent of Wal-Mart's purchases were shipped to Wal-Mart's own distribution centers from where they were distributed in Wal-Mart trucks. The system that operated in 2002 was fundamentally the same as that which a Harvard Business School case described in 1994:

> Each store received an average of five full or partial truckloads a week, and because Wal-Mart stores were grouped together, trucks could resupply several on a single trip. Returned

merchandise was carried back to the distribution center for consolidation, and since many vendors operated warehouses or factories within Wal-Mart's territory, trucks also picked up new shipments on the return trip. Roughly 2,500 people drove Wal-Mart's fleet of 2,000 trucks, which ran more than 60 percent full on backhauls. A store could select one of four options regarding the frequency and timing of shipments, and more than half accepted night deliveries. For stores located within a particular distance from the distribution center, an accelerated delivery plan was available, which allowed merchandise to be delivered within 24 hours.[12]

A typical distribution center spanned a million square feet and was operated 24 hours a day by a staff of 700 associates. It was highly automated and designed to serve the needs of about 150 stores within a radius of 200 miles. When orders were pulled from stock, an automated "pick to light" system guided associates to the correct locations.

Since the mid-1990s, Wal-Mart continued upgrading its distribution system. It was an early adopter of "cross-docking" – a system where goods arriving on inbound trucks were unloaded and reloaded on outbound trucks without first sitting in warehouse inventory.

In-Store Operations

Wal-Mart's management of its retail stores was based upon its objective of creating customer satisfaction by combining low prices, a wide range of quality products carefully tailored to customer needs, and a pleasing shopping experience. Wal-Mart's management of its retail stores was distinguished by the following characteristics:

- *Merchandising.* Wal-Mart stores offered a wide range of nationally branded products. Although Wal-Mart also sold its own brand – especially in clothing – it gave less emphasis to own brand products than other retailers (e.g., Sears). Each selection of merchandise was carefully tailored to the characteristics of the local market – point-of-sale data for individual stores greatly assisted responsiveness to local needs (see below).
- *Decentralization of store management.* Individual store managers were given considerable decision-making authority in relation to product range, product positioning within stores, and pricing. This differed from most other discount chains where decisions over pricing and merchandising were made either at head office or at regional offices. Decentralized decision-making power was also apparent within stores, where the managers of individual departments (e.g., toys, health and beauty, consumer electronics) were expected to develop and implement their own ideas for increasing sales and reducing costs.
- *Customer service.* Most Wal-Mart discount stores were open 9 a.m. to 9 p.m. six days a week, with shorter hours on Sundays. Supercenters were open continuously. Despite the fanatical emphasis on cost efficiency, Wal-Mart went to great lengths to engage with its customers at a personal level. Stores employed "greeters" – often retired individuals – who would welcome customers and hand out shopping baskets. Within the store, all employees were expected to

look customers in the eye, smile at them, and offer a verbal greeting. In order to encourage customer loyalty, Wal-Mart maintained a "Satisfaction Guaranteed" program. This program assured customers that Wal-Mart would accept returned merchandise on a no-questions-asked basis.

Marketing

Wal-Mart's marketing strategy rested primarily upon disseminating its policy of low prices and customer commitment. Central to its marketing was the communication of its slogan "Everyday Low Prices" – the concept that Wal-Mart's price cutting strategy was not restricted to particular products or to particular time periods, but was a basic principle of Wal-Mart's business.

As a result of its customer-focused, value-for-money approach, Wal-Mart was able to rely upon word-of-mouth communication of its merits, and was able to spend comparatively little on advertising and promotion. Advertising spending was limited to one advertisement circular per month per store and some television advertising. During the early 1990s, Wal-Mart spent only 0.5 percent of every sales dollar on advertising, compared to 2.5 percent for Kmart and 3.5 percent for Sears Roebuck and Company. In 2004, Wal-Mart's advertising sales ratio was 0.4 percent, compared with Target's 2.6 percent.

Wal-Mart placed strong emphasis on patriotism and national causes. During the mid-1980s, at a time of increased public concern about the mounting trade deficit, Wal-Mart launched its "Buy American" program. However, despite its flag waving, Wal-Mart's ability to undercut its competitors rested heavily upon low-cost imports. Its purchases from China amounted to $15 billion annually.[13]

Information Technology

With each of its business functions and between functions, Wal-Mart was a pioneer in applying information and communications technology to support decision-making and promote efficiency and customer responsiveness. In 1974, Wal-Mart was among the first retailers to use computers for inventory control. In 1977, Wal-Mart initiated electronic data interchange (EDI) with its vendors. In the following year Wal-Mart introduced bar code scanning for point-of-sale and inventory control. To link stores and cash register sales with supply chain management and inventory control, Wal-Mart invested $24 million in its own satellite in 1984. By 1990, Wal-Mart's satellite system was the largest two-way, fully integrated private satellite network in the world, providing two-way interactive voice and video capability, data transmission for inventory control, credit card authorization, and enhanced EDI.

By the end of the 1990s Wal-Mart was pioneering the use of data-mining for retail merchandising:

At Wal-Mart, information technology gives us that knowledge in the most direct way: by collecting and analyzing our own internal information on exactly what any given shopping cart contains. The popular term is "data-mining," and Wal-Mart has been doing it since about 1990. The result, by now, is an enormous database of purchasing information that enables us to place the right item in the right store at the right price. Our computer system receives 8.4 million updates every minute on the items that customers take home – and the relationship between the items in each basket. Our merchants use this database to understand what customers want – and to find ways to help them get it into their carts with as much convenience, and at as low a cost, as possible. In any given week, for example, typical Wal-Mart's highest-selling items will include videotapes of *Sleeping Beauty*, Folgers® coffee, bananas and toilet paper – although the chances are that no single shopping cart contains all of those items. That kind of information has significant value in and of itself. Consider Wal-Mart's ability to keep the shelves stocked with exactly what customers want most, but still be able to keep inventories under tight control. The computerized transmission of transactions to our systems, which keep track of what merchandise is needed where, is a key tool as Wal-Mart merchants work to serve our customers. And that's only the beginning. For example, imagine a receipt that records a customer's purchase of Clearasil®, a Backstreet Boys CD and lip gloss. It's a safe guess that this customer's household has a teenage girl in it, and where there are teenagers, there is merchandising to be done.[14]

Point-of-sale data analysis also assisted in planning store layout:

There are some obvious purchasing patterns among the register receipts of families with infants and small children. Well-thought-out product placement not only simplifies the shopping trip for these customers – with baby aisles that include infant clothes and children's medicine alongside diapers, baby food and formula – but at the same time places higher-margin products among the staples.

Seasonal merchandising – a key Wal-Mart focus – offers many opportunities for product placement based on customer buying patterns. For example, as pre-Halloween displays of costumes go up, they can be accompanied by a selection of flashlights – a valuable reminder for busy parents who might not have thought to stop by the hardware department for that important piece of trick-or-treating equipment.

Customers who buy suitcases are likely to be looking for other items they might need for traveling too – such as travel alarms and irons, which now, logically enough, can be found displayed alongside luggage at many Wal-Mart stores.

The common thread is simple: We are here to serve the customer; and customers tend to buy from us when we make it easy for them. That sounds like a simple idea. But first you must understand the customer's needs. And that's where information comes in.[15]

Most important was the role of IT in linking and integrating the whole of Wal-Mart's value chain:

Wal-Mart's web of information systems extends far beyond the walls of any one store. Starting from the basic information compiled at the checkout stand, at the shelves, and gathered by associates equipped with hand-held computer monitors, Wal-Mart works to manage its supplies and inventories not only in the stores, but all the way back to the original source. Wal-Mart has given suppliers access to some of our systems, which enables them to know exactly what is selling, and to plan their production accordingly. This not only helps us keep inventories under control, but also helps the supplier deliver the lowest-cost product to the customer. With sales and in-stock information transmitted between

Wal-Mart and our supplier-partners in seconds over the internet, buyers and suppliers are privy to the same facts and negotiate based on a shared understanding – saving a significant amount of time and energy over more traditional, low-tech systems. Our buyer benefits from the supplier's product knowledge, while the supplier benefits from Wal-Mart's experience in the market. Combine these information systems with our logistics – our hub-and-spoke system in which distribution centers are placed within a day's truck run of the stores – and all the pieces fall into place for the ability to respond to the needs of our customers, before they are even in the store. In today's retailing world, speed is a crucial competitive advantage. And when it comes to turning information into improved merchandising and service to the customer, Wal-Mart is out in front and gaining speed. In the words of Randy Mott, Senior Vice President and Chief Information Officer, "The surest way to predict the future is to invent it."[16]

Early in 2004, Wal-Mart was pioneering radio-frequency identification (RFID) – a system of locating and tracking cases of merchandise by means of electronic tags.

Human Resource Management

Wal-Mart's human resource policies were based closely upon Sam Walton's ideas about relations between the company and its employees and between employees and customers. All employees – from executive-level personnel to checkout clerks – were known as "associates." Wal-Mart's relations with its associates were founded upon respect, high expectations, close communication, and effective incentives.

Although Wal-Mart's employees received relatively low pay (in common with most of the retail trade), Wal-Mart offered strong profit incentives for employees and encouraged them to share in its wealth creation through its stock ownership scheme. Numerous employees have retired as millionaires as a result of their participation in the plan. Most of these were managers; however, in 1989, the first millionaire hourly associate retired from the company.

Wal-Mart resisted the unionization of its employees in the belief that union membership created a barrier between the management and the employees in furthering the success of the company and its members. Despite strenuous efforts by unions to recruit Wal-Mart employees, union penetration remained low. Between 2000 and 2004, the United Food and Commercial Workers together with AFL-CIO fought a concerted campaign to recruit Wal-Mart workers, but to little effect.[17]

Associates enjoyed a high degree of autonomy and received continuous communication about their company's performance and about store operations. Every aspect of company operations and strategy was seen as depending upon the close collaboration of managers and shop-floor employees. To control "shrinkage" (theft), the company instituted a bonus system whereby each associate could receive up to $200 if a store met corporate goals. Wal-Mart's shrinkage was estimated to be just above 1 percent, versus an industry average of 2 percent.

Wal-Mart's approach to employee involvement made heavy use of orchestrated demonstration of enthusiasm and commitment. The central feature of Wal-Mart meetings from corporate to store level was the "Wal-Mart Cheer" – devised by Sam Walton after a visit to Korea. The call and response ritual ("Give me a W!" "Give me an A!"

. . .), included the "Wal-Mart squiggly," which involved employees shaking their backsides in unison.

Fortune suggested that the Wal-Mart cheer's mixture of homespun and corporate themes provided an apt metaphor for what it called "the Wal-Mart paradox:"

> The paradox is that Wal-Mart stands for both Main Street values and the efficiencies of the huge corporation, aw-shucks hokeyness and terabytes of minute-by-minute sales data, fried-chicken luncheons at the Waltons' Arkansas home and the demands of Wall Street.
>
> Critics of Wal-Mart call the homespun stuff a fraud, a calculated strategy to put a human face on a relentlessly profit-minded corporation. What is paradoxical and suspect to people outside Wal-Mart, however, is perfectly normal to the people who work there. It reflects a deal that Sam Walton, Wal-Mart's founder, made with the people who worked for him.
>
> The deal was a lot more than just a matter of the occasional visit from Mr. Sam. Wal-Mart demonstrated its concern for workers in many ways that were small but specific: time and a half for work on Sundays, an "open door" policy that let workers bring concerns to managers at any level, the real chance of promotion (about 70% of store managers started as hourly associates).
>
> Sam Walton died in 1992, but the language of that deal still peppers the dialogue of Wal-Mart executives and the company's official literature. A quote that runs, in large type, across the top of a page in Wal-Mart's associate handbook is typical: "The undeniable cornerstone of Wal-Mart's success can be traced back to our strong belief in the dignity of each individual." Or listen to Wal-Mart spokesman Jay Allen: "If we didn't practice respect for the individual, didn't operate in an open-door environment, we would not be living up to the expectations that our associates have of us." In an interview with *Fortune* two years ago, Coleman Petersen, Wal-Mart's human resources chief, made much the same point: "The higher up in the organization you go, the more of a servant you need to become because of the respect and expectations that Wal-Mart associates have of you as a leader."[18]

Organization and Management Style

Wal-Mart's management structure and management style had been molded by Sam Walton's principles and values. As Wal-Mart grew in size and geographical scope, Walton was determined that corporate executives should keep closely in touch with customers and store operations. The result was a structure in which communication between individual stores and the Bentonville headquarters was both close and personal. Wal-Mart's regional vice presidents were each responsible for supervising between ten and fifteen district managers (who, in turn, were in charge of eight to twelve stores). The key to Wal-Mart's fast-response management system was the close linkage between the stores and headquarters. Former CEO, David Glass explained the system:

> The idea is very simple. Nothing very constructive happens in the office. Everybody else had gone to regional offices – Sears, Kmart, everybody – but we decided to send everybody from Bentonville out to the stores Monday though Thursday. And bring them back Thursday night. On Friday morning we'd have our merchandising meetings. But on Saturday morning we'd have our sales for the week. And we'd have the other information from people who'd been out in the field. They're telling us what our competitors are doing, and

[handwritten margin notes: "Staff culture strategy", "Staff Strength"]

we get reports from people in the regions who had been traveling though the week. So we decide then what corrective action we want to take. And before noon on Saturday the regional manager was required to be hooked up by phone to all his district managers, giving them direction as to what we were going to do or change. By noon on Saturday we had all our corrections in place. Our competitors, for the most part, got their sales results on Monday for the week prior. Now, they're already ten days behind, and we've already made the corrections."[19]

Wal-Mart placed a strong emphasis on management development. Most senior managers were recruited internally, and there was a strong emphasis placed upon developing managers through moving them between line and staff positions and between functions: "We have always moved our best and brightest talent around the organization to build the broad skills and experience that will carry Wal-Mart into the future. A few years ago we took our CIO, Bobby Martin, and asked him to run our International business. Three years ago we asked Tom Coughlin, who had run our Sam's business and was then running our Specialty Division, to head up our Wal-Mart store operations. At the same time, Lee Scott moved from Logistics to lead our Merchandising team. These are three examples of this cross-pollination that occurs throughout our company."[20] Many senior managers were long-serving Wal-Mart veterans and almost all had spent their entire careers in retailing (see table 5.6).

■ COMPETITION ■

Wal-Mart's expansion had brought it into closer rivalry with a broader range of competitors. When Sam Walton had opened his first discount stores in the rural south, Wal-Mart's competitors were mostly small mom-and-pop stores. Wal-Mart's expansion throughout the US and now internationally had brought Wal-Mart face to face with more powerful competitors. During 2000–04, Wal-Mart's new US stores were located primarily in the suburbs where they faced much greater competition than in their small-town locations. This competition comprised not just other discount chains – Target, Kmart, and Dollar General – but also specialist mass-retailers – particularly the "category killers" that dominated specific product markets: Home Depot in home improvement products, Toys-R-Us in toys, Office Depot in home office supplies, Best Buy in appliances and consumer electronics.

As Wal-Mart expanded the range of goods and service offerings, so it expanded its competitive front. Its expansion into Supercenters meant competition with supermarket chains (Kroger, Safeway, Giant). Its establishment of gas stations at its stores resulted in its competing with Exxon Mobil and Shell. Its wal-mart.com online shopping business competed with a wide range of Internet retailers.

In most overseas markets, Wal-Mart was far from being market leader. In Britain, its Asda subsidiary was the No. 2 supermarket chain after Tesco; in Brazil, it was No. 3 in the market; but in Germany, Argentina, and China the company was a relatively minor player.

Up until 2004, there was little evidence that increasing competition had dented Wal-Mart's performance – gross margins and net margins were little changed between 1994 and 2004 (see table 5.4). Looking ahead, could Wal-Mart continue to find new sources

Table 5.6 Wal-Mart's executive team

Name	Position	Joined W-M	Education
M. Susan Chambers	EVP, Risk Management, Benefits Administration, Aviation and Travel	1999	Wm. Jewell College. MO.
Robert F. Connolly	EVP, Marketing and Consumer Communications	1989	Rochester Institute of Technology
Thomas M. Coughlin	Vice Chairman of the Board	1978	California State University
Douglas J. Degn	EVP Food Merchandising	1983	University of Kansas
David J. Dibleis	EVP, Specialty Group	1971	Ft. Hays State University, KS
Linda M. Dillman	Chief Information Officer	1991	–
Michael T. Duke	CEO, Wal-Mart Stores Division	1995	Georgia Tech.
Joseph J. Fitzsimmons	Treasurer	1995	BS, University of Notre Dame; MS University of Chicago
Rollin L. Ford	EVP, Logistics and Supply Chain	1983	Taylor University, IN
David D. Glass	Chairman, Executive Committee of Board	1976	Southwest Missouri State University
James H. Haworth	EVP, Operations	1984	Central Missouri State University
Craig R. Herkert	COO, Wal-Mart International Division	2000	St. Francis College; Northern Illinois University
Charles M. Holley	Controller	1994	University of Texas; University of Houston

Table 5.6 *continued*

Name	Position	Joined W-M	Education
Thomas D. Hyde	Corporate Secretary	2001	University of Kansas; University of Missouri
C. Douglas McMillon	EVP, Merchandising, Sam's Club	1984	University of Arkansas; University of Tulsa
John B. Menzer	CEO, International Division	1995	Loyola University, Chicago
Coleman H. Peterson	Chief Human Resource Officer	1994	Loyola University, Chicago
Thomas M. Schoewe	CFO	2000	Loyola University, Chicago; University of Chicago
H. Lee Scott	CEO	1978	Pittsburgh State University
Gregory E. Spragg	EVP, Operations, Sam's Clubs	1998	North Carolina State University
Celia M. Swanson	EVP, Membership, Marketing and Administration, Sam's Clubs	1994	University of Nebraska
B. Kevin Turner	CEO, Sam's Clubs	1984	East Central University
S. Robson Walton	Chairman of the Board	1969	Wooster College; Columbia University
Claire A. Watts	EVP, Merchandising, Wal-Mart Stores	1997	University of Cincinnati

Source: "About Wal-Mart: Wal-Mart's Senior Officers" (www.walmartstores.com).

of cost efficiency that would allow it to undercut its competitors? Some competitors had adopted many of Wal-Mart's efficient practices, while offering differentiation through quality and more luxury goods – Target positioned itself as an up-market Wal-Mart, while Costco is an up-market Sam's Club. *The Economist* suggested that Wal-Mart's cost competitiveness might suffer from difficulties in maintaining its labor-cost advantage over other retailers and mounting legal and labor compliance costs.[21] At any one moment Wal-Mart faced about 8,000 lawsuits – mainly personal injury claims from employees but also class-action suits alleging violations of the Fair Labor Standards Act. Legal actions and compliance issues were not only a growing cost item for Wal-Mart, but were the most visible evidence of the risk of size and success for Wal-Mart's famed entrepreneurial culture.

APPENDIX
The Wal-Mart Culture

As Wal-Mart continues to grow into new areas and new mediums, our success will always be attributed to our culture. Whether you walk into a Wal-Mart store in your hometown or one across the country while you're on vacation, you can always be assured you're getting low prices and that genuine customer service you've come to expect from us. You'll feel at home in any department of any store . . . that's our culture.

■ SAM WALTON'S THREE BASIC BELIEFS ■

Sam Walton built Wal-Mart on the revolutionary philosophies of excellence in the workplace, customer service and always having the lowest prices. We have always stayed true to the Three Basic Beliefs Mr. Sam established in 1962:

Respect the Individual
" 'Our people make the difference' is not a meaningless slogan – it's a reality at Wal-Mart. We are a group of dedicated, hardworking, ordinary people who have teamed together to accomplish extraordinary things. We have very different backgrounds, different colors and different beliefs, but we do believe that every individual deserves to be treated with respect and dignity." – Don Soderquist, Senior Vice Chairman, Wal-Mart Stores, Inc.

Service to Our Customers
We want our customers to trust in our pricing philosophy and to always be able to find the lowest prices with the best possible service. We're nothing without our customers.
    "Wal-Mart's culture has always stressed the importance of Customer Service. Our Associate base across the country is as diverse as the communities in which we have Wal-Mart stores. This allows us to provide the Customer Service expected from each individual customer that walks into our stores." – Tom Coughlin, President and chief executive officer, Wal-Mart Stores division.

Strive for Excellence
New ideas and goals make us reach further than ever before. We try to find new and innovative ways to push our boundaries and constantly improve. "Sam was never satisfied that prices were as low as they needed to be or that our product's quality was as high as they deserved – he believed in the concept of striving for excellence before it became a fashionable concept." – Lee Scott, President and CEO.

■ EXCEEDING CUSTOMER EXPECTATIONS ■

Years ago, Sam Walton challenged all Wal-Mart associates to practice what he called "aggressive hospitality." He said "Let's be the most friendly – offer a smile of welcome and assistance to all who do us a favor by entering our stores. Give better service – over and beyond what our customers expect. Why not? You wonderful, caring associates can do it and do it better than any other retailing company in the world . . . exceed your customers' expectations. If you do, they'll come back over and over again."

As Wal-Mart associates we know it is not good enough to simply be grateful to our customers for shopping in our stores – we want to demonstrate our gratitude in every way we can! We believe that doing so is what keeps our customers coming back to Wal-Mart again and again.

■ HELPING PEOPLE MAKE A DIFFERENCE ■

Sam Walton believed that each Wal-Mart store should reflect the values of its customers and support the vision they hold for their community. As a result, Wal-Mart's Community Outreach Programs are guided by local Associates who grew up in the area and understand its needs. In addition, Wal-Mart Stores, Inc., has launched several national efforts to help the larger, US community.

Locally, Wal-Mart:

- Underwrites college scholarships for high-school seniors.
- Raises funds for nearby children's hospitals through the Children's Miracle Network Telethon.
- Provides money and manpower for fund raisers, school benefits and churches, Boy and Girl Scouts, park projects, police and fire charities, food banks, senior citizen centers, and more.
- Educates the public about recycling and other environmental topics with the help of a "Green Coordinator," a specially trained Associate who coordinates efforts to make an environmentally responsible store.

On the national scope, Wal-Mart Stores, Inc.:

- Provides industrial development grants each year to towns and cities that are attempting to bolster their economic base.
- Encourages American companies to bring offshore manufacturing operations "back home" and bolster the US job base through our Buy American Program.

■ SAM'S RULES FOR BUILDING A BUSINESS ■

People often ask, "What is Wal-Mart's secret to success?"

In response to this ever-present question, in his 1992 book *Made in America*, Sam Walton compiled a list of ten key factors that unlock the mystery. These factors are known as "Sam's Rules for Building a Business."

Rule 1. Commit to your business. Believe in it more than anybody else. I think I overcame every single one of my personal shortcomings by the sheer passion I brought to my work. I don't know if you're born with this kind of passion, or if you can learn it. But I do know you need it. If you love your work, you'll be out there every day trying to do it the best you possibly can, and pretty soon everybody around will catch the passion from you – like a fever.

Rule 2. Share your profits with all your Associates, and treat them as partners. In turn, they will treat you as a partner, and together you will all perform beyond your wildest expectations. Remain a corporation and retain control if you like, but behave as a servant leader in a partnership. Encourage your Associates to hold a stake in the company. Offer discounted stock, and grant them stock for their retirement. It's the single best thing we ever did.

Rule 3. Motivate your partners. Money and ownership alone aren't enough. Constantly, day-by-day, think of new and more interesting ways to motivate and challenge your partners. Set high goals, encourage competition, and then keep score. Make bets with outrageous payoffs. If things get stale, cross-pollinate; have managers switch jobs with one another to stay challenged. Keep everybody guessing as to what your next trick is going to be. Don't become too predictable.

Rule 4. Communicate everything you possibly can to your partners. The more they know, the more they'll understand. The more they understand, the more they'll care. Once they care, there's no stopping them. If you don't trust your Associates to know what's going on, they'll know you don't really consider them partners. Information is power, and the gain you get from empowering your Associates more than offsets the risk of informing your competitors.

Rule 5. Appreciate everything your Associates do for the business. A paycheck and a stock option will buy one kind of loyalty. But all of us like to be told how much somebody appreciates what we do for them. We like to hear it often, and especially when we have done something we're really proud of. Nothing else can quite substitute for a few well-chosen, well-timed, sincere words of praise. They're absolutely free – and worth a fortune.

Rule 6. Celebrate your successes. Find some humor in your failures. Don't take yourself so seriously. Loosen up, and everybody around you will loosen up. Have fun. Show enthusiasm – always. When all else fails, put on a costume and sing a silly song. Then make everybody else sing with you. Don't do a hula on Wall Street. It's been done. Think up your own stunt. All of this is more important, and more fun, than you think, and it really fools the competition. "Why should we take those cornballs at Wal-Mart seriously?"

Rule 7. Listen to everyone in your company. And figure out ways to get them talking. The folks on the front lines – the ones who actually talk to the customer – are the only ones who really know what's going on out there. You'd better find out what they know. This really is what total quality is all about. To push responsibility down in your organization, and to force good ideas to bubble up within it, you must listen to what your Associates are trying to tell you.

Rule 8. Exceed your customers' expectations. If you do, they'll come back over and over. Give them what they want – and a little more. Let them know you appreciate them. Make good on all your mistakes, and don't make excuses – apologize. Stand behind everything you do. The two most important words I ever wrote were on that first Wal-Mart sign, "Satisfaction Guaranteed." They're still up there, and they have made all the difference.

Rule 9. Control your expenses better than your competition. This is where you can always find the competitive advantage. For 25 years running – long before Wal-Mart was known as the nation's largest retailer – we ranked No. 1 in our industry for the lowest ratio of expenses to sales. You can make a lot of different mistakes and still recover if you run an efficient operation. Or you can be brilliant and still go out of business if you're too inefficient.

Rule 10. Swim upstream. Go the other way. Ignore the conventional wisdom. If everybody else is doing it one way, there's a good chance you can find your niche by going in exactly the opposite direction. But be prepared for a lot of folks to wave you down and tell you you're headed the wrong way. I guess in all my years, what I heard more often than anything was: a town of less than 50,000 population cannot support a discount store for very long.

■ SUNDOWN RULE ■

One Sunday morning, Jeff, a pharmacist at a Wal-Mart store in Harrison, Ark., received a call from his store. A store associate informed him that one of his pharmacy customers, a diabetic, had accidentally dropped her insulin down her garbage disposal. Knowing that a diabetic without insulin could be in grave danger, Jeff immediately rushed to the store, opened the pharmacy and filled the customer's insulin prescription. This is just one of many ways your local Wal-Mart store might honor what is known by our associates as the Sundown Rule.

It's a rule we take seriously at Wal-Mart. In this busy place, where our jobs depend on one another, it's our standard to get things done today – before the sun goes down. Whether it's a request from a store across the country or a call from down the hall, every request gets same-day service. These are our working principles.

The Sundown Rule was our founder, Sam Walton's, twist on that old adage "why put off until tomorrow what you can do today." It is still an important part of our Wal-Mart culture and is one reason our associates are so well known for their customer service. The observation of the Sundown Rule means we strive to answer requests by sundown on the day we receive them.

Source: "The Wal-Mart Culture" from www.walmartstores.com (includes "Sam's Rules for Building a Business", from Sam Walton and John Huey, *Made in America*, Doubleday, 1992).

NOTES

1. Sam Walton, *Sam Walton: Made in America*, New York: Bantam Books, 1992.
2. *Forbes*, August 16, 1982, p. 43.
3. G. C. Strachan, *The State of the Discount Store Industry*, Goldman Sachs, April 1994 (quoted in *Wal-Mart Stores, Inc.*, Harvard Business School Case 9–974–024, 1994).
4. From the Wal-Mart web site: www.walmart.com.
5. Sam Walton, *Sam Walton: Made in America*, New York: Bantam Books, 1992.
6. http://www.walmart.com/cservice/aw_samsway.gsp.
7. Wal-Mart Stores, Inc. Annual Report, 2002.
8. Wal-Mart Stores, Inc. Annual Report, 2000.
9. This description of Wal-Mart's retailing operations refers primarily to its US discount stores division.
10. Bill Saporito, "A week aboard the Wal-Mart Express," *Fortune*, August 24, 1992, p. 79.
11. Ibid.
12. "Wal-Mart Stores' Discount Operations," Harvard Business School Case No. 9-387-018, 1989, p. 3.
13. "Special Report: Wal-Mart," *The Economist*, April 17, 2004, pp. 67–9.
14. Wal-Mart Stores, Inc. Annual Report, 1999, p. 9.
15. Ibid., p. 9.
16. Ibid., p. 11.
17. "Unions vs. Wal-Mart: Up against the Wal-Mart," *Fortune*, May 17, 2004.
18. "Sam Walton made us a promise," *Fortune*, March 18, 2002.
19. "The Most Underrated CEO Ever," *Fortune*, April 5, 2004, pp. 242–8.
20. "Steady as she grows" (interview with David Glass), Wal-Mart Annual Report, 1999, p. 6.
21. "Special Report: Wal-Mart," *The Economist*, April 17, 2004, p. 67–9.

Eastman Kodak: Meeting the Digital Challenge

Robert M. Grant

January 2004 marked the beginning of Dan Carp's fifth year as Eastman Kodak Inc.'s chief executive officer. By late February, it was looking as though 2004 would also be his most challenging.

The year had begun with Kodak's dissident shareholders becoming louder and bolder. The critical issue was Kodak's digital imaging strategy that Carp had presented to investors in September 2003. The strategy called for a rapid acceleration in Kodak's technological and market development of its digital imaging business and the commitment of some $3 billion in investment – financed in part by slashing Kodak's dividend. Of particular concern to Carp was Carl Icahn who had obtained clearance to acquire 7 percent of Kodak stock. Icahn was not known for his patience or long-term horizons. He was famous for his role as a greenmailer and an initiator of boardroom putschs and leveraged buyouts. Opposition to Carp's strategy was based upon skepticism over whether the massive investments in digital imaging would ever generate returns to shareholders. Shareholder activist Bert Denton had an entirely different vision for Kodak. He viewed Kodak's traditional photography business as a potential cash cow. If Kodak could radically cut costs, a sizable profit stream would be available to shareholders. If shareholders wanted to invest in digital imaging they could then invest their money in more promising bets in the digital imaging field – Olympus, Canon, or Hewlett-Packard.

The release of Kodak's full-year results on January 22, 2004 added fuel to the flames. Top-line growth was anemic while, on the bottom line, net income was down by almost two-thirds. In presenting the annual results to investors and analysts, Carp's focus was on the future rather than the past. In updating Kodak's 2002–06 strategy he emphasized the distinct strategies for Kodak's "traditional businesses" and its "digital businesses." The traditional businesses would be "managed for cash to maximize value." This meant revenue contraction of around 7 percent per year together with aggressive cost cutting. During 2004–06, between 12,000 and 15,000 jobs would be axed and one-third of traditional factory space would close.[1]

For digital businesses the strategy was to "invest for profitable growth." With a projected average annual growth rate of 26 percent, the balance of Kodak's business would shift: in 2002 "traditional" had accounted for 70 percent of Kodak's revenues. By 2006 this would be down to 40 percent. As evidence of Kodak's ambitions, Carp announced the acquisition of Scitex, a producer of commercial ink-jet printers, PracticeWorks, a dental imaging company, and Chinon, a Japanese camera manufacturer.

While Kodak's cost-cutting and downsizing in its traditional chemical imaging business were welcomed by the stock market, skepticism was expressed over Kodak's growth targets for its digital businesses. As the *Financial Times'* Lex column observed:

> . . . Two key problems remain. The first is that, as Kodak extends its imaging technology into consumer electronics, it will encounter severe competition from existing camera makers and the brutal profit margins of a business where prices seem in perpetual freefall. If prices continue to plummet, it may still all be too little too late. Though few would question Kodak's technological expertise, its relative lack of experience in hardware was shown by its pride in attending the Las Vegas consumer electronics show for the first time this year. It has also been hit by a failure to develop new models fast enough and has tended to focus on the ultra-competitive entry-level market. . . .
>
> The other potential problem stems from predicting that descent curve for film. Much hope has been placed on growing demand for old-fashioned film cameras in emerging markets like China, India and Russia. So far, sales in the rest of the world as a whole have been declining at the same speed as the US . . .[2]

■ FROM START-UP TO MATURITY ■

When George Eastman told a co-worker at the Rochester Savings Bank that he had made plans for a vacation to Santo Domingo, the co-worker suggested that Eastman take photographs to remember it by. Eastman heeded the advice and purchased a state-of-the-art 3-by-4-foot camera, along with essential accessories and materials: developing plates, glass tanks, developing tents, chemicals, distilled water, tripod, phosphoric flashes, and photographic emulsions. Eastman never made it to Santo Domingo with his heavy load, but he did fall in love with photography and set about the challenge of creating amateur photography as a more convenient and affordable pastime.

Between 1880 and 1888 Eastman developed a new type of dry photographic plate, silver halide photographic film, and the first fully portable camera in 1888. In 1901 he changed the name of his company from the Eastman Dry Plate Company to Eastman Kodak Company. Kodak's strategy was to provide a fully integrated photographic service supplying the camera and film through to processing and printing. Its first advertising slogan was "You push the button, we do the rest." The business principles established by Eastman were:

- Mass production at low cost
- International distribution
- Extensive advertising
- A focus on the customer
- Fostering growth and development through continuing research

- Treating employees in a fair, self-respecting way
- Reinvesting profits to build and extend the business

By the time George Eastman died in 1932, he had created a vast new market which Eastman Kodak dominated.

By the end of the 1970s, Kodak was facing a series of new challenges. In cameras, Kodak's leadership in amateur cameras was undermined by the rise of the Japanese camera industry with its sophisticated yet easy-to-use 35mm cameras. In film too, Japanese competition was a growing problem as Fuji Photo Film Company stepped onto the world stage. Fuji's combination of cost leadership, high quality, and market aggressiveness forced Kodak to retaliate through price cuts and bigger advertising budgets. Fuji's sponsorship of the 1984 Los Angeles Olympic Games proclaimed its presence in Kodak's backyard. In instant photography, Polaroid was the dominant player – especially after Kodak's withdrawal following its violation of Polaroid's patents.

In response to these reversals, a new management team led by Colby Chandler and Kay Whitmore launched a series of diversification initiatives during 1983–93 in two main areas: imaging and life sciences.

Imaging and Data Storage Products

The 1980s were years of rapid development of imaging technologies and new printing and reprographic products. Chastened by its having passed up the opportunity to acquire Chester Carlson's xerography patents (these were bought by Haliod Corp., which renamed itself Xerox Corp.), Kodak was determined not to be sidelined by new technological opportunities. Chandler and Whitmore pioneered Kodak's expansion beyond the confines of chemical-based photographic imaging and into electrostatic imaging, electromagnetic imaging, electronic imaging, and thermal printing. For example:

- Eikonix Corp., acquired in 1985, gave Kodak a leading position in commercial imaging systems that scanned, edited, and prepared images for printing.
- Kodak developed the world's first megapixel electronic image sensor with 1.4 million pixels (1986). This was followed by a number of new products for electronic publishing, scanning, and editing for the printing and publishing industry, including Imagelink for document imaging and Optistar for micrographic digital image capture (1989).
- Kodak became a leader in image storage and retrieval systems. Its KAR4000 Information System provided computer-assisted storage and retrieval of microfilm images (1983). The Ektaprint Electronic Publishing System and Kodak Image Management System offered integrated systems to edit, store, retrieve, and print text and graphics (1985).
- Kodak became involved in a range of data storage products including floppy disks (Verbatim was acquired in 1985), a 14-inch optical disk capable of storing 6.8 billion bytes of information (1986), and magnetic recording heads for disk drives (through the 1985 acquisition of Garlic Corp.).

- Through a joint venture with Matsushita, Kodak began supplying alkaline batteries and videocassettes.

Most of these new imaging initiatives were directed towards the commercial sector. However, by the end of the 1980s, Kodak was developing electronic imaging products for the consumer market. As a result of its collaboration with Philips, Kodak announced its Photo CD system in 1990. Photo CDs allowed digitized photographic images to be stored on a compact disk, which could then be viewed and manipulated on a personal computer.

Life Sciences

The second area of development built upon Kodak's capabilities in chemical technology. Eastman Chemicals had been established in the 1920s to supply photographic chemicals both to Kodak's film and processing division and to third-party customers. By the 1980s, Eastman was a major international supplier of photographic chemicals, fibers, plastics (especially for soft-drink packaging), printing inks, and nutrition supplements.

Building on its capabilities in chemicals and its existing healthcare activities (e.g., nutritional supplements and diagnostic equipment), Kodak established its Life Sciences Division in 1984. The new division forged joint ventures and alliances with a number of pharmaceutical and biotech companies to pursue research and new products in the areas of antiviral compounds, nucleic acid, and recombinant proteins. In 1986 Kodak established Eastman Pharmaceuticals and greatly expanded its pharmaceutical interests with the acquisition of Sterling Drug in 1988 and a series of joint ventures with Sanofi during 1991–2. In addition, Kodak expanded its range of medical imaging products.

■ CREATING A DIGITAL STRATEGY: GEORGE FISHER, 1993–2000 ■

Few of the new initiatives produced major revenue growth and return on capital fell way below cost of capital. In 1993 the Kodak board ousted Whitmore and replaced him with George Fisher, then CEO of Motorola.[3]

Hiring Fisher was a major coup for Kodak. His success at implementing total quality management at Motorola and building a leading position in hardware for wireless telephony had made him one of the most highly regarded CEOs in America. He was viewed as one of the leaders of America's resurgence in high technology and was on every headhunter's list. He had already turned down the opportunity to become IBM's CEO (IBM's Board subsequently turned to Lou Gerstner). Moreover, with a doctorate in applied mathematics and ten years of R&D experience at Bell Labs, he had a scientist's grasp of electronic technology. As chairman and CEO of Eastman Kodak from November 1993 to December 2000, Fisher established a digital imaging strategy for Kodak that was to set the direction of the company up until 2004.

Refocusing on Imaging

From the outset, Fisher's strategic vision for Kodak was as an imaging company: "We are not in the photographic film business or in the electronics business, we are in the picture business."[4] In order to focus Kodak's efforts and lower debt, Fisher immediately approved proposals to spin off Eastman Chemical Company. This was followed by a string of other divestments. In 1994 the divestment of all healthcare businesses (other than medical imaging) was announced, the most important being the Sterling Winthrop pharmaceutical company. Sterling had been acquired at a cost of $5.1 billion in 1988; it was sold to SmithKline Beecham for $2.9 billion. The funds generated were used mainly to pay off debt.

The intention of the divestments was to enable Kodak to focus all of its resources on its core imaging business. However, developing a coherent strategy for digital imaging business was not easy. After reviewing the company's financials, Fisher was shocked to learn that Kodak had poured several billion dollars into digital imaging research since the mid-1980s yet had little to show for it in terms of world-beating products.

Digital Imaging Strategy

Fisher's digital strategy was to create greater coherence among Kodak's multiple digital projects, in part through creating a single digital projects division headed by newly hired Carl Gustin (previously with Apple Computer and DEC). Having established greater coherence, Fisher's digital strategy emphasized three key themes.

AN INCREMENTAL APPROACH

"The future is not some harebrained scheme of the digital Information Highway or something. It is a step-by-step progression of enhancing photography using digital technology," declared Fisher.[5] This recognition that digital imaging was an evolutionary rather than a revolutionary change would be the key to Kodak's ability to build a strong position in digital technology. If photography was to switch rapidly from the traditional chemical-based technology to a wholly digital technology where customers took digital pictures, downloaded them on to their computers, edited them, and transmitted them through the Internet to be viewed electronically, then undoubtedly Kodak would face an extremely difficult time. Apart from Kodak's positions in digital cameras and picture-editing software, most of this digital chain was in the hands of computer hardware and software companies. However, fortunately for Kodak, the whole of the 1990s and the early part of the next decade featured only selective incursions of digital technology into traditional photographic imaging. During the 1990s, digital cameras achieved only limited market penetration; the vast majority of photographic images were still captured on traditional film. The critical advantages of digital imaging were in image manipulation and image transmission.

Hence, central to Kodak's strategy was a hybrid approach where Kodak introduced those aspects of digital imaging that could offer truly enhanced functionality for users. Thus, in the consumer market, Kodak recognized that image capture would continue to be dominated by traditional film for some time – digital cameras did not offer the same sharpness of resolution as conventional photography. However, digital imaging offered the potential for image manipulation and transmission that were quite beyond traditional photography.

This hybrid approach involved Kodak in providing facilities in retail outlets for digitizing and editing images from conventional photographs, then storing, transmitting and printing these digital images. Kodak's first walk-up, self-service systems were its CopyPrint Station and Digital Enhancement Station. In 1994, Kodak launched its Picture Maker which allowed digital prints to be made from either conventional photo prints or from a variety of digital inputs. Picture Maker allowed customers to edit their images (zoom, crop, eliminate red-eye, and add text), and print them in a variety of formats. By the end of 2000, some 30,000 retail locations worldwide offered Picture Maker facilities. A particular advantage of these retailer-based digital photography systems was that they allowed Kodak to exploit a key resource – its extensive distribution presence. Ultimately, digital imaging had the potential to bypass retailers and photofinishers completely; however, during the transition period, Kodak viewed its huge retail presence as a means of bringing digital imaging to the mass market.

Kodak also used digital technology to enhance the services offered by photofinishers. Thus, the Kodak I.Lab system offered a digital infrastructure to photofinishers that digitized every film negative and offered better pictures by fixing common problems in consumer photographs. Kodak's Picture Center was introduced to improve the process of customer drop-off and pick-up, allowing fast self-service ordering of processing and print ordering.

Central to Kodak's digital strategy has been using the World Wide Web to allow consumers to post their photographs and order prints online. Picture Vision's PhotoNet system replaced Kodak's own Picture Network (first introduced in 1997). This allowed consumers to drop off film at retail locations and view their digitized images on Kodak's PhotoNet web site from which prints could be ordered. In addition, Kodak partnered with AOL to offer *You've Got Pictures* which allowed AOL members to send photographic images to one another.

Kodak's hybrid approach was also evident in introducing digital enhancement of conventional film. In February 1996, Kodak unveiled its Advantix brand of advanced photo system films. Advanced photo system was the result of agreement between Kodak and Fuji on technical standards for cameras and film that store both chemical film images and data that can be downloaded electronically. The system combined the resolution of conventional film with the versatility and communicability of digital imaging.

In addition, Kodak introduced a wide range of purely digital photographic products that extended from image capture to image printing. From 1995, these were launched under the Kodak Digital Science brand name, to help bring attention to Kodak's positioning and strengths in digital imaging technology.

- Image capture. Kodak developed digital cameras for both the top end and the bottom end of the market. In January 1994, Kodak launched a Professional Digital Camera (the camera alone costing $8,500) and the Apple Quicktake computer camera (manufactured by Kodak, marketed by Apple Computer), which, at $75, was the cheapest digital camera available at the time. In March 1995, Kodak introduced the first full-featured digital camera priced at under $1,000. During the subsequent six years, Kodak continued to bring out new, more sophisticated digital cameras, including professional cameras developed in conjunction with Canon. By 2000, Kodak offered a wide range of digital cameras. At the top end was its DC4800 camera with 3.1 megapixel resolution, at the other a PalmPix camera that allowed a Palm personal digital assistant to be used as a digital camera.

- Image scanning. During the late 1990s, Kodak introduced a range of high-resolution image scanners designed for photographic-quality digital imaging. By the end of 2001, Kodak's focus was almost entirely upon scanners for the business and professional market.

- Image storage and editing. After the failure of its initial launch of the Photo-CD system, based on a Photo-CD player that could store digital images on compact disks, in February 1995 Kodak introduced the next-generation Photo-CD imaging workstation, which targeted commercial laboratories, photo processors, and PC users. The system consisted of a CD-player capable of reading high-resolution digital images, viewing them on a TV or computer monitor, and uploading images for editing and subsequent printing.

- During the 1990s, Kodak introduced a broad range of printers including thermal printers for the professional market, laser printers for the professional and medical markets, and inkjet printers (manufactured by Lexmark) for the consumer market.

- These products were supported by a range of software products. These included: DSL software that allowed the editing and printing of digital images in retail photo-finishing labs, Access software that permitted the reading and display of Photo-CD disks, Photo-CD Player software that allowed photographic images to be merged with text, graphics and sound, and Kodak's Color Management System for color reproduction.

- Finally, digital imaging created a growing market for one of Kodak's traditional product areas: specialty papers for printing photographic images. During 2000, sales of Kodak's inkjet papers and media business increased by 30 percent. Kodak's new products for photographic printing included its Ultima range of picture paper.

DISTINCT STRATEGIES FOR CONSUMER AND COMMERCIAL MARKETS

Kodak's approaches to consumer and commercial markets were different. Kodak's incremental strategy – providing a pathway for customers from traditional to digital photography – was most evident in the consumer market. Here Kodak focused upon the mass market rather than leading-edge users and sought to exploit the strengths of the Kodak brand and Kodak's huge retail presence to provide consumers with the security and reliability they needed to voyage into the uncharted waters of digital photography.

> Four years ago, when we talked about the possibilities of digital photography, people laughed. Today, the high-tech world is stampeding to get a piece of the action, calling digital imaging perhaps the greatest growth opportunity in the computer world. And it may be. We surely see it as the greatest future enabler for people to truly "Take Pictures. Further."
>
> We start at retail, our distribution stronghold. Here consumers are at the peak moment of satisfaction, when they open their photofinishing envelopes. We believe the widespread photo-retailing infrastructure will continue to be the principal avenue by which people obtain their pictures. Our strategy is to build on and extend this existing market strength which is available to us, and at the same time be prepared to serve the rapidly growing, but relatively small, pure digital market that is developing. Kodak will network its rapidly expanding installed base of *Image Magic* stations and kiosks, essentially turning these into nodes on a massive, global network. The company will allow retailers to use these work stations to bring digital capability to the average snapshooter, extending the value of these images for the consumers and retailers alike, while creating a lucrative consumable business for Kodak.[6]

It was in the commercial and professional markets where Kodak launched its major innovations in digital imaging. The sophisticated needs of the government in satellite imaging, planning military campaigns, weather forecasting, and surveillance activities favored digital technologies for transforming, transmitting, and storing images; medical imaging (especially CT, MRI, and ultrasound) required digital technologies for 3D imaging, diagnosis, and image storage; publishers and printers needed digital imaging to complement the new generation of computerized publishing and printing systems for newspapers and magazines. For commercial applications ranging from journalism, to highway safety, to real estate, digital imaging provided the linkage to the Internet and sophisticated IT management systems.

The role of the commercial and professional segment as the lead market for Kodak's new digital products was reinforced by the huge price premium for professional products as compared with mass-market consumer products. In photography, the divide between the professional and the consumer segments remained wide, despite the continuous trickle-down of advanced digital technologies and product features from the professional to the consumer market. Most manufacturers – including Kodak – maintained clearly differentiated product ranges for each segment, which was reflected in clear price differentials. During 1999, price multiples between professional and consumer models were as much as 150 times for cameras ($30,000 vs. $200), 100 times for scanners ($10,000 vs. $100), and 15 times for color laser printers ($30,000 vs. $2,000).

In addition to the sophisticated digital cameras that Kodak released first to the professional market, Kodak established a leading position in digital imaging systems for medical diagnosis and commercial printing. For example:

- In the medical field, Kodak's Ektascan Imagelink system, which included the capability of converting medical images to digital images which could then be transmitted via phone lines to local hospitals, was launched in 1995. Kodak established world leadership in medical laser imaging through its Ektascan laser printer, introduced in 1996. This leadership was extended with the acquisition of Imation's Dry View laser imaging business in 1998. By the end of the 1990s, Kodak had built a powerful position in digital health imaging based upon both laser imaging and digital radiography. In 2000, Kodak launched its Application Service Provider business to the medical community allowing images to be captured and managed via Kodak's digital systems to Intel Online Services' data center.
- In the US space program, Kodak cameras and imaging equipment accompanied a number of missions, including the Mars probe and the IKONOS Earth-orbiting satellite.
- Elsewhere in the public sector, Kodak's digital scanning and document management systems were used in national censuses in the US, UK, France, Australia, and Brazil. At a unit of the German post office, a Kodak team achieved a world record, creating digitized copies of 1.7 million documents in 24 hours.
- In commercial printing and publishing, Kodak held a strong position in high-quality, high-speed digital printing systems. Kodak's involvement in this market was increasingly through NexPress, a joint venture between Kodak and Heidelberg which developed and supplied a range of printing and copying machines.
- In moving pictures, Kodak's traditional role as a supplier of cinematography was extended into the digital field through Kodak's services for digitizing conventional movie films, providing digital formats for cinema and TV film, and generating visual effects.

ALLIANCES

In its traditional photographic business, Kodak had been exceptionally vertically integrated. It had dominated the photographic value chain from basic research through to the processing of customers' photographic film. In digital imaging such dominance was impossible. Unlike silver halide imaging where Kodak had pioneered the development of the film, the cameras, and the chemicals and paper for film processing, the digital imaging field was already populated by some dominant companies. In computers there were Dell, Compaq, Toshiba, and many others; in operating systems and browsers Microsoft dominated; in image formatting software Adobe Systems was the key player; in printers Canon and HP led the field. If Kodak was to provide an integrated solution for its customers, it would need to partner with companies that were already well established in key digital technologies and in key markets for component software and hardware. Under Fisher's leadership, Kodak forged a series of joint ventures and strategic alliances. The partnerships with Canon, Lexmark, AOL, and Heidelberg have already been mentioned; in addition, Kodak established the following alliances:

- Kodak's Picture CD was developed with and co-marketed with Intel Corporation. Kodak's long-standing alliance with Intel also extended to the development of an ASP system for archiving and downloading medical images on a pay-per-use basis.
- Hewlett-Packard played a key role as a source of inkjet technology for Kodak. Phogenix Imaging, a joint venture between Kodak and HP, was established to develop high-quality inkjet solutions for micro and mini photo-finishing labs. The systems utilized Kodak's DLS software.[7] In addition, HP had collaborated with Kodak (as well as Microsoft and Live Picture Inc.) in developing the Flash-Pix image storage system for digital cameras.
- Kodak's collaboration with Microsoft also included cooperation to establish standards for Windows-based Picture Transfer Protocols and cooperation in the development of Photo-CDs.
- A cross-licensing agreement with Olympus to share digital camera technology and to join forces in developing a common approach to web-based storage and printing of photographs. The press release accompanying the announcement noted that Kodak had over a thousand patents related to digital cameras and digital photographic systems, while Olympus also possessed over a thousand patents with particular strengths in high-resolution digital cameras. A similar cross-licensing deal was agreed with Sanyo.
- Several of Kodak's alliances were primarily oriented towards opening Kodak's worldwide distribution system to partner companies. For example, in 2001 Kodak agreed to distribute Better Light Inc.'s top-of-the-line, high-resolution digital cameras as part of its professional range.

A key element of George Fisher's legacy was the recognition that, in every segment of the digital imaging market (consumer, professional, entertainment, and commercial), Kodak could only achieve a prominent market position if it forged partnerships with those companies that already possessed leadership at particular stages of the digital imaging value chain, whether it was Intel in semiconductors, AOL in consumer Internet services, HP in inkjet printers, or Heidelberg in commercial printing systems. Willy Shih, head of Kodak's digital imaging products from 1997 to 2003, observed: "We have to pick where we add value and commoditize where we can't."[8] The difficult decision was identifying the activities and product areas where it could add value, and those that were best left to other companies.

■ THE DIGITAL TRANSFOMATION GATHERS PACE: DAN CARP, 2000–2004 ■

Daniel A. Carp succeeded George Fisher as CEO on January 1, 2000. Unlike Fisher, Carp was a Kodak veteran. He started as a statistical analyst at Kodak in 1970 and had worked in several divisions and several functions as well as heading up Kodak's regional businesses in Latin America and Europe. As chief executive, his approach had been to develop and refine the strategic direction established by Fisher, to build on areas of strength, and to respond quickly to developments in the market for digital imaging

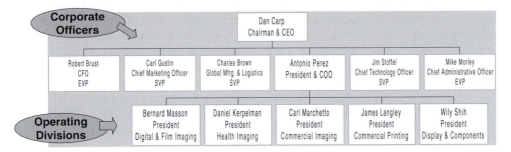

Figure 6.1 Kodak's organizational structure, February 2004

products. Carp's approach maintained the distinct strategies for the consumer and commercial market. The result was to establish some clear areas of focus for Kodak – especially in the professional and commercial sector. Carp's strategy was reflected in the organizational structure of Kodak, shown in figure 6.1.

The Commercial Sector

In the commercial sector, Carp's approach was to focus on a few markets which were both attractive and where Kodak's distinctive capabilities gave it a competitive edge. By late 2003, Kodak's commercial business was organized around three divisions:

- *Health Imaging.* This was viewed as an especially attractive segment by Carp on the basis of the margins available and Kodak's potential to carve out a strong niche in medical imaging products using both chemical and digital technologies. In 2000 alone, 45 new health imaging products were introduced, including digital radiography systems and a new dental radiography film. It also acquired Lumisys, a provider of desktop radiography systems, and PracticeWorks, a producer of dental practice management software.
- *Commercial Imaging.* Kodak's strength in commercial imaging has been built around its leadership in certain types of hardware (notably, high-speed scanners), its ability to supply integrated document management systems (allowing images of paper-based documents to be created, archived, referenced, and retrieved), and its relationships with customers (both commercial and public sector).
- *Commercial Printing.* Under Dan Carp Kodak had built up a strong presence in several parts of the commercial printing business – chiefly through joint ventures and acquisitions. These included: (a) Polychrome Graphics (a JV with Sun Chemical), which produces offset printing plates and proofing equipment; (b) NexPress (a JV with Heidelberg[9]) that makes high-end digital printers; (c) the production of inkjet printers by Encad (a producer of wide-format inkjet printers) and Versamark (previously Scitex Digital Printing) that makes

high-speed, narrow-format inkjet printers. Commercial printing products were focused on specific market segments, notably short-run "on-demand" printing and "transactional printing" (e.g. bills, statements, checks, and invoices). Government sales were an important component of commercial printing revenues. Commercial printing was seen as an important market opportunity for Kodak: the shift to digital printing was creating serious disruption and Kodak was able to offer a comprehensive range of hardware, consumables, and customer support.

The Consumer Market

In the consumer market, Kodak took a broader approach, consistent with its efforts to provide a transition path for consumers from traditional to digital imaging. This had meant a hybrid approach offering an integrated service where consumers could digitize conventional photographs, edit digitized images and obtain printed photographs in a variety of formats. What changed during the early years of the twenty-first century was the speed with which the transition from conventional to digital photography occurred.

The transition to digital had been slowed by the fact that digital imaging was not unambiguously superior to conventional film-based photography. In particular, with the exception of the most sophisticated (and expensive) professional cameras, digital cameras did not offer such fine resolution as conventional film. And, while digital images could be electronically stored and transmitted, the sizes of image files meant that storage was highly memory intensive and transmission was slow. Rapid developments in the technologies for sensors, memories, image compression, and broadband communication together with steep price declines for digital imaging hardware eliminated most of these constraints. During 2001–03, sales of conventional cameras and film declined sharply, while sales of digital cameras accelerated. However, rapid growth of sales volume meant only modest growth in sales revenue due to steep price reductions. A key feature of almost all sectors of the market for digital imaging was intense competition. Digital imaging resulted in a convergence of many previously distinct products and uses, the effect being to bring companies from very different product and industry backgrounds into direct competition.

The central theme of Kodak's consumer strategy was to provide ease-of-use. "For Kodak, digital photography is all about ease of use and helping people get prints – in other words, getting the same experience they're used to from their film cameras," said Martin Coyne, head of Kodak's Photographic Group, at the 2002 Kodak Media Forum. He supported his argument with data showing that while 90 percent of consumers were satisfied with the pictures obtained from traditional photography, for digital photography the numbers were only between 50 and 70 percent.[10]

Achieving ease of use required a systems approach rather than a product approach – Kodak recognized that most consumers have neither the time nor the patience for reading instructions and integrating different devices and software. Kodak's EasyShare system launched in 2001 was, according to Willy Shih, head of digital and applied imaging, intended to:

Table 6.1 Brand shares of the world market for digital still cameras (by units)

Brand	2003	2002	2001	2000
Sony	18%	20%	25%	26%
Canon	16%	14%	10%	9%
Olympus	13%	16%	11%	18%
Kodak	12%	10%	14%	11%
Hewlett-Packard	n.a.	3%	8%	7%
Fujifilm	10%	15%	14%	12%
Total units sold	48 m	28 m	17 m	n.a.

Source: Compiled from different newspaper articles.

... provide consumers with the first easy-to-use digital photography experience. ... Digital photography is more than just about digital cameras. This is just the first step. ... People need to get their pictures to their PCs and then want to share by printing or e-mail. So we developed a system that made the full experience as easy as possible.[11]

By 2003, most of the main elements of the EasyShare system were in place.

* Kodak had a broad range of EasyShare digital cameras.
* EasyShare camera docks allowed the transfer of digital images from camera to PC at the touch of a button.
* EasyShare software allowed the downloading, organization, editing, and emailing of images, as well as ordering online prints. EasyShare software was bundled with Kodak's cameras as well as being available for downloading for free from Kodak's web site.
* EasyShare printer docks enabled photographic prints to be made direct from the camera without the need for downloading to a PC.

The EasyShare initiative took Kodak into the following highly competitive areas where it lacked a strong market position initially:

* *Digital cameras.* Casio had been the early leader, with over half the world market during the early 1990s. By 1998, 45 companies were offering digital cameras. Suppliers including long-established camera manufacturers (Canon, Kodak, Fuji, Olympus), electronics companies (Casio, HP), and – most recently – manufacturers of wireless handsets (Nokia, Motorola, Samsung, and others). When Kodak entered the digital camera business it was already weak in conventional cameras and lacked the electronic imaging capabilities of Canon, Sony, and HP. Its EasyShare range resulted in substantial market share gains – by the fourth quarter of 2003 it was among the top 3 market leaders in the US, western Europe, and China. (See table 6.1 for market share data.)

- *Software.* Software for digital imaging comprised editing software for manipulating images, color control software, file format and storage software, and software for transferring image files between computers through the Internet. Editing software ranged from programs to fulfill basic image manipulation, such as Microsoft's Picture It, to more comprehensive picture editing and formatting software where Adobe's Photoshop dominated the market. Kodak's main strengths were in its color management software and its DLS System Management and Enhanced Services Software for managing retail processing and printing operations. In 2003 – despite Adobe Systems' domination of the market for image display, formatting, and editing with its Photoshop and Acrobat products – Kodak released its EasyShare software. Adobe quickly followed with PhotoShop Album – a $49 derivative of its PhotoShop software.
- *Printers.* Although a more mature market than digital cameras, home and office printers featured many suppliers and aggressive price competition. Kodak was positioned at the high end, producing commercial, medical, and professional printers using thermal, inkjet, and laser technologies. In 2002, Kodak acquired Scitex, a leader in continuous flow inkjet printing, in order to augment its capabilities in variable data digital printing. According to COO, Antonio Perez: "If a company wants to be a leader in digital imaging, it necessarily has to participate in digital output."[12] Initially, Kodak sourced inkjet printers from Lexmark. The 2003 EasyShare dock printer represented a major step forward for Kodak: a combined printer and camera dock that offered "one touch simple" thermal-dye printing either with a PC or direct from the camera.
- *Photographic paper.* To complete its home printing system, Kodak offered a number of technical advances in inkjet printing paper designed to place it ahead of the competition. Most significant was its Colorlast technology designed to preserve the fidelity and vibrancy of photographic prints for a hundred years or more.

Kodak's EasyShare system represented the third integrated system of digital photography for the consumer market. Its other two systems were its retail store-based system of processing and its online photographic services. Both of these systems developed significantly during 2001 to 2003:

- *Kodak's retail-based processing.* By 2003, Kodak was the clear leader in retail-based digital printing services with 24,000 installed Kodak Picture Makers in the US alone – including 2,000 at CVS drugstores. The kiosks offered consumers a number of scanning, editing, and printing services, with particular emphasis on the scanning of conventional photographic images. During 2004, Kodak began installing its G3 PictureMaker kiosk with the ability to print pictures in as little as five seconds.
- *Kodak's online digital imaging services.* Under Dan Carp and Willy Shih, the Internet was accorded a central role in Kodak's strategy for the consumer market. According to Shih: "the next Killer App . . . is when photography meets the network effect. Or, in other words when the internet is coupled with

digital photography." In 2001, Kodak increased its presence in online photographic processing by acquiring Ofoto, the leading online photographic company. In addition to offering online processing whereby consumers emailed their digital images and received their photographic prints by mail, Ofoto allowed members to build online albums through which family and friends could view and order prints for themselves. Kodak's press release stated: "Ofoto will serve as a critical connection between Kodak's film scanning and uploading services and Kodak's output capabilities through labs operated by its Qualex Inc. subsidiary. These capabilities will give customers and consumers unlimited flexibility in storing, sharing, enhancing and printing pictures." Several of Kodak's dot.com rivals in online photographic services struggled – PhotoPoint and Zing.com exited the market in 2002 – leaving Shutterfly, Snapfish, Wal-Mart, and Fuji as Kodak's main rivals. Kodak's online presence was also extended to "mobile photography." Alliances with Cingular, Nokia, and AT&T allowed users of wireless camera-phones to phone their digital still and video images to Kodak for storage, sharing, and processing.

Kodak's Resources and Capabilities

The central issue facing Kodak's digital imaging business was that its competitive position was totally different from that in traditional photography. In silver-halide photography Kodak had been the pioneer, and had gone on to dominate the photographic industry. In digital imaging, Kodak was but one of many companies that had entered digital imaging as a result of the convergence of imaging and electronics. Kodak, like Fuji, had entered digital imaging to protect itself against the threat that digital technologies presented to photographic film (by 2000, film sales had stagnated; by 2003, they were in decline). Canon, Olympus, and Minolta had entered from their positions in cameras. Casio, Ricoh, and Hewlett-Packard entered from office electronics and printing, while Sony came out of consumer electronics. All these companies possessed different sets of resources and capabilities with strengths and weaknesses in different areas. Kodak's bid to establish leadership in the new world of digital imaging required it to marshal its considerable base of resources and organizational capabilities, while building the additional capabilities needed to succeed in this technologically fast-moving field.

BRAND AND DISTRIBUTION

Foremost among Kodak's resource strengths were its brand equity and distribution presence. After almost a century of global leadership in the photographic industry, Kodak possessed brand recognition and worldwide distribution reach that was unrivaled in the photographic industry. Kodak could bring new products to consumers' attention and support these products with one of the world's best-known and most widely respected brand names, giving the company a huge advantage in a market where technological change created uncertainty for consumers. Kodak's brand reputation was supported by its massive, worldwide distribution presence – primarily through retail photography stores, film processors, and professional photographers. This retail presence was critical to Kodak's entire digital strategy, which was built around providing consumers with a pathway to digital imaging using services offered through retail stores and photo-finishers.

To what extent would Kodak's distribution and brand strengths continue to be a source of competitive advantage in digital imaging? Kodak's retail network was a depreciating asset as consumers' own home-based computer, email, and print capabilities increased. The brand, according to Chief Marketing Officer Carl Gustin, would continue to be Kodak's most valuable asset: "I have always said our brand is almost bulletproof when it comes to images, to memories, to trust, reliability, family values, and more." In studies of digital imaging products, Kodak's brand had ranked either No. 1 or No. 2 in recent years. However, the huge changes in the market might necessitate changes in Kodak's brand strategy. As Gustin remarked: "Does the Kodak name go everywhere, or is a variance of the Kodak name required? Does the name need some tagline? Multiple taglines? Does it mean the same in the commercial and services sector as it does in the consumer sector? That's all being investigated."[13] Nor was it clear that the Kodak brand would carry the same weight in digital as in traditional photography – especially when it was competing against brands such as Canon, Hewlett-Packard, and Sony. In relation to professional, commercial, medical, and government markets, Dan Carp believed that Kodak's market presence might be more secure. The long-established relationship between Kodak and its corporate and institutional customers and the range of support services that Kodak was able to supply provided a greater barrier to consumer electronics companies and high-tech upstarts.

TECHNOLOGY

In technology too, Kodak came to digital imaging with some well-established strengths. Its huge R&D investments in digital imaging since the early 1980s had created proprietary technologies across a broad front. Despite R&D cutbacks during the late 1990s, Kodak maintained one of the world's biggest research efforts in imaging. At its research labs in the US, UK, France, Japan, China, and Australia, Kodak employed more than 5,000 engineers and scientists, including more than 600 PhDs. In 2003, Kodak filed more than 900 patent applications and received 748 US patents, an increase of 11 percent over 2002.

Moreover, its century of innovation and development of photographic images gave Kodak tremendous depth of understanding of recording and processing images and a consultant to Kodak during the 1990s believed that these imaging capabilities transcended specific imaging technologies. Central to Kodak's imaging capability was its color management capability. In the digitizing of color and transferring digital images to paper, Kodak possessed a powerful set of complementary technologies in sensing, color management, and thermal printing. As *Business Week* observed when Fisher joined Kodak: "The basic know-how of combining electronic image capture and color management has been Kodak's for years. Kodak is a world-beater in electronic sensors, devices that see and capture an image, and has a raft of patents in color thermal printing. It also has the best understanding of color management software, which matches the colors you see on the screen with what's on the printed page."[14] By the late 1990s, Kodak was a world leader in color science, which studied the production, control, measurement, specification, and visual perception of color. In particular, Kodak pioneered the field of "colorimetry," which it used to measure and quantify the initial visual response to a stimulus of light.

At the image-capture stage, Kodak developed a leading position in sensors. In charge coupled device (CCD) image sensors for digital cameras, Kodak was a leader in both technology and market share. Kodak's CCD sensors were used by a number of its competitors. In 2001, Olympus selected Kodak's 5.1 million pixel sensor for its E-1 single lens reflex digital camera. In 2002, Kodak launched its 16 million pixel sensor that was adopted in a number of professional digital cameras, inducing those made by Imacon, Jenoptik, Phase One, Megavision, and Sinar.

In the field of image processing, Kodak deployed complex statistical methods and artificial intelligence to develop algorithms for processing digital images. These were used for automatic color balancing, object and text recognition, and image enhancement and manipulation across a wide range of digital imaging applications, including systems for digital photo-finishing where electronically scanned film images or direct-capture digital images could automatically adjust for scene reflectance and lighting conditions, noise, and sharpness – while operating at thousands of frames per hour. Kodak's image processing technology also included algorithms for image compression. In commercial imaging satellites, such proprietary algorithms were used to transmit richly detailed image files back to earth more efficiently than would be possible with non-compressed files.

In image storage, Kodak had a long history of pioneering research and product development, including floppy disks for PCs (1984), 14-inch optical disks (1986), and compact disks (Photo-CD was first announced in 1990). Kodak was a leading member of the consortium of firms (which also included Microsoft, Intel, Adobe, Canon, Fuji, HP, and IBM) that developed and promoted FlashPix for digital camera image storage.

In document and image management, Kodak had led the way in developing systems that store, retrieve, edit, and print text and graphics for organizations such as government departments, banks, and insurance companies, all of which handle thousands of documents a day. The capabilities that Kodak developed in designing these complex, large-scale document and image management systems for its commercial and institutional customers have also been relevant to the creation of digital imaging systems for the consumer market. In creating digital imaging systems for retailers and photo-finishers, Kodak has been involved in integrating various types of hardware and software in systems that must combine quality, versatility, and reliability. A key feature of such systems is that they require Kodak to partner and cooperate with other hardware and software companies whose products either form part of the Kodak system or with which the Kodak system must be compatible. As Kodak has increasingly used the Internet as an infrastructure for linking itself with customers and photo-finishers, so Kodak's capabilities in creating and integrating complex systems for editing, processing, storing, and communicating images are extended to a new dimension.

One of Kodak's most promising opportunities was its proprietary technology for OLED (organic light emitting diode) displays. To commercialize this technology Kodak formed SK Display Corporation with Sanyo to supply OLED screens to Kodak and other manufacturers. Kodak believed that its OLED display screens would displace liquid crystal displays (LCDs) in digital cameras and a range of other electronic products.

Supporting Kodak's digital system design capabilities was its predictive system modeling that allowed it to measure the characteristics of imaging systems and predict the performance of entire systems of digital and hybrid imaging that included optics, image sensors, scanners, image-processing operations, printers, display media, and human visual responses. Such modeling allowed developers to quickly evaluate competing design proposals and select product features delivering the highest value to the customer.

At the image-output level, Kodak believed that consumers would continue to demand printed photographs. In print media, particularly specialty coated papers, Kodak was world leader. During 2000–03, Kodak introduced a number of new inkjet papers embodying new technologies.

NEW PRODUCT DEVELOPMENT

Despite Kodak's strengths in basic and applied research and its long history of successful new product launches, Carp was acutely aware of the criticisms that had been leveled at Kodak for its weaknesses in bringing new products to market: Kodak was too slow and its marketers had little understanding of the digital world.

Kodak's product development process still reflected the company's origins in chemistry. Product development traditionally began with basic research where innovations were exploited through a long and meticulous product development process before being rolled out on to the world market. One of George Fisher's major initiatives as Kodak chairman and CEO had been to streamline and speed Kodak's cumbersome product development process. In place of Kodak's sequential "phases and gates" development process, Fisher transferred approaches that had worked well at Motorola – greater decentralization of new product development and the use of cross-functional development teams to accelerate cycle times. Speed also required collaboration to access the technologies and capabilities of outside companies. Kodak had no problem in establishing collaborative agreements with other companies – its size, brand name, and technological strength were sufficient to make it a highly attractive partner for small, technology-intensive firms in digital imaging. The real challenge was for Kodak to overcome a long history of insularity and hierarchical control in order to make its newfound alliances fruitful. Kodak's track record of alliances and joint ventures was mixed. Its Phogenix joint venture with HP to develop digital minilabs for film and image processes was dissolved in May 2003 after three years.

Under Dan Carp, Kodak has greatly increased the flow of new digital imaging products to the markets. To enhance Kodak's ability to develop successful new products, Carp continued Fisher's strategy of hiring senior executives from leading edge IT companies. Table 6.2 shows the backgrounds of Kodak's senior executives. In addition, Carp

Table 6.2 Eastman Kodak's senior management team, March 2004

Name	Position	Joined Kodak	Prior company experience
Corporate Officers			
Daniel Carp	Chairman & CEO	1970	–
Antonio Perez	President & COO	2003	CEO, HP Inkjet Imaging
Robert Brust	Chief Financial Officer	2000	Unisys, General Electric
Michael Morley	Chief Admin. Officer	1964	–
Gary Graafeiland	General Counsel	1979	–
Charles Brown	Director, Global Manufacturing & Logistics	1973	–
Carl Gustin, Jr.	Chief Marketing Officer	1994	DEC, Apple Computer
Henri Petit	Director, International	1975	–
James Stoffel	Chief Technology Officer	1997	Xerox
William Lloyd	Director, Inkjet Systems	2003	Inwit, Gemplus, HP
Daniel Meek	Director, Operating System	1973	–
Kim VanGelder	Chief Information Officer	1984	–
Divisional Presidents			
Bernard Masson	Digital & Film Imaging	2002	Lexmark
Daniel Kerpelman	Health Imaging	2002	GE Medical Systems
Carl Marchetto	Commercial Imaging	1996	Lockheed Martin
James Langley	Commercial Printing	2003	HP
Willy Shih	Display & Components	1997	Silicon Graphics

Source: Eastman Kodak Annual Report, 2003; www.kodak.com.

increased the pace of Kodak's acquisitions of companies that could fill key gaps in its own know-how. Despite these positive developments, there were lingering doubts as to whether a former monopolist of the photographic industry, with its activities heavily concentrated on Rochester, New York, could ever adapt to the fast-cycle product development practices of Silicon Valley.

FINANCES

One of Kodak's key advantages in withstanding the uncertainties and rapid technological changes of the market for digital imaging was its size and financial security. In contrast to the many start-up companies that sought to establish themselves in the sector, Kodak was independent of venture capitalists and the vagaries of the IPO market. In contrast even to some of its large and well-established rivals, Kodak had the security of cash flows from its traditional photographic business.

By the beginning of 2004, Eastman Kodak remained a financially strong company, but it was no longer the financial powerhouse of yesteryear. Since the late 1990s, debt has risen considerably, and retiree healthcare benefits represented a substantial long-term liability. Meanwhile, profitability has declined substantially between 2000 and 2003 – both because of the deterioration of the core photography business, and because of the restructuring charges that were becoming a regular feature of Kodak's income statement. As a result, some analysts doubted Kodak's ability to finance its "digital growth strategy," which involved investing some $3 billion in capital expenditures and acquisitions during 2004–06. However, tables 6.3 and 6.4 summarize Kodak's recent financial results.

■ LOOKING FORWARD ■

On February 12, Dan Carp prepared notes for his talk to the annual convention of the Photo Marketing Association as part of the Executive Visionaries Panel. As he reviewed his four years as CEO, he was satisfied that – 20 years after Kodak has begun diversifying beyond silver-halide imaging – Kodak strategy for digital imaging was finally showing both coherence and results.

In the medical and commercial sector, the company had strong, profitable positions in several markets where Kodak possessed particular technical strengths and strong customer relationships. However, it was in the consumer photographic sector that Carp felt that the many themes in Kodak's digital strategy were beginning to fit together. Kodak was finally a full-system supplier – not just to consumers using Kodak's retail stores, but also to consumers who did their own editing, transfer, and printing of digital images. In addition, Kodak had established strongholds in a number of key technologies – CCD sensors, OLED screens, image compression algorithms, color management systems, inks, and specialty inkjet papers. Kodak's efforts to establish itself as a leading supplier of digital cameras had been especially impressive.

Despite this encouraging progress, Carp realized that the 2004–06 period would be critical for Kodak – especially in the consumer sector. In every consumer product market that Kodak was competing, it faced tough competition. As always, Kodak's most direct competitor was Fuji Film. While Kodak had experienced stagnant revenues for the past four years, Fuji had grown rapidly and had achieved much higher operating earnings than Kodak.[15] Fuji was strongly positioned across a broad range of the technologies relevant to the new world of digital imaging: digital image-processing software, nano-technology, pigmentation technology, CCD technology, lenses, and lasers. Its "Vision 75" strategy (culminating in Fuji's 75th anniversary in 2007) planned for heavy investment and rapid sales growth. Many of the targeted markets were precisely the same as those where Kodak was also focusing: digital cameras, flat panel displays, print-on-demand digital commercial printing, digital minilabs, and the Chinese market.

Apart from Fuji, a number of other competitors – well established in the electronics industry – were growing their presence in digital imaging: Hewlett-Packard, Sony, and Canon to mention a few. Given the tendency for most of the standards in the industry to be open rather than proprietary, it seemed likely that competition would continue to be aggressive with no one company building a dominant position.

Given this outlook, what were Kodak's prospects for gaining a satisfactory rate of return on its investments in digital imaging? Given the pressure from activist shareholders should Kodak continue to position itself as a broad-line supplier of digital

Table 6.3 Eastman Kodak: selected financial data, 1997–2003 ($ million)

	2003	2002	2001	2000	1999	1998	1997
From income statement							
Sales	13,317	12,835	13,234	13,994	14,089	13,406	14,713
Costs:							
Cost of goods sold	9,033	8,225	8,670	8,019	7,987	7,293	7,979
Selling, general, and admin.	2,648	2,530	2,627	2,977	3,295	3,303	3,912
R&D costs	781	762	779	784	817	922	1,044
Operating earnings	238	793	345	2,214	1,990	1,888	1,778
Interest expense	148	173	219	178	142	110	98
Other income (charges)	51	101	(18)	96	261	328	(1,441)
Restructuring and other costs	484	98	659	(44)	350	–	1,441
Provision for income taxes	(66)	153	32	725	717	716	48
Net earnings	265	770	76	1,407	1,392	1,390	5
From balance sheet							
Total current assets	5,455	4,534	4,683	5,491	5,373	–	5,475
Including:							
Cash and cash equivalents	1,250	569	448	246	20	–	728
Receivables	2,389	2,234	2,337	2,653	2,537	–	2,271
Inventories	1,075	1,062	1,137	1,718	1,519	–	1,252
Property, plant, and equipment	5,094	5,420	5,659	5,919	6,189	–	5,509
Other noncurrent assets	4,269	3,540	2,072	1,767	1,801	–	1,231
Total assets	14,818	13,494	13,362	14,212	14,370	–	13,145
Total current liabilities	5,307	5,502	5,354	3,275	3,832	–	5,177
Including:							

Table 6.3 *continued*

	2003	2002	2001	2000	1999	1998	1997
Payables	3,707	3,351	3,276	3,403	1,163	–	3,832
Short-term borrowings	946	1,442	1,378	2,058	612	–	611
Other liabilities:							
Long-term borrowings	2,302	1,164	1,666	1,166	936	–	585
Post employment liabilities	3,344	3,412	2,728	2,610	2,776	–	3,075
Other long-term liabilities	601	639	720	671	859	–	1,019
Total liabilities	11,554	10,717	10,468	10,784	10,458	–	9,984
Shareholders' equity	3,264	2,777	2,894	3,428	3,912	–	3,161
Total liabilities (& equity)	14,818	13,494	13,362	14,212	14,370	–	13,145
From cash flow statement							
Cash flows from operating activities:							
Earnings from continuing operations	265	770	76	1,407	1,392	1,390	5
Adjustments for non-cash items	1,361	1,448	1,989	(425)	541	93	2,075
Net cash provided by operating activities	1,645	2,204	2,065	982	1,933	1,483	2,080
Cash flows from investing activities:							
Additions to properties	(506)	(577)	(743)	(945)	(1,127)	(1,108)	(1,485)
Proceeds from sale of businesses/assets	26	27	0	277	422	238	(85)
Acquisitions, net of cash acquired	(679)	(72)	(306)	(130)	(3)	(949)	(341)
Net cash used in investing activities	(1,267)	(758)	(1,074)	(783)	(685)	(1,839)	(1,896)
Net cash flows from financing activities	270	(1,331)	(804)	(314)	(1,327)	77	(1,198)
Number of employees (thousands)	63.9	70.0	75.1	78.1	80.7	86.5	97.5

Source: Eastman Kodak Annual Reports.

Table 6.4   Eastman Kodak: results by business segments, 1999–2003 ($ millions)

	2003	2002	2001	2000	1999
Net sales:					
Photography	9,232	9,002	9,403	10,231	10,265
Health Imaging	2,431	2,274	2,262	2,220	2,159
Commercial Imaging	1,559	1,456	1,454	1,417	1,479
All other	95	103	110	126	186
Consolidated total	13,317	12,835	13,229	13,994	14,089
Earnings from operations:					
Photography	418	771	787	1,430	1,709
Health Imaging	481	431	323	518	483
Commercial Imaging	166	192	172	233	257
All other	(78)	(28)	(60)	(11)	(109)
Total of segments	987	1,366	1,222	2,170	2,340
Net earnings:					
Photography	347	550	535	1,034	1,261
Health Imaging	382	313	221	356	324
Commercial Imaging	99	83	84	90	178
All other	(73)	(23)	(38)	(2)	(61)
Total of segments	755	923	802	1,478	1,702
Total assets:*					
Photography	8,905	8,798	9,225	7,100	6,875
Health Imaging	2,600	2,011	2,038	1,491	1,229
Commercial Imaging	1,396	1,405	1,438	1,045	963
All other	10	66	(16)	(92)	(123)
Total of segments	12,911	12,280	12,715	9,544	8,944

*Net operating assets for 1999 and 2000.

imaging solutions that went from digital cameras to photographic paper, or should Kodak focus on the areas where its traditional strengths lay – photo-finishing services and the supply of consumables such as paper and ink?

NOTES

1. Eastman Kodak Company, Fourth Quarter 2003 Report and 2004 Outlook, January 22, 2004.
2. Lex, "Kodak Focuses on Digital Future," *Financial Times*, January 23, 2004.
3. Linda Grant, "Can Fisher focus Kodak?" *Fortune*, January 13, 1997.
4. Address to the Academy of Management, Boston, August 1997.
5. "Kodak's New Focus," *Business Week*, January 30, 1995, pp. 62–8.
6. Eastman Kodak Company, "Kodak leaders outline road ahead to get Kodak 'back on track'," Press Release, November 11, 1997.
7. Eastman Kodak Company, "Kodak and HP joint venture to be named Phogenix Imaging," Press Release, August 1, 2000.

8. "Why Kodak still isn't fixed," *Fortune*, May 11, 1998.
9. In March 2004, Kodak agreed to purchase Heidelberg's 50 percent share of NexPress, together with Heidelberg's digital black and white printing systems (see Annual Report for 2003, p. 17).
10. Eastman Kodak Company, "The Big Picture: Kodak and Digital Photography," www.Kodak.com/US/en/corp/presscenter/presentations/020520mediaforum3.shtml.
11. Ibid.
12. Interview with Antonio Perez, President and COO, Kodak, www.photomarketing.com/0204_PEREZ.htm.
13. Interview with Carl Gustin, Chief Marketing Officer, Kodak, www.photomarketing.com/0204_Gustin.htm.
14. "Kodak's New Focus," *Business Week*, January 30, 1995, pp. 62–8.
15. Fuji's ratio of operating income to sales was 11.0% in 2000, 10.8% in 2001, 7.0% in 2002, and 7.3% in 2003.

Organizational Restructuring within the Royal Dutch/Shell Group

Robert M. Grant

At the beginning of 2000, the Royal Dutch/Shell Group of Companies (Shell) was emerging from one of the most ambitious and far-reaching organizational restructurings of its 93-year history. The restructuring had involved the shift from a geographically based to a primarily business sector-based structure, the elimination of over 1,000 corporate positions, the sale of much of its London headquarters, and the redesign of its systems of coordination and control. The restructuring had been precipitated by the realization that Shell would need to change the way it did business if it was to retain its position as the world's largest energy and chemicals company and offer an adequate return to shareholders in an increasingly turbulent industry environment.

By the end of 1999, it was clear that the changes were bearing fruit. Head office costs had been reduced and the increased coordination and control that the new sector-based organization permitted were helping Shell to control costs, focus capital expenditure, and prune the business portfolio. Return on capital employed (ROCE) and return on equity (ROE) for 1999 were their highest for ten years. However, much of the improvement in bottom-line performance was the result of the recovery in oil prices during the year. Once the benefits of higher oil prices were stripped out, Shell's improvements in financial performance looked much more modest.

At the same time, Shell's competitors were not standing still. BP, once government-owned and highly bureaucratized, had become one of the world's most dynamic, profitable, and widely admired oil majors. Its merger with Amoco quickly followed by its acquisition of Atlantic Richfield had created an international giant of almost identical size to Shell. In the meantime, Shell's longtime archrival, Exxon, was merging with Mobil. Shell was no longer the world's biggest energy company – its sales revenues lagged some way behind those of Exxon Mobil. Other oil and gas majors were also getting caught up in the wave of mergers and restructurings. In particular, Shell's once-sluggish European rivals were undergoing extensive revitalization. The merger of Total, Fina, and Elf Aquitaine in September 1999 had created the world's fourth "super-major" (after Exxon Mobil, Shell, and BP Amoco). Also asserting itself on the world stage was Italy's privatized and revitalized Eni SpA.

The reorganization that had begun in 1994 under chairman of the Committee of Managing Directors, Cor Herkstroter, and continued under his successor, Mark Moody-Stuart, had transformed the organizational structure of Shell. From a decentralized confederation of over 200 operating companies spread throughout the world, a divisionalized group with clear lines of authority and more effective executive leadership had been created. Yet, Shell remained a highly complex organization that was a prisoner of its own illustrious history and where corporate authority remained divided between The Hague, London, and Houston. Had enough been done to turn a sprawling multinational empire into an enterprise capable of deploying its huge resources with the speed and decisiveness necessary to cope with an ever more volatile international environment?

■ HISTORY OF THE ROYAL DUTCH/SHELL GROUP ■

The Royal Dutch/Shell Group is unique among the world's oil majors. It was formed from the 1907 merger of the assets and operations of the Netherlands-based Royal Dutch Petroleum Company and the British-based Shell Transport and Trading Company. It is the world's biggest and oldest joint venture. Both parent companies trace their origins to the Far East in the 1890s.

Marcus Samuel inherited a half share in his father's seashell trading business. His business visits to the Far East made him aware of the potential for supplying kerosene from the newly developing Russian oilfields around Baku to the large markets in China and the Far East for oil suitable for lighting and cooking. Seeing the opportunity for exporting kerosene from the Black Sea coast through the recently opened Suez Canal to the Far East, Samuel invested in a new tanker, the *Murex*. In 1892, the *Murex* delivered 4,000 tons of Russian kerosene to Bangkok and Singapore. In 1897, Samuel formed the Shell Transport and Trading Company, with a pecten shell as its trademark, to take over his growing oil business.

At the same time, August Kessler was leading a Dutch company to develop an oilfield in Sumatra in the Dutch East Indies. In 1896 Henri Deterding joined Kessler and the two began building storage and transportation facilities and a distribution network in order to bring their oil to market.

The expansion of both companies was supported by the growing demand for oil resulting from the introduction of the automobile and oil-fueled ships. In 1901 Shell began purchasing Texas crude, and soon both companies were engaged in fierce competition with John D. Rockefeller's Standard Oil. Faced with the might of Standard Oil, Samuel and Deterding (who had succeeded Kessler as chairman of Royal Dutch) began cooperating, and in 1907 the business interests of the two companies were combined into a single group, with Royal Dutch owning a 60 percent share and Shell a 40 percent share (a ratio that has remained constant to this day).

The group grew rapidly, expanding East Indies production and acquiring producing interests in Romania (1906), Russia (1910), Egypt (1911), the US (1912), Venezuela (1913), and Trinidad (1914). In 1929 Shell entered the chemicals business, and in 1933 Shell's interests in the US were consolidated into the Shell Union Oil Corporation. By 1938, Shell crude oil production stood at almost 580,000 barrels per day out of a world total of 5,720,000.

The post-war period began with rebuilding the war-devastated refineries and tanker fleet, and continued with the development of new oilfields in Venezuela, Iraq, the Sahara, Canada, Colombia, Nigeria, Gabon, Brunei, and Oman. In 1959, a joint Shell/Exxon venture discovered one of the world's largest natural gas fields at Groningen in the Netherlands. This was followed by a series of major North Sea oil and gas finds between 1971 and 1976.

During the 1970s, Shell, like the other majors, began diversifying outside of petroleum:

- In 1970 it acquired Billiton, an international metals mining company, for $123 million.
- In 1973 it formed a joint venture with Gulf to build nuclear reactors.
- In 1976–7 it acquired US and Canadian coal companies.
- In 1977 it acquired Witco Chemical's polybutylene division.

By the beginning of the 1980s, Shell had built global metals and coal businesses and established several smaller ventures including forestry in Chile and New Zealand, flower growing in the Netherlands, and biotechnology in Europe and the US.

The 1980s saw a reversal of Shell's diversification strategy, with several divestments of "non-core businesses" and a concentration on oil and gas – especially upstream. One of Shell's major thrusts was to increase its presence within the US. After acquiring Belridge Oil of California, it made its biggest investment of the period when it acquired the minority interests in its US subsidiary Shell Oil for $5.4 billion.

■ SHELL'S ORGANIZATION STRUCTURE PRIOR TO 1995 ■

Shell's uniqueness stems from its structure as a joint venture and from its internationality – it has been described as one of the world's three most international organizations, the other two being the Roman Catholic Church and the United Nations. However, its organizational structure is more complex than either of the other two organizations. The structure of the Group may be looked at in terms of the different companies that comprise Royal Dutch/Shell and their links of ownership and control, which Shell refers to as *governance responsibilities*. The Group's structure may also be viewed from a management perspective – how is Royal Dutch/Shell actually managed? The day-to-day management activities of the Group, which Shell refers to as *executive responsibilities*, are complex, and the structure through which the Group is actually managed does not correspond very closely to the formal structure.

The Formal Structure

From an ownership and legal perspective, the Royal Dutch/Shell Group of Companies comprised four types of company:

- *The parent companies*. Royal Dutch Petroleum Company N.V. of the Netherlands and the Shell Transport and Trading Company plc of the UK owned the shares of the group holding companies (from which they received dividends) in the proportions 60 percent and 40 percent. Each company had its shares separately listed on the stock exchanges of Europe and the US, and each had a separate Board of Directors.
- *The group holding companies*. Shell Petroleum N.V. of the Netherlands and The Shell Petroleum Company Ltd of the UK held shares in both the service companies and the operating companies of the Group. In addition, Shell Petroleum N.V. also owned the shares of Shell Petroleum Inc. of the US – the parent of the US operating company, Shell Oil Company.
- *The service companies*. During the early 1990s, there were nine service companies located either in London or The Hague. They were:
  - Shell Internationale Petroleum Maatschappij B.V.
  - Shell Internationale Chemie Maatschappij B.V.
  - Shell International Petroleum Company Limited
  - Shell International Chemical Company Limited
  - Billiton International Metals B.V.
  - Shell International Marine Limited
  - Shell Internationale Research Maatschappij B.V.
  - Shell International Gas Limited
  - Shell Coal International Limited.

The service companies provided advice and services to the operating companies but were not responsible for operations.

- *The operating companies* (or "opcos") comprised more than 200 companies in over 100 countries (the 1993 annual report listed 244 companies in which Shell held 50 percent or more ownership). They varied in size from Shell Oil Company, one of the largest petroleum companies in the US in its own right, to small marketing companies such as Shell Bahamas and Shell Cambodia. Almost all of the operating companies operated within a single country. Some had activities within a single sector (exploration and production (E&P), refining, marketing, coal, or gas); others (such as Shell UK, Shell Canada, and Norske Shell) operated across multiple sectors. Figure 7.1 shows the formal structure of the Group.

Coordination and Control

Managerial control of the Group was vested in the Committee of Managing Directors (CMD), which forms the Group's top management team. The Committee comprised five

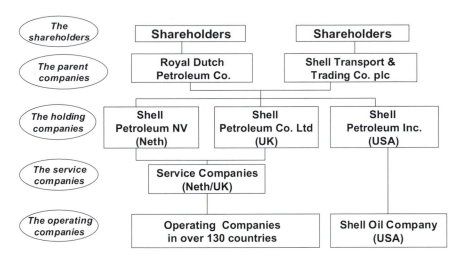

Figure 7.1 The formal structure of the Royal Dutch/Shell Group

Managing Directors. These were the three-member Management Board of Royal Dutch Petroleum and the Chairman and Vice Chairman of Shell Transport and Trading. The chairmanship of CMD rotated between the President of Royal Dutch Petroleum and the Managing Director of Shell Transport and Trading. Thus, in 1993, Cor Herkstroter (President of Royal Dutch) took over from J. S. Jennings (Managing Director of Shell Transport and Trading) as Chairman of CMD, and Jennings became Vice Chairman of CMD. Because executive power was vested in a committee rather than a single chief executive, Shell lacked the strong individual leadership that characterized other majors (e.g., Lee Raymond at Exxon and John Browne at BP).

The CMD provided the primary linkage between the formal (or *governance*) structure and the management (or *executive*) structure of the Group. The CMD also linked together the two parent companies and the group holding companies.

The combination of diffused executive power at the top together with operating authority and financial responsibility dispersed through 244 operating companies meant that, compared with every other oil major, Shell was highly decentralized. However, the technical and economic realities of the oil business limited the autonomy of each operating company – interdependence resulted from linkages between upstream and downstream, between refining and chemicals, and from common financial and technological needs. It was the job of the service companies to provide the necessary coordination. During the early 1960s, Shell created, with the help of McKinsey & Company, a matrix structure within its service companies to manage its operating companies. This structure was viewed as a critical ingredient of Shell's ability to reconcile the independence of its operating companies with effective coordination of business, regional, and functional commonalities. This matrix organization continued into the 1990s (see figure 7.2).

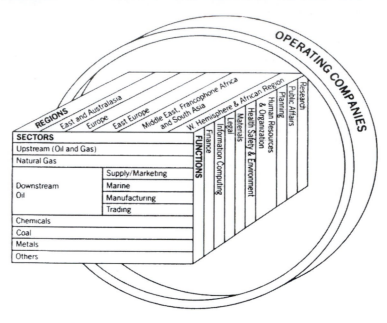

Figure 7.2 The Shell Matrix (pre-1996)

The three dimensions of this matrix were represented by the principal executives of the service companies, who were designated "coordinators." Thus, the senior management team at the beginning of 1995 included the following:

Committee of Managing Directors
- Chairman
- Vice-Chairman
- three other Managing Directors.

Principal executives of the service companies
- Regional coordinators:
  - Europe
  - Western Hemisphere and Africa
  - Middle East, Francophone Africa, and South Asia
  - East and Australasia
- Sector coordinators:
  - E&P Coordinator
  - Chemicals Coordinator
  - Coal/Natural Gas Coordinator
  - Metals Coordinator
  - President – Shell International Trading
  - Marine Coordinator
  - Supply and Marketing Coordinator

- Functional coordinators:
  - Director of Finance
  - Group Treasurer
  - Group Planning Coordinator
  - Manufacturing Coordinator
  - Group HR and Organization Coordinator
  - Legal Coordinator
  - Group Public Affairs Coordinator
  - Group Research Coordinator
  - Director of The Hague Office
  - Director of the London Office

Strategic Planning at Shell

Within this three-way matrix, the geographical dimension was traditionally the most important. The fact that the operating companies were national subsidiaries provided the basis for the geographical emphasis of operational and financial decision making. This was reinforced through the strategic planning process, which put its main emphasis on planning at the national and regional levels.

Shell's planning system lay at the heart of its management system. It was viewed as one of the most sophisticated and effective of any large multinational. It was much discussed and widely imitated. Its main features were the following:

- A strong emphasis upon long-term strategic thinking. Shell's planning horizon extended 20 years into the future – much further than the four- or five-year planning that most companies engage in. Unlike most other companies, the basis for these strategic plans was not *forecasts* but *scenarios* – alternative views of the future which allowed managers to consider strategic responses to the different ways in which the future might unfold.
- A breadth of vision, and emphasis on the generation and application of ideas rather than a narrow focus on financial performance. Shell's planning department was receptive to concepts and ideas drawn from economics, psychology, biochemistry, biology, mathematics, anthropology, and ecology. As a consequence, Shell pioneered many new management techniques, including multiple scenario analysis, business portfolio planning, cognitive mapping, and the application of organizational learning concepts to planning processes.
- More generally, Shell was in the vanguard of the transition from the role of the strategy function as *planning* towards one where the primary roles of strategy were encouraging *thinking about the future*, developing the capacity for *organizational learning*, promoting *organizational dialogue*, and facilitating organizational *adaptation* to a changing world.

Planning at Shell was primarily bottom-up. The CMD identified key issues, set strategic direction, and approved major projects, and the planning department formulated the scenarios. However, most strategic decisions and initiatives originated among the operating companies. The role of the planning staff and the regional and sector coordinators was to coordinate the operating company strategic plans.

■ FORCES FOR CHANGE ■

Between the early 1970s and the early 1990s, the world petroleum industry was transformed by a number of fundamental changes.[1] The growing power of the producer countries was seen not just in the sharp rise in crude oil prices during the first oil shock of 1974, but even more fundamentally in the nationalization of the oil reserves of the international majors. By the 1990s, the list of the world's top 20 oil and gas producers was dominated by state-owned companies such as Saudi Aramco, Petroleos de Venezuela, Kuwait Oil, Iran National Oil Company, Pemex (Mexico), and Russia's Gasprom and Lukoil. In addition, the old-established majors faced competition from other sources. The "new majors," integrated oil companies such as Elf Aquitaine (France), Total (France), Eni (Italy), Nippon Oil (Japan), Neste (Finland), and Respol (Spain), were expanding rapidly, while in North America and the North Sea independent E&P companies such as Enterprise Oil, Triton, and Apache were becoming significant global players. Between 1970 and 1990, the share of world oil production of the "Seven Sisters" fell from 31 percent to 7 percent.[2] The loss of control over their sources of crude oil was a devastating blow for the majors – their whole strategy of vertical integration had been based around the concept of controlling risk through owning the downstream facilities needed to provide secure outlets for their crude oil. As market transactions for crude oil and refinery outputs became increasingly important, so prices became much more volatile. Between 1981 and 1986, crude prices fell from $42 a barrel to $9 before briefly recovering to $38 in the wake of the Iraqi invasion of Kuwait, and then resuming their downward direction.

Between 1985 and 1993, almost all the world's oil majors underwent far-reaching restructuring. Restructuring involved radical simultaneous changes in strategy and organizational structure in a compressed time-frame. Key features of restructuring by the oil majors were:

- Reorienting their goals around shareholder value maximization.
- Greater selectivity in their strategies, involving the divestment of unprofitable businesses, refocusing around core petroleum and gas businesses, withdrawing from countries where investments were not justified by the returns being earned, and outsourcing those activities that could be performed more efficiently by outside suppliers.
- Cutting back on staff, especially at the corporate level. (Table 7.1 shows changes in numbers of employees among the majors.)
- Reducing excess capacity through closures of refineries and filling stations.
- Decentralization of decision making from corporate to divisional levels and from divisional to business unit levels at the same time as giving divisions and business units full profit and loss responsibility.
- Shifting the basis of organizational structure from geographical organization around countries and regions to worldwide product divisions (many of the

Table 7.1 Employment among the oil majors ('000)

	1999	1996	1993	1990	1985
Shell	99	101	117	136	142
Elf Aquitaine[c]	81	85	94	92	78
ENI	79	83	106	128	125
Exxon[a]	79	79	91	101	147
Total[c]	57	57	50	43	41
BP[b]	99	53	73	118	132
Mobil[a]	–	43	62	68	72
Amoco[b]	–	42	46	53	48
Chevron	39	41	48	50	62
Texaco	25	29	33	40	57
Arco[b]	17	23	25	28	31

Notes:
[a] Exxon merged with Mobil in 1998.
[b] Amoco merged with BP in 1997. BP acquired Arco in 1999.
[c] Total merged with Fina in 1998 and with Elf Aquitaine in 1999.
Source: *Fortune Global 500*, 2000, 1997, 1994, 1991, and 1996.

majors formed worldwide divisions for upstream activities, downstream activities, and chemicals).

- "Delayering" through eliminating administrative layers within hierarchical structures. For example, Amoco broke up its three major divisions (upstream, downstream, and chemicals) and had 17 business groups reporting direct to the corporate center. Mobil also broke up its divisional structure, and created 13 business groups. (The Appendix shows the organization structure of several of the majors.)

■ SHELL IN THE EARLY 1990s ■

Shell was the only major oil company that did not undergo radical restructuring between 1985 and 1993. The absence of restructuring at Shell appeared to reflect two factors:

- Shell's flexibility had meant that Shell had been able to adjust to a changing oil industry environment without the need for discontinuous change. For example, Shell had been a leader in rationalizing excess capacity in refining and shipping, in upgrading its refineries with catalytic crackers, in establishing arm's-length relationships between its production units and its refineries, in moving into natural gas, and in taking advantage of opportunities for deepwater exploration.

- Because of Shell's management structure, in particular the absence of a CEO with autocratic powers, Shell was much less able to initiate the kind of top-down restructuring driven by powerful CEOs such as Larry Rawl at Exxon, Jim Kinnear at Texaco, Serge Tchuruk at Total, or Franco Bernabè at Eni.

Nevertheless, during the early 1990s, a combination of forces was pushing the CMD towards more radical top-down change. The most influential of these pressures was dissatisfaction over financial performance. The early 1990s were difficult years for the industry. The fall in oil prices to the mid-teens meant that returns from the traditional fount of profit – upstream – were meager. At the same time, refining and chemicals suffered from widespread excess capacity and price wars. Meanwhile, investors and the financial community were putting increased pressure on companies for improved return to shareholders. The CMD was forced to shift its attention from long-term development to short-term financial results. Against a variety of benchmarks, Shell's profit performance looked less than adequate:

- Cost of capital was the most fundamental of these – during the early 1990s Shell was earning a return on equity that barely covered the cost of equity.
- Long-term stability was a further goal. Top management asked, "What rate of return is needed to provide the cash flow needed to pay dividends and replace assets and reserves?" The returns of 1990–4 were somewhat below this figure.
- Shell's rates of return, margins, and productivity ratios were below those of several leading competitors.

Table 7.2 shows Shell's financial performance during the 1990s.

Evidence of the potential for performance improvement through restructuring was available from inside as well as from outside the Group. During the late 1980s and early 1990s, several Shell operating companies – notably those in Canada, the US, UK, South Africa, Germany, Malaysia, and France – showed the potential for organizational restructuring, process redesign, and outsourcing to yield substantial cost savings and productivity improvements.

The operating company executives that had been in the vanguard of cost cutting were increasingly resentful of the corporate structure. By 1994, Shell employed 6,800 people in its central organization (in London and The Hague) and in its corporate research and support functions. Even allowing for the differences in organizational structure between Shell and its competitors, this was bigger than the corporate and divisional administration of any other oil and gas major. As the operating companies struggled to reduce their own costs and improve their bottom-line performance, so they became antagonistic towards what they saw as a bloated corporate center whose support and services offered little discernable value. A major gripe was the failure of Shell's elaborate matrix structure to provide effective coordination of the operating companies. Lack of coordination in Europe resulted in UK refineries selling into Spain and Portugal, the Marseilles refinery supplying Belgium, natural geographical units such as Scandinavia split between different operating companies, and difficulties in launching Europe-wide initiatives such as the Shell credit card.

As Chairman Cor Herkstroter noted:

Table 7.2 Royal Dutch/Shell Group: performance data, 1992–9

	1999	1998	1997	1996	1995	1994	1993	1992
Gross sales ($ bill.)	149.7	138.3	171.7	172.0	150.7	129.1	125.8	128.4
Operating profit ($ bill.)	15.2	3.1	15.3	17.1	12.5	9.6	8.9	9.2
Net income ($ bill.)	8.6	0.4	7.8	8.9	6.9	6.2	4.5	5.4
Cash flow from operations ($ bill.)	11.1	14.7	16.7	16.6	14.9			
ROCE (%)	12.1	2.8	12.0	12.0	10.7	10.4	7.9	9.0
ROE (%)	15.4	0.7	12.8	15.1	11.8	11.5	8.7	9.7
Capital expenditure ($ bill.)	7.4	12.9	13.4	12.1	11.8	10.5	9.5	10.4
Employees ('000)	99	102	105	104	106	107	117	127

(The data are for continuing operations only. Hence, Shell's numbers of employees shown in Table 7.1 differ from those here because of acquisitions and disposals.)

> Many Operating Companies are sending us clear signals that they feel constrained by the management processes of the Service Companies, that the support and guidance from them is ineffective or inefficient, and that the services are too costly. They do not see the eagerness for cost reductions in the Operating Companies sufficiently mirrored in the center.[3]

The essential issue, however, was to prepare Shell for an increasingly difficult business environment:

> While our current organization and practices have served us very well for many years, they were designed for a different era, for a different world. Over the years significant duplication and confusion of roles at various levels in the organization have developed. Many of you notice this on a day-to-day basis.
>
> We anticipate increasingly dynamic competition. We see the business conditions of today, with flat margins and low oil prices continuing into the future. In addition, there will be no let up on all players in the industry to strive for higher productivity, innovation quality and effectiveness.
>
> Our vision of the future is one of increasing competitive surprise and discontinuity, of increasing change and differentiation in skills required to succeed; and of increasing demands by our people at the front line for accountability within a framework of clear business objectives, and with access to a global source of specialist expertise.[4]

The Change Process

Within Shell, proponents of organizational change, including the heads of several of the operating companies, the finance function, and Group Planning, had had little success in persuading the Committee of Managing Directors of the need for large-scale change. In May 1993, Cor Herkstroter took over as Chairman of the CMD. A Dutch accountant, who had spent his entire career at Shell, Herkstroter was an unlikely pioneer of change. Fellow executives described him as a private, Old World personality without much charisma, and with a preference for written communication. Nevertheless, Herkstroter was widely respected for his intelligence and courage. "He's Shell's Gorbachev," said Philip Mirvis, a consultant working with Noel Tichy at Shell.[5]

Faced with growing evidence of suboptimal financial performance and an over-complex, inward-looking organizational structure, Herkstroter called a meeting of Shell's 50 top managers at Hartwell House, an English country manor, in May 1994. The meeting was a shock for the CMD. The request for frank discussions of the reasons for Shell's lagging return on capital provided a series of barbed attacks on top management and sharp criticism of the service company organization. The corporate center was castigated for taking months to approve operating company budgets and for the general laxness of financial controls. E&P coordinator Robert Sprague tossed a blank transparency onto the overhead projector and commented, "I don't know what to report, this issue is really a mess." The meeting had a powerful impact on the CMD: "We were bureaucratic, inward looking, complacent, self-satisfied, arrogant," observed then-Vice Chairman John Jennings. "We tolerated our own underperformance. We were technocratic and insufficiently entrepreneurial."[6] The outcome was the appointment of a high-level team to study Shell's internal organization and come up with options for redesign.

The team, set up in July 1994, was headed by Ernst van Mourik-Broekman, the head of HR, together with Basil South from Group Planning, Group Treasurer Stephen Hodge, an executive from Shell France, and the head of Shell's gas business in the Netherlands. The internal team was joined by three senior consultants from McKinsey & Company: two from the Amsterdam office and one from the London office.

The starting point for the internal team was a program of interviews with 40–50 managers at different levels within the company. This provided a basis both for assessing the existing structure and for generating ideas for change. The role of the McKinsey consultants was to provide perspective, to challenge the ideas of the Shell team, to introduce the experiences of other large multinationals (ABB for instance), to provide the backup research needed to refine and test out ideas and concepts, and to organize the program of work and consultation.

By October 1994, the group had prepared a diagnosis of the existing Shell structure together with a suite of options for reorganization. During October and November, a series of workshops was conducted, mainly in London, to explore in greater detail the specific dimensions of change and to clarify and evaluate the available options. Each workshop team provided input on a specific area of change. The results of this exercise were written up towards the end of November, and a report was submitted to the CMD. It identified the areas for change and the options.

During December 1994, the team spent two "away days" with the CMD to identify the objects of change and how the different options related to these. The result was a blueprint which the team wrote up mid-December. After six or seven drafts, the report was approved by the CMD during the weekend of Christmas. At the beginning of January, the report was circulated to the chief executives of the main opcos and the coordinators within the service companies with a request for reactions by the end of January. In the meantime, Chairman Herkstroter gave a speech, directed to all company employees, to prepare them for change, but without any specifics as to the organizational initiatives that were likely to occur.

The driving force behind the redesign was the desire to have a simpler structure with clearer reporting relationships, thereby allowing the corporate center to exert more effective influence and control over the operating companies. A simpler structure would help eliminate some of the cost and inertia of the head office bureaucracies that had built up around Shell's elaborate committee system. There was also a need to improve coordination between the operating companies. This coordination, it was felt, should be based upon the business sectors rather than geographical regions. Globalization of the world economy and the breakdown of vertical integration within the oil majors had meant that most of the majors had reorganized around worldwide business divisions. As was noted above, most of the majors formed upstream, downstream, and chemicals divisions with worldwide responsibility. For Shell, achieving integration between the different businesses within a country or within a region was less important than achieving integration within a business across different countries and regions. For example, in exploration and production, critical issues related to the development and application of new technologies and sharing of best practices. In downstream, the critical issues related to the rationalization of capacity, the pursuit of operational efficiency, and the promotion of the Shell brand.

By the end of January, a broad endorsement had been received. In February a two-day meeting was held with the same group of Shell's 50 senior managers that had initiated the whole process some ten months earlier. The result was a high level of support and surprisingly little dissent. The final approval came from the two parent company Boards. On March 29, 1995, Cor Herkstroter, Chairman of the Committee of Managing Directors, gave a speech to Shell employees worldwide outlining the principal aspects of a radical reorganization of the Group, which were to be implemented at the beginning of 1996.

In the meantime, two totally unexpected events only increased the internal momentum for change. While Shell faulted itself on its ability to produce a return on capital to meet the levels of its most efficient competitors, in managing health, safety, and the environment and in responding to the broader expectations of society, it considered itself the leader of the pack. Then came the Brent Spar incident. A carefully evaluated plan to dispose of a giant North Sea oil platform in the depths of the Atlantic produced outcry from environmental groups, including Greenpeace. Consumer boycotts of Shell products resulted in massive sales losses, especially in Germany. Within a few months, Shell was forced into an embarrassing reversal of its decision.

A few months later the Nigerian military regime executed Ken Saro-Wiwa, a prominent Nigerian author who had protested Shell's poor environmental record in his country. Again, Shell was found to be flat-footed and inept at managing its public relations over the incident. The handling of the Brent Spar and Nigerian incidents convinced many that Shell's top management was both unresponsive and out of touch. "We had to take a good look at ourselves and say, 'Have we got it right?'" said Mark Moody-Stuart, then a Managing Director. "Previously if you went to your golf club or

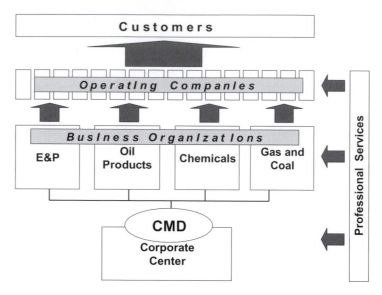

Figure 7.3 Shell's management structure, 1996

church and said, 'I work for Shell,' you'd get a warm glow. In some parts of the world that changed a bit."[7]

■ THE NEW SHELL STRUCTURE ■

The central feature of the reorganization plan of 1995 was the dismantling of the three-way matrix through which the operating companies had been coordinated since the 1960s. In its place, four business organizations were created to achieve closer integration within each business sector across all countries. It was intended that the new structure would allow more effective planning and control within each of the businesses, remove much of the top-heavy bureaucracy that had imposed a costly burden on the Group, and eliminate the power of the regional fiefdoms. The new structure would strengthen the executive authority of the Committee of Managing Directors by providing a clearer line of command to the business organizations and subsequently to the operating companies, and by splitting central staff functions into a Corporate Center and a Professional Services Organization. The former would support the executive role of the CMD; the latter would produce professional services to companies within the Group. Figure 7.3 shows the new structure.

At the same time, the underlying principles of Shell's organizational structure were reaffirmed:

- The decentralized structure based on the autonomy of the Shell operating companies vis-à-vis the Group was to be maintained.

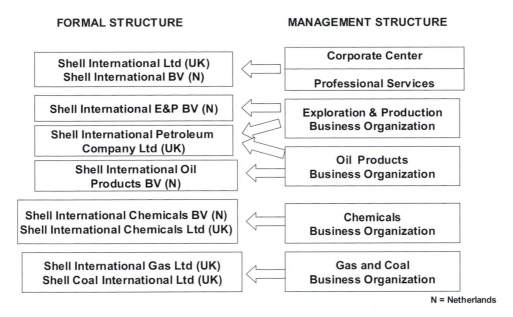

Figure 7.4 The service companies in 1996: links between the formal structure and the management structure

- The new structure continued the distinction between *governance* and *executive responsibility* which was described above. Thus, the formal structure of parent companies, holding companies, operating companies, and service companies was continued without significant changes. The Boards of these companies discharged the governance functions of the Group, including exercise of shareholder rights, the fulfillment of the legal obligations of the companies, and the appointment and supervision of the managers who fulfill executive responsibilities. It was the management structure where the major changes occurred, especially within the service companies.

The Formal Structure

As noted, the formal corporate structure shown in figure 7.1 was little changed. The principal changes in the formal structure were changes involving the identities and roles of the service companies to create a closer alignment with the new management structure. Thus, the new Corporate Center and Professional Services Organization were housed within Shell International Ltd (in London) and Shell International B.V. (in The Hague). Other service companies housed the new Business Organizations. Figure 7.4 shows the relationship between the new management structure and Shell's formal legal structure.

The Management Structure

The new organizational structure can be described in terms of the four new organizational elements – the Business Organizations, the Corporate Center, Professional Services, and the Operating Units – together with the two organizational units that continued from the previous structure, the operating companies and the Committee of Managing Directors.

THE BUSINESS ORGANIZATIONS

The central features of the new organization structure were the new Business Organizations. The CMD was supported by four Business Organizations: E&P ("upstream"), oil products ("downstream"), chemicals, and gas and coal. The Business Organizations were headed by Business Committees made up of a number of Business Directors appointed by the CMD. These Business Directors included:

- Business Directors with responsibility for particular business segments. For example, among the members of the E&P Business Committee in 1998 were J. Colligan, Regional E&P Business Director for Asia-Pacific and South America, H. Roels, Regional E&P Business Director for Middle East and Africa, and R. Sprague, Regional E&P Business Director for Europe.
- Certain of the operating companies were so important that their Chief Executives were also Business Directors. For example, in 1998, the E&P Business Committee included A. Parsley, Managing Director of Shell E&P International Venture B.V., while the Oil Products Business Committee included M. Warwick, President of Shell International Trading and Shipping Co. Ltd, and P. Turberville, President of Shell Europe Oil Products B.V.
- A Business Director for Research and Technical Services.
- A Business Director for Strategy and Business Services.

The Business Committees were accountable to CMD for:

- the strategy of their business area;
- endorsing the capital expenditure and financial plans of the operating companies and business segments within their business area;
- appraising operating company and business segment performance; and
- the availability of technical, functional, and business services to the operating companies within their business sector.

Chairing each of the Business Committees was a member of the CMD. Thus, in early 1998, E&P reported to Managing Director P. B. Watts, Oil Products to Managing Director S. L. Miller, Chemicals to Vice Chairman M. Moody-Stuart, and Gas and Coal to Managing Director M. van den Bergh.

THE CORPORATE CENTER

This supported the CMD in its role in:

- setting the direction and strategy of the Group;
- growing and shaping the Group's portfolio of investments and resources;
- enhancing the performance of Group assets;
- acting as custodian of the Group's reputation, policies, and processes; and
- providing internal and external communication.

Apart from supporting the work of the CMD, the Corporate Center assisted the parent companies and the Group holding companies in managing their financial, tax, and corporate affairs. The Corporate Center represented the other two dimensions of Shell's former matrix organization. For example, the Director for Planning, Environment and External Affairs chaired the meetings of Shell's Technology Council and Health, Safety and Environment Council. Also, the Corporate Advice Director undertook ad hoc country reviews.

The Corporate Center comprised six directorates:

- Planning, Environment and External Affairs
- Corporate Advice (supporting each of the Managing Directors in their regional roles as well as responsibility for IT, security, contracting and procurement)
- Group Treasurer
- Group Controller
- Human Resources
- Legal

In addition to these directorates, the Corporate Center also included the Head of Group Taxation, the Chief Information Officer, the Head of Intellectual Property, the Head of Contracting and Procurement, the Head of Group Security, the Head of Learning, and the Secretary to the CMD.

PROFESSIONAL SERVICES

These new units provided functional support for the operating companies and service companies within the Group. They offered their services on an arm's-length basis and competed with external service providers for the business of the operating companies. They were also able to provide services to third-party customers outside the Group. The services provided included:

- Finance (e.g., treasury services, accounting, tax advice)
- HR (e.g., recruitment, training)
- Legal

- Intellectual property (intellectual property protection, licensing)
- Contracting and procurement
- Group Security (security advice)
- Shell Aircraft Ltd (corporate jets)
- Office services (e.g., accommodation, personnel services)
- Health (medical services, environmental and occupational health advice)

Each Professional Services unit was headed by the relevant director from the Corporate Center. For example, HR was headed by the HR Director; legal and intellectual property services were headed by the Legal Director.

THE OPERATING COMPANIES

In the new organizational structure, the operating companies retained their role as the primary business entities within Shell. Each operating company was managed by a Board of Directors and a Chief Executive. The Chief Executive of an operating company was responsible to his/her Board and to his/her Business Director for the effective management of the operating company. The Chief Executive's responsibilities included the following:

- setting the company's strategic aims against the backdrop of any guidelines established by the Business Committee;
- providing leadership to put the strategic aims into effect and instill an entrepreneurial company culture;
- setting internal financial and operating targets and overseeing their achievement;
- supervising the management of the business and setting priorities;
- effective reporting on the company's activities and results to the Group.[8]

OPERATING UNITS

The superimposition of the Business Organizations on top of the operating companies created a problem for Shell because the operating companies were defined by country rather than by business sector and included activities which crossed business sectors. Hence, to achieve alignment between the new Business Organizations and the operational activities of the Group, Operating Units were created:

> In the context of the Group organizational structure, Operating Unit refers to the activities in one of the Group Businesses which are operated as a single economic entity. An Operating Unit can coincide with an Operating Company, be a part of an Operating Company or straddle part or all of several Operating Companies.[9]

Thus, where an operating company was in one business only, the operating company was the relevant Operating Unit. However, multi-business operating companies, such as Shell UK and Shell Australia, which included upstream, downstream, chemical, and gas businesses, were divided into separate Operating Units in order to align operating activities with the new Business Organizations. Each of these Operating Units was headed by a manager with executive responsibilities who reported to the relevant Business Director. Where several Operating Units operated in a country under different Chief Executives, the Managing Director with responsibilities for that particular region appointed one of them as a "country chairman" to fulfill country-level responsibilities (with regard to matters of taxation, conformity with national legislation, national government relations, and the like).

In addition, some Operating Units spanned several operating countries. In order to achieve more effective integration across countries and to save on administrative and operating costs, the trend was to form Operating Units which combined businesses in several countries. Thus, in Europe there was a desire to run chemicals and oil products as single business entities.

Changing Culture and Behavior

Changes to the formal organizational structure were only one dimension of the organizational changes of this period. If Shell was to improve its operational and financial performance and improve its responsiveness to the multitude of external forces that impacted its many businesses, then change needed to go beyond formal structures. The criticisms leveled at Shell for being bureaucratic, inward looking, slow, and unresponsive were not about organizational structure, they were about behavior and attitudes. In any organizational change, a new structure may provide the right context, but ultimately it is the effects on individual and group behavior that are critical.

During 1996 and 1997, the Shell management development function moved into a higher gear. Organizational development and change consultants included Noel Tichy from Michigan Business School, Larry Selden from Columbia, McKinsey & Company, Boston Consulting Group, and Coopers & Lybrand. These were in addition to Shell's internal change management team, known as LEAP (Leadership and Performance Operations). The result was a substantial increase in Shell's management development and organizational development activities. *Fortune* magazine reported:

> This army has been putting Shell managers through a slew of workshops. In early February, teams from the gasoline retailing business in Thailand, China, Scandinavia and France spent six hours in a bitter Dutch downpour building rope bridges, dragging one another through spider webs of rope, and helping one another climb over 20-foot walls.
>
> The Shell managers especially liked Larry Selden. He teaches people to track their time and figure out whether what they're doing contributes directly to growth of both returns and gross margins. Selden calls this "dot movement," a phrase he has trademarked and which means moving the dot on a graph of growth and returns to the north-east. "The model is very powerful," says Luc Minguet, Shell's retail manager in France. "It's the first time I've seen such a link between the conceptual and the practical. And I realized I was using my time very poorly."

In a particularly revealing exercise, the top 100 Shell executives in May took the Myers–Briggs personality test, a widely-used management tool that classifies people according to 16 psychological types. Interestingly, of its top 100 managers, 86% are "thinkers," people who make decisions based on logic and objective analysis. Of the six-man CMD, 60% are on the opposite scale. They are "feelers" who make decisions based on values and subjective evaluation. No wonder all those "thinkers" had such a hard time understanding the emotion behind Nigeria and Brent Spar. And no wonder the CMD gets frustrated with the inability of the lower ranks to grasp the need for change.[10]

■ FURTHER DEVELOPMENTS, 1996–9 ■

Cost Cutting and Restructuring

The most evident short-tem impact of the reorganization was a substantial reduction in Service Company staffs. Towards the end of 1995, Shell began shrinking its head offices in London and The Hague in anticipation of the introduction of the new organizational structure at the beginning of 1996. During 1996, the downsizing of central services and administrative functions within the Service Companies accelerated. During 1996, one of the two towers at the London Shell Centre was sold and was converted into residential apartments.

The quest for cost reductions did not stop at the Service Companies but extended to the operating companies as well. Between 1995 and 1997, unit costs were reduced by 17 percent in real terms, and between 1994 and 1997, savings in procurement costs amounted to $600 million each year. A priority for the Group was rationalization of capacity and reductions in operating costs in its downstream business. To facilitate this, Shell embarked upon three major joint ventures:

- the amalgamation of Shell Oil's downstream assets in the western US with those of Texaco;
- the amalgamation of Shell's European downstream businesses with those of Texaco; and
- the merging of Shell's Australian downstream business with that of Mobil.

Restructuring in Shell's other businesses included a swap of oil and gas properties with Occidental and the creation of a single global chemicals business. The chemicals business demonstrated clearly the benefits of global integration. In addition to cost savings of around 7 percent each year, investment decisions became better coordinated. "The Center's full control over chemicals, for instance, led Shell to put a new polymer plant closer to customers in Geismar, Louisiana, instead of near the existing plant in Britain. Two years ago that plant automatically would have been added to the UK fiefdom."[11]

Further Organizational Changes under Moody-Stuart

In June 1998, Mark Moody-Stuart succeeded Cor Herkstroter as Chairman of the CMD against a background of declining oil and gas prices and weakening margins in refining and chemicals. With Shell's operating profit and ROCE falling well below the projections for 1998, it was clear that further organizational change and cost reduction would be essential. In September he announced a series of restructuring measures aimed at reducing Shell's cost base while reaffirming Shell's commitment to the target of 15 percent ROACE (return on average capital employed) by 2001. Refinery cutbacks included the closure of Shellhaven refinery and partial closure of Berre refinery in France. The national head offices in the UK, Netherlands, Germany, and France would be closed.[12]

A key element of the organizational changes pushed by Moody-Stuart was the desire to replace Shell's traditional consensus-based decision making with greater individual leadership and individual accountability. To this end, the Business Committees that had been set up to manage the new business sectors were replaced by Chief Executives:

> From today we have CEO's and executive committees running each of our businesses. We have entered a new period where executive decisions have to be made rapidly and business accountability must be absolutely clear. So we have changed our structures.
>
> The major change we announced is establishing executive structures, with CEO's, in Oil Products and Exploration and Production. CEO's already run our other businesses: Gas and Coal, Chemicals and Renewables, as well as Shell Services International. Now we are structured to make rapid progress to our objective in each of our businesses.
>
> Business Committees served us in good stead in a period of transition but as from today they are a thing of the past. We will still have discussion, but we will make business decisions rapidly.[13]

The trend towards executive power and personal accountability was also apparent in the Committee of Managing Directors. In place of the traditional "committee of equals," Moody-Stuart recast the CMD more as an executive group where individual members had clearly defined executive responsibilities.

Moody-Stuart also accelerated the integration of Shell's US subsidiary, Shell Oil Inc., into its global structure. By the end of 1998, the chemicals sector was a truly global division and by early 1999 upstream operations in the US had been integrated into the global exploration and production sector. During 1999, the historically separate Shell Oil corporate office in Houston became integrated within Shell's Corporate Center and Professional Services organization. Thus, Shell Oil's Human Resource function staff became part of a new global Shell People Services organization, while Finance, Tax, Legal, and Corporate Affairs also integrated with their counterparts in London. The President and CEO of Shell Oil, Inc. became a de facto member of the CMD.

Figure 7.5 shows Shell's management structure under Mark Moody-Stuart's leadership.

■ TOWARDS A SECOND CENTURY ■

As Royal Dutch/Shell approached the second century of its corporate life, there was a clear consensus within the company that the organizational changes made during 1995–9 had created a structure that was much better able to respond to the uncertainties and discontinuous changes that affected the oil industry. Outside the company,

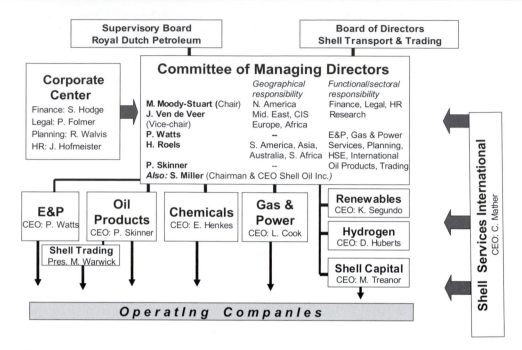

Figure 7.5 Shell's management structure, 2000

Shell-watchers both in the investment community and in other oil companies had little doubt that the 1996 reorganization had contributed substantially to the efficient and effective management of the Group. The stripping away of much of the administrative structure in the Group head offices in London and The Hague, the elimination of the regional coordinating staffs, and the closure of some of Shell's biggest national head-quarters not only reduced cost, but seemed to be moving Shell towards a swifter, more direct style of management. The restructuring of chemicals and downstream busi-nesses revealed both a tough-mindedness and a decisiveness that few had associated with the Shell of old.

The former Vice-Chairman of the CMD outlined the way in which the changes in organization had impacted Shell's business portfolio and its strategic management:

> We used to have a complex regional matrix system – with multiple reporting lines. In com-pensation relatively modest annual raises were awarded – and more often than not expected – without being strictly tied to performance. Our businesses were tightly linked to national markets and then to regions. Accountability was, through the matrix system, diffuse. It wasn't a bad system. When it was launched – in 1958 – it was an excellent system. But, by the early 90s, it had definitely reached its 'use by' date. Hurdle rates were used – good guides – but they allowed unbridled investment growth, which tended to ex-acerbate portfolio weaknesses. Jobs were for life in the old Shell and virtually all recruit-ment was internal.

By the early 90s we had a problem. There was no crisis – which in some ways was part of the problem. But ROACE was not good enough and it was obvious that something needed to be done. In the middle of the 90s we instituted something we called "transformation". As you can see here there were results, things were improving, but not really as quickly as they should have been. Then, in 1999 we had a particularly difficult environment, which galvanized us to rapidly complete the transformation process. Tough decisions were made, write-downs taken and the whole process accelerated.

As a consequence, today we have global businesses, headed by personally accountable CEOs. Reporting lines are direct, uncomplicated. Incentive pay and stock options are the norm. Every project has to compete globally for capital. Everyone in the organization can compete for any job – and we also actively hire from outside.

This has resulted in a significantly improved profile. Earnings are up on basically stable net revenues. Oil production is up, as are gas, chemical and oil product sales. The number of employees required has declined.

Capital has moved away from the poor performers and declining areas to new opportunities.[14]

The new organization had permitted far-reaching restructuring of Shell's downstream and chemicals businesses:

In the early 1990s we operated refineries in all parts of the world and our refining cover was over 80%. We have been closing or selling refineries . . . Our goal in this effort is twofold – one is to reduce our refinery cover to a range of 65%–70% by 2001. The other is to achieve a return on average capital employed of 15% by 2001 . . .

At the beginning of the nineties we had [chemical] plants scattered across the globe with 30 plants in Europe, 7 in Asia Pacific, and 17 in America. The plants produced products that were sold through some 22 different product groups, each having profit and loss responsibility. Today we are concentrating on a few, world-scale plants and a much more limited product line. We will have 7 plants in Europe, 6 in Asia Pacific and 4 in America and products will be sold through 12 product groups.[15]

The question in most people's minds was whether Shell was moving ahead of the pack or playing catch up. For all Shell's pride in being a pioneer of modern management ideas – from scenario analysis to organization learning – Shell had created by year 2000 a business-sector-based organization of a kind that most other diversified multinationals had created decades before. Moreover, some of Shell's leading competitors were moving away from such structures. BP – hailed by many to be the most dynamic and responsive of any of the petroleum majors – had abandoned its traditional divisional structure in favor of a flatter structure in which individual business units reported directly to the corporate center.

In addition, Shell still retained some relics of the old structure that could compromise the new philosophy of responsiveness and single-point accountability. For example, Shell was still a joint venture rather than a single corporation. Its Committee of Managing Directors was still composed of board members from its dual parent companies. The principle of rotating leadership between the two parents with fixed single terms of office for the CMD Chairman was still intact. While Shell had been consumed with its internal restructuring, other companies had been transforming themselves through mergers and acquisitions. Had Shell missed out on the Great Oil Patch M&A

Boom? Probably, but if Royal Dutch/Shell was to get serious about mergers, its first priority should be to merge with itself, noted the *Financial Times'* Lex column.

APPENDIX
The Organizational Structures of Other Oil Majors

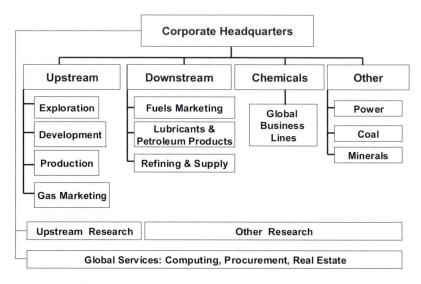

Figure 7.A1   Exxon Mobil

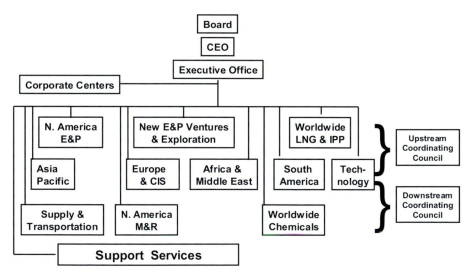

Figure 7.A2   Mobil (prior to merger with Exxon)

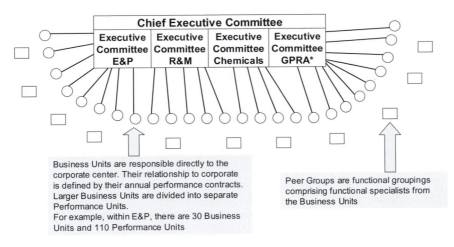

Business Units are responsible directly to the corporate center. Their relationship to corporate is defined by their annual performance contracts. Larger Business Units are divided into separate Performance Units.
For example, within E&P, there are 30 Business Units and 110 Performance Units

Peer Groups are functional groupings comprising functional specialists from the Business Units

Figure 7.A3 BP

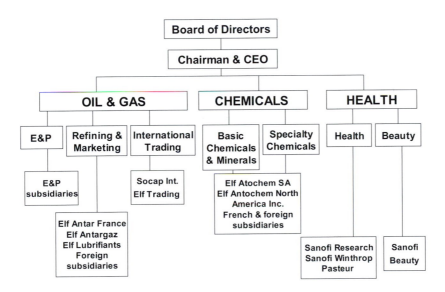

Figure 7.A4 Elf Aquitaine (prior to merger with Total-Fina)

NOTES

1. This section draws from R. Cibin and R. M. Grant, "Restructuring among the world's largest oil majors," *British Journal of Management*, December 1996.
2. The "Seven Sisters" were the original international oil majors: Shell, Exxon, Mobil, BP, Chevron, Texaco, and Gulf. (Gulf was acquired by Chevron in 1984.)

3. C. A. J. Herkstroter, "Right for the times and right for Shell," Speech delivered in London, March 29, 1995.
4. Ibid.
5. "Why is the world's most profitable company turning itself inside out?" *Fortune*, August 4, 1997, pp. 121–5.
6. Ibid.
7. Ibid.
8. *Reference Guide to Group Organizational Structure*, Shell International Ltd, August 1996.
9. Ibid., p. 17.
10. "Why is the world's most profitable company turning itself inside out?" *Fortune*, August 4, 1997, pp. 121–5.
11. Ibid.
12. "Shell shapes up for future," Speech by M. Moody-Stuart, San Francisco, September 18, 1998 (www.shell.com).
13. M. Moody-Stuart, Changes in Shell's organization: comments to the Shell Global Leadership Conference, London December 10, 1998.
14. Marten van den Bergh; "Strengthening the Portfolio," Shell Press Release, April 3, 2000.
15. Ibid.

case eight

Harley-Davidson, Inc., February 2004

Robert M. Grant

You've shown us how to be the best. You've been leaders in new technology. You've stuck by the basic American values of hard work and fair play . . . Most of all, you've worked smarter, you've worked better, and you've worked together . . . as you've shown again, America is someplace special. We're on the road to unprecedented prosperity . . . and we'll get there on a Harley.

President Ronald Reagan, speech at Harley-Davidson plant, York, PA, May 6, 1987

The recovery of this company since the 1980s has been truly remarkable. When you were down in the dumps, people were saying American industry was finished, that we couldn't compete in the global economy, that the next century would belong to other countries and other places. Today, you're not just surviving – you're flourishing, with record sales and earnings; and one of the best-managed companies in America. . . . one of the reasons you're the best-managed company in America is that you have a genuine partnership between labor and management, where all employees are valuable and expected to make good decisions on their own for the benefit of the common enterprise. And I thank you for setting that example. I wish every manufacturer in America would model it.

President Bill Clinton, speech at Harley-Davidson plant, York, PA, November 10, 1999

It's one thing to have people buy your products. It's another for them to tattoo your name on their bodies.

www.harley-davidson.com

As Harley-Davidson's chairman and CEO, Jeff Bleustein, reviewed the company's full year financial results for 2003, he realized that the past financial year would be a difficult act to follow. The 100th anniversary of Harley-Davidson's in August 2003 set the stage for a year-long program of festivities that would attract over a million participants – most of them Harley owners. Harley shipped 291,147 motor-cycles – a 10.4 percent increase over the previous year – and sales and profits broke previous records for the eighteenth consecutive year. It was a far cry from the early 1980s, when Bleustein was head of engineering and Harley was producing less than 40,000 bikes a year and struggling to remain solvent under a mountain of debt.

During the early months of 2004, Bleustein had little opportunity to remi-nisce about the joys of Harley's centennial celebrations. His thoughts were fixed firmly on the future. Wall Street's expectations of Harley-Davidson's profit per-formance had been fueled not only by the company's remarkable 18-year record-breaking run, but also by the strategic goals set by the company. On the basis of annual unit sales growth of 7 percent to 9 percent, Bleustein set a target of 400,000 motorcycles to be sold in 2007. Profit targets were even more ambitious – with continuing productivity gains and increased sales of parts, accessories, general merchandise and financial services, Bleustein set the goal of annual earning growth "in the mid-teens."

As Bleustein prepared for a strategy review with his top management team, he pondered the different forces that might throw Harley-Davidson off course. Bleustein's greatest concerns related to the world economy. Despite reviving economic prospects in both the US and Japan, combined federal and trade deficits together with record levels of consumer debt represented a continuing threat to the stability of the US economy. For any company selling leisure products priced between $6,500 and $22,000, any slowdown in US consumer spending represented a significant predica-ment. Competition was not a primary concern. Harley had demonstrated its ability to hold its own against similarly styled V-twins produced by rivals (including the big Japanese producers: Honda, Yamaha, Kawasaki, and Suzuki). They might be able to replicate the look of the Harley Hog, but none could replicate the "Harley Experience." But what if motorcycle riders began to look for a different type of experience? Harley's share of the US heavyweight market had held constant at just under 50 percent for the past seven years. What if the appeal of the heavyweight cruiser waned and buyers became attracted to the European-styled sports models pro-duced by Ducati, Aprilia, Triumph, and BMW, or the high-performance Japanese machines? The disappointing sales of Harley's Buell range of sports motorcycles sug-gested that Harley's potential to compete in other segments of the motorcycle industry was limited. Longer term, Bleustein was concerned over the demographic trends. Harley's popularity was closely associated with the baby-boom generation. As this gen-eration aged, so did Harley's customers. How would Harley appeal to younger genera-tions? Other threats were internal. Harley's success had been built upon a drive for success and a collaborative work culture that had been forged during the difficult cir-cumstances of the 1980s, but, as Harley went from strength to strength and expanded its employee base, would complacency set in?

Table 8.1 Annual production of motorcycles by Harley-Davidson

Year	Production	Year	Production
1901	3	1990	62,500
1903	150	1992	76,500
1913	12,904	1994	95,811
1920	28,189	1995	105,104
1933	3,700	1996	118,771
1936	9,812	1997	132,285
1948	31,163	1998	150,818
1953	14,050	1999	177,187
1966	36,310	2000	204,592
1975	75,403	2001	234,500
1981	41,586	2002	263,700
1986	36,700	2003	291,147

Source: www.harley-davidson.com.

■ THE HISTORY OF HARLEY-DAVIDSON ■

1903–1981: From Birth to Maturity

Harley-Davidson, Inc. was founded in 1903 by William Harley and brothers William Davidson, Arthur Davidson, and Walter Davidson. Harley's 1903 model was made in the Davidson family shed and had a three-horsepower engine. In 1909 Harley introduced its first two-cylinder, V-twin engine, featuring the deep, rumbling sound for which Harley motorcycles are renowned. During the 1920s the US motorcycle industry consolidated. In 1910 there were some 150 US motorcycle producers; by 1929, Indian, Excelsior, and Harley accounted for the majority of US motorcycle sales. The Great Depression killed Excelsior, and Indian closed in 1953, leaving Harley the sole American manufacturer of motorcycles. Table 8.1 shows Harley's production over the century.

The post-war era was one of opportunity lost for Harley-Davidson. Growing affluence and the rise of youth culture created a growing demand for motorcycles. However, this was satisfied primarily by imports. By 1959, Harley was still market leader, but British imports amounted to about 30,000 bikes a year, with BSA, Triumph, and Norton taking 49 percent of the US market.[1] In 1959, Honda entered the US market. The result was the rebirth of motorcycling in the US. Although Harley initially benefited from the rapid expansion of the market, soon Honda and the other Japanese producers moved up-market into the heavyweight sector. In 1969 Honda introduced its four-cylinder CB750, a huge technical advance on anything produced by Harley or the British. In the same year, Harley-Davidson was acquired by AMF, which proceeded to expand production capacity with the building of the York, Pennsylvania assembly plant. Boosting capacity to 75,000 units annually had disastrous consequences for product quality. A company audit in the mid-1970s revealed that more than half the cycles coming off the line were missing parts.[2] By the end of the 1970s, Honda had replaced Harley as market leader in heavyweight motorcycles in the US.

1981–2003: Rebirth

In 1981 Harley-Davidson's senior managers, led by Vaughn Beals, organized a leveraged buyout. Harley emerged as an independent, privately owned company, but heavily laden with debt. The buyout coincided with a severe recession and soaring interest rates – especially troublesome for a highly leveraged business. Registrations of heavyweight motorcycles fell during 1981 and 1982 while Harley's own sales plummeted. By 1982 its sales of bikes were down by more than a third from 1979. During 1981 and 1982, Harley-Davidson lost a total of $60 million. Redundancies came thick and fast: 30 percent of office staff was dismissed with similar cutbacks among hourly workers.

While battling to stay solvent, the new management team also devoted themselves to rebuilding production methods and working practices in order to cut costs and improve quality. Managers visited several Japanese automobile plants and carefully studied Toyota's just-in-time (JIT) system. Less than four months after the buyout, Harley management began a pilot JIT inventory and production-scheduling program called "MAN" (Materials As Needed) in its Milwaukee engine plant. The objective was to reduce inventories and costs and improve quality control. Within a year, all Harley's manufacturing operations were being converted to JIT: components and sub-assemblies were "pulled" through the production system in response to final demand.

The revolution in production methods and new spirit of cooperation between workers and management – plus help from the US government in the form of a temporary 49 percent tariff on imports of Japanese heavyweight motorcycles – soon fed through into both the top line and bottom line of Harley's income statement. To fuel the continuing development of the company, Harley-Davidson went public in 1986. Between 1986 and 1990, Harley's share of the heavyweight market expanded steadily from about 30 percent to over 60 percent, with demand outstripping production. During this time, management improved the quality and reliability of its product, and began to explore growth opportunities in retail clothing and international sales.

The 1990s saw year-on-year uninterrupted growth in the heavyweight motorcycle market and a continued increase in Harley's market share. The company's biggest challenge continued to be balancing production capacity with surging demand for its products. In order to overcome this constraint, in 1996, the company announced the ambitious Plan 2003. Plan 2003 was a vision to dramatically increase production capacity over the eight years preceding the company's 100th anniversary. New production plants in Kansas City and York, Pennsylvania, the launching of several new models, and international expansion resulted in sales approaching 300,000 in 2003 – an eightfold increase on 1983.

Table 8.2 Harley-Davidson's motorcycle registrations (1995–2003)*

	1995	1996	1997	1998	1999	2000	2002	2003
United States (total)	163,100	178,500	205,400	246,200	297,800	363,400	442,300	461,200
Harley-Davidson	77,800	86,800	101,200	119,400	146,000	168,300	209,900	228,400
Market share (651+cc)	47.7%	48.6%	49.3%	48.5%	49.0%	46.3%	47.5%	49.5%
Europe (total)	207,200	224,700	250,300	270,200	306,700	293,400	331,800	323,100
Harley-Davidson	15,400	15,300	16,100	17,300	19,900	21,800	23,500	26,300
Market share (651+cc)	7.4%	6.8%	6.4%	6.4%	6.5%	7.4%	7.1%	8.1%
Japan/Australia (total)	39,400	37,417	58,880	69,200	63,100	62,700	63,900	58,900
Harley-Davidson	7,900	8,400	10,100	10,800	12,300	12,900	13,600	15,200
Market share (651+cc)	20.1%	22.4%	17.2%	15.6%	19.6%	20.5%	21.2%	25.8%

* Includes Buell.

Source: www.harley-davidson.com.

■ THE HEAVYWEIGHT MOTORCYCLE MARKET ■

The heavyweight segment (over 650 cc) was the most rapidly growing part of the world motorcycle market between 1990 and 2003, with the US accounting for a major part of this growth. Sales of heavyweight motorcycles in the major markets of the world increased from 322,400 units in 1991 to 877,400 in 2003. North America was the largest market for big bikes, representing 56 percent of the sales in the major world markets. Between 1999 and 2003, sales of heavyweight motorcycles increased by 14 percent annually in North America, compared with about 2 percent growth in Europe and Asia.

In North America, Harley increased its market share rapidly during the 1980s. Between 1993 and 2003, its market share was relatively stable, varying between 46.2 percent and 48.2 percent. Elsewhere, Harley was unable to replicate the market dominance it achieved within its home market. However, during 2000–03, Harley achieved the remarkable feat of becoming heavyweight market leader in Japan, pushing Honda into second place. In Europe, on the other hand, Harley lagged behind its Japanese competitors and BMW (see tables 8.2 and 8.3).

The heavyweight motorcycle market comprised three segments:

- *Cruiser motorcycles:* These were "big, noisy, low riding, unapologetically macho cycles,"[3] typically with V-twin engines and an upright riding position. Their design reflected the dominance of styling over either comfort or speed. For the urban males (and some females) in Los Angeles, New York, Paris, and Tokyo, the cruiser motorcycle was practical transportation in congested metropolises, but was primarily a statement of style. The cruiser segment was practically created by Harley and was preeminent in the US, representing over half of the heavyweight market. Most of Harley's competitors in this segment had imitated the main features of traditional Harley design: V-twin engines (many

Table 8.3   Market shares in heavyweight motorcycles (651cc+), 2000 and 2003 (%)

	North America		Europe		Japan/Australia	
	2003	2000	2003	2000	2003	2000
Harley-Davidson	48.1	46.3	8.1	7.4	25.8	20.5
Honda	18.6	19.1	16.7	21.8	17.8	21.8
Kawasaki	7.1	9.1	10.0	9.4	13.8	18.9
Suzuki	10.3	9.5	15.5	14.3	10.7	10.4
Yamaha	9.1	9.0	16.0	17.3	11.4	17.0
BMW	2.8	3.2	15.3	13.0	6.2	4.0
Ducati	–	1.9	6.0	6.3	6.6	4.6
Triumph	–	–	3.7	4.2	–	–
Other	4.0	1.9	8.7	6.3	7.7	4.2

Source: Harley-Davidson *Annual Report*, 2000, 2003.

with engine displacements that exceeded those of small family cars), low-torque power, an upright riding position, and a low center of gravity.

- *Touring bikes:* These included cruisers especially equipped for longer-distance riding and bikes specially designed for comfort over long distance (including the Honda Goldwing and the bigger BMWs). These tourers featured luxuries such as audio systems, two-way intercoms, and heaters. While Harley led this segment on the basis of style and image, Honda and BMW had engineered their motorcycles for greater smoothness and comfort over long distances through the use of multi-cylinder, shaft-drive engines, and advanced suspension systems.
- *Performance models:* These were based upon racing bikes, with high-technology, high-revving engines, an emphasis on speed, acceleration, and race-track styling; minimal concessions were provided for rider comfort. The segment was the most important in the European and the Asian/Pacific markets, representing 62 percent and 66 percent of total heavyweight bike sales respectively. The segment was dominated by Japanese motorcycle companies, with a significant representation of European specialists such as Ducati and Triumph. Harley entered the performance segment in 1993 through its involvement in Buell Motorcycles, which it fully acquired in 1998.

It is worth noting that the conventional segmentation into lightweight, middleweight, and heavyweight did not clearly define Harley-Davidson's market. Harley's strength lay in just one part of the heavyweight market: the *super-heavyweight* segment, comprising bikes with cylinder displacement of more than 850cc. The only motorcycle that Harley-Davidson produced with an engine size of less than 850cc was the Buell Blast.

■ HARLEY-DAVIDSON IN 2004 ■

The Brand

The Harley-Davidson image and the loyalty it engendered among its customers were its greatest assets. Harley-Davidson was one of the archetypes of American style. The famed spread eagle signified not just the brand of one of the world's oldest motorcycle companies, but an entire lifestyle with which it was associated. Harley has been described as "the ultimate biker status symbol . . . a quasi religion, an institution, a way of life."[4] Together with a few other companies – Walt Disney and Levi Strauss – Harley had a unique relationship with American culture. The values that Harley represented – individuality, freedom, and adventure – could be traced back to the cowboy and frontiersman of yesteryear, and before that to the motives that brought people to America in the first place. As the sole surviving American motorcycle company from the pioneering days of the industry, Harley-Davidson represented a tradition of US engineering and manufacturing.

This appeal of the Harley brand was central, not just to the company's marketing, but to its strategy as a whole. The central thrust of the strategy was reinforcing and extending the relationship between the company and its consumers. Harley-Davidson had long recognized that it was not selling motorcycles, it was selling the Harley experience. Prominent in annual reports of recent years were pictures and prose depicting the Harley Experience:

> A chill sweeps though your body, created by a spontaneous outburst of pure, unadulterated joy. You are surrounded by people from all walks of life and every corner of the globe. They are complete strangers, but you know them like your own family. They were drawn to this place by the same passion – the same dream. And they came here on the same machine. This is one place you can truly be yourself. Because you don't just fit in. You belong.[5]

If the appeal of the Harley motorcycle was the image it conveyed and the lifestyle it represented, then the company had to ensure that the experience matched the image. To increase Harley's involvement in its consumers' riding experience it formed the Harley Owners' Group in 1983. Through HOG, the company became involved in organizing social and charity events. Employees, from the CEO down, were encouraged to take an active role in HOG activities. HOG's website described the kind of emotion and atmosphere that the company was trying to deliver to customers through its HOG organization: "the feeling of being out there on a Harley-Davidson motorcycle links us like no other experience can. It's made HOG like no other organization in the world . . . The atmosphere is more family reunion than organized meeting."[6] The continued growth of the Harley Owners' Group throughout the 1990s was particularly important in encouraging repurchase and upgrading by Harley owners. During 1999–2003, about one half of all sales were to customers who had owned a Harley previously, while about 20 percent were first-time motorcycle buyers.

During the 1980s and 1990s, the demographic and socioeconomic profile of Harley customers shifted substantially. Traditionally, Harley owners were blue-collar men in their 20s and 30s. By 2002, the median income of a Harley owner was $78,600, up from $38,400 in 1987. The average age grew to 45 in 2002, up from 35 in 1987. Also, by 2002, 9 percent of Harley consumers were female, up from 2 percent in 1987. Harley-Davidson's ability to capture the imagination – and spending power – of the baby-boomers was critical to its financial success. As the prices of Harley principal motorcycle models rose towards the $20,000 mark, middle-aged professionals became the most attractive target demographic for the company.

The Products

Broadening Harley's market appeal had major implications for product policy and design. The Harley image was linked closely to its big, throaty, V-twins. Ever since its disastrous foray into small bikes during the AMF years, Harley had recognized that its competitive advantage lay with super-heavyweight bikes. Here it stuck resolutely to the classic styling that had characterized Harleys since its early years. At the heart of the Harley motorcycle was the air-cooled V-twin engine that had been Harley's distinctive feature since 1909. Harley's frames, handlebars, fuel tanks, and seats also reflected traditional designs.

Harley's commitment to traditional design features may be seen as making a virtue out of necessity. Its smaller size and scale compared to its competitors limited its ability to invest in technology and new products. As a result, Harley lagged far behind its competitors in the application of automotive technologies: its motorcycles not only looked old-style, much of the technology was old-style. When Harley introduced its new Twin Cam 88 engine in 1998, *Motorcycle* magazine reported:

> Honda comes out with an average of two new (or reworked) motors every year. The other Japanese manufacturers are good for about one. Count on Ducati and BMW to do something every few years. That leaves only Moto Guzzi and Harley. So it goes to say that when either of these two old farts gets off the pot, they really raise a stink, so to speak.
>
> The Twin Cam 88 is Harley's first new engine since the Evolution Sportster motor of 1986, and their first new Big Twin motor since the original Evolution, released in 1984. Fifteen years between engines is not really that long a span for Harley. The Evo's predecessor, the Shovelhead lasted 19 years (with a revision after five), and the Panhead lasted nearly as long.[7]

Yet, despite the fanfare, Harley's Twin Cam 88 engine was hardly innovative. It was a 1,450 cc traditional V-twin with push rods and was air-cooled, a decade after Japanese manufacturers had introduced multivalve, liquid-cooled, overhead camshaft engines. BMW's R1200C cruiser model (launched in 1997 with a starring role in the James Bond movie *Tomorrow Never Dies*) featured shaft drive, a multivalve, fuel-injected engine, triple-disk, anti-lock brakes, and "road-hugging" cornering from its advanced suspension system. While BMW and the Japanese manufacturers applied the latest automotive technology to their new models, Harley concentrated upon incremental refinements to its engines, frames, and gearboxes aimed at improving power delivery, reliability, increasing braking power, and reducing vibration. This continual upgrading of its technology and its quality was an essential requirement of Harley shifting its customer base from blue-collar enthusiasts to middle-aged professionals who lacked the time, inclination, and expertise to tune and maintain their bikes and needed "luxuries" such as electric starters and vibration control.

Harley used alliances as a means of accessing advanced automotive technologies. In 1997, it established a joint venture with Porsche AG to source and assemble motorcycle components and to access Porsche's expertise in engine emission compliance. For its VF1000 Superbike race team, Harley collaborated with Cosworth Racing, Ford, and Gemini Racing Technologies.

In recent years, Harley-Davidson increased its commitment to innovation and more radical product design. The V-Rod introduced in October 2001 featured innovative styling and an all-new liquid-cooled engine. The Buell range also offered Harley engineers an opportunity to be more technically innovative. The 2002 Buell Firebolt featured a new engine, an all-aluminum frame, and the "naked" styling pioneered by Ducati.

Reconciling product differentiation with scale economies was a continuing challenge for Harley. Personalization is an essential requirement for the Harley owner. Hence, Harley offered a wide model range, and a broad set of options regarding paint, accessories, and trim. At the same time, economies in engineering, manufacturing, and purchasing required standardizing components across the model range. The result was that Harley continually broadened its range of models (its 2004 lineup offered over 30 separate models) and for each model offered a range of options. At the same time, it based this range of product offerings upon three engine types (Evolution XL, Twin Cam 88, and Revolution), four basic frames, four styles of gas tank, and so on.

The Harley product line also covered a wide price range. The Sportster model was positioned as an entry level bike, priced at a mere $6,495, less than one-third of the price of the Ultra Classic Electra Glide with two-tone paint at $20,405 (see table 8.4).

Buell

Harley's involvement in Buell represented an attempt to broaden its customer base and its market appeal – especially overseas. In 1997, Harley set up a working group to explore ways of attracting new, younger motorcycle riders. Market research found that many potential riders were put off by motorcycles being "hard to learn," and big cruisers and touring bikes were viewed as "intimidating" or "something an old guy would ride." Founded by ex-Harley engineer Erik Buell, Buell Motor Company developed bikes that synthesized the comfort and style of a Harley cruiser with the high-performance attributes of a sports bike. Harley acquired complete ownership of Buell in 1998. Buell bikes used Harley engines and other components, but mounted them on a lighter, stiffer frame. The lighter weight and superior handling and acceleration of Buell models were seen as appealing to younger motorcyclists and also to the European market, where customers put greater emphasis on sporty performance and a cheaper price tag. In the

Table 8.4 Heavyweight motorcycles: price comparisons, 2004

Manufacturer and model	Engine	Recommended retail price ($)
Harley-Davidson		
XL 800 Sportster	V-twin, air-cooled, 883cc	6,495
Fat Boy FLSTF	V-twin, air-cooled, 1,540cc	16,245
V Rod VRSCB	V-twin, liquid-cooled, 69 cu. in.	17,295
Heritage Softail Classic	V-twin, air-cooled, 1,450cc	17,580
H-D Ultra Classic Electra Glide	V-twin 1,450cc, injection (2-tone)	20,405
Honda		
Shadow Spirit	V-twin, OHC, 705cc	5,999
VTX1300	V-twin, liquid-cooled, 1300cc	9,199
VTX1800	V-twin, liquid-cooled, 1800cc	12,599
Suzuki		
Marauder 800	V-twin, liquid-cooled, OHC, 805cc	5,999
Intruder 1400	V-twin, air-cooled, 1,462cc	8,399
Marauder 1800	V-twin, liquid-cooled, OHC, 1800cc	10,999
Kawasaki		
Vulcan 800	V-twin, 8-valve, OHC	6,499
Vulcan Classic	V-twin, air-cooled, 1,470cc	8,999
Yamaha		
V Star Classic 1100	V-twin, OHC, 1100cc	8,349
Road Star Warrior	V-twin, OHC air-cooled, 1670cc	12,099
BMW		
R1200 Classic	1,170cc, horizontal twin, air-cooled	14,650
BMW R1200 Tourer	1,170cc, horizontal twin, air-cooled	16,250
Polaris		
Victory Classic Cruiser	V-twin, 4-valve OHC, 1,507cc	13,699

Source: Websites of different motorcycle manufactures.

US, the age of the typical Buell customer was seven years younger than that of Harley buyers, and the price was about $10,000 compared with an average Harley price of $16,000. As with Harley, Buell attempted to foster close relations with its customers. The Buell Riders Adventure Group (BRAG) was modeled after HOG.

Buell's production rose from 4,462 units in 1997 to 10,943 in 2002 (see table 8.5), boosted by new models such as the Buell Blast, an entirely new model with a 490cc single cylinder engine and a price tag of $4,595. With the Buell Firebolt, Harley moved even more into direct competition with Japanese and European producers of high-performance sports bikes. Despite heavy investments in developing and launching new products, Buell's unit sales fell by about 9 percent in 2003 due to a fall-off in sales of the Buell Blast.

Table 8.5 Harley-Davidson shipments 1997–2003

	1997	1998	1999	2000	2001	2002	2003
Motorcycle shipments							
United States ('000s)	96.3	110.9	135.6	158.9	188.3	215.7	242.9
Export ('000s)	36.1	39.9	41.6	45.8	46.2	48.0	48.2
Motorcycle product mix							
Sportster	23.8%	22.5%	23.6%	22.6%	21.7%	19.4%	19.7%
Custom	53.5%	51.3%	49.6%	49.3%	49.8%	46.9%	46.7%
Touring	22.8%	26.2%	26.8%	28.1%	27.9%	26.8%	28.4%
VRSL	–	–	–	–	0.7%	6.8%	5.3%
Buell motorcycle shipments							
Worldwide ('000s)	3.1	5.5	6.8	6.9	9.9	10.9	10.0

Source: Harley-Davidson Annual Reports.

Distribution

Upgrading Harley's distribution network was a key aspect of its development strategy during the 1980s and 1990s. Many of Harley's 620 US dealerships were poorly managed shops, operated by enthusiasts, with erratic opening hours, a poor stock of bikes and spares, and indifferent customer service. If Harley was in the business of selling a lifestyle and an experience, then dealers were the primary point of contact between the company and its customers. Moreover, if Harley's future lay with professionals who possessed the disposal income to lay out $17,000 on a motorcycle for occasional leisure rides, then the retail environment had to be appropriate to the requirements of this customer group.

Harley's dealer development program increased support for dealers while imposing higher standards of pre- and after-sales service, and requiring better dealer facilities. The dealers were obliged to carry a full line of Harley replacement parts and accessories, and to perform service on Harley bikes. Training programs helped dealers to meet the higher service requirements, and encouraged them to recognize and meet the needs of the professional, middle-class clientele that Harley was now courting. Harley had taken the lead over other motorcycle companies in introducing new services to customers. These included test ride facilities, rider instruction classes, motorcycle rental, assistance for owners in customizing their bikes through dealer-based "design centers" and "chrome consultants," and insurance services. Eighty-one percent of Harley dealerships in the US were exclusive – a higher percentage than for any other motorcycle manufacturer.

Given the central role of dealers in the relationship between Harley-Davidson and its customers, dealer relations continued to be a strategic priority for Harley. Its Retail Environments Group provides retail planning advice with a goal of bringing the same retail experience to customers everywhere in the world. Harley-Davidson University was established to "enhance dealer competencies in every area from customer satis-

Table 8.6 Harley-Davidson's sales of parts, accessories, and general merchandise, 1992–2003 ($ million)

	1992	1993	1994	1995	1996	1997	1998	1999	2000	2001	2002	2003
Parts and accessories	103.6	127.8	162.0	192.1	210.2	241.9	297.1	362.6	447.9	509.6	629.2	712.8
General merchandise	52.1	71.2	94.3	100.2	90.7	95.1	114.5	132.7	151.4	163.9	231.5	211.4

Source: Harley-Davidson financial statements (www.harley-davidson.com).

faction to inventory management, service proficiency, and front-line sales." Harley's relationships with its dealers were particularly important for the continued growth of Harley's sales of financial services, parts and accessories, and general merchandise. Harley believed that its dealer strategy was an important explanation for the fact that, despite a fivefold increase in production capacity since the beginning of the 1990s, demand for Harley motorcycles continued to outstrip supply. Every motorcycle that Harley made in 2003 had been sold long before it came off the production line. For many models, would-be buyers joined a waiting list. One result was that used bikes frequently sold at higher prices than new bikes. More generally, the rate of price depreciation of used Harleys was very low.

Other Products

Sales of parts, accessories, and "general merchandise" (clothing and collectibles) represented 20 percent of total revenue in 2000 – much higher than for any other motorcycle company (see table 8.6). Clothing sales included not just traditional riding apparel, but a wide range of men's, women's, and children's leisure apparel.

Only a small proportion of the clothing, collectibles, and other products bearing the Harley-Davidson trademark were sold through the Harley dealership network. Most of the "general merchandising" business represented licensing of the Harley name and trademarks to third-party manufacturers. For example, Nice Man Merchandising supplied Harley-Davidson children's clothes; a giftware company supplied Harley holiday bulb ornaments, music boxes, and a Road King pewter motorcycle replica; L'Oréal offered a line of Harley-Davidson cologne; Harley-Davidson Cafés operated in Manhattan and Las Vegas.

Harley-Davidson Financial Services was established to supply credit, insurance, and extended warranties to Harley dealers and customers. Between 2000 and 2003 it was Harley's most rapidly growing source of profits, accounting for 15 percent of total operating income in 2003.

International Expansion

A key part of Harley-Davidson's growth strategy was expanding sales outside of the US. "A few years ago," said Harley CEO Bleustein, "our prime focus was the domestic market, and the rest was gravy. That view had to change. If our growth is to continue, Europe will have to play a significant part." A critical issue for international marketing was the extent to which the products and the Harley image needed to be adjusted to meet the needs of overseas markets. Harley's image was rooted in American culture, and was central to its appeal to European and Asian customers. "The US and Harley are tied together," observed Hugo Wilson of Britain's *Bike* magazine, "the guy who's into Harleys here is also the guy who owns cowboy boots. You get a Harley and you're buying into the US mystique."[8] At the same time, the composition of demand and the customer profiles were different in overseas markets.

Europe was the focal point of Harley's overseas ambitions, simply because it was the second largest heavyweight motorcycle market in the world. Europe was also a huge challenge for Harley. Unlike in the US, Harley had never had a major position in Europe and it had to fight to take market share from the established leaders in the heavy bike segment: BMW, Honda, Kawasaki, and Yamaha. The European motorcycle market differed significantly from the American market in that 70 percent of the heavy motorcycle market was for performance bikes, while the touring/cruiser bikes such as those Harley made accounted for only 30 percent. European buyers tended to be knowledgeable and highly style conscious. Also, European roads and riding style were different from the US. As a result, Harley modified some of its models to better meet the needs and tastes of its European customers. The US Sportster, for example, had a straight handlebar instead of curled buckhorns and a new suspension system to improve cornering. The name was also changed to the "Custom 53." The Harley Softail also received a new look, becoming the "Night Train." As in the US, HOG played a critical role in building brand image and customer loyalty. Harley's anniversary celebration in Barcelona on June 2003 attracted some 150,000 people, including Harley owners from all over Europe. Central to Harley's international strategy was building its dealer network. Between 2000 and 2003, Harley expanded its dealership network in Europe and Asia, acquired several distributors, and built a new European headquarters in Oxford, England. At the beginning of 2004, Harley had 383 dealers in Europe (including the Middle East and Africa), 221 in Asia, and 30 in Latin America. In the US there were 648 Harley dealerships and in Canada 75.

Operations

Since emerging as an independent company in 1981, Harley-Davidson had continuously upgraded its manufacturing operations. This involved continuous investment in plant and equipment, both to introduce advanced process technologies and to expand capacity. Even more important was the development of manufacturing capabilities through total quality management, just-in-time scheduling, CAD/CAM, and the devolution of responsibility and decision making to the shopfloor.

At the beginning of 2004, Harley's engine and component manufacturing was clustered around its Milwaukee headquarters, with assembly concentrated at York, Pennsylvania and Kansas City, Missouri. (See table 8.7.)

Despite the enormous strides in implementing state-of-the-art manufacturing methods and expanding production to offset the problems of small-scale production, Harley's low production volumes relative to Honda and the other Japanese manufac-

Table 8.7 Harley-Davidson's main facilities, 2004

Location	Function	Square feet
Wisconsin		
Milwaukee	Corporate headquarters	515,000
Wauwatosa	Product development center	397,000
Wauwatosa	Engine manufacturing	422,000
Menomonee Falls	Engine and transmission production	479,000
Franklin	Parts/accessories distribution center	250,000
Tomahawk	Fiberglass parts production/painting	189,000
Pennsylvania		
York	Final assembly plant, parts and painting	1,331,000
Missouri		
Kansas City	Manufacturing, painting	330,000
Brazil		
Manaus	Manufacturing	30,000

Source: Harley-Davidson 10K l Report, 2003.

turers imposed significant cost disadvantages. A key factor in this volume-related cost disadvantage was in the purchasing components. Bought-in, customized components accounted for a large proportion of manufacturing costs and Harley did not possess the same buying power as Honda or even some of the smaller manufacturers. Thus, despite its smaller volume of motorcycle production, BMW was able to leverage the buying power of its automobile business.

To meet this challenge, Harley placed purchasing managers at senior levels within its management structure and fostered close relations with its key suppliers. In 1992, Harley extended its program of quality improvement to encompass its suppliers. It established a supplier advisory council (SAC) to expose supplier executives to the best practices of other suppliers in the Harley network.[9] Harley's director of purchasing, Garry Berryman, commented: "Through the SAC, we're able to take some of the entrepreneurial aspects of our smaller, privately held suppliers and inject that enthusiasm, spirit, and energy into those that may be larger, publicly held companies. In this way, the SAC serves not only to improve purchasing efficiency, but also provides a forum to share information, ideas, and strategy." The SAC, noted Berryman, was a way "to leverage the successes that occur in one area across the broader organization."[10] Suppliers were also included in Harley's new product development process. Leroy Zimdars, Harley's director of purchasing development, noted: "We want suppliers to be deeply involved, at an early stage, in new product development. We'll use the SAC as a sounding board for how the supply base accepts the new structure, and we can react to it."[11]

People and Management Processes

A key feature of Harley's turnaround during the 1980s was the quest for a new relationship between management and employees. Following the management buyout,

Harley's new management team systematically rethought management–employee relationships, employee responsibilities, and organizational structure. The result was a transformation in employee commitment and job satisfaction. "What other company has employees who tattoo the company name on their bodies? Or offers not just a job but a lifestyle?" queried an assembly-line worker at Harley's Milwaukee plant. Harley had a no lay-off policy, 12 weeks of paid maternity leave, and unlimited sick days for staffers.

The process of management innovation was a continuing one. Harley's new Northland Plant in Kansas City featured a management structure and working methods designed to promote employee commitment and self-management. "I'm not aware of anybody anywhere doing anything that emulates this," said plant chief Karl Eberle.[12] In contrast to the traditional layout of Harley's other plants, the Northland Plant did not have a management space that overlooked the floor production from a glassed-in office upstairs. Instead, the plant manager and other administrators worked in a "bullpen area" on the production floor of the 330,000 square-foot building.

In an effort to engage and motivate the entire plant workforce, management developed a novel operating structure different from anything else within the company. The structure comprised three types of teams:

- *Natural work groups* – every worker belonged to a work group, with 8–15 people per group.
- *Process operating groups* – comprised representatives from each work group. There were four process operating groups; one for each of the plant's four operating divisions: paint, assembly, fabrication, and engine production.
- *Plant leadership group* – a 14-member committee, responsible for governing the facility. It comprised the plant manager, the presidents of both unions representing the plant workforce, four elected representatives from the process groups, an elected representative from maintenance, and six administrators.

Harley's belief in the effectiveness of non-hierarchical, team-based structures in fostering motivation and accelerating innovation and learning was evident throughout the company. The Harley-Davidson Operating System was a philosophy and a methodology for continuous improvement involving team-based efforts to identify wasted steps, pare costs, and enhance quality throughout manufacturing.

The movement toward a flatter, more team-based organizational structure extended to Harley's corporate headquarters. "In our new organization," explained Clyde Fessler, VP for business development, "the Harley-Davidson Motor Company has been divided into three broad, functional areas called Circles. They are: the Create Demand Circle (CDC), the Produce Product Circle (PPC), and the Provide Support Circle (PSC). Each Circle is composed of the leaders representing the functions within it. The flexibility of the organization extends even to the decision of which functional areas are identified within a given circle. It is quite possible that Circle definitions may shift from time to time, depending on the demands of the business."[13] Each Circle operated as a team with leadership moving from person to person, depending on the issue being addressed.

Overall coordination was provided by the Strategic Leadership Council (SLC) comprising individuals nominated by each of the three Circles. Explained Fessler:

> The role of the SLC is to resolve issues that have not been settled previously by consensus in Circle meetings. Leadership of the Council also rotates, shifting to the Circle representative who "owns" the topic being discussed . . . The Circle format is especially valuable in that it facilitates systems thinking in our strategy implementation. If the marketing function plans to focus on a specific product, the Circles provide an opportunity to get feedback from manufacturing about timing and availability. If the Manufacturing function needs to shut down its operations to upgrade equipment, the Circle structure allows all the affected functions to be involved in the decision. . . . Defining the roles and responsibilities of each functional Circle and each Circle member has brought clarity, which in turn stimulates dialogue, trust, and eventually, non-threatening confrontation . . . Collaborative interdependent teams may not be able to move as quickly as the single decisive leader in a hierarchy, but they can be more innovative and resourceful and, ultimately, more effective in today's complex business climate.[14]

■ COMPETITION ■

Despite Harley's insistence that it was supplying a unique Harley experience rather than competing with other motorcycle manufacturers, the more Harley took market share from other manufacturers, the more it was engaged in a brutally competitive market. By broadening its market, Harley came into closer competition with its Japanese and European rivals – Buell's mission was to compete directly with them. And the more successful was the Harley brand, the more it could expect its bigger competitors to target its own market niche. Honda, Suzuki, Yamaha, and Kawasaki had long been offering V-twin cruisers styled closely along the lines of the classic Harleys – but at lower prices, with more advanced technologies, and in some dimensions, superior performance. In competing against Harley, the Japanese manufacturers' key advantage was their sales volume. Harley's single-segment focus and concentration on the US market meant that it produced a much smaller volume of bikes than any of the Japanese producers. The most striking comparison was between Harley-Davidson and Honda: Harley's total of 291,000 bikes in 2003 was dwarfed by Honda's 5 million bikes in the same year. These volume differences had important implications for Harley's ability to access economies of scale and for its vulnerability to factors influencing its dominant market – the US market for heavyweight motorcycles.

In addition, Harley lacked the diversification of its rivals. Honda, BMW, and Suzuki were important producers of automobiles and more than one-third of Yamaha's turnover came from boats and snowmobiles. These companies could benefit from sharing technology, engineering capabilities, and marketing and distribution know-how across their different vehicle divisions. In addition, sheer size conferred greater bargaining power with suppliers.

Also, Harley was facing competition from other specialists producing retro-styled cruiser bikes. In recent years Excelsior, Polaris (Victory), and Big Dog had all entered Harley's markets during the late 1990s, but with only limited success.

Appendix 2 gives profiles of several competitors of Harley, while table 8.4 shows price comparisons.

■ MEETING THE CHALLENGES OF TOMORROW ■

The Strategic Plan for Sustainable Growth, which emerged at the end of February 2004, offered a ten-year roadmap for Harley's future development. Bleustein recognized that the targets set – unit sales growth of 7 to 9 percent annually and annual earnings growth "in the mid-teens" – were ambitious. However, with growing sales of parts, accessories, and financial services and continued productivity increases from improved business processes, Bleustein considered these targets well within Harley's grasp. At the heart of the strategy were two core principles – *growing value* and *strengthening the brand*. Implementing these principles required a systematic approach to developing Harley's differentiation advantage, while working strenuously to contain costs. Throughout the whole range of Harley-Davidson's activities—from designing new motorcycles to interfacing with customers – Bleustein was satisfied that Harley had built a management system that was dedicated to excellence and continuous improvement. What concerned him were the possible potholes that the company might encounter on the road forward. In Donald Rumsfeld's words, what were the "unknown unknowns" that might throw Harley-Davidson off course?

In thinking through Harley's possible vulnerabilities, Bleustein grappled with some of the implications of a strategy that emphasized selling an experience rather than selling a product. The problem of selling experiences was that they were dependent upon the social and psychological identity and aspirations of the customer. Were the values embodied in the "Harley Experience" universal and enduring or were they the result of cultural, social demographic phenomena that were particular to the United States during the past two decades? To date, the market had absorbed Harley's additional production with no signs of indigestion. Would an additional 100,000 motorcycles per year be absorbed just as willingly, or would the very ubiquity of Harley bikes undermine the individuality that was closely linked to "The Experience"? While Harley's marketing emphasized the experience of motorcycling, Bleustein was acutely aware that purchasing a Harley was, for many of its owners, more a statement of style than a desire to ride the great American wilderness.

With the baby-boomers graduating from motorcycles to retirement homes, Harley would no longer be benefitting from favorable US demographic trends. In these circumstances Harley's ability to maintain its market share would depend increasingly on its ability to recruit new and younger customers. To date, Harley had had little success in selling to younger riders. Similar comments could be made about Harley's other potential growth market – overseas. For all its building of distribution networks and marketing efforts outside the US, Harley's overseas performance had been patchy: very successful in Japan, but only modest sales growth in Europe.

APPENDIX 1

Harley-Davidson, Summary of Financial Statements, 1994–2003

Table 8.A1 Harley-Davidson: selected items from financial statements, 1994–2000 ($ million, except per-share data)

	1994	1995	1996	1997	1998	1999	2000	2001	2002	2003
Income statement										
Net sales	1,159	1,350	1,531	1,762	2,064	2,453	2,906	3,407	4,091	4,624
Gross profit	358	411	490	586	691	836	991	1,153	1,418	1,666
R&D	28	30	37	53	59	70	76	130	140	150
Selling, admin., engineering	204	234	269	329	377	448	513	552	639	684
Operating income	154	181	228	270	334	416	515	663	883	1,149
Of which:										
Financial services	–	4	8	12	20	28	37	61	104	168
Interest income	2	0	3	8	4	8	18	17	17	23
Other income	1	(5)	(4)	(2)	(1)	(3)	16	(7)	(13)	(6)
Income before taxes	156	176	228	276	336	421	549	673	886	1,166
Provision for income taxes	60	65	84	102	123	154	n.a.	236	306	405
Net income	104	112	166	174	213	267	348	438	580	761
Earnings per share (diluted)	$0.62	$0.73	$0.94	$1.13	$1.38	$1.73	$1.13	$1.41	$1.90	$2.50
Balance sheet										
Assets:										
Cash and cash equivalents	59	31	142	147	165	183	419	n.a.	281	812
Finance receivable, (current portion) net	–	170	184	249	319	355	581	n.a.	856	1,002
Accounts receivable, net	143	134	141	103	113	102	98	n.a.	109	112
Inventories	173.4	84.4	101.4	117.5	155.6	168.6	191.9	n.a.	218	208
Total current assets	406	337	613	704	845	949	1,297	n.a.	2,067	2,729
Property, plant, equipment	263	285	409	529	628	682	n.a.	n.a.	1,033	1,046
Total assets	739	1,001	1,230	1,599	1,920	2,112	2,436	n.a.	3,861	4,928
Liabilities:										
Current liabilities										
Current portion of debt	18	3	9	91	147	181	89	n.a.	383	324
Accounts payable	64	103	101	106	123	138	n.a.	n.a.	227	224
Total current liabilities	216	233	251	362	468	518	498	n.a.	990	956
Non-current liabilities										
Debt	0	164	258	280	280	280	355	n.a.	380	670

Table 8.A1 *continued*

	1994	1995	1996	1997	1998	1999	2000	2001	2002	2003
Other long-term liabilities	90	109	70	62	67	65	97	n.a.	123	86
Post-retirement benefits	n.a.	n.a.	66	68	72	76	81	n.a.	105	127
Total stockholders' equity	433	495	663	827	1,030	1,161	1,406	n.a.	2,233	2,958
Total liabilities & equity	739	1,001	1,230	1,599	1,920	2,112	2,436	n.a.	3,861	4,923
Cash flows										
Operating activities	81	169	228	310	318	416	565	750	776	936
Capital expenditures	(95)	(113)	(179)	(186)	(183)	(166)	(204)	(290)	(324)	(227)
Total investing activities	(97)	(188)	(214)	(406)	(340)	(300)	(171)	(764)	(1,014)	(485)
Financing activities	(3)	(10)	96	102	40	(98)	(158)	34	80	81
Net increase in cash	(18)	(26)	(111)	5	(18)	18	236	20	(158)	532

Source: Harley-Davidson financial statements (www.harley-davidson.com).

APPENDIX 2

Harley-Davidson's Competitors

Table 8.A2 Comparative financial data for Harley-Davidson, Honda and BMW ($ million, except per-share data)

	Honda		Yamaha Motor		BMW		Harley-Davidson	
	2003	2002	2003	2002	2003	2002	2003	2002
Revenue	67,479	55,253	8,454	7,138	52,122	44,316	4,624	4,091
Gross profit margin	34.9%	34.2%	28.3%	25.9%	22.7%	25.4%	40.3%	39.0%
SGA expense	15,845	12,660	1,825	1,571	7,634	7,716	774	725
Operating income	5,837	4,798	565	281	4,209	3,541	892	693
Net income after tax	3,614	2,722	216	61	2,444	2,117	761	580
Net margin	5.4%	4.9%	2.5%	1.0%	4.7%	4.8%	16.5%	14.2%
Operating income/total assets	9.0%	9.2%	9.7%	10.5%	5.5%	8.2%	18.1%	17.9%
Return on equity	16.2%	14.1%	13.3%	5.8%	12.1%	14.6%	25.7%	26.0%
Operating cash flow	5,825	5,628	703	591	9,880	7,599	936	780
Cash flow from investing activities	(9,088)	(6,653)	(329)	(352)	(14,097)	(10,182)	(485)	(1,018)
R&D expenditure	3,698	n.a.	486	n.a.	2,694	n.a.	150	n.a.
Advertising expenditure	1,987	n.a.			n.a.	n.a.	51	n.a.
Employees	126,900	n.a.	32,066		104,342	n.a.	8,800	n.a.

Source: www.hoovers.com.

■ HONDA ■

Honda Motor Co. has been manufacturing motorcycles since 1947 as a second tier player in an expansion cycle of the Japanese motorcycle industry given the need for cheap transportation means after World War II. The company entered the US market in 1959, first with cheaper, lightweight bikes, before quickly moving into the higher priced segments such as performance and touring bikes. The company leveraged the experience obtained in its domestic market in advertising and distribution in its entrance to the US. Given its initial dependency on an exclusive dealership network in Japan, it decided to go directly to retailers. Moreover, it invested heavily in advertising directly to consumers, which gave Honda excellent results in its domestic market.[15] It achieved an extraordinary growth in the US market, increasing sales from $500 million in 1960 to $77 million in 1965 and shared with Yamaha and Suzuki 85 percent of the US market by 1966.[16] Honda has been the world's largest motorcycle manufacturer since 1959, with 5,190,000 bikes produced in 2000 (vs. 54,000 made by BMW and 204,592 made by Harley).[17] The company holds 26.5 percent of the total US motorcycle market, and enjoys the number one market share position. The firm's motorcycle sales grew by 20 percent in 1999, reaching 296,479 American Honda units sold in the US (20 percent increase) compared to 158,817 sold by Harley, and 174,376 motorcycles in year 2000 (a record 34.5 percent increase) in an industry in which sales grew 27.3 percent.

Honda Motor's worldwide sales reached 5.16 million motorcycles in year 2000 and the company has the objective of achieving the 7 million mark by March 2004.[18] Worldwide sales have increased by approximately 20 percent and the decline in unit sales in Japan and Europe has been more than offset by the volume growth in Asian countries (especially India, Indonesia, and Thailand), as well as in North America.[19] Honda is the Japanese car and motorcycle manufacturer most dependent on the US market. Above 50 percent of its consolidated revenues in year 1999 derived from its US operations.

Honda is a superior engineering company and its motorcycles have traditionally been "on the leading edge of technology."[20] "Honda is, above all, an engine company,"[21] and the world's leader in four-stroke technology. The firm was capable of transferring these capabilities into a broad product offering (motorcycle, automobiles, and power products). Its performance bikes have dominated motorcycle racing for decades and are associated with the world's greatest racers. The innovations achieved from racing were adapted to its motorcycle products. In the early 1970s the company also had great success with street and touring bikes with the introduction of the style-setting CB750K0 in 1969 and the Goldwing, the world's first long-distance touring bike, in 1975.[22] Honda's capabilities of product innovation together with heavy investment in R&D, economies of scale, and efficient distribution enable it to develop technical superiority at a lower price. The firm has also committed the largest advertising budget in the industry and established, from early on, the largest dealership network in the US.[23] Its scale advantage together with high growth rates resulted in superior productivity that was translated into lower prices. Honda has experienced steep learning curves of 75–87 percent that enable the company to achieve real price reductions of around 50 percent or more over time.[24]

■ YAMAHA ■

Yamaha Motor Company was established in 1955. Its first product was a 125 cc two-stroke motorcycle. By 2003 it was producing 2.6 million motorcycles a year – with scooters forming a major portion of its sales. Motorcycles made up about 55 percent of sales revenue. Yamaha's other products were watercraft, power products (including all-terrain vehicles and marine engines), and swimming pools. Yamaha's biggest market was south east Asia, where it owned motorcycle manufacturing plants in China, Indonesia, Vietnam, Thailand, and India. Yamaha has a long history of designing and manufacturing V-twin heavyweight cruisers. Its Virago 750 cc V-twin was introduced into the US in 1981 and was a leading seller for almost 20 years. The Yamaha Road Star is designed to compete directly with Harley's retro-look cruisers. The Road Star, with its 1600 cc V-twin engine, has the biggest engine in this category of motorcycles. Yamaha is known for its advanced motorcycle technologies. It introduced the first five-valves per cylinder motorcycle engine, the first four-stroke mass-production motocross bike, and the Yamaha Induction Control System for increased fuel efficiency.

■ BMW ■

Even though motorcycles made only about 2.6 percent of total BMW sales income in 2000,[25] the company is committed to supporting and developing its line of bikes. With annual sales of 74,614 bikes in 2000, the company exported 69 percent of its motorcycles abroad, compared with 66 percent in 1999.

BMW Motorcycles celebrated its 75th anniversary in 1998 and its bikes have led the way to technical innovation, pioneering such things as advanced suspension systems, anti-lock brakes, and fuel injection.[26] Because of these technological innovations, BMW motorcycles have lower operating costs than the competition. In a comparison of Kawasaki and BMW touring bikes, the California Police Department estimated an operating cost of 1.9 cents per mile for the Kawasaki model tested, compared with an operating cost of 1.7 cents per mile for the BMW model tested.[27] The company has always been associated with a high technical and quality standard, and its motorcycles are also known for reliability, safety, and comfort.

BMW offers a full line of performance, touring, and cruiser bikes. Recently it has introduced its new concept model C1, which is designed to unite the mobility of the bike with safety of the car. The first cruiser, BMW R1200C, was introduced in 1997 as part of the latest James Bond movie, *Tomorrow Never Dies*,[28] and became BMW's best-selling bike in its first model year.[29] The R1200C includes the latest technological innovations and safety features; however, it departs from the retro look favored by other producers. In creating the bike, BMW assumed that in the future "high performance cruisers will replace retro-look customs with a sportier look and feel."[30] The R1200C was the first in this category. At a price of $14,500, the cruiser is priced about $1,000 below the range of comparable Harley models and provides superior features such as anti-lock disk brakes, superior acceleration technology, and a liquid-cooled engine.[31] Half of R1200C buyers are those who already own a Harley, and the other half are those who own a Japanese motorcycle.

BMW introduced the new luxury touring model K1200LT in 1999. This model also represents the "new" design concept of the modern look. Compared with the competing models it offers superior comfort and user friendliness.

BMW motorcycles are positioned as a source of "undeniable pleasure and excitement of riding." The underlying idea is that BMW should provide the functionality of the bike with improved comfort and reliability features. In order to achieve this goal the company leverages the innovative car-building technologies of its 70,000 sq ft R&D campus in Munich. As a result, BMW motorbikes have anti-lock braking system (ABS), close to car-comfort seats as well as enhanced cooling and battery systems to increase reliability of the engine during various riding conditions. Most of the BMW motorcycles are manufactured in the single plant located in the vicinity of Berlin. During 2002, the plant was expanded to 2,400 workers (additional 320) to achieve the capacity of 400 items per day. A new C1 model is currently being built in the Carrozzeria Bertone factory.

■ EXCELSIOR HENDERSON MOTORCYCLE MANUFACTURING COMPANY (EXCELSIOR) ■

In the early 1990s two brothers, Dave and Dan Hanlon, bought the trademarks to a pre-war motorcycle manufacturer, Excelsior and Henderson. Formed in 1876, Excelsior Supply Co. was one of the top three US motorcycle manufacturers at the turn of the century along with Indian Motorcycle and Harley-Davidson. Its motorcycle was the first to break the 100 mph barrier. The company was liquidated during the Depression in 1931 and ever since the Hanlon brothers have been trying to resuscitate its image by manufacturing, marketing, and selling cruisers and touring bikes under the Excelsior brand name, evoking "an authentic American motorcycling heritage and lifestyle."[32]

The Hanlons have developed a prototype of a retro-style cruiser with the latest technology and accessories, such as electronic fuel injection, a four-valve cylinder, and an overhead cam engine. Named The Super X, it is to be sold at a sticker price between $17,000 and $20,000.

With no revenue generation and with reported losses of $5.9 million and $2.5 million in 1997 and 1996 respectively, the firm went public in 1997, raising $28 million in proceeds. These IPO funds, together with a $1.7 million State of Minnesota equipment financing bond, financed the construction of the company's new administrative and manufacturing facility in Belle Plain, Minnesota. Production started in 1998 (with 5,500 units of backorders), to be stopped in late 1999 when the firm filed Chapter 11 bankruptcy protection.

E. H. Partners, Inc. acquired the firm from Chapter 11 in September 2000 (the firm's public stockholders and founders did not retain an equity interest) and announced a reorganization plan that consisted in its restructuring, no manufacturing during 2001, and resumption of motorcycle production for the 2002 year with the complete re-launch of the firm. Moreover, its dealership networks, owing to lack of support from the firm, have lost huge amounts in warranty repairs not reimbursed and the current availability of parts is almost terminated.

■ POLARIS ■

A leading snowmobile (world's largest manufacturer), ATV (all-terrain vehicle), and personal watercraft maker since the 1950s, and currently one of the largest US manufacturers, the firm has past success with taking on Japanese competitors. In the early 1990s, Polaris entered the personal watercraft and the ATV markets, both dominated by Japanese competitors – Kawasaki and Honda respectively. Since then, Polaris has gained the number two market share in ATV sales (37 percent of revenue), and challenged Kawasaki's dominance of the personal watercraft market by gaining significant market share and brand recognition.

Polaris launched a new cruiser, the Polaris Victory, in the spring of 1998 with a retro look and new technology, and targeting the high-margin, high-growth cruiser market dominated by Harley. High-tech engineering has "eliminated some of the noise and vibration associated with a Harley."[33] The Victory was positioned to compete with technologically advanced Honda, Suzuki, Kawasaki, and Yamaha cruisers on a price level above Japanese models. Polaris "competes with Japanese on price, quality, and technology." The company stresses its "made in the USA" appeal to attract customers away from these foreign competitors and is counting on its previous experience making personal watercraft and ATVs to beat the competition. According to CEO Wendel, "We met these guys in snowmobiles and ATVs and we beat their asses off."[34]

Polaris is a very efficient and aggressive company with high-tech manufacturing capabilities and a combined distribution network of 2,000 dealers for all of its products (Victory Motorcycles are available at 300 dealers in the US, Canada and the UK). It reported twelve consecutive years of record net income, totaling $82.8 million in 2000 (8 percent increase) and sales totaled a record $1,425.7 million (7 percent increase).

The firm entered the motorcycle industry leveraging its resources and capabilities: large distribution network, cross-selling opportunities, engineering and manufacturing capabilities, and low production costs. Engineering of the new cruiser was performed in-house, lowering development costs. Production and assembly takes place at two plants that had extra capacity, and the firm reaches break-even at 4,000 motorcycles per year (3 percent of the current cruiser market). Victory motorcycles sales more than tripled in 1999 and grew by 50 percent in year 2000.

Polaris anticipated becoming a significant player in the motorcycle market, developing a line of touring, cruiser, and performance bikes with projected sales of $500 million by 2003 and expanded capacity of 40,000–50,000 per year. Polaris is known as an efficient, low-cost manufacturer.

■ TRIUMPH ■

Triumph,[35] a British manufacturer, began motorcycle production in 1902. By 1909 the company was producing 3,000 bikes per year and by the 1950s became one of the world's most renowned motorcycle brands (in part thanks to its appearance as Marlon Brando's bike in the classic movie *The Wild One*).

However, by the 1970s the company faced financial problems and was forced to liquidate in 1983. Primarily due to the efforts of its current head, John Bloor, the company revived in the early 1990s and began development and production of new models. In 1996 the company surpassed the 50,000 bikes production level (touring, cruisers) and unveiled plans to introduce a new performance motorcycle.

"Triumph is the greatest name, and only survivor, of the once internationally dominant British motorcycle industry." Triumph is about glamour and rebellion, about speed and performance. The company's most popular model (25 percent of production capacity) is a cruiser, the Thunderbird. Thunderbird's styling is similar to that of the 1960s Triumph model with the same name and the bike is positioned to capture a part of the lucrative heavyweight cruiser market.

NOTES

1. Boston Consulting Group, "Strategy alternatives for the British motorcycle industry," Her Majesty's Stationery Office, London, July 30, 1975; quoted in Richard T. Pascale, "Perspectives on strategy: the real story behind Honda's success," *California Management Review*, March 23 (Spring 1984), 47–72.
2. Peter Reid, "How Harley beat back the Japanese," *Fortune*, September 25, 1989.
3. Gary Strauss, "Born to be bikers," *USA Today*, November 5, 1997.
4. Marc Ballon, "Born to be wild," *Inc*, November 1997, p. 42.
5. Harley-Davidson, Inc. Annual Report, 2000.
6. http://www.harley-davidson.com/experience/family/hog.
7. *Motorcycle* magazine, February 1998.
8. Marco R. della Cava, "Motorcycle maker caters to the continent," *USA Today*, April 22, 1998.
9. Kevin R. Fitzgerald, "Harley's supplier council helps deliver full value," *Purchasing*, September 5, 1996.
10. Ann Millen Porter, "One focus, one supply base," *Purchasing*, June 5, 1997.

11. Kevin R. Fitzgerald, "Harley's supplier council helps deliver full value," *Purchasing*, September 5, 1996.
12. Stephen Roth, "Harley's goal: unify union and management," *Kansas City Business Journal*, May 16, 1997.
13. Clyde Fessler (Harley VP for Business Development), "Rotating leadership at Harley-Davidson: from hierarchy to interdependence," *Strategy & Leadership*, July 17, 1997.
14. Ibid.
15. Honda (B) Harvard Business School, Case No. 9-384-050.
16. Honda (A) Harvard Business School, Case No. 9-384-049.
17. http://www.honda.com; http://www.bmw.com; and table 8.1.
18. American Honda Reports Record Motorcycle Sales For 2000, February 2, 2001 (www.americanmotor.com).
19. Honda's Q2 2000 Motorcycle Sales Up – Overall Net Income Down, November 16, 2000 (www.americanmotor.com).
20. Adrian Blake, "Two motorcycle giants celebrate anniversaries," *The Toronto Star*, April 11, 1998.
21. American Honda Reports Record Motorcycle Sales For 2000, February 2, 2001 (www.americanmotor.com).
22. Ibid.
23. Honda (A) Harvard Business School, op. cit.
24. Ibid.
25. http://www.bmw.com.
26. Richard Truett, "Motorcycling has long run in the BMW family," *The Orlando Sentinel*, March 5, 1998.
27. John O'Dell, "Giving chase: BMW wants to break Kawasaki's and Harley's hold on the police market," *Los Angeles Times*, September 21, 1997.
28. "BMW in control with Bond bike cruiser," *The San Diego Union Tribune*, March 14, 1998.
29. Truett, "Motorcycling has long run in the BMW family," op. cit.
30. Blake, "Two motorcycle giants," op. cit.
31. "Comparison of dealers" suggested retail prices in table 8.4.
32. "Excelsior Henderson selects J. D. Edwards to provide smooth ride to growth," *Business Wire*, March 24, 1998.
33. Macario Juarez, "City business to help debut American Harley rival," *Albuquerque Tribune*, December 18, 1997.
34. Paul Klebnikov, "Clear the roads, here comes Victory," *Forbes*, October 20, 1997.
35. http://www.georgian.net/rally/triumph.

case nine

Online Broking Strategies: Surviving the Downturn at Merrill Lynch, Charles Schwab, and E*Trade

Anjali Bakhru and Ann Brown

■ INTRODUCTION ■

The advent of online broking in the mid 1990s re-drew the map of the broking industry. New entrants included both established brokers and new firms attracted by the potential of reaching new customer segments drawn to the on-line brokerage business model. However, the rapidly growing on-line brokerage industry, estimated to include up to 150 firms in the United States, was soon faced with a different market environment. Following the downturn in technology stocks in May 2000, global stock markets remain weak. The once buoyant brokerage industry has been reeling from the decrease in market volumes at the end of a decade-long bull market, intensifying competition in a dwindling market. Investor confidence has been further eroded by a series of extraordinary events that include accountancy scandals and potential conflicts of interest in financial houses acting as advisors to companies whose shares they are also selling.

The three companies – Merrill Lynch ("Merrill"), Charles Schwab ("Schwab") and E*Trade – described in this case represent the main types of entrant in the online broking industry.

Merrill is a successful traditional full-service brokerage firm, while Schwab has its origins in the 1970s as a pioneer of the discount brokerage model. Finally, E*Trade is a pure play entrant and a pioneer of online trading. The three companies have pursued successful, albeit different, strategies during the emergence of the online broking market. Given prolonged market weakness, this case examines the strategy pursued by each firm in the years since the beginning of 2001. With no immediate prospect of an

This case was prepared by Anjali Bakhru of Open University Business School and Ann Brown of Cass Business School, City University. Copyright © 2005 Anjali Bakhru and Ann Brown upturn to share trading, it remains to be seen how well their strategies will serve them in the future.

■ CHANGING THE MAP OF THE BROKING INDUSTRY WITH ONLINE TRADING ■

The early expectations for the power of the Internet to transform share trading were high. Even the survival of traditional brokerages was considered to be under threat. It is not too difficult to appreciate the basis for these views, when the characteristics of the Internet are so well-suited to trading shares. The Internet offers a new channel through which trades can be transacted – the core operations of a broker – but it also offers a rich medium for communication, where customers are able to access and manipulate information. The web's reach and the potential to offer a 24-hour broking service reduce the limitations of geography and maximize customer convenience respectively. The business model is an efficient one with the potential to simplify operations through the electronic capture and transmission of transaction data, thereby offering cheaper administrative costs and, hence, lower fees for the execution of trades. New investors can enter the market with far lower capital resources than had previously been possible. Any Internet user can obtain real-time stock market information, previously only available to professionals, and existing investors can manage their own portfolio directly through the Internet.

The broking industry can be considered to consist of three main market segments: advisory, discretionary, and execution-only. Although brokers tend to specialize in one of these three segments, some are full-service brokers, such as Merrill Lynch, offering all the main types of service. Advisory services are where clients receive personalized advice on their investment strategies including advice on stock selection, while discretionary services tend to be offered to high net worth investors, where brokers are responsible for managing the client's equity portfolio. Finally, execution-only services are essentially "no frills" services: in return for lower costs, investors do not receive investment advice and a broker will simply act upon the investor's trading instructions. Essentially, online broking is a sub-segment of the execution-only segment (see figure 9.1).

The online brokers at their most basic level of service, offer support for their customers to manage their own investments ("DIY" model of investing) and execute trades as specified by the client. Contact with the company is mainly online, where customer support includes access to research and market data as well as software-based investment tools. Key to this business model is customer confidence in the reliability and security of the IT systems that execute trades and the quality of customer support.

However, the threat to the traditional broking industry has never materialized as expected. On one level, the threat posed by alternative electronic trading systems, such as Direct Access Trading ("DAT"), has yet to develop. DAT allows a client to trade directly with an exchange such as NASDAQ or through an Electronic Communication Network ("ECN"), where the latter are essentially private trading systems that potentially will provide the platform for global access to 24 hours-a-day, real-time trading.[1] Similarly, while the onset of Internet trading witnessed the growth in new online entrants, few traditional brokers disappeared and few new entrants were start-up firms. The online

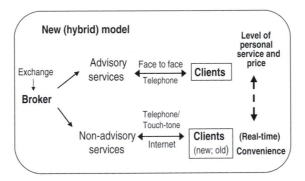

Figure 9.1 Broker business models

market developed primarily through existing firms enhancing their existing offerings to include online broking services. New online business models appeared to co-exist successfully with other more traditional broker models.

While the online business model has an intrinsic appeal to more active, semi-professional investors or "day traders," many of whom were already clients of the discount brokers, the appeal to other customer segments of the online business model has been significant. The attraction of online investing has created an expansion in the retail customer segment with new customers, who have never dealt directly in stocks and shares, now opening online accounts with brokerages. The development of web sites, like www.fool.com, www.stockhouse.com, www.moneyextra.com, that not only offer stock market information and comment but have also created chat rooms for their registered visitors, is another new feature of the market. The ordinary investor can now talk to others and exchange experiences. They can further follow company news and obtain research and analysis at a time and pace of their own choosing. At the same time, the development of online broking coincided with the growth in the mass affluent segment of the population. The mass affluent have been generally defined as those households that have at least £70,000 or approximately $100,000 to invest in the market. This group began to be identified in the late 1990s as a potentially lucrative market. More than 10 percent of all households in developed economies fall into this category. However, the long-term impact on the market of these growing customer segments is far from clear; it is still an open question as how best to service each of these customer segments to meet their needs and generate profits for the broker.

■ ACHIEVING COMPETITIVE SUCCESS ■

Like other dot.com companies, new entrants in the online broking market accepted the need to go for growth in customer accounts. They spent hugely on marketing to obtain brand recognition and market share. In general, marketing spend has seemed to yield results in terms of growth in the number of customer accounts. The argument for this strategy however was based on more solid grounds than for many other dot.com companies in other industries. Traditional brokers generate income from three main sources: commission on trades, interest income derived from the difference between interest payments to clients on their cash balances and the interest earned on margin loans, and a portion of the market-maker's bid–ask spread. It is the same for online brokers. In other words, total income is significantly affected by trading volumes and the size of clients' investment assets. At the same time, the automation of transaction processing implies high fixed costs but relatively low marginal costs and, hence, economies of scale exist. In addition, there is the critical mass argument. There is a point at which brokerages can reach a critical number of accounts such that the firm breaks even in terms of costs and revenues with zero trades and, hence, without the benefit of commission income. With a growth in the number of client accounts, non-commission revenues increase, although admittedly at a diminishing rate. However, the firm's marginal costs are also decreasing, usually at a faster rate. It was thought that firms achieving a critical mass of accounts first would be in a dominant position. This led to further speculation that only a small number of online brokers would survive when this point was reached. Price competition was fierce in the early years; E*Trade alone cut commissions seven times in the four years up to 1998. The lower costs of transactions online made this possible but the strong belief in the need for volume fueled the entrant firms' commitment to this policy.

The most exploited aspect of the Internet – its ability to disseminate information to any number of individuals simultaneously and almost instantaneously – is central to the online business model. The growth in the range and scope of information provided both by online brokers to clients and by investors to other investors is one of the most extraordinary features of the online broking sector. Even the distributive power of the Internet has been exploited. Investors can download or access software tools, like portfolio management packages, that help them manage their own investments. The importance of the performance of the technology supporting online transactions was recognized early. Customers valued security, reliability, speed, ease of use, and integrity of data records. System failure for any reason could be a major factor in losing clients.

■ THE MAJOR EVENTS OF THE DOWNTURN ■

Since May 2000, retail investors' faith in equity investment has been challenged with the dot.com bubble bursting, persistent stock market weakness, concerns over company reporting, and the issue of corporate governance in general. "It's no surprise that the bear market has taken its toll, but the sheer intensity of investors' gloominess is remarkable," observed *BusinessWeek*.[2] According to a survey held by the magazine at the end of 2002, investors were tired of investing in stock markets following a three-year bear market. Investor pessimism appeared to have reached new lows, with 36 percent of investors regarding the stock market as overpriced despite the market's low levels, and only 24 percent of investors were planning to invest "a lot" or "somewhat" more in stocks or mutual funds in the following six months (down from 47 percent in 1999).

The dot.com collapse marked a new era for Internet companies with a shakeout of firms in many online sectors. At the same time, venture capital (VC) investment in online firms was significantly reduced and there was a collapse in the number of firm

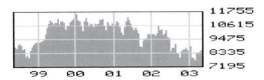

Figure 9.2   Performance of Dow Jones Index

IPOs (Initial Public Offerings). The potential for unprecedented share price rises was no longer an added attraction for investors new to equity investment. Other sectors were not left unscathed, and the bursting of the dot.com bubble was closely followed by the news of massive over-investment in the telecoms sector, creating conditions in which share prices soared and then fell by unprecedented amounts along with many company failures. Investors were left with the bewildering impression that VC and company management lacked an understanding of the business they were in. Moreover, the continuing high level of directors' fees or severance pay, even as the firm reported losses, left many commentators disillusioned. With the growth in stock market indices slowing (see figure 9.2), and even going negative, other problems began to emerge, notably dubious accounting practices that had tended to overvalue some share prices. This culminated in a series of highly public company scandals of which Enron and WorldCom are probably the best known. In both cases, the accounts of the late 1990s had been shown to overstate profits and assets, leaving Enron bankrupt and Worldcom on its knees. The courts have yet to decide the degree of criminal behavior that was carried out by the top management of these companies, but many senior managers have been charged. Many investors in the United States, however, have suffered twice – from the consequences of direct share investment as well as from the impact on 401(k) pension plans that are heavily invested in the firms they are working for. Perhaps one of the most spectacular events was the demise in 2002 of Andersen, auditor to Enron and one of the major accounting firms, as a result of their apparent collusion in the fraudulent accounting at Enron. The public discussion of accounting standards has underlined the problems of conflict of interest for auditors and the difficulty of representing a firm's intangible assets in particular. The Sarbanes-Oxley Act was passed by the US Congress with the intention of cleaning up the auditing process. This act became law in July 2002. The investment banks have also been subject to fierce criticism in relation to their investment recommendations. The inherent conflicts of interest for a bank when it acts both as a corporate broker for a company and as an investment advisor to other clients became acute in the dot.com boom and crash. In the publicity surrounding the aftermath, it seems likely that many shares were knowingly misrepresented.

The average investor, reading the business press and watching his or her shares lose value, is left with the perception that corporate management has little interest in protecting the shareholder, that accounting standards are inadequate, and that accounts may fail to represent the true position of a firm, while analysts are likely to have a vested interest in overselling shares.

■ THE THREE COMPANIES ■

For those companies that have embraced Internet share dealing, the reduction in trading volumes over the past two years has been serious. Their revenue and business growth were based on growth in transactions. The loss of volume has adversely affected both revenue and marginal costs. In the following subsections, we describe recent developments at each of the three brokers Merrill Lynch, Charles Schwab, and E*Trade in terms of two periods, where the end of 2000 can be considered to mark the impact of market decline on the broking firms. Figure 9.3 compares the share price performance of the three firms over the period since 1998.

Merrill Lynch

Investment banking giant Merrill Lynch & Co., Inc. has offices around the globe, total client assets of around US$1.46 trillion, and its origins date back to 1820. For a private client broker like Merrill, with its army of 17,000 brokers, online broking would seem a threat to its core business. It was a late mover and it was not until December 1999 that a web-based service was developed, helped along by the acquisition of D. E. Shaw's discount brokerage in early 1999.

PERIOD ONE: MARKET GROWTH

For Merrill, the opportunity provided by the Internet has effectively been twofold. Development of online services has enabled it to retain its existing client base as well as attract new clients from the fast-growing affluent customer segment and, additionally, the knock-on effects of embracing Internet technology have tended to be significant for Merrill's institutional business. Merrill has two main online services: Merrill Lynch OnLine and Merrill Lynch Direct. The former service offers clients, by its own admission, the best of both worlds – the convenience of online account access and the advice of a Merrill Lynch Financial Advisor – while the advisory service is not offered with the latter. Product pricing is simple: for fee-based, full-service customers using Merrill Lynch OnLine, trading is free; while for clients of Merrill Lynch Direct, the cost is $29.95 per trade for US equities, where clients can also have online access to cash management services and Merrill's research (see table 9.1). With regard to the former, a fee is charged at a blended rate of 1 percent of equity and mutual fund assets and 0.3 percent of cash/fixed income assets for a minimum annual fee of $1,500, with fee percentages declining as assets grow. In return for this fee, clients receive a personalized service from a Merrill financial advisor as well as unlimited broking transactions at no additional charge, where orders can be placed via a consultant, the telephone or Internet.

Merrill offers a variety of sophisticated tools, such as personalized *watch lists* and *securities trackers*. Clients can also consolidate information from all their financial service providers on "My Financial Picture," which is regarded as an easy way of

Merrill Lynch

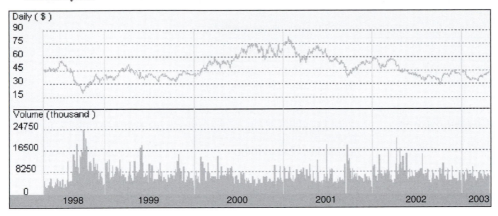

Charles Schwab

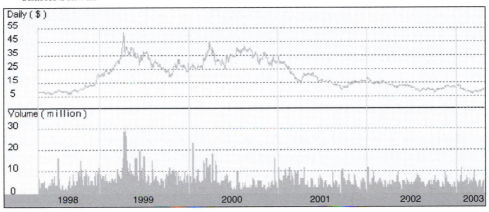

E*Trade

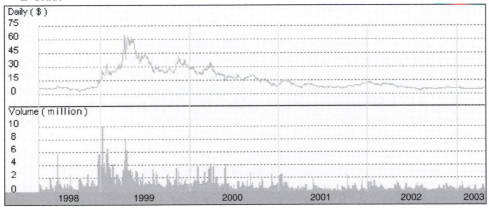

Figure 9.3 Comparison of broker share prices
Source: www.morningstar.com.

Table 9.1 Comparison of broking fees at April 2003

	Trade commission	Other
Merrill Lynch	For fee-based, full-service customers, trading is free; for anyone else, $29.95 per trade.	
Charles Schwab	$29.95 per online trade; $54.95 for broker-assisted trades; $49.95 for automated phone trades.	Schwab Account's service fee of $45 per quarter per account for investors with account size less than $10,000; no service fee for accounts larger than $50,000.
E*Trade	$19.99 for listed and Nasdaq stock trades. Additional $3 order-handling fee for customers trading fewer than 27 times per quarter.	Minimum margin of $1,000 for cash accounts.

sharing this information with their advisors to enhance the level of advice and guidance received. Research and information can also be received in a wireless version from Merrill Mobile. Since new customers are likely to be those drawn to the Merrill Lynch Direct service, Merrill offers the Merrill Lynch Educational Channel on its web site, to afford investors the opportunity to learn the basics of financial planning and investing. Given that Merrill is already a full-service broker, which is part of a larger investment banking group, its online services have been largely developed internally. However, at the end of 2000, Merrill outsourced its mortgage origination and servicing operations to Cendant on a private label basis to provide an enhanced array of services to its clients nationwide.

PERIOD TWO: MARKET DECLINE

Merrill is one of the most successful and largest securities houses, although group net earnings of $2.6 billion compare unfavorably with those of nearly $4 billion in 2000 (see table 9.2). The group was not left unscathed by the market downturn in 2001, with Merrill stating at the end of June that second quarter revenues would be approximately 15 percent lower than first quarter revenues in 2001.[3] Although market weakness negatively affected trading volumes, Merrill is protected to some extent by its pricing system with a large part of brokerage earnings being fee-based rather than transaction-based.

2001 was a difficult year for Merrill. It was caught in the scandal over analysts misleading clients over share recommendations; the private opinions of analysts appeared to differ substantially from the bullish share recommendations that they issued. The

Table 9.2 Merrill Lynch: consolidated statement of earnings (in millions, except per share amounts)

	Year ended December 31			
	2002	2001	2000	1999
Revenues:				
Commissions	4,626	5,266	6,977	6,355
Asset management fees and admin.	4,914	5,351	5,688	4,753
Investment banking	2,444	3,539	4,049	3,614
Interest revenue, net of interest expense	3,533	3,266	3,111	2,101
Principal transactions	2,340	3,930	5,995	4,752
Other	751	528	967	746
Total	18,608	21,880	26,787	22,321
Expenses excluding interest:				
Compensation and benefits	9,426	11,269	13,730	11,337
Communications and technology	1,741	2,232	2,320	2,053
Occupancy and related depreciation	909	1,077	1,006	953
Brokerage, clearing and exchange fees	727	895	893	779
Advertising and market development	540	703	939	783
Professional fees	552	545	637	571
Office supplies and postage	258	349		
Goodwill amortization	–	207	217	227
Other	611	902	1,328	1,412
Research-related expenses	211	–	–	–
(Recoveries)/expenses related to Sep 11	(212)	131	–	–
Restructuring and other charges	8	2,193	–	–
Total	14,771	20,503	21,070	18,115
Income before income taxes and dividends	3,837	1,377	5,717	4,206
Income taxes	1,069	609	1,738	1,319
Net income	2,577	573	3,784	2,693
Diluted earnings per share	$2.69	$0.57	$4.11	$3.11
No. of private client advisors	n/a	16,400	20,200	18,600
No. of employees	50,900	57,400	72,000	67,900

firm finally settled a case brought by the State of New York, agreeing to pay a $100 million fine in May. By the end of 2001, Merrill's newly appointed President, Stanley O'Neal, was offering thousands of non-brokerage employees a buyout package. This led to a reduction in the firm's workforce from a peak of 72,000 to 55,000. At the same time, the group announced its strategy to exit unprofitable businesses at a time of a slowing global economy. The direct results of this new strategic emphasis included the sale of its South African brokerage division to Investec and its Canadian brokerage and asset management business to the Canadian Imperial Bank of Commerce. The firm's overseas online operations were also targeted. In May 2001, Merrill set up a new UK online banking and stock broking joint venture with HSBC (www.mlhsbc.co.uk) aimed at the mass affluent, self-directed investor. Potential investors were required to make a minimum investment of £10,000 in cash and/or shares. Clients had access to their accounts online, by telephone, as well as through a physical network of investment centers. Within a short period of time, the venture had expanded its operations to other countries, including Australia and Canada, and had planned to operate in 21 countries by 2004. However, as early as December 2001, the winding down of the venture was announced, even though the joint venture was not expected to make a profit for four years, given that fewer than 4,000 investors had been attracted to the service since its May launch.[4] Merrill finally pulled out of the joint venture in May 2002 after a total investment of $200 million. Since the beginning of 2002, Merrill's rationalization plans are unchanged and its brokerage operations in Japan have been severely reduced with the closure of several branches.

Prolonged market weakness has forced Merrill to question its overall strategy and reassess its online strategy. The company appears to have exited unprofitable businesses with a renewed focus on its core operations. While the company maintains a commitment to a multichannel strategy, it remains to be seen how central its online strategy is to maintaining the customer relationships that are the heart of its private client business.

Charles Schwab

Charles Schwab was incorporated in 1971 and entered the discount brokerage business in 1974 prior to the US Securities and Exchange Commission's abolition of fixed commissions in 1975. Always a leader rather than a follower, Schwab began online trading in 1984, although it didn't go live with Internet trading until 1996. At the end of September 2002, Schwab had more than 8.0 million active customer accounts with total assets worth $727 billion. Of these accounts, 4.1 million were online with 84 percent of all trades conducted online. (See table 9.3.)

Schwab pursues a multichannel strategy, aimed at providing a wide selection of choices for its clients' investment needs and offering online and telephone broking through to advisory services provided via its network of offices. Telephone access is provided in two forms: through automated telephone channels or through a service that allows customers to talk to a firm representative. The latter is organized primarily through regional client telephone service centres and online client support centres that operate both during and after market hours. Online broking services for retail clients

Table 9.3 The Charles Schwab Corporation: consolidated statement of income (in millions, except per share amounts)

	Year ended December 31			
	2002	2001	2000	1999
Revenues:				
Commissions	1,206	1,355	2,294	1,875
Asset management fees and admin.	1,761	1,675	1,583	1,220
Interest revenue, net of interest expense	841	929	1,237	820
Principal transactions	184	255	570	500
Other	143	139	104	71
Total	4,135	4,353	5,788	4,486
Compensation and benefits	1,854	1,875	2,414	1,888
Other compensation	22	56	39	
Occupancy and equipment	471	490	415	307
Communications	262	339	353	279
Advertising and market development	211	246	332	248
Depreciation and amortization	321	338	255	169
Professional services	177	193	255	184
Commissions, clearance and floor brokerage	71	92	138	100
Merger-related goodwill and other impairment charges	61	–	69	–
Goodwill amortization	–	66	53	12
Restructuring and other charges	373	419		
Other	144	104	234	200
Total	3,967	4,218	4,557	3,387
Income before income taxes	168	135	1,231	1,099
Income taxes	71	57	513	433
Net income	109	199	718	666
Weighted average common shares outstanding – diluted	1,375	1,399	1,404	1,373
Diluted earnings per share	$0.07	$0.06	$0.51	$0.49
Dividends declared per common share	$0.0440	$0.0440	$0.0407	$0.0373
No. of employees	16,700	19,600	26,300	20,100

primarily centre on www.schwab.com, although there is also CyberTrader, an integrated software-based trading platform for highly active investors, which the firm is continuing to develop, and its wireless service PocketBroker, which has not taken off as expected.

PERIOD ONE: MARKET GROWTH

The launch of Internet technology provided Schwab with an opportunity to tap into new customer markets, where it pursued a "bricks-and-clicks" strategy, with more than 70 percent of new accounts being opened at its branches. Customer education was a key component of Schwab's online offering. WebShops, which were introduced in 1999, were the first in a series of educational workshops designed to help investors increase their skills in using Schwab's online services. However, Schwab began to reorient its customer focus to include the growing mass affluent customer market both in the US and overseas. Surveys showed that up to a quarter of mass affluent investors are prepared to make their own financial decisions with little or no advice, with almost half of these wired to the Internet.[5] Since the launch of its Signature Services program in 1999, Schwab has designed new products targeted at mass affluent investors. SchwabAdvisorSource was also launched, which refers customers with more investable assets who seek a higher level of investment advice. In this case, clients must have a minimum of $100,000 to use the service, which offers referral to over 400 advisors. Schwab does, however, face a number of hurdles with regard to its market repositioning: its acquisition of US Trust in mid-2000 could be viewed as direct competition to Schwab's substantial investment advisor client base. Schwab provides custodial, trading and support services to nearly 6,000 independent investment managers, who had guided the investments of around 1 million Schwab accounts containing $224.2 billion in assets at the end of March 2001.

Technology has been core to Schwab's online strategy, ensuring that the company is able to expand and improve upon existing services, such as Mutual Fund One Source. This makes nearly 1,300 funds available from around 250 fund families with no-load, no-transaction fees. During 2001, StockExplorer was developed as an online screening tool which enables clients to identify equities that meet certain screening criteria according to the investment strategy selected. Essentially, it is a tool that mimics the advisory function of a personal broker. At the same time, systems have to respond to the challenge of varying capacity demands. 1999 was a major growth year for Schwab, with total customer assets up 48 percent on the previous year to $725 billion, and with the number of new accounts opened up by 1.5 million to a total of 6.6 million accounts at the year end. This growth was reflected in a $126 million investment in systems capacity, which doubled trade processing capabilities as well as enabling the web site to handle single-day records of 78 million hits in December of that year.

It is not surprising that, given Schwab's focus on multichannel delivery, the company has tended to focus on internal development of its technology to ensure a greater level of control. Its move to work more with outside providers was justified by the company's need to enhance existing services; its MyAccounts service utilized technology provided by Yodlee Inc. to aggregate online financial information for clients and enable them to analyze and manage that information in one password-protected site. And most notably, in 2000 Schwab entered into a technology alliance with Ericsson to develop wireless trading applications.

PERIOD TWO: MARKET DECLINE

Weakness in equity markets tends to have a negative impact on retail brokers. Clients of retail brokerages, unlike wealthier private clients, are likely to have share portfolios that are a much smaller percentage of their total investments and, hence, are more likely to withdraw from equity markets in a downturn. Schwab is a successful company with net income of over $718 million in 2000 (table 9.3). However, Schwab's trading revenues in the first quarter of 2001 were down 51 percent year-on-year, with total revenues down 30 percent. In addition, the total number of daily average trades was down substantially during the same period.

For Schwab, the impact of market weakness was first felt in early 2001, when Schwab began encouraging its employees to take time off in an attempt to avoid layoffs. By March, however, the trading situation had worsened, and Schwab announced that it was going to fire 13 percent of its employees. By the end of 2001, the firm had reduced its workforce by nearly a quarter, the first layoffs since the market crash of 1987. The one exception to all this was the marketing budget; it was reported that Schwab was still going to spend the same amount on marketing in 2001 – around $330m – as it did the previous year.[6] Trading volumes did not, however, recover in 2002, with Schwab announcing that the number of trades in August was down 25 percent on July. The company continued to lay off staff throughout 2002. With the total number of employees at 16,700 at the end of 2002, Schwab had laid off approximately 35 percent of its workforce since the end of 2000. While the reduction in staff in 2001 was aimed at reducing capacity in its retail business and technology units, along with the sale of substantial amounts of computer hardware, the firm said that the recent staff cuts were focused on streamlining the company's structure and eliminating middle management.[7]

Despite continued market weakness and ongoing conflicts of interest with its advisor client base, the firm continues to confirm its commitment to target the mass affluent customer segment. In May 2002, Charles Schwab himself announced moves aimed at capturing the most profitable customers of the likes of Merrill, Morgan Stanley Dean Witter, Salomon Smith Barney, and UBS Paine Webber – affluent clients with $500,000 to $5 million to invest. As a result of this, the company has launched its own private client service, where, for a flat fee, customers can talk with a personal advisor on a wide range of issues from asset allocation to stock selection as well as receive equity research from investment bank Goldman Sachs. Clients pay an annual fee of 0.6 percent of assets subject to a minimum fee of $1,500, although the advice offered does not cover legal, tax, or estate-planning advice. These clients constitute an estimated $11 trillion investment market, or about half of all the investments made by Americans.[8]

Other new services include a stock-rating system to aid investment decisions. More than 3,000 stocks are graded on an A to F scale based on 24 measures, such as a company's cash flow and sales growth. The company claims that the potential of the system to outperform the S&P500 stock index is proven in recent trials. At the same time, since the beginning of 2002, Schwab's marketing campaign has emphasized that its brokers are not paid on a commission basis and has focused on the impartiality of the firm's investment advice given that the firm is not part of an investment banking group. The company further plans to launch insured banking products, aimed at encouraging nervous investors back into the equity markets. However, cost pressures have caused the company to reappraise its fee structure, with an extra $3 transaction fee being added to online trades.

To date, Schwab has pursued a successful multichannel strategy, where the use of technology has been central to its strategy of enhancing its offering. Given continued market weakness, the firm's positioning towards the mass affluent investor does, however, carry risks. Will it maintain its leading position as a retail broker or will investors view it as a diluted version of a private client broker, unable to compete with rivals like Merrill Lynch?

E*Trade

E*Trade is both the pioneer of Internet trading and a "pure-play" entrant. Its success has been rapid; transaction revenues were over $739 million in 2000 (see table 9.4) and the company was listed on the New York Stock Exchange (from NASDAQ) in early 2001, less than five years since its IPO on August 16, 1996. From a reported 91,000 customer accounts at the time of listing, E*Trade reported 3.725 million active customer accounts with total customer assets of $47.9 billion and 3,800 employees by March 2001, when the level of customer accounts had approximately doubled over the previous year. Despite the market downturn, the firm has continued to expand and diversify. By early 2003, the company described its principal activities as offering ". . . *personalised and fully integrated financial services solutions that includes investing, banking, lending, planning and advice."*

PERIOD ONE: MARKET GROWTH

The company launched its new financial portal site, Destination E*Trade, in late 1998 along with a "state-of-the-art" new customer support centre. This was followed by the opening of a Knowledge Centre in 1999 for the benefit of customers, many of whom were young and new to investing. Clients were offered two types of accounts: an E*Trade account or a PowerE*Trade account. The latter is for more active investors in which the more you trade, the lower your commissions, with these as low as $4.95 per trade for 75 trades or more per calendar quarter. However, the company has continued to expand the services it offers. It acquired Private Accounts to provide low cost, direct access to nationally recognized money managers and timely access to portfolio information. It also launched E*Trade Personal Money Management, an online investment resource that allows investors to search for, compare, and hire professional money managers via the Internet – a service that is available to customers with a minimum of $100,000 to invest.

Table 9.4 E*Trade: consolidated statement of operations (in thousands, except per share amounts)

	Year ended December 31		Year ended September 30	
	2002	2001	2000	1999
Revenues:				
Transaction revenues			739,078	355,830
Net interest			359,496	153,622
International			166,061	124,233
Other			107,686	40,546
Provision for loan losses			(4,003)	(2,783)
(Post-2000)				
Brokerage Revenues:				
Commissions	301,778	377,704		
Principle transactions	216,544	157,949		
Other brokerage related	178,744	156,690		
Brokerage interest income	182,103	305,581		
Brokerage interest expense	(12,515)	(86,489)		
Net Brokerage Revenue	866,654	911,435		
Banking Revenue:				
Gain on sales of orig. loans	128,506	95,478		
Gain on loans held	83,953	75,836		
Other banking related	46,184	38,587		
Banking interest income	763,890	854,290		
Banking interest expense	(548,659)	(692,786)		
Provision for loan losses	(14,664)	(7,476)		
Net Banking Revenue	459,210	363,929		
Net Revenues	1,325,864	1,275,364	1,368,318	671,448
Cost of Services	567,224	595,590	515,571	302,342
Operating Expenses:				
Sales and marketing	203,613	253,422	521,532	325,449
Technology developments	55,712	88,717	142,914	79,935
General and administrative	210,646	236,353	209,436	102,826
Amortization of intangibles	28,528	43,091	22,764	2,915
Merger-related expenses	11,473	11,174	36,427	7,174
Facility re-structuring/non-recurring	16,519	202,765		
Executive loan settlement	(23,485)	30,210		
Total operating expenses	502,736	865,732	933,073	518,299
Total cost	1,069,960	1,461,322	1,448,644	820,641
Operating Income (Loss)	255,904	(185,958)	(80,326)	(149,193)
Income taxes	85,121	(19,885)	85,478	(31,288)
Extraordinary items	1,555	480	(181)	4,651
Net income (Loss)	(186,405)	(241,532)	19,152	(56,769)
Weighted average common shares outstanding – diluted	361,051	339,315	301,926	272,832
Diluted earnings per share	$0.52	$0.73	$0.06	$(0.21)
No. of Employees	3,500	3,500	3,800	2,000

E*Trade's origins stem from its development of proprietary transaction processing technology, and the company's technological infrastructure is based on a modular architecture which is scaleable to handle increasing transaction volumes. Enhancements to its broking service included the development of E*Trade AccountExpress (the first real-time account opening and funding service that allowed customers to open and fund an account electronically) by increasing the cash amount that new customers could initially invest as well as enabling faster and easier transfer of additional funds to E*Trade. MarketCaster, a new applet product which provides brokerage customers with free, streaming, real-time stock quotes, was also introduced. With this product customers are able to set up one or more customized watch lists and monitor the performance of stocks without having to refresh their computer screen. MarketTrader is a tool providing all PowerE*Trade customers with streaming NASDAQ Level II quotes, integrated trading, and personal account information on a single screen. It is offered to the most active traders, namely those who trade more than 30 (PowerE*Trade) and 75 times (Platinum Level) per quarter respectively. Convenience of access has been central to E*Trade's strategy. Customer access has been enabled via the Internet, CompuServe, Prodigy Internet, Microsoft Investor, WebTV, direct modem connection, and TELE*MASTER, their touchtone and speech recognition telephone investing system. An integrated wireless banking and brokerage service was launched in October 2000.

Expansion of services has been afforded by the company's emphasis on developing content, technology and distribution alliances including Bond Exchange (bond trading), Instinet (after-hours trading), Briefing.com (research), InsWeb (insurance), Critical Path (e-mail services), and EveryPath (wireless application provider). At the same time, E*Trade acquired a number of companies including Private Accounts (which provides low-cost, direct access to nationally recognized money managers), VERSUS Technologies (software supplier for global cross-border trading), Card Capture Services (to expand the array of financial transactions and, ultimately, online brokerage via ATMs), Telebanc (the nation's largest pure-play Internet bank), and ClearStation (a financial media site that integrates technical and fundamental analysis with community discussion to offer investors ideas, analysis and opinion). Also, E*Trade together with Ernst and Young announced a joint venture in 2000 to provide a personal electronic advisory service to help prepare clients for major financial events such as buying a home, tax/estate planning, funding a child's education and preparing for retirement.

PERIOD TWO: MARKET DECLINE

At the beginning of 2001, E*Trade's average customer balance was $17,500 vs. $106,000 for Schwab and $180,000 for Merrill.[9] The firm is vulnerable to a reliance on brokerage commission, especially given that its low trading prices imply a higher "critical mass" (i.e. the point at which the firm is profitable while charging no commissions at all). The company increased its physical broking presence in the US, including the development of E*Trade Zones, in conjunction with retailer Target. The firm is further attempting to diversify its sources of revenues. The company has expanded geographically, predominantly via joint ventures and acquisitions, with operations across the globe serving customers in many countries including Australia, Canada, Denmark, Hong Kong, Israel, Japan, Korea, Norway, South Africa, Sweden, the UK, and the US through branded web sites. Telebanc, acquired in 2000, was relaunched as E*Trade Bank, the largest pure-play Internet bank in the USA. Integrated banking and broking services were provided with access to the third largest ATM network in the USA (with around 9,600 ATMs). The success of the bank is owed, in part, to gains from cross-selling efforts to the broking customer base. Mitchell Caplan, Head of Banking Division, said in April 2002:

> Last quarter, half our new bank accounts came from existing brokerage customers and 29 percent of the mortgage business came from existing banking and brokerage customers.

Since the beginning of 2001, E*Trade has nevertheless suffered a significant decrease in broking volumes and revenues. It has sought to expand its broking services. Following the public condemnation of research analysts at investment banks like Merrill, E*Trade has taken the opportunity to provide its own research to clients, given that it is not compromised by the potential conflicts of interest facing investment banks. In May 2002, the firm hired a group of analysts from investment bank Credit Lyonnais to provide clients with unbiased advice. However, its core broking business remained under pressure and, by October 2002, the firm began to extend an offer of $9.99 per trade to those customers averaging 27 trades per quarter. It is not surprising that Christos Cotsakos, CEO, came under criticism from shareholders for the very large compensation package awarded to him for 2001, an unprofitable year for the company. Despite relinquishing part of his compensation package, his final pay still stood at $64m, the highest in the US broking industry.

E*Trade has come a long way since its pure-play origins. The company has sought to extend and adapt its broking service in line with changes in customer tastes and in response to the market environment. At the same time, the firm has sought to grow and protect its revenues by diversifying its online financial services offerings. The firm has successfully managed to survive the market downturn so far. The question remains: how long will it take for the company to translate this once again into profits?

■ SUMMARY ■

The application of Internet technologies to traditional markets has led to the emergence of new, online markets, where new customer segments have been created by the transformation of existing business models. What is interesting about the broking industry is how all segments of the retail broking industry appear to have embraced the new technology and added new online services to their existing service offering. However, private client brokers, such as Merrill, may prove to be the exception in terms of the direction of their online strategy, given the greater resilience exhibited by the very rich than the mass affluent in the current market downturn.

■ QUESTIONS ■

1. What has been the impact of the Internet on the broking industry?
2. During the period of market growth, how did each of the three brokers compete?
3. E*trade can be considered to be an Internet-based e-commerce business. Identify the type of e-business model that it has developed over the growth period. Is this a viable model?
4. How well has each company performed during the downturn?
5. How have each of the three brokers responded to the market downturn? Do you think they will be successful in surviving the downturn and why?

■ USEFUL WEB SITES ■

US Securities and Exchange Commission: http://www.sec.gov/cgi-bin/srch-edgar (Edgar Archives)

Company websites: www.ml.com
www.schwab.com
www.etrade.com

NOTES

1. http://www.tradefreedom.com/features/freedom.html.
2. *BusinessWeek*, 30/12/02.
3. Merrill Press Release, 06/26/01.
4. *Financial Times*, 12/07/01.
5. *Financial Times*, 06/22/01.
6. *Financial Times*, 03/28/01.
7. *Financial Times*, 18/9/02.
8. *BusinessWeek*, 3/6/02.
9. *Forbes Global*, 10/01/01.

EMI and the CT Scanner [A] and [B]

Christopher A. Bartlett

■ CASE A ■

In early 1972 there was considerable disagreement among top management at EMI Ltd, the UK-based music, electronics, and leisure company. The subject of the controversy was the CT scanner, a new medical diagnostic imaging device that had been developed by the group's Central Research Laboratory (CRL). At issue was the decision to enter this new business, thereby launching a diversification move that many felt was necessary if the company was to continue to prosper.

Complicating the problem was the fact that this revolutionary new product would not only take EMI into the fast-changing and highly competitive medical equipment business, but would also require the company to establish operations in North America, a market in which it had no prior experience. In March 1972 EMI's board was considering an investment proposal for £6 million to build CT scanner manufacturing facilities in the United Kingdom.

Assistant Professor Christopher A. Bartlett prepared this case as a basis for class discussion rather than to illustrate either effective or ineffective handling of an administrative situation. Information was obtained from public sources and third parties. Although employees of the subject company discussed with the researcher events referred to in the case, they did not participate in the preparation of the document. The analysis, conclusions, and opinions stated do not necessarily represent those of the company, its employees or agents, or employees or agents of its subsidiaries. Thorn EMI plc, on its own behalf and on behalf of all or any of its present or former subsidiaries, disclaims any responsibility for the matters included or referred to in the study.

Development of the CT Scanner

COMPANY BACKGROUND AND HISTORY

EMI Ltd traces its origins back to 1898, when the Gramophone Company was founded to import records and gramophones from the United States. It soon established its own manufacturing and recording capabilities, and after a 1931 merger with its major rival, the Columbia Gramophone Company, emerged as the Electric and Musical Industries, Ltd. EMI Ltd quickly earned a reputation as an aggressive technological innovator, developing the automatic record changer, stereophonic records, magnetic recording tape, and the pioneer commercial television system adopted by the BBC in 1937.

Beginning in 1939, EMI's R&D capabilities were redirected by the war effort toward the development of fuses, airborne radar, and other sophisticated electronic devices.

The company emerged from the war with an electronics business, largely geared to defense-related products, as well as its traditional entertainment businesses. The transition to peacetime was particularly difficult for the electronics division, and its poor performance led to attempts to pursue new industrial and consumer applications. EMI did some exciting pioneering work, and for a while held hopes of being Britain's leading computer company.

Market leadership in major electronics applications remained elusive, however, while the music business boomed. The 1955 acquisition of Capitol Records in the United States, and the subsequent success of the Beatles and other recording groups under contract to EMI, put the company in a very strong financial position as it entered the 1970s. In 1970 the company had earned £21 million before tax on sales of £215 million, and although extraordinary losses halved those profits in 1971, the company was optimistic for a return to previous profit levels in 1972 (see exhibits 10.1 to 10.3 for EMI's financial performance).

Exhibit 10.1 EMI Limited: profit and loss statement, 1969–71 (£ thousands)

Years Ended June 30	1969	1970	1971
Sales			
Music	110,554	129,439	128,359
Leisure	20,960	32,651	35,798
Television	4,640	10,625	13,593
Electronics	40,170	42,571	52,819
Total	176,324	215,286	230,569
Profit (loss) before Interest and Taxation			
Music	13,293	16,427	1,970
Leisure	1,691	3,875	4,146
Television	733	992	3,833
Electronics	3,741	3,283	3,090
Subtotal	19,458	24,577	13,039
Property	–	(20)	939
Total	19,458	24,557	13,978

Exhibit 10.1 *continued*

Years Ended June 30	1969	1970	1971
Sales			
United Kingdom	63,144	89,069	103,824
Europe	25,987	27,017	39,673
North America	65,528	74,622	58,989
Other countries	21,665	24,578	28,083
Total	176,324	215,286	230,569
Profit (loss) before Interest and Taxation			
United Kingdom	8,301	10,465	13,113
Europe	3,176	3,230	3,113
North America	5,525	7,627	(5,754)
Other countries	2,456	3,235	3,506
Subtotal	19,458	24,557	13,978
Net interest payable	(1,857)	(3,599)	(5,010)
Total	17,601	20,958	8,968
As a percentage of net assets	15.8%	17.3%	7.4%
Taxation	8,407	10,443	3,541
As a percentage of profit	47.8%	49.8%	39.5%
Profit after taxation	9,194	10,515	5,427
As a percentage of net assets	8.3%	8.7%	4.5%

Exhibit 10.2 EMI Group consolidated balance sheet, 1972

Employment of Capital		
Goodwill		80,814
Fixed assets		104,174
Other investments		14,354
Current assets		
Inventories	45,508	
Films, programs, and rights	7,712	
Accounts receivable	82,483	
Liquid funds	20,086	
	155,789	
Less		
Current liabilities		
Accounts payable	96,942	
Bank borrowings	14,168	
Taxes payable	17,174	
Dividends declared	4,202	
	132,486	
Net current assets		23,303
Total		222,645
Capital Employed		
Share capital		40,937
Reserves		90,239
Minority shareholders' interests		14,992
Loan capital		76,011
Deferred taxes		466
Total		222,645

Exhibit 10.3 EMI Group projected funds flow, 1972 (£ thousands)

Sources of Funds	
Profit before tax	18.3
Depreciation	6.7
Sale of fixed assets	5.5
Sale of investments	5.4
Loan capital	0.3
Decrease in working capital	4.5
Total	40.7
Uses of Funds	
Tax payments	5.9
Dividends paid	5.6
Fixed asset additions	13.0
Repayment of loan capital	3.4
Reduction in short-term borrowings	12.8
Total	40.7

Around that time, a change in top management signaled a change in corporate strategy. John Read, an accountant by training and previously sales director for Ford of Great Britain, was appointed chief executive officer after only four years in the company. Read recognized the risky, even fickle, nature of the music business, which accounted for two-thirds of EMI's sales and profits. In an effort to change the company's strategic balance, he began to divert some of its substantial cash flow into numerous acquisitions and internal developments.

To encourage internal innovation, Read established a research fund that was to be used to finance innovative developments outside the company's immediate interests. Among the first projects financed was one proposed by Godfrey Hounsfield, a research scientist in EMI's Central Research Laboratories (CRL). Hounsfield's proposal opened up an opportunity for the company to diversify in the fast-growing medical electronics field.

CT SCANNING: THE CONCEPT

In simple terms, Hounsfield's research proposal was to study the possibility of creating a three-dimensional image of an object by taking multiple X-ray measurements of the object from different angles, then using a computer to reconstruct a picture from the data contained in hundreds of overlapping and intersecting X-ray slices. The concept became known as computerized tomography (CT).

Although computerized tomography represented a conceptual breakthrough, the technologies it harnessed were quite well known and understood. Essentially, it linked X-ray, data processing, and cathode ray tube display technologies in a complex and precise manner. The real development challenge consisted of integrating the mechanical, electronic, and radiographic components into an accurate, reliable, and sensitive system. Figure 10.1 provides a schematic representation of the EMI scanner,

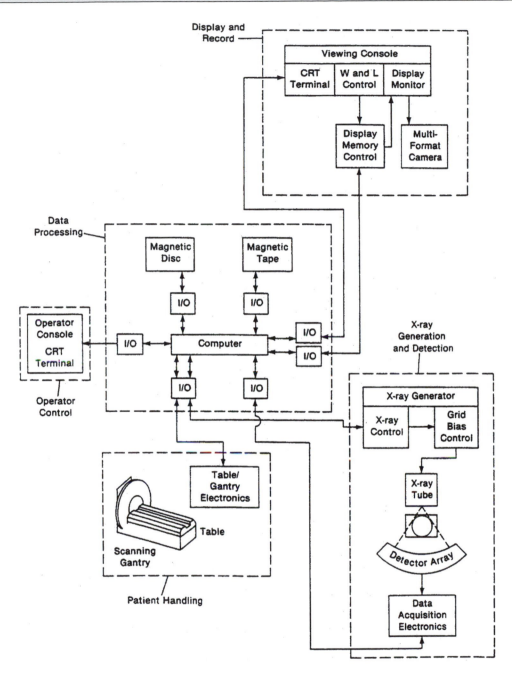

Figure 10.1 Schematic drawing of scanner system

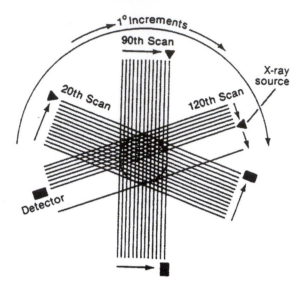

Figure 10.2 Translate-rotate CT scanning

illustrating the linkage of the three technologies, as well as the patient handling table and X-ray gantry.

Progress was rapid, and clinical trials of the CT scanner were under way by late 1970. To capture the image of multiple slices of the brain, the scanner went through a translate-rotate sequence, as illustrated in figure 10.2. The X-ray source and detector, located on opposite sides of the patient's head, were mounted on a gantry. After each scan, or "translation," had generated an X-ray image comprising 160 data points, the gantry would rotate 1° and another scan would be made.

This procedure would continue through 180 translations and rotations, storing a total of almost 30,000 data points. Since the detected intensity of an X-ray varies with the material through which it passes, the data could be reconstructed by the computer into a three-dimensional image of the object that distinguished bone, tissue, water, fat, and so on.

At about the time of the CT clinical trials, John Powell, formerly managing director of Texas Instrument's English subsidiary, joined EMI as technical director. He soon became convinced that the poor profitability of the nonmilitary electronics business was due to the diffusion of the company's 2,500-person R&D capability over too many diverse small-volume lines. In his words, "EMI was devoted to too many products and dedicated to too few."

Because the CT scanner project built on the company's substantial and well-established electronics capability, Powell believed it gave EMI an important opportunity to enter an exciting new field. He felt that this was exactly the type of effort in which the company should be prepared to invest several million pounds.

Diagnostic Imaging Industry

During the first half of the twentieth century, diagnostic information about internal organs and functions was provided almost exclusively by conventional X-ray examination, but in the 1960s and 1970s, several new imaging techniques emerged. When the CT scanner was announced, three other important technologies existed: X-ray, nuclear, and ultrasound.

EMI management believed its CT scanner would displace existing diagnostic imaging equipment in only a few applications, specifically head and brain imaging.

X-RAY

In 1895 Wilhelm Roentgen discovered that rays generated by a cathode ray tube could penetrate solid objects and create an image on film. Over the next 40 to 50 years, X-ray equipment was installed in almost every healthcare facility in the world. Despite its several limitations (primarily due to the fact that detail was obscured when three-dimensional features were superimposed on a two-dimensional image), X-rays were universally used. In 1966 a Surgeon General's report estimated that between one-third and one-half of all crucial medical decisions in the United States depended on interpretation of X-ray films. That country alone had more than 80,000 X-ray installations in operation, performing almost 150 million procedures in 1970.

The X-ray market was dominated by five major global companies. Siemens of West Germany was estimated to have 22 percent of the world market, N. V. Philips of the Netherlands had 18 percent, and Compagnie Generale de Radiologie (CGE), subsidiary of the French giant Thomson Brandt, held 16 percent. Although General Electric had an estimated 30 percent of the large US market, its weak position abroad gave it only 15 percent of the world market. The fifth largest company was Picker, with 20 percent of the US market, but less than 12 percent worldwide.

The size of the US market for X-ray equipment was estimated at $350 million in 1972, with an additional $350 million in X-ray supplies. The United States was thought to represent 35–40 percent of the world market. Despite the maturity of the product, the X-ray market was growing by almost 10 percent annually in dollar terms during the early 1970s.

A conventional X-ray system represented a major capital expenditure for a hospital, with the average system costing more than $100,000 in 1973.

NUCLEAR IMAGING

In the mid-1960s a nuclear diagnostic imaging procedure was developed. Radioisotopes with a short radioactive life were projected into the body, detected and monitored on a screen, then recorded on film or stored on a tape. Still in an early stage of development, this technology was used to complement or, in some instances, replace a conventional X-ray diagnosis. Both static and dynamic images could be obtained.

Table 10.1 Numbers of hospitals in the United States, 1972

Number of beds	Short-term	Long-term (chronic)	Total
Less than 100	3,110	375	3,485
100–299	1,904	385	2,289
300–499	574	141	715
More than 500	537	91	628
Total	6,125	992	7,117

Following the pioneering development of this field by Nuclear-Chicago, which sold the first nuclear gamma camera in 1962, several other small competitors had entered the field, notably Ohio Nuclear. By the late 1960s larger companies such as Picker were getting involved, and in 1971 GE's Medical Systems Division announced plans to enter the nuclear medicine field.

As new competitors, large and small, entered the market, competition became more aggressive. The average nuclear camera and data processing system sold for about $75,000. By 1973, shipments of nuclear imaging equipment into the US market were estimated to be over $50 million.

ULTRASOUND

Ultrasound had been used in medical diagnosis since the 1950s, and the technology advanced significantly in the early 1970s, permitting better-defined images. The technique involves transmitting sonic waves and picking up the echoes, which when converted to electric energy could create images. Air and bone often provide an acoustic barrier, limiting the use of this technique. But because the patient was not exposed to radiation, it was widely used as a diagnostic tool in obstetrics and gynecology.

In 1973 the ultrasound market was very small, and only a few small companies were reported in the field. Picker, however, was rumored to be doing research in the area. The cost of the equipment was expected to be less than half that of a nuclear camera and support system, and perhaps a third to a quarter that of an X-ray machine.

US MARKET POTENTIAL

Because of its size, sophistication, progressiveness, and access to funds, the US medical market clearly represented the major opportunity for a new device such as the CT scanner. EMI management was uncertain about the sales potential for their new product, however.

As of 1972, there were around 7,000 hospitals in the United States, ranging from tiny rural hospitals with fewer than 10 beds to giant teaching institutions with 1,000 beds or more (see table 10.1).

Since the price of the EMI Scanner was expected to be around $400,000, only the largest and financially strongest short-term institutions would be able to afford one. But the company was encouraged by the enthusiasm of the physicians who had seen and worked with the scanner. In the opinion of one leading American neurologist, at least 170 machines would be required by major US hospitals. Indeed, he speculated, the time might come when a neurologist would feel ethically compelled to order a CT scan before making a diagnosis.

During the 1960s the radiology departments in many hospitals were recognized as important money-making operations. Increasingly, radiologists were able to commission equipment manufacturers to build specially designed (often esoteric) X-ray systems and applications. As their budgets expanded, the size of the US X-ray market grew from $50 million in 1958 to $350 million in 1972.

Of the 15,000 radiologists in the United States, 60 percent were primarily based in offices and 40 percent in hospitals. Little penetration of private clinics was foreseen for the CT scanner. Apart from these broad statistics, EMI had little ability to forecast the potential of the US market for scanners.

EMI's Investment Decision

CONFLICTING MANAGEMENT VIEWS

By late 1971 it was clear that the clinical trials were successful and EMI management had to decide whether to make the investment required to develop the CT scanner business. One group of senior managers felt that direct EMI participation was undesirable for three reasons. First, EMI lacked medical product experience. In the early 1970s EMI offered only two very small medical products, a patient-monitoring device and an infrared thermography device, which together represented less than 0.5 percent of the company's sales.

Second, they argued that the manufacturing process would be quite different from EMI's experience. Most of its electronics work had been in the job shop mode required in producing small numbers of highly specialized defense products on cost-plus government contracts. In scanner production, most of the components were purchased from subcontractors and had to be integrated into a functioning system.

Finally, many believed that without a working knowledge of the North American market, where most of the demand for scanners was expected to be, EMI might find it very difficult to build an effective operation from scratch.

Among the strongest opponents of EMI's self-development of this new business was one of the scanner's earliest sponsors, Dr Broadway, head of the Central Research Laboratory. He emphasized that EMI's potential competitors in the field had considerably greater technical capabilities and resources. As the major proponent, John Powell needed convincing market information to counter the critics. In early 1972 he asked some of the senior managers how many scanners they thought the company would sell in its first 12 months. Their first estimate was five. Powell told them to think again. They came back with a figure of 12, and were again sent back to reconsider. Finally, with an estimate of 50, Powell felt he could go to bat for the £6 million investment, since at this sales level he could project handsome profits from year one. He then prepared an argument that justified the scanner's fit with EMI's overall objectives, and outlined a basic strategy for the business.

Powell argued that self-development of the CT scanner represented just the sort of vehicle EMI had been seeking to provide some focus to its development effort. By definition, diversification away from existing product-market areas would move the company into somewhat unfamiliar territory, but he firmly believed that the financial and strategic payoffs would be huge. The product offered access to global markets and an entry into the lucrative medical equipment field. He felt the company's objective should be to achieve a substantial share of the world medical electronics business not only in diagnostic imaging, but also through the extension of its technologies into computerized patient planning and radiation therapy.

Powell claimed that the expertise developed by Hounsfield and his team, coupled with protection from patents, would give EMI three or four years, and maybe many more, to establish a solid market position. He argued that investments should be made quickly and boldly to maximize the market share of the EMI scanner before competitors entered. Other options, such as licensing, would impede the development of the scanner. If the licensees were the major X-ray equipment suppliers, they might not promote the scanner aggressively since it would cannibalize their sales of X-ray equipment and consumables. Smaller companies would lack EMI's sense of commitment and urgency. Besides, licensing would not provide EMI with the major strategic diversification it was seeking. It would be, in Powell's words, "selling our birthright."

THE PROPOSED STRATEGY

Because the CT scanner incorporated a complex integration of some technologies in which EMI had only limited expertise, Powell proposed that the manufacturing strategy should rely heavily on outside sources of those components rather than trying to develop the expertise internally. This approach would not only minimize risk, but would also make it possible to implement a manufacturing program rapidly.

He proposed the concept of developing various "centers of excellence" both inside and outside the company, making each responsible for the continued superiority of the subsystem it manufactured. For example, within the EMI UK organization a unit called SE Labs, which manufactured instruments and displays, would become the center of excellence for the scanner's viewing console and display control. Pantak, an EMI unit with a capability in X-ray tube assembly, would become the center of excellence for the X-ray generation and detection subsystem. An outside vendor with which the company had worked in developing the scanner would be the center of excellence for data processing. Finally, a newly created division would be responsible for coordinating these subsystem manufacturers, integrating the various components, and assembling the final scanner at a company facility in the town of Hayes, not far from the CRL site.

Powell emphasized that the low initial investment was possible because most of the components and subsystems were purchased from contractors and vendors. Even internal centers of excellence such as SE Labs and Pantak assembled their subsystems from purchased components. Overall, outside vendors accounted for 75–80 percent of the scanner's manufacturing cost. Although Powell felt his arrangement greatly reduced EMI's risk, the £6 million investment was a substantial one for the company, representing about half the funds available for capital investment over the coming year. (See exhibit 10.2 for a balance sheet and exhibit 10.3 for a projected funds flow.)

The technology strategy was to keep CRL as the company's center of excellence for design and software expertise, and to use the substantial profits Powell was projecting from even the earliest sales to maintain technological leadership position.

Powell would personally head up a team to develop a marketing strategy. Clearly, the United States had to be the main focus of EMI's marketing activity. Its neuroradiologists were regarded as world leaders and tended to welcome technological innovation. Furthermore, its institutions were more commercial in their outlook than those in other countries and tended to have more available funds. Powell planned to set up a US sales subsidiary as soon as possible, recruiting sales and service personnel familiar with the North American healthcare market. Given the interest shown to date in the EMI scanner, he did not think there would be much difficulty in gaining the attention and interest of the medical community.

Getting the $400,000 orders, however, would be more of a challenge. In simple terms, Powell's sales strategy was to get machines into a few prestigious reference hospitals, then build from that base.

THE DECISION

In March 1972 EMI's chief executive, John Read, considered Powell's proposal in preparation for a board meeting. Was this the diversification opportunity he had been hoping for? What were the risks? Could they be managed? How? If he decided to back the proposal, what kind of an implementation program would be necessary to ensure its eventual success?

■ CASE B ■

The year 1977 looked like it would be a very good one for EMI Medical Inc., a North American subsidiary of EMI Ltd. EMI's CT scanner had met with enormous success in the American market. In the three years since the scanner's introduction, EMI medical electronics sales had grown to £42 million. Although this represented only 6 percent of total sales, this new business contributed pretax profits of £12.5 million, almost 20 percent of the corporate total (exhibit 10.4). EMI Medical Inc. was thought to be responsible for about 80 percent of total scanner volume. And with an order backlog of more than 300 units, the future seemed rosy.

Despite this formidable success, senior management in both the subsidiary and the parent company were concerned about several developments. First, this fast-growth field had attracted more than a dozen new entrants in the past two years, and technological advances were occurring rapidly. At the same time, the growing political debate over hospital cost containment often focused on $500,000 CT scanners as an example

Exhibit 10.4 EMI Limited: P&L statement, 1969–76

Years ended 30 June	1969 £'000	1970 £'000	1971 £'000	1972 £'000	1973 £'000	1974 £'000	1975 £'000	1976 £'000
Sales								
Music	110,554	129,439	128,359	137,755	169,898	213,569	258,343	344,743
Leisure	20,960	32,651	35,798	37,917	45,226	53,591	66,566	81,428
Television	4,640	10,625	13,593	17,165	22,011	22,814	29,107	38,224
Electronics – other than medical	40,170	42,571	52,819	58,215	83,516	104,811	128,644	164,943
Medical electronics	–	–	–	–	321	5,076	20,406	42,104
	176,324	215,286	230,569	251,052	320,972	399,861	503,066	671,442
Profit (loss) before interest and taxation								
Music	13,293	16,427	1,970	9,333	16,606	26,199	19,762	27,251
Leisure	1,691	3,875	4,146	4,983	4,255	2,639	5,981	5,619
Television	733	992	3,833	5,001	6,104	4,465	2,982	5,646
Electronics – other than medical	3,741	3,283	3,090	1,353	5,264	5,835	5,378	13,937
Medical electronics	–	–	–	–	(67)	1,242	9,230	12,502
	19,458	24,577	13,039	20,670	32,162	40,380	43,333	64,955
Property	–	(20)	939	2,118	1,842	402	(103)	–
	19,458	24,557	13,978	22,788	34,004	40,782	43,230	64,955
Sales								
United Kingdom	63,144	89,069	103,824	113,925	142,945	165,641	198,153	241,972
Europe	25,987	27,017	39,673	52,541	82,405	105,251	134,450	170,385
North America	65,528	74,622	58,989	53,151	55,143	67,141	78,154	128,798
Other countries	21,665	24,578	28,083	31,435	40,479	61,828	92,309	130,287
	176,324	215,286	230,569	251,052	320,972	399,861	503,066	671,442
Profit (loss) before interest and taxation								
United Kingdom	8,301	10,465	13,113	15,447	19,287	16,784	16,494	21,802
Europe	3,176	3,230	3,113	3,133	6,133	9,043	9,679	14,521
North America	5,525	7,627	(5,754)	1,091	3,555	6,412	7,065	13,067
Other countries	2,456	3,235	3,506	3,117	5,029	8,543	9,992	15,565
	19,458	24,557	13,978	22,788	34,004	40,782	43,230	64,955
Net interest payable	1,857	3,599	5,010	4,452	6,386	5,690	8,258	5,604
Profit before taxation	17,601	20,958	8,968	18,336	27,618	35,092	34,972	59,351
As a percentage of net assets	*15.8*	*17.3*	*7.4*	*14.4*	*18.9*	*22.8*	*21.2*	*31.2*
Taxation	8,407	10,443	3,541	8,575	13,227	18,666	19,549	31,224
As a percentage of profit	*47.8*	*49.8*	*39.5*	*46.8*	*47.9*	*53.2*	*55.9*	*52.6*
Profit after taxation	9,194	10,515	5,427	9,761	14,391	16,426	15,423	28,127
As a percentage of net assets	*8.3*	*8.7*	*4.5*	*7.7*	*9.8*	*10.7*	*9.3*	*14.8*
Extraordinary items	–	–	–	–	843	264	(14,472)	(146)
Profit attributable to ordinary stockholders	7,259	8,736	4,562	7,297	10,864	13,327	13,124	24,399

of questionable hospital spending. Finally, EMI was beginning to feel some internal organizational strains.

Entry Decision

PRODUCT LAUNCH

Following months of debate among EMI's top management, the decision to go ahead with the EMI Scanner project was assured when John Read, the company CEO, gave his support to Dr Powell's proposal. In April 1972 a formal press announcement was greeted by a response that could only be described as overwhelming. EMI was flooded with inquiries from the medical and financial communities, and from most of the large diagnostic imaging companies wanting to license the technology, enter into joint ventures, or at least distribute the product. The response was that the company had decided to enter the business directly itself.

Immediately action was implemented to put Dr Powell's manufacturing strategy into operation. Manufacturing facilities were developed and supply contracts drawn up with the objective of beginning shipments within 12 months.

In May, Godfrey Hounsfield, the brilliant EMI scientist who had developed the scanner, was dispatched to the US accompanied by a leading English neurologist. The American specialists with whom they spoke confirmed that the scanner had great medical importance. Interest was running high in the medical community.

In December, EMI mounted a display at the annual meeting of the Radiological Society of North America (RSNA). The exhibit was the highlight of the show, and boosted management's confidence to establish a US sales company to penetrate the American medical market.

US MARKET ENTRY

In June 1973, with an impressive pile of sales leads and inquiries, a small sales office was established in Reston, Virginia, home of the newly appointed US sales branch manager, Mr Gus Pyber. Earlier that month the first North American head scanner had been installed at the prestigious Mayo Clinic, with a second machine promised to the Massachusetts General Hospital for trials. Interest was high, and the new sales force had little difficulty getting into the offices of leading radiologists and neurologists.

By the end of the year, however, Mr Pyber had been fired in a dispute over appropriate expense levels, and James Gallagher, a former marketing manager with a major drug company, was hired to replace him. One of Gallagher's first steps was to convince the company that the Chicago area was a far better location for the US office. It allowed better servicing of a national market, was a major center for medical electronics companies, and had more convenient linkages with London. This last point was important since all major strategic and policy decisions were being made directly by Dr Powell in London.

During 1974, Gallagher concentrated on recruiting and developing his three-man sales force and two-man service organization. The cost of maintaining each salesman on the road was estimated at $50,000, while a serviceman's salary and expenses at that time were around $35,000 annually. The production rate for the scanner was running at a rate of only three or four machines a month, and Gallagher saw little point in developing a huge sales force to sell a product for which supply was limited, and interest seemingly boundless.

In this seller's market the company developed some policies that were new to the industry. Most notably, they required that the customer deposit one-third of the purchase price with the order to guarantee a place in the production schedule. Sales leads and enquiries were followed up when the sales force could get to them, and the general attitude of the company seemed to have somewhat of a "take it or leave it" tone. It was in this period that EMI developed a reputation for arrogance in some parts of the medical profession.

Nonetheless, by June 1974 the company had delivered 35 scanners at $390,000 each, and had another 60 orders in hand.

Developing Challenges

COMPETITIVE CHALLENGE

Toward the end of 1974, the first competitive scanners were announced. Unlike the EMI scanner, the new machines were designed to scan the body rather than the head. The Acta-Scanner had been developed at Georgetown University's Medical Center and was manufactured by a small Maryland company called Digital Information Sciences Corporation (DISCO). Technologically, it offered little advance over the EMI scanner except for one important feature. Its gantry design would accommodate a body rather than a head. While specifications on scan time and image composition were identical to those of the EMI scanner, the $298,000 price tag gave the Acta-Scanner a big advantage, particularly with smaller hospitals and private practitioners.

The DeltaScan offered by Ohio Nuclear (ON) represented an even more formidable challenge. This head and body scanner had 256×256 pixels compared with EMI's 160×160, and promised a $2\frac{1}{2}$-minute scan rather than the $4\frac{1}{2}$-minute scan time offered by EMI. ON offered these superior features on a unit priced $5,000 below the EMI scanner at $385,000.

Many managers at EMI were surprised by the speed with which these products had appeared, barely two years after the EMI scanner was exhibited at the RSNA meeting in Chicago, and 18 months after the first machine was installed in the Mayo Clinic. The source of the challenge was also interesting. DISCO was a tiny private company, and ON contributed about 20 percent of its parent Technicare's 1974 sales of $50 million.

To some, the biggest surprise was how closely these competitive machines resembled EMI's own scanner. The complex wall of patents had not provided a very enduring defense. ON tackled the issue directly in its 1975 annual report. After announcing that $882,200 had been spent in Technicare's R&D Center to develop DeltaScan, the report stated:

Patents have not played a significant role in the development of Ohio Nuclear's product line, and it is not believed that the validity or invalidity of any patents known to exist is material to its current market position. However, the technologies on which its products are based are sufficiently complex and application of patent law sufficiently indefinite that this belief is not free from all doubt.

The challenge represented by these new competitive products caused EMI to speed up the announcement of the body scanner Dr Hounsfield had been working on. The new CT 5000 model incorporated a second-generation technology in which multiple beams of radiation were shot at multiple detectors, rather than the single pencil beam and the single detector of the original scanner (see figure 10.3). This technique allowed the gantry to rotate 10° rather than 1° after each translation, cutting scan time from $4\frac{1}{2}$ minutes to 20 seconds. In addition, the multiple-beam emission also permitted a finer image resolution by increasing the number of pixels from 160×160 to 320×320. Priced over \$500,000, the CT 5000 received a standing ovation when Hounsfield demonstrated it at the radiological meetings held in Bermuda in May 1975.

Despite EMI's reassertion of its leadership position, aggressive competitive activity continued. In March 1975, Pfizer Inc., the \$1.5 billion drug giant, announced it had acquired the manufacturing and marketing rights for the Acta-Scanner.

By June 1975, managers at EMI estimated competitors' cumulative orders as follows:

	Total shipped	*On order*
EMI	122	110
Ohio Nuclear	2	50 (est.)
Pfizer	0	20 (est.)

EMI was then operating at an annual production rate of 150 units, and ON had announced plans to double capacity to 12 units per month by early 1976. Pfizer's capacity plans were unknown. The most dramatic competitive revelation came at the annual RSNA meeting in December 1975, when six new competitors displayed CT scanners. Although none of the newcomers offered immediate delivery, all were booking orders with delivery dates up to 12 months out on the basis of their spec sheets and prototype or mock-up equipment exhibits.

Some of the new entrants (Syntex, Artronix, and Neuroscan) were smaller companies, but others (General Electric, Picker, and Varian) were major medical electronics competitors. Perhaps most impressive was the General Electric CT/T scanner, which took the infant technology into its third generation (see figure 10.3). By using a 30°-wide pulsed fan X-ray beam, the GE scanner could avoid the time-consuming "translate-rotate" sequence of the first- and second-generation scanners. A single continuous 360° sweep could be completed in 4.8 seconds, and the resulting image was reconstructed by the computer in a 320×320 pixel matrix on a cathode ray tube. The unit was priced at \$615,000. Clinical trials were scheduled for January, and shipment of production units was being quoted for mid-1976.

The arrival of GE on the horizon signaled the beginning of a new competitive game. With a 300-person sales force and a service network of 1,200, GE clearly had market-

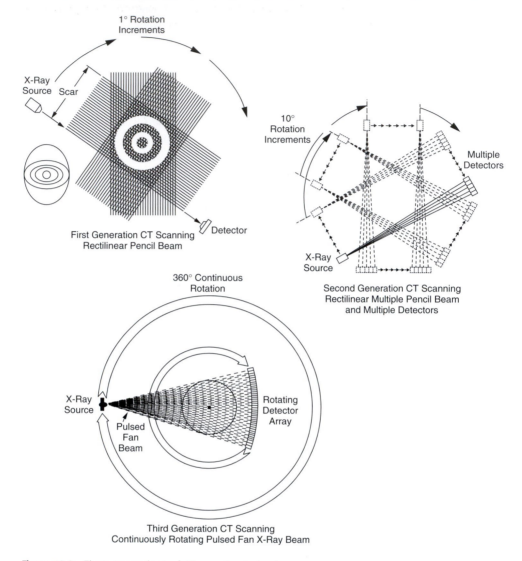

Figure 10.3 Three generations of CT scanning technology

ing muscle. They had reputedly spent $15 million developing their third-generation scanner, and were continuing to spend at a rate of $5 million annually to keep ahead technologically.

During 1975, one industry source estimated, about 150 new scanners were installed in the US, and more than twice as many orders entered. (Orders were firm, since most were secured with hefty front-end deposits.) Overall, orders were split fairly evenly between brain and body scanners. EMI was thought to have accounted for more than 50 percent of orders taken in 1975, ON for almost 30 percent.

MARKET SIZE AND GROWTH

Accurate assessments of market size, growth rate, and competitors' shares were difficult to obtain. The following represents a sample of the widely varying forecasts made in late 1975:

- Wall Street was clearly enamored with the industry prospects (Technicare's stock price rose from 5 to 22 in six months) and analysts were predicting an annual market potential of $500 million to $1 billion by 1980.
- Frost and Sullivan, however, saw a US market of only $120 million by 1980, with ten years of cumulative sales only reaching $1 billion by 1984 (2,500 units at $400,000).
- Some leading radiologists suggested that CT scanners could be standard equipment in all short-term hospitals with 200 beds or more by 1985.
- Technicare's president, Mr R. T. Grimm, forecast a worldwide market of over $700 million by 1980, of which $400 million would be in the US.
- Despite the technical limitations of its first-generation product, Pfizer said it expected to sell more than 1,500 units of its Acta-Scanner over the next five years.

Within EMI, market forecasts had changed considerably. By late 1975, the estimate of the US market had been boosted to 350 units a year, of which EMI hoped to retain a 50 percent share. Management was acutely aware of the difficulty of forecasting in such a turbulent environment, however.

INTERNATIONAL EXPANSION

New competitors also challenged EMI's positions in markets outside the US. Siemens, the $7 billion West German company, became ON's international distributor. The distribution agreement appeared to be one of short-term convenience for both parties, since Siemens acknowledged that it was developing its own CT scanner. Philips, too, had announced its intention to enter the field.

Internationally, EMI had maintained its basic strategy of going direct to the national market rather than working through local partners or distributors. Although all European sales had originally been handled out of the UK office, it quickly became evident that local servicing staffs were required in most countries. Soon separate subsidiaries were established in most continental European countries, typically with a couple of salesmen, and three or four servicemen. Elsewhere in the world, salesmen were often attached to EMI's existing music organization in that country (e.g., in South Africa, Australia, and Latin America). In Japan, however, EMI signed a distribution agreement with Toshiba which, in October 1975, submitted the largest single order to date: a request for 33 scanners.

EMI in 1976: Strategy and Challenges

EMI'S SITUATION IN 1976

By 1976 the CT scanner business was evolving rapidly, but, as the results indicated, EMI had done extremely well financially (exhibit 10.4). In reviewing developments since the US market entry, the following was clear:

- While smaller competitors had challenged EMI somewhat earlier than might have been expected, none of the big diagnostic imaging companies had brought its scanner to market, even four years after the original EMI scanner announcement.
- While technology was evolving rapidly, the expertise of Hounsfield and his CRL group, and the aggressive reinvestment of much of the early profits in R&D, gave EMI a strong technological position.
- While market size and growth were highly uncertain, the potential was unquestionably much larger than EMI had forecast in their early plans.
- In all, EMI was well established, with a strong and growing sales volume and a good technical reputation. The company was unquestionably the industry leader.

Nonetheless, in the light of all the developments, the strategic tasks facing EMI in 1976 differed considerably from those of earlier years. The following paragraphs outline the most important challenges and problems facing the company in this period.

STRATEGIC PRIORITIES

EMI's first sales priority was to protect its existing highly visible and prestigious customer base from competitors. When its second-generation scanner was introduced in mid-1975, EMI promised to upgrade without charge the first-generation equipment already purchased by its established customers. Although each of these 120 upgrades was estimated to cost EMI $60,000 in components and installation costs, the US sales organization felt that the expense was essential to maintain the confidence and good faith of this important core group of customers.

To maintain its leadership image, the US company also expanded its service organization substantially. Beginning in early 1976, new regional and district sales and service offices were opened with the objective of providing customers with the best service in the industry. A typical annual service contract cost the hospital $40,000 per scanner. By year's end, the company boasted 20 service centers with 150 service engineers – a ratio that represented one serviceman for every two or three machines installed. The sales force by this time had grown to 20, and was much more customer oriented.

Another important task was to improve delivery performance. The interval between order and promised delivery had been lengthening; at the same time, promised delivery dates were often missed. By late 1975, it was not unusual for a 6-month promise to convert into a 12- or 15-month actual delivery time. Fortunately for EMI, all CT manufacturers were in backorder and were offering extended delivery dates. However, EMI's poor performance in meeting promised dates was hurting its reputation. The company responded by substantially expanding its production facilities. By mid-1976 there were six manufacturing locations in the UK, yet because of continuing problems with component suppliers, combined capacity for head and body scanners was estimated at less than 20 units a month.

ORGANIZATIONAL AND PERSONNEL ISSUES

As the US sales organization became increasingly frustrated, they began urging top management to manufacture scanners in North America. Believing that the product had reached the necessary level of maturity, Dr Powell judged that the time was ripe to establish a US plant to handle at least final assembly and test operations. A Northbrook, Illinois site was chosen.

Powell had become EMI's managing director and was more determined than ever to make the new medical electronics business a success. A capable manager was desperately needed to head the business, particularly in view of the rapid developments in the critical North American market. Consequently, Powell was delighted when Normand Provost, who had been his boss at Texas Instruments, contacted him at the Bermuda radiological meeting in March 1975. He was hired with the hope that he could build a stronger, more integrated US company.

With the Northbrook plant scheduled to begin operations by mid-1976, Normand Provost began hiring skilled production personnel. A Northbrook product development center was also a vision of Provost's to allow EMI to draw on US technical expertise and experience in solid state electronics and data processing, and the company began seeking people with strong technological and scientific backgrounds.

Having hired Provost, Dr Powell made several important organizational changes aimed at facilitating the medical electronics business's growth and development. In the UK, he announced the creation of a separate medical electronics group. This allowed the separate operating companies, EMI Medical Ltd (previously known as the X-Ray Systems Division), Pantak (EMI) Ltd, SE Labs (EMI) Ltd, and EMI Meterflow Ltd, to be grouped together under a single group executive, John Willsher. (See figure 10.4.) At last, a more integrated scanner business seemed to be emerging organizationally.

The US sales subsidiary was folded into a new company, EMI Medical Inc., but continued to operate as a separate entity. The intention was to develop this company as an integrated diversified medical electronics operation. Jim Gallagher, the general manager of the US operations, was fired and Bob Hagglund became president of EMI Medical Inc. While Gallagher had been an effective salesman, Powell thought the company needed a more rounded general manager in its next phase of expansion. Hagglund, previously

In mid-1976, the company announced its intention "to protect its inventions and assert its patent strength," and subsequently filed suit against Ohio Nuclear claiming patent infringement. However, at the same time, EMI issued a statement proclaiming that "it was the company's wish to make its pioneering scanner patents available to all under suitable licensing arrangements."

At the annual RSNA meeting in December 1976, sixteen competitors exhibited scanners. The year's new entrants (including CGR, the French X-ray giant; Hitachi from Japan; and G. D. Searle, the US drug and hospital equipment company) were not yet making deliveries, however. The industry's potential production capacity was now estimated to be over 900 units annually.

GE's much-publicized entry was already six months behind their announced delivery date, but it was strongly rumored that production shipments of GE's third-generation scanner were about to begin. EMI Medical Inc. awaited that event with some trepidation. (A summary of major competitors and their situations as of 1976 is presented in table 10.2.)

REGULATORY PROBLEMS

By mid-1976 there were indications that government might try to exert a tighter control over hospital spending in general, and purchase of CT scanners in particular.

The rapidly escalating cost of healthcare had been a political issue for years, and the National Health Planning and Resources Development Act of 1974 required states to control the development of costly or unnecessary health services through a mechanism known as the Certificate of Need (CON) procedure. If they wished to qualify for Medicare or Medicaid reimbursements, healthcare facilities were required to submit documentation to their state's department of health to justify major capital expenditures (typically in excess of $100,000).

Before 1976, the CON procedures had generally been merely an administrative impediment to the process of selling a scanner, delaying but not preventing the authorization of funds. However, by 1976, the cost of medical care represented 8 percent of the gross national product and Jimmy Carter made control of the "skyrocketing costs of healthcare" a major campaign issue. One of the most frequently cited examples of waste was the proliferation of CT scanners. It was argued that this $500,000 device had become a symbol of prestige and sophistication in the medical community, so that every institution wanted its own scanner, even if a neighboring facility had one that was grossly underutilized.

In response to heightened public awareness of the issue, five states declared a moratorium on the purchase of new scanners, including California, which had accounted for over 20 percent of total US scanner placements to date. In November, Jimmy Carter was elected president.

ORGANIZATIONAL PROBLEMS

Perhaps most troublesome to Dr Powell were the organizational problems. Tensions within the EMI organization had been developing for some time, centering on the issues

Table 10.2 Selected competitive data

Company	Product line	Price	Delivery (months)	Company strengths/weaknesses
EMI	2nd generation Head and body 20 second scan Multiple models for various applications 320 × 320 pixels 2nd generation	$395 K (head) $550 K (body) 20% deposit	10	Original innovator – some base in ultrasound $10 M per annum in R&D $1.2 B sales: $85 M in medical Strong service base Modular product line Strong customer base Rapid follower
Ohio Nuclear	Head and body 20 second scan 256 × 256 pixels	$385 K (head) $525 K (body) 20% deposit	10	R&D increased to $8–10 M per annum Technicare sales $100 M; scanners 50% Had nuclear; acquired ultrasound co. Strong marketing
Pfizer	1st generation (announced 2nd generation) Head and body 30+ second scan 3rd generation	$295 K (head) $475 K (body) $25 K deposit	9	Acquired technology – slow developing Company sales $1.6 B; scanners 2% No other diagnostic imaging Strong R&D capability
General Electric	Head and body 3 second scan 320 × 320 pixels	$315 K (head) $595 K (body) $15 K with order $75 K on mfg. start	15	Leader in diagnostic imaging (X-ray, nuclear, entering ultrasound) $16 B sales: Medical Systems $400 M Very strong sales and service base
Picker	Hybrid 3rd generation (announced) Body only 20 second (est.) Expected on market mid-1977	$550 K	10–12	Good design and development skills Late entrant – but strong performance expected Leader in X-ray, nuclear, and ultrasound Strong marketing and service base $300 M sales

of manufacturing and product design. Managers in the US company felt that they had little control over manufacturing schedules and little input into product design, despite the fact that they were responsible for 80 percent of corporate scanner sales. In their view, the company's current market position was being eroded by the worsening manufacturing delivery performance from the UK, while its longer-term prospects were threatened by the competitive challenges to EMI's technological leadership.

Although the Northbrook plant had been completed in late 1976, US managers were still not satisfied they had the necessary control over production. Arguing that the quality of subassemblies and components shipped from the UK was deteriorating and delivery promises were becoming even more unreliable, they began investigating alternative supply sources in the US.

UK-based manufacturing managers felt that much of the responsibility for backlogs lay with the product engineers and the sales organizations. Their unreliable sales forecasts and constantly changing design specifications had severely disrupted production schedules. The worst bottlenecks involved outside suppliers and subcontractors that were unable to gear up and down overnight. Complete systems could be held up for weeks or months awaiting a single simple component.

As the Northbrook plant became increasingly independent, US managers sensed that the UK plants felt less responsibility for them. In tight supply situations they felt there was a tendency to ship to European or other export customers first. Some US managers also believed that components were increasingly shipped from UK plants without the same rigid final checks they normally received. The assumption was that the US could do their own QC checking, it was asserted. Both these assertions were strongly denied by the English group.

Nonetheless, Bob Hagglund soon began urging Dr Powell to let EMI Medical Inc. become a more independent manufacturing operation rather than simply a final assembly plant for UK components. This prospect disturbed John Willsher, managing director of EMI Medical Ltd, who argued that dividing manufacturing operations could mean duplicating overhead and spreading existing expertise too thin. Others felt that the "bootleg development" of alternative supply sources showed a disrespect for the "center of excellence" concept, and could easily compromise the ability of Pantak (X-ray technology) and SE Labs (displays) to remain at the forefront of technology.

Product development issues also created some organizational tension. The US sales organization knew that GE's impressive new third-generation "fan beam" scanner would soon be ready for delivery, and found customers hesitant to commit to EMI's new CT 5005 until the GE product came out. For months telexes had been flowing from Northbrook to EMI's Central Research Laboratories asking if drastic reductions in scan time might be possible to meet the GE threat.

Meanwhile, scientists at CRL felt that US CT competition was developing into a specifications war based on the wrong issue, scan time. Shorter elapsed times meant less image blurring, but in the trade-off between scan time and picture resolution, EMI engineers had preferred to concentrate on better-quality images. They felt that the 20-second scan offered by EMI scanners made practical sense since a patient could typically hold his breath that long while being diagnosed.

CRL staff were exploring some entirely new imaging concepts and hoped to have a completely new scanning technology ready to market in three or four years.

Dr Hounsfield had conducted experiments with the fan beam concept in the early 1970s and was skeptical of its ability to produce good-quality images. To use sodium iodide detectors similar to those in existing scanners would be cost prohibitive in the large numbers necessary to pick up a broad scan; to use other materials such as xenon gas would lead to quality and stability problems, in Hounsfield's view. Since GE and others offering third-generation equipment had not yet delivered commercial machines, he felt little incentive to redirect his staff to these areas already researched and rejected.

There were many other demands on the time and attention of Hounsfield and his staff, all of which seemed important for the company. They were in constant demand by technicians to deal with major problems that arose that nobody else could solve. Sales people wanted him to talk to their largest and most prestigious customers, since a visit by Dr Hounsfield could often swing an important sale. They were also involved in internal training on all new products. The scientific community wanted them to present papers and give lectures. And increasingly, Dr Hounsfield found himself in a public relations role as he accepted honors from all over the globe. The impact was to greatly enhance EMI's reputation and to reinforce its image as the leader in the field.

When it appeared that CRL was unwilling or unable to make the product changes the US organization felt it needed, Hagglund made the bold proposal that the newly established research laboratories in Northbrook take responsibility for developing a three- to five-second-scan "fan beam"-type scanner. Dr Powell agreed to study the suggestion, but was finding it difficult to evaluate the relative merits of the US subsidiary's views and the CRL scientists' opinions.

By year's end, Dr Powell had still been unable to find anybody to take charge of the worldwide medical electronics business. By default, the main decision-making forum became the Medical Group Review Committee (MGRC), a group of key line and staff managers which met, monthly at first, to help establish and review strategic decisions.

Among the issues discussed by this committee were the manufacturing and product development decisions that had produced tensions between the US and UK managers. Powell had hoped that the MGRC would help build communications and consensus among his managers, but it soon became evident that this goal was unrealistic. In the words of one manager close to the events:

> The problem was there was no mutual respect between managers with similar responsibilities. Medical Ltd was resentful of Medical Inc.'s push for greater independence, and were not going to go out of their way to help the Americans succeed.

As the business grew larger and more complex, Dr Powell's ability to act both as corporate CEO and head of the worldwide medical business diminished. Increasingly, he was forced to rely on the MGRC to address operating problems as well as strategic issues. The coordination problem became so complex that, by early 1977, there were four subcommittees of the MGRC, each with representatives of the US and UK organizations, and each meeting monthly on one side of the Atlantic or the other. Committees included Manufacturing and Operations, Product Planning and Resources, Marketing and Sales Programs, and Service and Spares.

POWELL'S PROBLEMS

As the new year opened, Dr Powell reviewed EMI's medical electronics business. How well was it positioned? Where were the major threats and opportunities? What were the key issues he should deal with in 1977? Which should he tackle first, and how?

These were the issues he turned over in his mind as he prepared to note down his plans for 1977.

Rivalry in Video Games

Robert M. Grant

In May 2002, the video games industry was entering into the growth phase of a new cycle of expansion stimulated by the launch of 128-bit video games consoles. This was the fifth such cycle since the late 1970s, each of them associated with a new generation of technology. With each cycle, the industry had surpassed its previous sales peak. Industry forecasts suggested that the fifth-generation 128-bit machines would be no exception – worldwide sales of video games consoles were expected to peak at around 45 million in 2003. However, the major part of the industry's revenues – and virtually all of its profit – was generated by software. The production of video games software had emerged as one of the most important and profitable aspects of the entertainment industry. With retail sales increasing from about $15 billion in 2001 to $19 billion in 2003, the games software industry was comparable in revenues to the motion picture industry.

For the three main players in the industry, the key issue was how revenues and profits would be split among them. Sony had taken an early lead in new generation of 128-bit consoles, and its PlayStation2 was well positioned to repeat the dominance that its original PlayStation had achieved in the previous generation of 32- and 64-bit machines. However, by the summer of 2002 its continued market dominance was far from assured. Nintendo, with its powerful reputation among younger video games enthusiasts and its proven ability to create blockbuster games (*Super Mario Brothers, Zelda, Gran Turismo,* and *Pokémon*) was competing ferociously to take market share from Sony. In the meantime, newcomer Microsoft had launched the world's most powerful games console – the Xbox with massive computing power and graphics capability and equipped with broadband connections to allow fully interactive games playing.

The intensity of competition between the players was strongly influenced by the history of the industry. In every previous generation of machines, one company had successfully dominated the world market and had scooped the major part of the industry profit pool – the only exception being the third-generation 16-bit machines in which Sega and Nintendo had split the world market. Escalating development costs for both hardware and software would reinforce this tendency for video games to be a "winner-take-all" industry. Already Sega had exited the hardware market, its Saturn and Dreamcast machines having failed to establish viable market shares.

Yet, despite all the advantages of market leadership, the technological and creative dynamism of the industry had resulted in transitions of market leadership. Nintendo had taken over from Atari, Sony had displaced Sega and Nintendo. The key issue for Nintendo and Microsoft was to understand how to harness the forces of change – new technology, consumers' desire for novel games, and the complementarities between hardware and software – in strategies that would confer competitive advantage in the new product cycle. For Sony, the critical issue was how it could best exploit the advantages of incumbency – a vast installed base and massive library of games titles – to thwart the ambitions of the old challenger, Nintendo, and the new warrior, Microsoft.

Critical Issue

■ ATARI AND THE 4-BIT GAMES MACHINES: 1972–85 ■

The home video games market emerged during the late 1970s. Its origins lay in the video games machines designed for amusement arcades. The first of these electronic arcade video games was *Pong*, created by Nolan Bushnell in 1972. With $500, Bushnell and a friend formed Atari to market the game. This simple coin-operated table-tennis game caught on in bars and arcades, but Atari's failure to establish effective patent and trademark protection resulted in a flood of imitators. By 1973, Atari held 10 percent of the new video game industry, and the rest of the market was shared among the followers.

Meanwhile, several companies, including Magnavox, had developed home video game consoles with a few preprogrammed games, but these dedicated machines attracted little consumer interest. Atari itself introduced a home version of its *Pong* machine in 1975. The key innovation that permitted the development of the home video market was Fairfield's release of Channel F, the first home video game system to accept interchangeable cartridges. Interchangeable cartridges allowed games consoles to become versatile machines capable of playing a variety of games. Nolan Bushnell saw the potential of games consoles with interchangeable cartridges. Two months after the release of Channel F, he sold Atari to Warner Communications for $27 million to give him the financial backing required to develop and launch a new home games machine. In 1977, Atari (now a division of Warner) released its 2600 home video games console at a retail price of $200. The release of *Space Invaders* (1979) and *Pac-Man* (1981) unleashed a craze for video games. In 1982, both games were transferred from arcades to the Atari 2600: sales skyrocketed. During 1982 Atari held almost 80 percent share of the video game market.

However, competition in both hardware and software intensified in 1982. Mattel had entered the industry with its Intellivision system in late 1979, Coleco introduced ColecoVision, and former Atari employees set up Activision. Like the Atari 2600, all these competing consoles were 4-bit machines. During 1982, 20 new suppliers of Atari-compatible cartridges entered the market and 350 new game titles were released in that year. Atari was unable to prevent independent software developers from marketing games for the Atari 2600, though Atari was able to collect a royalty. The market became oversupplied, forcing software manufacturers with slow-selling game titles to liquidate their inventories at closeout prices during 1983 and 1984: on some games, prices were slashed from $40 to $4. Meanwhile, consumer interest was shifting from video games to personal computers. The collapse of sales forced Atari into burying truckloads of unsold video game cartridges in the Arizona desert, forcing parent Warner Communications to report a $539 million loss on its consumer electronics business in 1983. In 1984 Warner Communications and Mattel were driven to the brink of bankruptcy by the losses of their video game subsidiaries. Warner sold its Atari division that year, and in 1985 both Mattel and Coleco announced they were exiting the video game business. Industry sales of video games collapsed from $3 billion in 1982 to $100 million in 1985.

■ NINTENDO AND THE 8-BIT ERA: 1986–91 ■

Nintendo was established in 1889 in Kyoto, Japan as a playing card manufacturer. In 1922, Hiroshi Yamauchi, the great-grandson of Nintendo's founder, became the company's president at the age of 22 and led Nintendo's expansion into the toy business. In 1975, Yamauchi encouraged Nintendo's entry into video games, initially through licensing Magnavox's system. In 1983, Nintendo released the 8-bit Famicom home video system that used interchangeable cartridges. The ¥24,000 ($100) machine sold 500,000 units in Japan during its first two months.

In 1980, Nintendo established Nintendo of America to enter the $8 billion-a-year US arcade business. After a slow start, Nintendo had a hit in 1981 with *Donkey Kong*, created by Nintendo's legendary game developer, Sigeru Miyamota. In the fall of 1985, Nintendo test-marketed Famicom, which was renamed the Nintendo Entertainment System (NES), in New York. Despite the widespread belief that home video game systems were a fad that had seen its day, Nintendo sold over a million units in the US during its first year. By the end of 1987, three million games had been sold. *Legend of Zelda* became the first game to sell over a million copies and then, in 1986, *Super Mario Brothers* was launched, a game that would eventually sell 40 million copies worldwide. Miyamota developed both games. By 1988, Nintendo had an 80 percent market share of the $2.3 billion US video game industry. In 1989, Nintendo expanded its market with the launch of GameBoy, a portable video game system.

However, Nintendo learned a valuable lesson from Atari's failure: it was important to control the supply of the game cartridges to ensure quality and prevent fierce price competition. To this end, Nintendo required its game developers to follow strict rules regarding the creation and release of new games for its NES game players. Prior to release, Nintendo had to approve the content of a game. Every games cartridge incorporated a "security chip" that permitted it to operate on the Nintendo console. Nintendo controlled all manufacturing of cartridges and charged its independent games developers a 20 percent royalty and a manufacturing fee of $14 per cartridge (the subcontracted cost of manufacture to Nintendo was $7). The minimum order was 10,000 cartridges for the Japanese market and 50,000 for the US market – paid in advance.

Licensees were charged about twice the cost of manufacturing. Cartridges were delivered to licensees at the shipping dock at Kobe, Japan, and then distribution became the licensees' responsibility. Licensees were also limited to developing five NES games a year and could not release an NES game on a competing system for a period of two years. By 1983 only 30 percent of the NES cartridges sold were games developed by Nintendo; the rest were from licensed third-party developers.

Nintendo's stranglehold over its software developers resulted in the huge success of its NES console, but also reflected its massive marketing and distribution effort. Its advertising, which amounted to 2 percent of sales, was closely linked to new game releases. Its monthly magazine, *Nintendo Power*, had a readership of 6 million. Its retail presence was huge – in 1989, Nintendo products amounted to 20 percent of total US spending on toys and games. Retail distribution was tightly controlled. New games were released according to a carefully designed schedule and were quickly withdrawn once interest began to wane. Nintendo typically restricted shipments of its most popular games, and discouraged its retailers from carrying competitive products.

Between 1984 and 1992, Nintendo's sales rose from $286 million to $4,417 million. By 1990, one-third of US and Japanese households owned an NES and in both countries its share of the home video console market exceeded 90 percent. Nintendo's return on equity over the period was 23.1 percent – far above the average for large Japanese companies, while its stock market value exceeded that of both Sony and Nissan during most of 1990–1. Table 11.1 shows the sales of Nintendo and other manufacturers since 1990.

■ SEGA AND THE 16-BIT ERA: 1992–5 ■

Sega Enterprises Ltd (Sega) is a Japanese company founded by Americans. In 1951, two Americans in Tokyo, Raymond Lemaire and Richard Stewart, began importing jukeboxes to supply American military bases in Japan. In 1965, their company merged with Rosen Enterprises, founded by David Rosen, a former US airman who had been stationed in Japan. Not happy with the game machines available from US manufacturers, Rosen decided to make his own. The company's first hit was a submarine warfare arcade game called Periscope. Sega was acquired by Gulf & Western in 1969 and went public in 1974. Hayao Nakayama, a Japanese entrepreneur and former Sega distributor, was recruited to head Sega's Japanese operation; Rosen headed the US operation. During the video games industry's boom period of the 1970s and early 1980s, Sega's revenues grew rapidly, reaching $214 million in 1982. With the video game slump, Gulf & Western were keen to sell, and Nakayama and Rosen bought Sega's assets for $38 million in 1984, thus forming Sega Enterprises Ltd. The deal was backed by CSK, a large Japanese software company that in 1998 owned 20 percent of Sega. Nakayama became the chief executive, and Rosen headed the US subsidiary. Sega went public in 1986.

Like Nintendo, Sega had migrated from arcade games to home games; however, in Japan, Sega's 8-bit Master System lagged well behind Nintendo's Famicom. The US story was similar. Sega launched Master System in the US in 1986, but despite better graphics than Nintendo's NES, Sega achieved only a 15 percent market share. In Europe,

Table 11.1 US retail sales of hardware and software by console type, 1990–2001 ($, millions)

	1990	1991	1992	1993	1994	1995	1996	1997	1998	1999	2000	2001
Nintendo												
NintendoES	2,904	1,833	720	370	102	34	15	–	–	–	–	–
Super NES	–	560	1,733	1,890	1,471	823	514	243	137	20	0	–
N64	–	–	–	–	–	–	490	1,690	2,032	1,887	1,532	804
GameCube	–	–	–	–	–	–	–	–	–	–	–	–
Sega												
Genesis	280	586	1,090	1,706	1,490	719	294	180	0	0	–	–
Game Gear	–	91	162	219	318	135	77	34	13	0	–	–
Sega CD	–	–	61	232	215	30	0	–	–	–	–	–
32-X	–	–	–	–	107	63	0	–	–	–	–	–
Saturn	–	–	–	–	–	140	368	311	148	0	0	–
Dreamcast	–	–	–	–	–	–	–	–	–	1,160	820	182
Sony												
PlayStation	–	–	–	–	–	375	1,254	2,525	3,161	2,882	2,087	1,157
PlayStation2	–	–	–	–	–	–	–	–	–	–	493	3,762
Microsoft												
X-box	–	–	–	–	–	–	–	–	–	–	–	540
Other												
Atari Lynx	32	40	32	13	3	–	–	–	0	–	–	–
Atari Jaguar	–	–	–	7	64	52	0	0	0	0	–	–
3DO-based	–	–	–	29	238	252	24	0	50	50	10	0
Phillips CD-I	–	–	49	78	64	54	138	21	0	0	–	–
Total hardware & software	3,216	3,110	3,847	4,534	4,066	2,686	3,174	5,004	5,541	5,999	4,942	6,445
Sales composition												
Hardware	31%	37%	40%	37%	34%	34%	43%	43%	36%	22%	32%	46%
Software	69%	63%	60%	63%	66%	66%	57%	57%	64%	78%	68%	54%
Total	100%	100%	100%	100%	100%	100%	100%	100%	100%	100%	100%	100%

Sources: IDC, Gerard Klauer Mattison & Co., and case writer estimates.

where Nintendo sales had been slow to take off, Sega did better and Sega of Europe accounted for a large share of Sega's revenues.

In October 1988, Sega introduced its 16-bit Mega Drive home video system in Japan. Despite superior graphics and sound to the existing 8-bit systems and support from several of its arcade games, only 200,000 units were sold in the first year. In September 1989, the system, now renamed Genesis, was launched in the US priced at $190 with games selling at between $40 and $70. This was 16 months before Nintendo released its 16-bit Super NES player. In June 1991, Sega launched its *Sonic the Hedgehog* game and began bundling the game with its Genesis player.

The success of *Sonic* together with an advertising campaign built around the slogan "Genesis does what Nintendon't" established Sega's Genesis as the cool alternative to the Nintendo NES. In addition, Sega targeted a broader market than Nintendo, directing its appeal to adults as well as teenagers. The result was a surge of independent software developers who began writing games for Sega. By September 1991 there were 130 software titles available for the Genesis. Sega's licensing terms were similar to those of Nintendo, but there was no exclusivity clause and Sega's royalty charge was higher than Nintendo's – around $20 per cartridge. Support by games developers and retailers for Sega's Genesis was partly a result of the unpopularity that Nintendo had generated through its allegedly monopolistic practices.

Nintendo launched its 16-bit machine, the Nintendo Super-NES, in September 1991. It modified its licensing terms with games developers to match those of Sega: it raised its fees to $20 a cartridge and abandoned its exclusivity clause.

Despite Nintendo's huge installed base, brand awareness, and extensive distribution, the 16-bit market represented a new competitive arena where Sega was able to offer a wider variety of 16-bit games titles: by January 1993, Sega's library of 16-bit titles totaled 320, compared with 130 for Nintendo. During 1992–6, the two companies split the US market almost evenly. Elsewhere, the picture varied. In Japan, Nintendo held a commanding market position over Sega with the Super NES outselling Genesis by about nine to one. Nintendo maintained its market leadership in Europe – but barely. Sega was a market leader in several European countries and was a close follower in several others.

■ THE SONY PLAYSTATION AND THE 32/64-BIT GENERATION: 1995–8 ■

Established in Japan in May 1946, Sony Corporation emerged during the 1970s and 1980s as one of the world's most successful and innovative consumer electronics companies. In 1990, Sony began developing a 32-bit games machine that utilized software stored on CD-ROMs. Sony introduced its PlayStation in the Japanese market in December 1994 and in the US in September 1995. The European launch did not occur until the spring of 1997.

In the new generation of 32-bit video games using CD-ROM software, Sega was able to beat Sony to market. Sega's Saturn was launched in Japan a month before PlayStation, and in the US it had a three-month lead over PlayStation. Nevertheless, it was Sony that quickly became the market leader in the new generation of machines. Prior to its launch, Sony had built a large library of games titles. It had courted the top games developers, to the point of contributing financially for developing games on the Play-Station, and offering a broad range of game development tools, designing its hardware to facilitate game development.

Sony's ability to gain the support of both developers and retailers was also a result of Sony's stature and credibility. Despite Sony's lack of history in video game hardware or software, the company was considered a formidable competitor because of its global distribution capability, brand awareness, and the content potential of the movie libraries of Columbia Pictures and Tri-Star Entertainment (both Sony subsidiaries). Sony made few mistakes in launching its PlayStation: it came to market with a wider range of quality games, well-planned distribution, and a massive advertising budget.

By contrast, Sega, despite its solid reputation among video game consumers and its well-known brand, suffered from the ill-coordinated product launch of its Saturn system. Only a handful of game titles were available at the launch, the supply of machines was limited by lack of manufacturing capacity, and distribution was haphazard. Sony's machine attracted such a huge early following that Sega could not recover. Sega's US sales were sluggish throughout 1996 and 1997. At the end of 1997, Saturn had an estimated total installed base of fewer than 2 million units. Almost no third-party licensees published titles exclusively on the Saturn, and very few planned to publish any new titles for the Saturn system. Saturn's market failure was attributed to its comparatively high launch price, its lack of blockbuster exclusive titles, and a development system that many developers felt was inferior to that of the PlayStation. To bolster the declining market share of its Saturn player, Sega instituted rebate and incentive programs. Sega stopped marketing the Saturn in the United States in the spring of 1997.

Meanwhile, Nintendo attempted to recapture market leadership by leapfrogging Sony in technology. The N-64 system launched in Japan in May 1996, in the US in September 1996, and in Europe in the spring of 1997 used a 64-bit processor. One of its launch games – *Super Mario 64* – was acclaimed as one of the best games ever developed, while the James Bond game, *GoldenEye*, was a major draw that attracted customers to the N-64. Unlike Sony, Nintendo stuck with cartridges instead of CD-ROMs. Although this permitted cheaper hardware, it resulted in lower margins for developers and made distribution more cumbersome. Nintendo games were priced $15 to $20 above those of PlayStation games.

There was little doubt as to the winner of this competitive battle. Sony achieved market share leadership in Japan, the United States, and Europe. In early 1998, Sony's game division had sold more than 33 million PlayStation game players worldwide, along with 236 million games CDs. PlayStation was one of Sony's greatest product successes in its history.

From a consumer standpoint, Sony PlayStation's most attractive features (compared to those of Nintendo's N-64) were its lower software costs and greater library of titles. The average PlayStation title retailed for less than $45, whereas N-64 titles averaged close to $60. Hardware prices were comparable at $150.

From a software developer's point of view, the PlayStation system had both advantages and disadvantages. On the positive side, the manufacturing cost of PlayStation CD-ROMs was far lower than that of N-64 cartridges, and CD-ROMs containing a

Table 11.2 Relative costs: PlayStation and Nintendo 64, 1997

	PlayStation $	Nintendo 64 $
Hardware		
Graphics subsystem	35.83	29.11
Central electronics	51.51	78.16
Audio subsystem	25.71	10.02
Card MVA	16.27	10.98
CD-ROM subsystem	48.50	–
PCB	12.09	2.55
Other	23.54	29.10
Total	213.45	159.92
Software		
Cost to software	12.00	34.00
developer, of which:		
manufacturing cost	1.50	12.00
royalty fee	7.50	19.00
developer's variable cost	3.00	3.00
Wholesale price	30.00	45.00
Retail price	40.00	60.00

Source: CIBC Oppenheimer.

PlayStation video game could be pressed and shipped to retailers in much less time than Nintendo cartridges (which were made in Japan). Furthermore, N-64 cartridges had to be paid for at the time of order placement. The longer lead times for getting N-64 cartridges on retailer shelves also meant greater inventory and sales risks for Nintendo game developers. It was difficult to judge how quickly a title would sell, particularly in the case of newly introduced games. To keep from losing out on sales and from disgruntling both retailers and consumers, publishers of Nintendo games were motivated to order larger quantities in order to avoid retailer stock-outs of what might prove to be a popular-selling title. In contrast, retailers could normally be resupplied with additional copies of hot-selling PlayStation titles within a matter of days (the packaging and booklets took longer to complete than the CD pressing). If a PlayStation's title didn't sell well, no additional discs had to be pressed, and the costs associated with slow-selling inventories were minimized. Table 11.2 shows cost comparisons between PlayStation and the N-64 for both software and hardware.

Most software publishers liked developing PlayStation games because of their lower prices and short production lead times, features which gave them a lower break-even point for recovering development costs – the estimated break-even point for the N-64 was 190,000 units, versus 172,000 units for the PlayStation.

In terms of gaining the support of third-party developers, the competitive disadvantages Nintendo faced from higher cartridge costs and longer lead times to supply retailers had to be balanced against the advantages afforded by Nintendo's strategy of restricting the number of its game titles. Sony's PlayStation had over 300 titles vying

Table 11.3 Worldwide sales of 32-, 64-, and 128-bit hardware systems, 1994–2000 (millions of units)

	1994	1995	1996	1997	1998	1999	2000
Unit sales							
United States	–	1.0	4.8	11.8	13.5	9.0	7.3
Europe	–	0.6	1.9	4.4	6.4	6.4	4.7
Japan	0.8	3.6	6.6	7.0	6.9	6.6	5.1
Rest of world	0.0	0.3	0.8	1.5	1.9	2.0	1.8
Total	0.8	5.4	14.1	24.7	28.7	23.9	18.9
Cumulative installed base							
United States	–	1.0	5.8	17.6	31.1	40.1	47.5
Europe	–	0.6	2.4	6.9	13.2	19.6	24.3
Japan	0.8	4.4	11.0	18.0	24.9	31.4	36.5
Rest of world	0.0	0.3	1.1	2.6	4.6	6.6	8.4
Total	0.8	6.2	20.3	45.0	73.7	97.6	116.7

Sources: Gerard Klauer Mattison & Co., and IDC.

for shelf space. It was estimated that the average N-64 title sold over 400,000 units in 1997 whereas the average PlayStation game had sales of just over 69,000 copies. Hence, software developers had the potential to make more profit from a successful N-64 game than from a successful PlayStation game. Sony's ability to offer a vast library of titles for the PlayStation, assisted by its high ratio of games sold per console (called the *tie ratio*), was increasing. The PlayStation had a particularly attractive tie ratio (from a game developer's perspective). PlayStation's tie ratio was estimated to be 5.82:1 in 1997 and grew to about 6.40:1 in 1998. This compared to tie ratios of less than 5:1 for older systems during their prime and a 2.55:1 ratio for the N-64 titles.

In June 1997, in an effort to combat the cost disadvantage of its cartridges, Nintendo began cutting the prices it charged third-party licensees for N-64 cartridges from over $30 to as low as $21. Nintendo management believed that N-64's rapidly growing installed base and recently reduced software prices would attract more game developers and publishers. The fierce competition between Sony and Nintendo fueled further expansion in the market. During 1997 and 1998, worldwide sales of video games consoles reached unprecedented levels. (See table 11.3.)

■ THE BATTLE FOR THE 128-BIT GENERATION ■

The Sega Dreamcast

The failure of Saturn was a massive blow for Sega. During 1998, Sega began work on its Dreamcast games system, which it hoped would give it market leadership in the new generation of 128-bit machines. The key to Sega's strategy was to be first to market with a new 128-bit console, thus leapfrogging Sony and Nintendo in technology. By using PC-based technology for its hardware, Sega aimed to make it easy for game developers to create games for Dreamcast, and facilitate new versions of existing PC-based games. The company also wanted to pioneer Internet-based interactivity.

Dreamcast was launched in Japan at the end of 1998. A major feature of Dreamcast was in permitting interactive games playing through the Internet. The launch was seen as Sega's last chance: "This is the last roll of the dice for Sega. If it doesn't work it will have to pull out of the sector," said Stuart Dinsey of trade magazine *MCV*. Nick Gibson of stock broking and consulting firm Durlacher added: "Sega has to make this work; it has no contingency plans. It is heavily in debt to fund the marketing." The development and launch of Dreamcast strained Sega's financial resources to the limit. In the year to March, Sega made a net loss of ¥45 bn ($490 m) and was forced to cut costs, including the elimination of 1,000 jobs.

Sega's president, Shoichiro Irimajiri, set a target for Dreamcast at half the global market. This was seen as an ambitious goal, given Sega's 1998 market share of less than 5 percent of the world market coupled with Sony's brand strength. "PlayStation is an unbelievably strong brand; that's taken a lot of work and a lot of cash. It has done incredibly well and could sell even more this year than last. If Sony does its job properly it can keep PlayStation hot," said Stuart Dinsey. To undermine the impact of the Dreamcast launch, Sony provided advance publicity about its new version of PlayStation (PlayStation2). In particular, it emphasized Playstation2's technological superiority to Dreamcast (especially its use of DVD technology) and its backward compatibility (allowing consumers to use their existing PlayStation software).

Failure to produce adequate games had tripped up Sega in the past; it was a key factor in Saturn's failure: "The fact that there's a new machine with 128 bits is irrelevant to consumers to a large extent. Sega needs a killer application such as PlayStation's Lara Croft – and Sonic is not so sexy. It needs to woo developers to support the platform, something Sony has worked hard to do," said Jeremy Dale, commercial and marketing Director at Nintendo.

In Japan, Dreamcast achieved sales of 900,000 units by March 1999, just short of its target of a million. During 1999, Dreamcast was launched in both North America and Europe. In both regions, Dreamcast was able to establish a strong market foothold. With Sonic playing a prominent role in Sega's marketing, Sega's US market share of game machines grew to 15% in the fourth quarter of 1999 from just 0.1% a year before. Meanwhile, Nintendo and Sony lost ground: Sony dropped to a 53% market share, from 63% a year earlier; Nintendo (excluding GameBoy) slipped to a 32% share from 37%. Sega even exceeded its own expectations: it sold 1.5 million of its $199 Dreamcast machines and 4.5 million games in the US market in the last quarter of 1999 – garnering some $523 million in revenue. In software, Sony had 64% market share, the same as a year before, Nintendo had 29% market share compared with 35% in the previous year, while Sega had 7.1% compared with 0.6% a year earlier.

Yet, despite Dreamcast's successful launch, it was not the savior that Sega had hoped for. Its technical advances were significant; nevertheless, the advantages of 128-bit over 64-bit technology were much less evident than the advantages of 32-bit over 16-bit. As a result, PlayStation continued to sell strongly long after Dreamcast hit the market. In the fourth quarter of 1999, 3.3 million PlayStations were sold in North America compared with 3.9 million in fourth quarter 1998. Moreover, despite its lead in the new generation of machines, Dreamcast was always overshadowed by the hype and expectation that surrounded the forthcoming launch of PlayStation2.

PlayStation2

The launch of PlayStation2 on March 4, 2000 was the most eagerly anticipated event in the history of the Japanese consumer electronics industry. By 7 A.M. in the morning of the launch, lines of eager games enthusiasts formed outside Sony dealers and, in several instances, police had been called to control the would-be buyers. In 48 hours, all one million PlayStation2s were sold, ten times the number sold when the original PlayStation was released.

Ken Kutaragi, the maverick engineer who was the driving force behind Sony's entry into video games, had masterminded the design of PlayStation2. In the summer of 1996, Kutargari had assembled a team of engineers from Sony and its manufacturing partner, Toshiba, and asked them to design a games machine with performance that exceeded any PC and with graphics processing power ten times that of the original PlayStation.

At ¥39,800, PlayStation2 was a 128-bit machine offering cinematic-style graphics, a DVD player capable of showing films, and the potential for Internet connectivity. Nobuyuki Idei, Sony's president, aimed to make the PlayStation2 the main mechanism for consumers to access the Internet, offering online games, e-commerce, email, and the ability to download music, software, and video. As Kazuo Hirai, president of Sony US, enthused, "PlayStation 2 is not the future of video games entertainment, it is the future of entertainment, period." However, initially, PlayStation2 did not include a modem, a mistake according to Sega's president Shoichiro Irimajiri. Sony's Idei countered that modem technology was moving so fast that it was better to sell them as add-ons.

PS2 represented a huge investment for Sony. The company invested $1 billion in two plants, one a joint venture with Toshiba to make the main central processing unit (the "Emotion Engine"), and another to manufacture the graphics synthesizer. But the marketing expenses incurred in the global rollout of PS2 would dwarf investment in technology and manufacturing plants. Given these investments, and PS2's low price, analysts were forecasting that it would not be until 2002 that Sony's games division would exceed the ¥136 bn record operating profits it achieved in 1998. However, Sony was confident that the business model underlying its original PlayStation remained sound. "The great thing about the games console business is that products last for three years," said Mr. Idei. "In the world of the PC, a product is doing well if it lasts three months. With the PlayStation2 we have lots of time to recoup our investment." The product provided two profit streams: those generated by the sale of the console (the original PlayStation sold 71 million units) and the much bigger profit stream from software (Dresdner Kleinwort Benson estimated that almost half of Sony's ¥255 billion operating profit for 2000 would derive from games software). PS2 also offered the possibility of a third revenue stream: online usage.

Despite massive investments and careful planning, the launch of the PS2 was far from smooth. Shortages of two key components – the graphics synthesizer (made by Sony) and the "Emotion Engine" central processor – resulted in a shortage of PS2s for the critical US Christmas shopping period. PS2 was also handicapped by a shortage of software. The power and sophistication of PS2, together with a number of technical quirks, meant that it was a difficult machine for which to develop games. Hence, most of the early PS2 games were revisions of earlier titles.

Sega's Response

Despite good sales of Dreamcast in North America and Europe, as the launch of Sony's PlayStation2 approached, Sega's sales in Japan began to decline. Although Sega sold two million Dreamcast consoles in Japan between its launch in November 1998 and the first quarter of 2000, Sony sold 1.8 million PlayStation2s in just two months. During the first half of 2000, pessimism grew over Sega's prospects. Its share price more than halved between February and June 2000 and rumors circulated that Shoichiro Irimajiri, Sega's president, would resign because of the poor performance.

Facing the prospect of becoming an also-ran in the video game machine market, Sega initiated a bold new plan to grab market share: give away the hardware. Starting in August, Sega offered its Dreamcast console at no charge. The offer was available to customers who subscribed to a new Sega web service for two years at $21.95 a month. Customers who already owned a Dreamcast would get a free keyboard and a $200 check if they subscribed. Sega was betting on spurring revenues from software and Internet service: "We may give up $400 million in hardware revenue," said Peter Moore, Marketing VP at Sega of America, "but with two-year service contracts we can make $1 billion in Internet service-provider revenue." The key issue for Sega was whether sufficient numbers of game players wanted to hook their machines to their television sets and cruise the web. Despite the hype about accessing the web with video games consoles, the primary medium for the Internet is still the personal computer.

During summer 2000, Sega established Sega.com, an independent company headed by Brad Huang, a 35-year-old whiz kid and former hedge-fund manager who pitched the strategy to Sega Chairman Isao Okawa a year earlier. Sega's online-gaming web site, SegaNet, made its debut in August 2000. The web site provided Sega with a portal to the Internet and a gathering place for Sega fans, permitting Sega to sell space to other advertisers. Eventually, Sega hoped to provide games for which it would be able to charge a premium monthly fee. Gamers with Dreamcast consoles would be able to use any Internet service provider to access the SegaNet site. But Sega hoped to persuade them to sign up for its high-speed service, which would be provided by GTE Corp.'s GTE internetworking unit.

Sega's vision of using Internet connectivity as a basis to wrest market share from Sony was never fulfilled. By the fall of 2000, Sega's sales revenues were slipping, losses were mounting, and the company was carrying a debt burden of $500 million. In October 2000, Sega threw in the towel. It announced its withdrawal from video games hardware in order to concentrate upon games software.

Nintendo: the GameCube

Meanwhile, Nintendo continued fighting its corner in the video games market. During 1999 sales of the N-64 began to decline. In the fourth quarter, Nintendo sold 1.9 million units, compared with 2.4 million in fourth quarter 1998. Between its launch in 1996 and April 2000, it had sold 29.6 million Nintendo 64 machines, against 70 million PlayStations over the same five-year period. Increasingly, the N-64, which used bulkier games cartridges instead of the CD-ROMs or DVDs, was viewed as technologically outdated. However, Nintendo still dominated the hand-held market, and continued to be profitable. Like Sony, Nintendo tried to head-off declining sales by cutting console prices in the US from $129 to $99 in the fall of 1999.

In June 2000, it unveiled a new portable version of its Nintendo 64 console, quickly countering Sony's announcement of a smaller, portable version of its rival PlayStation console, known as the PSone. Both companies were targeting mobile Internet users of Japan's NTT DoCoMo's I-mode web phone service. Nintendo was also preparing to launch a new version of the GameBoy, its popular hand-held game machine.

However, Nintendo's major hopes for the future were pinned on the new Internet-ready 128-bit machine that was code-named Dolphin, but renamed GameCube prior to its release in 2001. The new system would offer unprecedented graphics capability and would feature state-of-the-art software, much of which would be developed internally by Nintendo's crack developers. The GameCube involved close collaboration with a number of hardware and software companies. The specially designed processor was developed by IBM from its PowerPC processor used in the Apple iMac. The graphics chip was supplied by ArtX – a start-up company founded by ex-Silicon Graphics engineers. To encourage software writers, it improved the financial terms available to third-party developers and made available a full set of development tools well in advance of the launch. Table 11.4 compares the features of GameCube with its rivals.

GameCube went on sale in Japan on September 14, 2001, with its US debut on November 18, occurring just three days after the launch of the Microsoft Xbox. Although its launch generated massive attention in Japan, sales of 240,000 during the first week fell short of a sell-out (initial shipments to retailers were 450,000). Despite Nintendo's internal development efforts and its wooing of external developers, only three games were available for GameCube at the time of its Japanese launch. To maximize its US market impact, Nintendo set a US marketing budget of $75 million for the fourth quarter of 2001, and set the retail price at $199 – a full $100 below that of the Microsoft Xbox and PS2. The GameCube's games library expanded during December and January. In addition to Nintendo's well-known characters, great hopes were placed on *Pikmin* – the latest creation of Nintendo's top game developer, Shigeru Miyamoto, whose earlier successes had included *Super Mario Brothers* and *Zelda*.

The Microsoft Xbox

Microsoft's decision to launch a video games console was the greatest bombshell to hit the industry in the new decade. Throughout 2000 and most of 2001, Microsoft's

Table 11.4 Comparison of the 128-bit games consoles

	Sega Dreamcast	Sony PlayStation2	Nintendo GameCube	Microsoft X-Box
CPU	200 MHz SH4 Hitachi-made RISC processor	294 MHz 0.18 micron custom CPU manufactured by Toshiba	485 MHz 0.18 micron IBM "Gecko" processor derived from Power PC	Intel P3 733 MHz
Polygons per second	3 million; 1 million with curved surfaces, fogging and lighting	66 million; 16 million with curved surfaces; 36 million with fogging and lighting	6 to 12 million real-world polygons	100 million with all effects on
Storage	1 gigabyte GD-ROM (a proprietary double-density CD-ROM)	4.7 gigabyte DVD-ROM	4.7 gigabyte DVD-ROM	DVD-ROM Also, hard drive
Graphics	128-bit 3D graphics	128-bit 3D graphics	128-bit 3D graphics	Nvidia NV-25 running 300 MHz 256-bit graphics pipeline
DVD movie player	No	Yes	No	Yes
Memory bus bandwidth	800+ megabytes/second	3.2 gigabytes/second	3.2 gigabytes/second	6.4 gigabytes/second
Modem	56 kbps	None	None	Broadband modem

Source: Nintendo Next Generation Comparison Chart.

development efforts were the subject of a frenzy of speculation by industry players, outside commentators, and games players. The software giant's entry was seen as symbolizing the emerging potential of video games consoles. Once viewed as children's toys, games consoles were emerging as the primary platform for electronic entertainment, with a potential to offer movies, music, and many of the communications functions performed by PCs.

The Xbox was designed to place Microsoft far ahead of any other games machine in terms of technological capabilities. The *Financial Times* described it as: "Arguably the most powerful games console ever made, developed after consultation with more than 5,000 gamers and games creators, it has a staggering array of features: an internal hard disk with a 733 MHz processor, 64 MB of memory, a DVD player, Dolby Digital 5.1 Surround Sound and an Ethernet port that makes it the only game console that's Internet-ready and broadband-enabled."[1]

However, despite its state-of-the-art technology, Xbox's technological advantages did not translate into a clearly superior user experience: "Although the Xbox is very good, it doesn't offer a sufficiently different gaming experience from existing consoles ... The technological difference between generations of consoles is getting smaller all the time, and all three consoles now on the market in the US (Xbox, GameCube, PS2) have great graphics. It's hard for the average player to tell the difference."[2] The industry had long recognized that blockbuster games generated console sales; this was becoming ever more true. And, as with all newcomers to the video games industry, software availability was Xbox's major weakness. When Xbox was launched in the US in November 2001, 19 games were available. Although this was substantially more than the GameCube, it paled in comparison to PS2's more than 200 titles. Moreover, Xbox also lacked the recognizable characters owned by its established rivals, such as Mario Brothers and Lara Croft. As Nick Gibson, games analyst at Durlacher, observed: "By the time Microsoft and Nintendo complete their global launches in 2002, Sony will have built up an installed base of over 25 million units compared to 4 million to 5 million for the others at best. This momentum, combined with strong developer and publisher support, gives Sony an unassailable lead in this console cycle."[3] Xbox's US launch was successful with 1.5 million sold in the six-week Christmas shopping period.

Xbox's biggest challenge was to make a major dent in PS2's market share in Japan. Microsoft's Japanese launch of Xbox was a major event for Microsoft. Bill Gates was present to sell the first Xbox in Japan, on February 22, 2002, and in the week prior to the launch, Microsoft released 12 new games for Xbox. Priced at ¥34,800 ($259.30), the Xbox cost 17 percent more than PS2 and 39 percent more than GameCube. However, Xbox's reception in Japan was disappointing for Microsoft. In its first three days, 150,000 units were sold of the 250,000 that were shipped (PS2 had sold 720,000 in its first three days). Soon after the launch, a number of consumers began making complaints that the Xbox was scratching their CDs and DVDs. Microsoft's hesitant response to these complaints alienated many Japanese consumers and retailers. Moreover, none of Xbox's initial games releases proved to be major hits with Japanese games players.

■ THE VIDEO GAMES MARKET IN MAY 2002 ■

Market Demand

As summer 2002 approached, the world video games industry was moving into a period of expectancy and uncertainty. Most forecasts showed the market to be on the threshold of its biggest-ever expansion phase. Each generation of games consoles had surpassed its predecessor in terms of unit sales. Despite their hesitant start, the fifth-generation 128-bit machines (PS2, GameCube, and Xbox) would surpass the unit sales of the 32/64-bit machines (PS1, Saturn, and N-64). Industry sales for 2002 were estimated at between $25 billion and $31 billion, although the breakdown between hardware and software sales varied greatly between different market analysts. There was consensus over the importance of the industry within the entertainment sector: sales

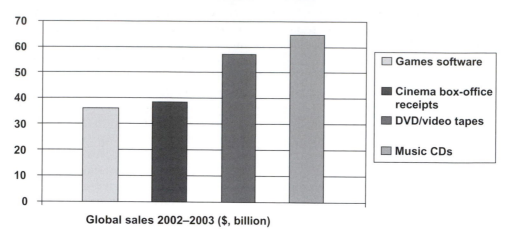

Figure 11.1 Estimated world entertainment sales by media type, 2002 and 2003
Source: Goldman Sachs.

of games software would soon exceed the film industry's box office receipts (see figure 11.1).

The increasing revenues generated by the industry throughout its history were a contrast to most of the high-tech sector, in which increasing unit sales were typically more than offset by declining unit prices. The prices of games consoles fell sharply within each generation of players, but across the generations prices had remained fairly steady. New products were typically introduced at around $200–$300, with prices eventually falling to between $100 and $200. However, by far the greater portion of revenues was generated by software whose unit prices remained around the $50 level.

Market expansion was primarily the result of the success of the hardware and software manufacturers in expanding the industry's user base. From its initial teen and pre-teen customers of Atari, games machines had gradually expanded their demographic penetration:

> Gaming is no longer the province of children and teenagers. According to a survey carried out by the Interactive Digital Software Association, 60 percent of Americans play games, either on consoles, hand-held devices, or PCs. Of those gamers, 61 percent are adults, 43 percent women, and the average age is 28. Figures from Europe and Japan tell a similar story. A generation that grew up with games has simply kept on playing. And as gamers age, their disposable income increases, making gaming an extraordinarily lucrative market.[4]

While children who grew up playing video games continued to do so as adults, game preferences changed greatly with age. Adolescents were more concerned with what was "in" and "hot." The adult market was composed of numerous niches, each with an interest in a different type of game. Adults liked titles that fit in with their lifestyle and interests. Sports-based games were very popular among adult males. Among older players, *The Sim*, which simulated family life, those based on TV shows (such as *Who Wants To Be a Millionaire?*), and those based on professional sports were popular.

Despite the breadth of the market, gaining market leadership depended critically upon gaining the support for the core, games-playing enthusiasts. This group numbered about 7 to 12 million individuals within the US. They were mostly males and between the ages of 12 and 30 years old. Many read game magazines like *EGM*, *GamePro*, and *Next Generation*, and were linked by their own web sites which communicated news, views, and reviews of new hardware and software.

The market key demo

Software

Video game console makers ("platform providers") each licensed third parties to develop software for use with their respective game-playing systems. Typically, the software developer submitted a prototype for evaluation and approval that included all artwork to be used in connection with packaging and marketing of the product. The platform providers usually retained the right to limit the number of games and approve timing of release under manufacturing and licensing arrangements. Home video game production was based on estimated demand for each specific title, with on-hand inventories depending on seasonal variations in demand during the market life of a specific game title. At the time that a newly developed game was approved for manufacturing, the developer had to provide the platform manufacturer with a purchase order for that product and an irrevocable letter of credit for 100 percent of the purchase price. Initial orders generally required 30 to 75 days to produce, depending on the platform. Reorders of cartridge games had required approximately 50 days for manufacturing. This figure had been reduced to 14 days for CD-ROM-based games. Shipping of orders required an additional 3–10 days, depending on the mode of transport and location of the software producer.

Increasing demand for multi-featured, action-packed game titles has driven up the cost of developing new game titles in the past five years. In the early 1990s, publishers customarily spent around $300,000 to develop a game for PC, Super NES, or Genesis systems. In 1998, the average budget was around $1 million per game, and many complex games, with all kinds of multimedia features, entailed even higher development costs. The development costs for some games had exceeded $10 million (e.g. Origin's *Wing Commander IV* was a high-profile example). The advent of 128-bit consoles had further added to the sophistication and cost of software development. By 2001–02, development costs were typically $2 million to $5 million per game. A successful title could bring in $200 million to $300 million – similar to box office revenues from a blockbuster movie. However, like movies, the success rate was low – a minority of games covered their development costs, while a mere handful provided the money-spinning blockbusters. Games software was almost entirely a sunk-cost business: development costs ran into the millions of dollars, but production costs were between $1 and $2 per copy.

The software side of the video game industry focused on several competitive weapons: product quality and features, compatibility of products with popular platforms, brand-name recognition, access to distribution channels, marketing effectiveness, reliability and ease of use, price, and technical support. Given the substantial cost of product development and of the marketing required to support best-selling titles, financial resources were becoming a critical competitive asset.

Increasing development costs were primarily the result of game players' demands for games of increased quality and sophistication. Development costs were also boosted by competition to license titles, themes, and characters from television, movies, and other media. Substantial non-refundable advance licensing fees and significant advertising expenses also increased the financial risk involved. Incorporating compelling story lines or game experiences with full-motion video, digital sound, and other lifelike technology added further to the cost equation.

The profits received by the console manufacturers were also derived – almost exclusively – from sales of software. The billions of dollars spent by each of the manufacturers on their 126-bit consoles were recouped through the sales of software rather than the sales of hardware: the selling price of the consoles failed to cover the cost of manufacture, let alone the cost of development. However, the licensing fees paid by the games publisher to the console manufacturer were typically about $10 per copy. The result was strongly cyclical earnings of the hardware companies. The launch of a new console would result in massive cash outflows. Even after a successful market launch, booming hardware sales would typically generate continuing losses since the manufacturers' revenues from consoles barely covered the cost of goods sold. It was not until a healthy installed base had been established that the manufacturer would begin to recoup the investment made. Thus, Sony's installed base of 30 million PS2s at the end of May 2002 and a similar number of its original PlayStations still in use gave it a huge financial advantage over Nintendo and Microsoft.

The development of video games required a blend of technology and creative talent. The development process included game development and design, prototyping, programming, art, computer graphic design, animation, sound engineering, technical writing, editorial review, and quality assurance. It took 12 to 24 months (occasionally longer) to complete a new title, and 6 to 14 months to make existing titles compatible for play on a different platform. Many games were based on characters and themes that were either owned by the game developer or licensed from third parties. Software companies had to grapple with several strategic issues when embarking upon a new development project: (1) what development and distribution agreements to arrange, (2) whether to acquire content from outsiders or create original content with an in-house group, (3) which game-playing platform to develop for, and (4) how to attract and retain their key creative and technical talent.

The most common strategy in creating a new title was for a software publisher to hire a developer. The developer was responsible for creating and programming the game and assuring the quality of the product. The publisher handled manufacturing, packaging, marketing, and distribution issues. The publisher bore the risk of unsold inventory if the title was a failure in the marketplace. Generally, game developers were paid a royalty based on wholesale revenues. Royalty payments varied greatly, but typically ranged from 5 to 15 percent.

Many developers were attempting to publish their own titles. Affiliated label and co-publishing programs had become a popular means for small companies to publish their own titles and maintain their independence. Under an affiliated label program, a developer handled marketing and publishing, while a co-publisher dealt with distribution. In return, the developer received a royalty of up to 75 percent of wholesale revenue. A variation on the affiliated label program was expected to become the distribution method of choice.

The licensing fees paid by software publishers for exclusive rights to the intellectual property of media companies and sports organizations grew substantially between 1998 and 2002. Securing the license to produce a game based on a hit movie (e.g. *Harry Potter*) could cost several millions of dollars. In the sports market, licenses paid to sports leagues (NFL, NHL, MLB, NBA, MLS) typically involved an up-front payment, plus a royalty of 5 to 15 percent of the wholesale price for each unit sold. Many large entertainment conglomerates were setting up interactive divisions to create titles based on their own property.

The Competitive Situation, May 2002

During spring 2002, competition in all three major markets – North America, Japan, and Europe – was intensifying. For Nintendo and Microsoft, the next six months would be critical. If they were to retain the support of software developers and retailers and recoup a significant proportion of their development and launch costs, it was essential that they grabbed a substantial share of new hardware sales in all three major markets. For Sony, the key was to utilize its incumbency advantage of installed base and huge library of titles to thwart its two rivals. In March 2002, Sony cut the US price of its PS2 from $299 to $199 and made similar cuts in other countries. Microsoft responded by cutting the price of its Xbox from $299 to $199, and Nintendo reduced its GameCube from $199 to $149. Despite PS2's problematic launch, it was clearly established as market leader with an installed base of 30 million worldwide as compared to about 4.5 million each for GameCube and Xbox. Estimates for the full year suggested that Sony would maintain its leadership of a very strong worldwide market for games consoles (see table 11.5).

However, it was too early to declare Sony the winner. The advent of network gaming had the potential to upset the competitive situation. Online games playing had become increasingly popular on PCs and most forecasters anticipated that interactivity would be the next big wave for dedicated games consoles. However, as the games have raced ahead in sophistication, dial-up modem links have become increasingly unsatisfactory in providing interactivity. The different manufacturers were pursuing different Internet strategies. Sony and Nintendo had developed adapters for their consoles that allowed Internet access, while leaving it to service providers, cable companies, and others to provide infrastructure and host games. Microsoft had adopted a more pioneering approach. It had announced the establishment of Xbox Live to support online games through a $2 billion dedicated network. Subscription fees would be paid directly to Microsoft.

While Sony and Nintendo's approach involved less capital outlay and greater flexibility to adjust to the network technologies and billing systems of different countries, other analysts viewed Microsoft's strategy as a potential winner. Not only would it give

Table 11.5   Estimate of the world video game market in 2002

	$, billions
Total industry sales	31
Of which, hardware	22
software	9
	Millions of units
Cumulative unit sales by model	
PlayStation2	48.4
GameCube	15.1
Xbox	6.9
	$, millions
Sales of PC games	8,500 (down 8.5% on 2001)
Sales of games for mobile phones, PDAs, and interactive TV	873 (100% increase on 2001)

Source: Informa Media Group.

Microsoft control over the provision of software, such a network would offer Microsoft a distribution system for a wide array of entertainment products, including movies and music.

APPENDIX

Table 11.A1   Financial data on the leading hardware manufacturers

NINTENDO											(Yen, billions)
	1992	1993	1994	1995	1996	1997	1998	1999	2000	2001	2002
Total sales	562	635	497	429	401	463	534	573	531	463	555
Operating income	157	181	104	86	133	115	172	156	145	85	119
Income taxes	94	90	59	50	74	50	88	165	108	71	77
Net income	87	88	53	42	60	65	84	86	56	97	106
Cash and cash equivalents	n.a.	n.a.	343	397	483	542	n.a.	639	594	825	895
Total current assets	n.a.	n.a.	519	498	571	660	n.a.	809	810	958	1,038
Total assets	517	n.a.	591	579	650	736	849	893	933	1,069	1,157
Total current liabilities	n.a.	n.a.	140	108	136	170	n.a.	189	169	225	212
Total liabilities	147	n.a.	110	137	172	n.a.	893	933	231	219	n.a.

Table 11.A1 *continued*

NINTENDO *(Yen, billions)*

	1992	1993	1994	1995	1996	1997	1998	1999	2000	2001	2002
Total shareholder equity	329	n.a.	444	465	513	564	633	700	757	835	935
Capital expenditures	n.a.	n.a.	162	224	252	298	388	354	436	n.a.	n.a.
ROA (%)	18.5	14.6	10.1	7.2	9.8	9.4	10.6	9.9	6.1	9.7	9.5
ROE (%)	30.0	21.9	13.2	9.2	12.3	12.1	14.0	12.9	7.7	12.2	12.0

SEGA *(Yen, billions)*

	1992	1993	1994	1995	1996	1997	1998	1999	2000	2001	2002
Net sales:	213	347	354	333	346	360	331	226	339	243	206
Consumer products	135	229	236	188	170	164	114	85	186	116	85
Amusement center operations	41	59	62	74	82	88	95	92	75	79	69
Amusement machine sales	36	58	52	61	85	98	124	91	74	52	53
Royalties on game software	0.4	1	4	9	10	9	4	2	n.a.	n.a.	n.a.
Cost of sales	151	252	270	257	271	285	271	202	290	218	145
Gross profit	62	95	84	76	75	75	60	24	49	25	62
Selling, general, and admin. expenses	23	33	37	45	46	44	64	62	89	77	47
Operating income	39	63	47	31	30	31	7	4	(40)	(52)	14
Net income	14	28	23	14	5	6	(36)	(32)	(52)	(418)	(18)
Total assets	226	295	301	426	441	387	369	426	375	284	244
Total shareholders' equity	90	117	165	176	178	179	122	81	81	92	84
ROA (%)	8.2	10.8	7.8	3.9	1.2	1.3	(9.7)	(8.1)	(15.7)	(115.2)	(7.5)
ROE (%)	16.7	27.1	16.5	8.3	3.0	3.1	(24.0)	(32.0)	(60.1)	(375.0)	(20.5)

SONY *(Yen, billions)*

	1993	1994	1995	1996	1997	1998	1999	2000	2001	2002
Return on average equity (%)	16.7	27.1	16.5	8.3	3.0	3.1	(24.0)	(32.0)	(60.1)	(375.0)	(20.5)
Sales and operating revenue	4,001	3,744	3,990	4,592	5,663	6,761	6,804	6,687	7,315	7,578

Table 11.A1 *continued*

SONY										(Yen, billions)
	1993	1994	1995	1996	1997	1998	1999	2000	2001	2002
of which:										
Games	n.a.	n.a.	n.a.	201	408	700	760	631	661	1,004
Operating income (loss)	131	107	(167)	235	370	526	348	241	225	135
of which:										
Games	n.a.	n.a.	n.a.	n.a.	n.a.	117	137	77	(51)	84
Pre-tax income	93	102	(221)	138	312	459	378	264	266	93
Income taxes	50	79	65	77	164	215	178	95	116	65
Net income (loss)	36	15	(293)	54	139	222	179	122	17	15
Capital expenditures	251	196	251	251	298	388	354	436	465	327
R&D expenses	232	230	239	257	283	318	375	394	417	433
Net working capital	367	616	538	816	844	1,151	1,127	974	831	779
Stockholders' equity	1,428	1,330	1,008	1,169	1,459	1,816	1,824	2,183	2,315	2,370
Total assets	4,530	4,270	4,224	5,046	5,680	6,403	6,299	6,807	7,827	8,186
ROA (%)	1.0	0.3	(6.9)	1.2	2.6	3.5	2.8	1.9	0.2	0.2
ROE (%)	2.9	1.3	(25.1)	5.0	10.5	13.5	9.8	6.1	0.7	0.6

Notes: ROA = Return on average assets; ROE = Return on average equity.
Source: Company annual reports.

NOTES

1. Sathnam Sanghera, "Out of the box at last," *Financial Times*, Creative Business section, November 20, 2001.
2. Ibid.
3. Ibid.
4. "Console wars," *The Economist*, June 22, 2002, pp. 71–2.

case twelve

Eni SpA: Building an International Energy Major

Robert M. Grant and Michael Ritter

February 15, 2003 marked the 50th anniversary of the founding of Eni SpA – Italy's largest company and the world's seventh biggest public petroleum company[1] – and the beginning of Vittorio Mincato's fifth full year as Chief Executive Officer. Under Mincato's leadership, Eni had experienced a period of continuous transition and development based upon a strategy of "growth of the core energy business." The results were impressive. Between 1998 and 2003, Eni's revenues and hydrocarbon production had both grown by more than half, operating income had more than doubled, and Eni's share price appreciation had been greater than any other oil major.

The first two months of 2003 saw no slackening of pace for Mincato. During January and February 2003, Eni finalized its acquisitions of Fortum Petroleum (a Norwegian oil and gas company) for 1.1 billion euros and the 56 percent of Italgas (an Italian gas distribution company) that it did not already own. In January, Eni also purchased a service station network in Spain and four Hungarian gas distribution companies. However, Mincato's main preoccupation was Eni's corporate plan for the next four years. On January 29, Mincato and his senior executives presented Eni's strategic plans to the investment community in London. During the next two weeks the roadshow visited the financial centers of Europe and America.

Mincato envisaged the next four years building upon the achievements of the previous four. The centerpiece of Eni's strategy for 2004–07 was continued upstream growth. During 1999–2002, Eni's oil and gas production had grown faster than most other majors. The target for the next four years was production growth of 5 percent per annum. Increased upstream output would be supported by downstream expansion – especially in the European gas market. As a result, Eni would build its position as one of the world's leading vertically integrated natural gas companies. At the same

This case was prepared by Robert Grant and Michael Ritter. We are grateful for the support and cooperation of Eni SpA, in particular from Leonardo Maugeri and Renato Cibin.

time, Eni would continue to reduce its investment in chemicals and other non-core businesses.

Mincato was well aware that Eni's position as one of the world's most profitable and fastest growing energy majors was vulnerable to the challenges of a complex and turbulent business environment. High energy prices were a major contributor to Eni's stellar financial performance. The price of oil remained vulnerable to increased supplies from Iran, Iraq, and the former Soviet Union, while massive investments in liquefied natural gas (LNG) threatened to depress European gas prices. Any major slowdown in the world economy would also undermine energy prices. Longer term, environmental issues clouded the outlook for fossil fuels. Relative to its peers, Eni lacked massive size and the international scope of the new "supermajors" – Exxon Mobil, BP-Amoco, TotalFinaElf, and ChevronTexaco – created during the merger wave of 1996–2001. Mincato was determined to avoid large-scale mergers and acquisitions: "We've always preferred to grow organically and in an orderly manner. That's our history," he told investment analysts in London.[2] If Eni was to continue to outperform its larger rivals, it would need to continue to hone a strategy that exploited its distinctive differences, and execute that strategy with enhanced effectiveness and efficiency.

■ MATTEI AND THE CREATION OF ENTE NAZIONALE IDROCARBURI, 1926–62[3] ■

Eni traces its origins to 1926 when the Italian Prime Minister, Benito Mussolini, established Agip (Azienda Generali Italiana Petroli) as a state-owned oil refining company.[4] In 1945 Enrico Mattei, a former partisan, was appointed head of Agip and was instructed to dismantle this relic of fascist economic intervention. Contrary to instructions, Mattei renewed Agip's exploration efforts and, in 1948, discovered a substantial gas field in Northern Italy's Po Valley. In 1949, Mattei also took over the management of SNAM, the Italian gas distribution company. With the opportunity to create a national energy system based on the newly found gas reserves, pipelines were laid at a frantic rate. "Mattei built the pipelines first and negotiated afterwards . . . He simply ignored private and public rights and the law . . . Much of the work was done at night on the theory that by morning the work would be so far along that there would not be very much that anybody could do about it."[5] At San Donato, outside Milan, Mattei created Metanopoli, a small town comprising offices, gas plants, and employees' homes. On February 10, 1953, the government merged Agip, SNAM, and other state-owned energy activities to form Ente Nazionale Idrocarburi (Eni) with the task of "promoting and undertaking initiatives of national interest in the fields of hydrocarbons and natural gases." Mattei was appointed its first chairman and chief executive. In fact, Eni's 36 subsidiaries extended well beyond oil and gas to include engineering services, chemicals, soap, and real estate.

Under Mattei's leadership, Eni became committed to building an integrated, international oil and gas company that would ensure the independence of Italy's energy supplies and make a substantial contribution to Italy's post-war economic regeneration. Mattei soon established himself as a national hero: "He embodied great visions for post-war Italy – antifascism, the resurrection and rebuilding of the nation, and the emergence of the 'new man' who had made it himself, without the old boy network."[6] Mattei's daring and resourcefulness was especially evident in Eni's international growth. Post-war recovery was accompanied by a quest for new sources of oil – especially in the Middle East. Eni's problem was that most leading oil-producing countries had agreements with the existing oil majors: Standard Oil New Jersey (later Exxon), Mobil, Standard Oil of California (later Chevron), Texaco, Royal Dutch/Shell, British Petroleum, and Gulf Oil. These "Seven Sisters" – as Mattei christened them – collaborated closely to tie-up oil supplies: the Arabian American Oil Company (Aramco) was jointly owned by Exxon, Chevron, Texaco, and Mobil; the Iranian Consortium involved all seven of the sisters together with Total of France.

The production agreement that Mattei signed with the Shah of Iran in 1957 marked the beginning of a fundamental shift of power from the oil majors to producer governments. It also established Eni as the *enfant terrible* of the international oil business. The Iranian agreement was revolutionary. It created a jointly owned exploration and production company headed by an Iranian chairman and with the proceeds shared between Eni and the Iranian National Oil Company. "This new approach opened the way to full control of energy resources for the producing countries and anticipated a trend that would become the basis of future agreements in the oil business."[7] The repercussions of the "Mattei formula" extended beyond the oil industry to international diplomacy. A 1957 US confidential progress report pointed to "the threat posed by Enrico Mattei to the political objectives of the United States." This "new deal" with producer countries allowed Eni to extend its upstream interests throughout North Africa. Between 1958 and 1960, Eni led the way in acquiring exploration and production rights in Libya, Egypt, Tunisia, and Algeria. Mattei continued to upset the status quo with deals to purchase crude oil from the Soviet Union. By the end of the 1950s, Italy had become the Soviet Union's biggest oil customer after China. Again, the deal was innovative and daring: Soviet oil was bartered for exports of synthetic rubber and other Italian products – in effect, Eni acquired Soviet oil at less than half of the prevailing world price.

Beyond Oil and Gas

Mattei's drive to build a corporate empire did not stop at hydrocarbons. By 1962, Eni was "engaged in industries as various as motels, highways, chemicals, soap, fertilizers, synthetic rubber, machinery, instruments, textiles, electrical generation and distribution, contract research, engineering and construction, publishing, nuclear power, steel pipe, cement, investment banking, and even education, to mention only a few."[8] This diversification resulted from Mattei's indefatigable deal making. As a state-owned enterprise dependent upon political support, many of Mattei's acquisitions were politically motivated. For example, Eni's acquisition of Lanerossi, a wool textile company in Veneto, appears to have been motivated by Mattei's desire to influence a local Christian Democratic politician.[9]

Other business developments were designed to support Eni's oil and gas businesses. In 1955 Snamprogetti was created to design and construct chemical and petrochemical plants and pipeline transportation systems. Saipem was added with operations focused on offshore construction, pipe laying and drilling. Pignone of Florence (later Nuovo Pignone) was acquired to produce equipment used in the oil and gas industry.

■ ENI AFTER MATTEI, 1962–1992 ■

Adjustment, Rebalancing, and Political Intervention[10]

Mattei died in a mysterious plane crash on October 27, 1962. He was 56 years old. He left a sprawling corporate empire whose strategy had been Mattei's vision and opportunism, and whose integrating force had been Mattei's charisma and personal decision-making authority. At the time of his death, Mattei was President not just of Eni but also of its main operating companies – Agip Mineraria, Agip, Snam, Anic, Stanic, and Agip Nucleare.[11] Filling the void as Eni's new president was Marcello Boldrini, a 72-year-old professor of statistics with very little hands-on management experience. At the same time, Eni faced problems on multiple fronts. Despite Mattei's innovative deal making, the company remained tiny by international standards. It was also short of oil – in 1962 Eni was producing a mere 32,000 barrels per day of crude with only 18 active wells outside of Italy. Meanwhile, Eni was in a perilous financial situation. The profits generated by Eni's monopoly position in the Italian gas market were dissipated throughout the company's diverse business interests. Most serious was Eni's high level of debt. In 1960, the Italian Central Bank had forbidden Eni from issuing new debt.[12]

Financial weakness resulted in Eni becoming increasingly dependent upon government. Increasing political control meant that Eni became an instrument of government economic, industrial, and employment policies. As a result, Eni continued to diversify into minerals and metals processing, chemicals, coal, and textile machinery – often to rescue failing companies. After 1975, the chairman of Eni lost direct control of the operating companies – their chief executives were appointed by government on the basis of political considerations. Nevertheless, during the 1960s and 1970s, Eni continued to expand its interests in oil and gas. Major initiatives included the purchase of natural gas from the Soviet Union (which involved Eni building a pipeline from the Austrian-Czechoslovak border to Italy), the Trans-Med Pipeline from Algeria and Tunisia to Italy, and the development of offshore projects in West Africa, Congo, and Angola.

1983–1992: Reform and Crisis

In 1983, Franco Reviglio was appointed chairman of Eni and quickly concluded that Eni could not continue down its present path. Its 335 operating companies spanned much of Italy's industrial sector. By 1982, losses totaled 1,501 billion lire ($1.28 billion) and debt had risen to over 19,000 billion lire ($14 billion). Reviglio's priorities were to reestablish Eni on solid financial ground, distance itself from political power, and to refocus on oil and gas. Between 1982 and 1989, Eni made considerable progress in reducing costs, eliminating losses, restructuring debt, and creating a more coherent and manageable business portfolio. Several businesses in nuclear power, minerals, and textiles were sold and Eni's chemical division, EniChem, was merged with Montedison's chemical division to create Enimont. By the time the chairmanship of Eni had passed from Reviglio to Gabriele Cagliari in 1989, Eni reported net income of 1,544 billion lire ($1.2 billion) on sales of 37,189 lire ($27.1 billion), and long-term debt was down to 9,850 billion lire ($7.9 billion). Table 12.1 shows Eni's growth and profitability since 1980.

Under Cagliari, Eni returned to an era of intense political interference, the result of which was to bring Eni to the verge of collapse. Between 1990 and 1992, Eni's capital investment and exploration expenditures were close to 150 percent of operating cash flow and long-term debt increased to 13,453 billion lire.

Meanwhile, the movement for far-reaching reforms of Italy's over-extended and inefficient public sector was gaining strength. Italy was facing increasing pressures from the European Commission and the new European Monetary Union to rein in public expenditures, reduce its public sector deficit, and free up industry from state intervention. In June 1992, a new government was formed under reformist Prime Minister Giuliano Amato. In July, the government announced the first steps in granting Eni greater autonomy: the Ministry for State Participation was dismantled, Eni and three other state-owned corporations were converted into joint-stock companies, and their relationships with the government were transferred to the Treasury.

■ THE BERNABÈ ERA: PRIVATIZATION AND TRANSFORMATION, 1992–1998 ■

The new legal structure had important governance implications for Eni. Henceforth, its board of directors was legally responsible to shareholders for the financial state of the company – even though the only shareholder was the Italian government. Top management responsibility was vested in a three-person board comprising Gabriele Cagliari as Chairman, Giuseppe Ammassari as government representative, and Franco Bernabè as CEO. The 44-year-old Bernabè was a surprise choice – an economist who headed up Eni's planning department, he lacked line management experience. The significance of Bernabè's appointment was that he was a prominent advocate of privatization, having already drawn up plans for a privatized Eni.

As CEO, Bernabè moved quickly to position himself, rather than Chairman Cagliari, as the primary decision maker and center of executive power within Eni. In a directive to operating company presidents he announced that, henceforth, they would each report to him. He followed up with a series of visits to Eni's operating companies in which he met with managers, discussed their businesses, and laid out his ideas for Eni's future. Central to his thinking was the belief that Eni needed to be privatized as an integrated oil, gas, and chemical company – shorn of its various diversified businesses, but otherwise a vertically integrated upstream–downstream company similar to other international energy majors.[13]

During the fall of 1992, Bernabè launched his restructuring plan. Beginning with the sale of Nuovo Pignone (Eni's gas turbine business) to General Electric, several non-core businesses were sold and the proceeds used to reduce debt. Throughout the entire company, subsidiaries were pressured to cut costs, establish tighter capital expenditure

Table 12.1 Eni's sales, profits, employment, and production, 1980–2003

	1980	1981	1982	1983	1984	1985	1986	1987	1988	1989	1990	1991
Sales (US$m)	31,440	32,532	30,677	29,221	29,542	24,328	22,557	24,464	25,220	27,105	41,764	n.a.
Net income (US$m)	116	–232	–1,280	–922	–36	406	42	544	1,006	1,176	1,697	n.a.
Employees ('000s)	n.a.	n.a.	140	136	n.a.	129	130	119	116	136	131	n.a.
Oil and gas production ('000s boe/day)	320	322	307	335	371	371	384	443	490	538	590	n.a.

	1992	1993	1994	1995	1996	1997	1998	1999	2000	2001	2002	2003*
Sales (US$m)	38,659	33,595	30,670	35,335	37,973	34,323	33,177	31,225	46,000	43,607	51,379	52,400
Net income (US$m)	–768	154	1,977	2,704	2,930	2,980	2,891	3,019	5,671	7,333	4,816	5,585
Employees ('000s)	126	109	92	86	83	80	79	72	70	71	81	77
Oil and gas production ('000s boe/day)	860	901	941	982	984	1,021	1,038	1,064	1,187	1,369	1,472	1,562

* 2003 sales and net income are in millions of euros

n.a. = not available.

Source: Eni annual reports for various years.

discipline, and raise profit aspirations. However, in the early stages of Bernabè's restructuring, Eni was plunged into crisis.

In March 1993, Eni became caught up in the corruption scandal that had swept the country. Dozens of Eni executives became indicted on corruption charges, including chairman Cagliari and the chief executives of several of Eni's main operating companies.[14] Between March 9 and 11, Cagliari and other top managers were arrested. The initial paralysis of Eni offered Bernabè the opportunity to clean house and restructure management. Later that March, Bernabè forced the resignation of the board and appointed a new, non-political board comprising technocrats and energy industry experts. In April, he demanded the resignation of all the board members of Eni's operating companies and embarked upon a process of selection and reappointment. Within two months, 250 board members were substituted.[15]

Management changes paved the way for an intensified program of restructuring. Bernabè's corporate strategy was "to reduce Eni from being a loose conglomerate to concentrate on its core activity of energy."[16] In the troubled chemicals sector, five large plants were closed and capacity halved. During 1993, Bernabè's first whole year as chief executive, 73 Eni businesses were closed or sold worldwide, employment fell by 15,000, cost savings and asset sales amounted to 1.7 trillion lire, and net income went from a loss of 946 billion lire in 1992 to a 304 billion lire profit.[17] Commenting on Eni's financial recovery, Bernabè noted: "One of the reasons why we have been able to achieve better results is that we have been able to operate without political interference. We have been able to manage our business on commercial criteria."[18]

Eni's Initial Public Offering

Eni's initial public offering of 15 percent of its total equity on November 21, 1995 raised 3.3 billion euros for the Italian Treasury and on November 28, Eni shares commenced trading on the Milan, London, and New York stock exchanges. After more than 40 years of looking to political leaders in Rome for guidance, Eni's top management had to adjust to a new set of masters – the investment community in the world's financial capitals.

For Bernabè, the IPO marked a fundamental change in Eni's goals and responsibilities, but it was a starting point rather than an end in itself. "A government-owned, politically controlled monopoly could not be turned into a competitive global integrated oil company overnight," he observed.[19] Commitment to maximizing shareholder value provided the impetus for reconfiguring its portfolio of assets: "Eni's strategy is to focus on businesses and geographical areas where, through size, technology, or cost structure, it has a leading market position. To this end, Eni intends to implement dynamic management of its portfolio through acquisitions, joint ventures, and divestments. Eni also intends to outsource non-strategic activities."[20]

Capital investments became increasingly focused upon upstream activities. In refining, marketing, and petrochemicals, costs were reduced and assets were sold. Organizationally, Bernabè combined centralization and decentralization. Subsidiary managers were given increased authority over human resource decisions and their authorization limits for capital expenditures were increased. At the same time, corporate planning systems were strengthened and financial discipline was increased. The merger of Agip into Eni in 1997 increased corporate control over Eni's most important subsidiary.

The results were striking. Between 1992 and 1998, Bernabè had halved Eni's debt, turned a loss into a substantial profit, and reduced the number of employees by some 46,000. However, 1998 was to be Bernabè's last year at Eni: his success at transforming Eni made him the obvious candidate to lead the turnaround of another newly privatized giant – Telecom Italia.

■ ENI UNDER MINCATO: FROM RESTRUCTURING TO GROWTH ■

Vittorio Mincato brought a different background and a different style of management to Eni. Twelve years Bernabè's senior, Mincato had already spent 42 years at Eni. His career included both corporate and line management positions, including 15 years as chairman of EniChem where he cut chemical plants from over 40 to 20 and eliminated chronic losses. Mincato brought a powerful reputation and intimate knowledge of the Eni group to the chief executive suite, but little was known about the strategy or management style he would pursue.

Despite massive changes under Bernabè, the Eni that Mincato inherited faced sizable problems. During 1998, the world economy was hit by the financial contagion that had spread from south east Asia to Latin America and Russia, and oil prices fell to below $10 a barrel. At home, Eni's gas monopoly was threatened by EU initiatives to liberalize energy markets. Meanwhile, the petroleum arm's competitive landscape was being transformed by mergers – BP's acquisition of Amoco was followed by Exxon's merger with Mobil. Eni itself remained unsettled after the momentous internal changes of the previous five years. Mincato described Eni as strong but tired: "like an athlete at the end of an extremely long, grueling race."[21]

Developing a Corporate Strategy

In confronting Eni's external challenges, Mincato recognized that Eni "still lacked a clear and courageous vision of its future." This lack of strategic focus was reinforced by Eni's internal weaknesses. Despite Bernabè's efforts to establish control over Eni's operating companies, the group still retained the features of a holding company. During his first few months as chief executive, Mincato developed his thinking about Eni's future and throughout 1999 he shaped the Group's strategic plan for 2000–03. The central theme of the strategy would be growth in Eni's core energy business. This would inevitably involve acquisition: "Our weakness is our size and our priority is to grow. The fastest way is through acquisition and we have ample financial means to do so."[22] Such growth would inevitably require further internationalization. In an interview with the *Financial Times*, Mincato spelled out the main thrusts of the strategy:

> The first phase of the company's strategy is complete. It involved refocusing the group on its core oil, gas and related activities and the disposal of all diversified lines. "We are now

entering phase two: this will involve concentrating on growth and further rationalization of the core businesses," he says.

The main target of rationalization is the group's chemical activities. Mr. Mincato, in charge of chemical operations before becoming CEO, said Eni was too small a player in the chemical sector. It needed alliances and joint ventures "even with a minority stake" to reduce the weight of the loss-making chemical business on the invested capital.

The next issue, he says, is to deal with the liberalization of Italy's domestic gas market. "The impact of liberalization should be marginal because we are planning to offset lower direct sales in Italy with increased volumes sold abroad." The group plans to sell gas to Croatia and Greece and is negotiating with other European countries.

Mr. Mincato is also keen to develop the group's presence in the electricity market. "Our interest is based on the possibility of a gas company becoming integrated downstream into power generation to stabilize or increase sales and revenues in the short term," he says.[23]

In Eni's annual report for 1999, Mincato explained Eni's strategy for 2000–03 in greater detail:

In 1999 the scenario in which Eni operates underwent deep changes . . . Two phenomena in particular affected the most important sectors of our core business: the consolidation of the oil industry globally and liberalization of the European and Italian gas markets. . . .

The four-year plan approved at the end of 1999 derives from a new strategic vision that features, on one side, an aggressive growth option in upstream activities and, on the other, a customer-oriented approach in the energy markets.

For the upstream sector we devised a plan calling for 50% growth in hydrocarbon production by 2003. Such an objective will be made up of two components. The first is represented by ordinary growth . . . the second component of growth is related to mergers and/or acquisitions . . .

In the natural gas sector, Eni has been active at three levels. First, it followed an internationalization strategy in downstream activities with the aim of selling at least 10 billion cubic meters of natural gas per year by 2003 in foreign growth markets . . . Second, with the creation of EniPower, Eni started to restructure its activities in the electricity sector, an area which represents a necessary step to strengthen its position in the gas chain, in view of the fact that most of the growth in demand for natural gas in Europe will come from the expansion of combined cycle electricity production.

To support the opening up of the natural gas market in Italy, we started to restructure our activities at Snam, separating . . . transport activities from supply and sale.

The scope of the changes affecting our industry will require on our part the achievement of strong efficiency improvements. For this reason, plans to cut costs have been revised, raising to 1 billion euro (an increase of 250 million euro) the amount of savings that Eni plans to achieve through cost cutting by 2003 . . . While costs will be cut across all sectors, strong measures will be taken in the Petrochemical sector – whose weight in terms of net capital will decline to 7% by 2003.[24]

Upstream Strategy

Mincato's boldest moves were in the upstream business. Once Eni had committed itself to a 50 percent increase in hydrocarbon output, acquisition became essential. Yet,

Table 12.2 Eni oil and gas production by area, 1997–2003 (thousands of barrels of oil equivalent per day)

	Italy	North Sea	North Africa	West Africa	Rest of World	World
Production						
2003	300	345	351	260	306	1,562
2002	316	308	354	238	256	1,472
2001	308	288	317	233	223	1,369
2000	333	168	306	225	155	1,187
1999	358	154	269	206	77	1,064
1998	394	156	236	196	56	1,038
1997	404	155	229	180	54	1,021
Reserves						
2003	996	912	2,024	1,324	2,016	7,272

Mincato was resolutely opposed to Eni participating in the wave of mega-mergers that was reshaping the global oil and gas industry. He saw large-scale mergers being driven by expectations of synergies and economies of scale that were seldom realized: "Eni carefully analyzed the history of major mergers of the last 30 years and was able to see that, in 80 percent of cases, these destroyed value, especially when they involved cultural problems."[25] Mincato also recognized Eni's limited experience in integrating acquired companies: Eni must be capable of "digesting" any acquisitions it made.[26] Furthermore, Eni's stock market valuation was relatively low compared with its peers; to avoid dilution, Eni's preferred medium of exchange was cash.

In May 2000, Eni made its first ever takeover bid for a listed company. It acquired British Borneo, a London-listed exploration and production company, for 1.3 billion euro (including debt). This was followed in December 2000 with the acquisition of another British-based upstream company, LASMO, for 4.1 billion euro (including debt). Mincato viewed these acquisitions as milestones for Eni: "We had never before bought foreign companies and the result has already helped internationalize our own internal culture."[27]

Eni also expanded its own exploration. In Kazakhstan, Eni took over the operatorship of the newly discovered Kashagan oilfield in the North Caspian Sea – the largest oil discovery of the past 30 years. Other major additions included reserves in Iran (South Pars and Baklal fields), in West Africa (notably Angola and Nigeria), in North Africa (mainly Libya and Algeria), and in the North Sea. By the end of 2002, Eni had already achieved its 2003 production targets. (Table 12.2 shows Eni's growth of production during 1997–2003.)

Eni also refocused its upstream portfolio. To exploit economies in infrastructure, Eni concentrated its E&P activities on a smaller number of countries, and to gain more effective control over its upstream investment it increasingly sought to be the operator of the oil and gas ventures in which it participated.

Vertical Integration in Natural Gas

If upstream (exploration and production) was to be the primary source of Eni's profit growth, natural gas was where the greatest opportunities lay. World demand for natural gas was expected to grow at twice the rate of that for oil. Moreover, Eni had the downstream market position essential for adding value to gas reserves. During 1999–2000, Eni embarked upon two massive natural gas projects. The biggest and most ambitious, the Blue Stream project, involved a joint venture between Eni and the Russian gas giant, Gazprom, to invest over 2 billion euros in building a gas pipeline from Russia to Turkey that would pass under the Black Sea. Widely derided as "Blue Dream" for its technical and environmental complexities, by the end of 2002, Saipem had completed the two-line pipeline. The second major project was the Greenstream pipeline from Libya to Italy.

At the same time that Eni was investing heavily in natural gas reserves and long-distance pipelines, its downstream domestic business was under threat. In May 2000, the Italian government implemented the European directive on competition in natural gas. Eni's share of the Italian gas market was limited to 75 percent of primary transportation and 50 percent of the final market. In addition, primary transportation of natural gas and its marketing and local distribution had to be undertaken by separate companies. Eni's response was, first, to restructure its downstream gas company (Snam) and, second, to explore growth opportunities in other European gas markets.

Snam was split into two businesses. Its primary gas transmission network was vested in a new company, Snam Rete Gas, 40 percent of which was offered in an IPO in November 2001. Its marketing and supply business was merged into Eni to form the main component of Eni's Gas and Power division. The legislative decree of May 2000 also required the separation of gas storage from gas production and marketing. Hence, Eni's gas storage system in Italy was vested in a new regulated company, Stoccaggi Gas Italia, which was wholly owned by Eni. The new competitive structure of the Italian gas market also gave Eni the opportunity to sell natural gas to the new domestic competitors. In 2001 Eni signed seven multiyear contracts involving total sales of 15 million cubic meters each year. Eni also established EniPower SpA to develop combined-cycle power generation plants. Electricity production offered Eni a new market for its natural gas that did not count as part of Eni's share of the Italian gas market for regulatory purposes.

Outside of Italy, Eni acquired several gas distribution companies including major stakes in Spain's Union Fenosa Gas (50 percent), GVS in Germany (50 percent), and Galp Energia in Portugal (33 percent). Eni also entered the downstream gas markets of Hungary, Greece, and Croatia. In addition, the Blue Stream project would involve gas sales to Turkey of 8 billion cubic meters each year.

Figure 12.1 shows the vertical integrated structure of Eni's natural gas and its oil businesses while Appendix 2 shows operating data over the period, including Eni's gas and power activities.

Refining and Marketing Strategy

Downstream, Eni pursued rationalization and cost reduction in both refining and distribution. Under Mincato's leadership refining capacity was reduced, and in 2002 Eni

NATURAL GAS (billion cubic meters)

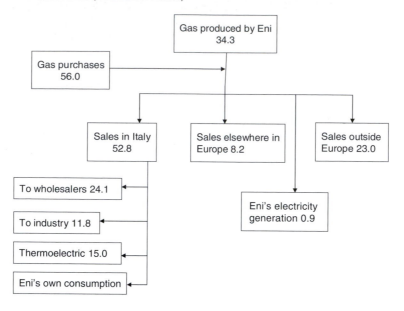

OIL (millions of tonnes)

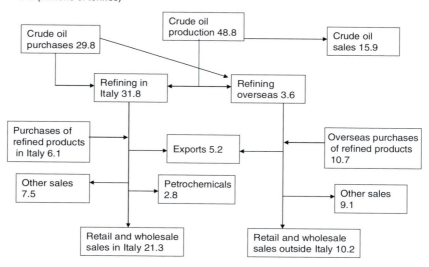

Figure 12.1 Eni's vertical chains in oil and gas
Source: Eni Fact Book, 2003.

sold an equity stake in its refinery complex in Sicily. At the retail level, 1,900 service stations were closed between 1999 and 2001. Outside of Italy, Eni pursued selective expansion, acquiring service stations in France, Spain, Czech Republic, and Brazil while withdrawing from countries where Eni possessed neither the market share nor the supply infrastructure to permit profitability. Appendix 2 shows Eni's refining and marketing output and sales.

Rationalization in Chemicals

Under Mincato's leadership, Eni continued its strategy of reducing capital employed in petrochemicals. Eni's return on its chemicals investments was dismal and, given EniChem's limited presence outside Italy, it would always be at a competitive disadvantage to global players such as Exxon Mobil, Shell, BP, Dow, and Du Pont. In 2001, Eni agreed to sell its polyurethane business to Dow Chemical and it consolidated its olefins, aromatics, styrene, and elastomer production within a separate company, Polimeri Europa, in preparation for its sale.

Internal Change

Some of Mincato's most important initiatives related to Eni's organization and management systems. While Bernabè had won the battle for Eni to be privatized as a single corporation and had initiated the merging of Agip into Eni, most of its principal businesses – Agip Petroli, Snam, Saipem, and Snamprogetti – were separate joint stock companies with their own boards of directors and a history of independence from corporate control. Between 2000 and 2003, Mincato transformed Eni from a holding company into a multidivisional corporation with the main operating companies reorganized into three divisions: exploration and production, gas and power, and refining and marketing. Appendix 3 describes Eni's main businesses.

Mincato recognized that reorganizing Eni as a single corporation would not cause Eni to act as a unified company. Hence, during 2000–03, Mincato introduced several initiatives to give Eni a clearer sense of identity and build a common culture. In May 2000, Eni announced major changes to its human resource policies. The "RES Program," introduced in June, 2001 inaugurated a new emphasis on human resources and their development:

> By means of the RES Program, Eni sets out to "capture" those who work in the group . . . trying to understand their abilities, their ambitions, how they can contribute to the success of the company, now and in the future. The approach is radically new: the policy of human resources management and development is centered on the person. Group employees will be considered not just as a collective entity (staff), but as individuals, each with his own merits and his own potential. This outlook means redefining methodologies, changing the model.[28]

The new HR policies included:

- Renewal of human resources through increased emphasis on professional and managerial development.
- Cost reduction through streamlining staff structures and developing greater flexibility in human resources management.
- Focusing Eni Corporation on its core functions of coordination and control and decentralizing human resource management and development.
- Internationalizing Eni's human resources.
- Establishing Eni Corporate University as a service company to provide human resource development.

In addition to increased internal dynamism, Eni also needed greater external recognition and clearer external identity – especially among international investors and host governments. In February, 2001 Mincato delivered a speech entitled "Eni's Way" in Houston Texas. The speech emphasized the role of technology and originality in Eni's development of new projects and its pursuit of new markets and reserves. During 2002, the term "Eni's Way" was adopted as the company's tag-line in a major campaign of corporate advertising. The meaning of "Eni's Way" remains vague, but the imagery used in the advertising suggested a commitment to technology, ethical and environmental responsibility, and a frontier spirit.

■ THE ENERGY SECTOR IN 2002 ■

Since the first oil shock of the 1970s, the oil and gas industry had been transformed by the emergence of new competitors (especially the national oil companies), the development of international markets for trading oil and gas, the growing power of producer countries, the opening of more countries to inward direct investment, and the advent of new technologies. At the beginning of the twenty-first century, these forces of change continued to be sources of turbulence and unpredictability.

Industry Consolidation

Between 1998 and 2002, a wave of mergers and acquisitions resulted in the emergence of an elite group of "supermajors," comprising Exxon Mobil, BP, Royal Dutch/Shell, ChevronTexaco, and TotalFinaElf (see table 12.3).

The stock markets responded favorably to most of these mergers and acquisitions – however, the extent to which they would generate real economic benefits was unclear. The primary motivation appeared to be the desire for growth – a particularly powerful motive when revenues and profits were depressed by low oil prices.[29] Once the merger wave began, it was sustained by companies' fear of being relegated to "second division" status within the industry. The positive stock market reaction to the mergers was surprising given "study after study across [other] industries shows that only a small minority of mergers achieve measurable gains, such as higher productivity, profits, or share prices over the long term." An important motive was spreading risks through maintaining a portfolio of major upstream projects: "Only well-capitalized firms that are big

Table 12.3 Major mergers and acquisitions in the oil and gas industry*

Leading oil and gas companies, 1995	Revenues in 1995 ($ bn)	Date merged	Leading oil and gas companies, 2002	Revenues in 2002 ($ bn)
Exxon	123.92		Exxon Mobil Corp.	182.47
Mobil	75.37	1999		
Royal Dutch/Shell Group	109.87		Royal Dutch/Shell Group	179.43
Enterprise Oil	1.18	2002		
British Petroleum	56.00		BP Amoco	178.72
Amoco	28.34	1998		
Arco	15.82	2000		
Chevron	31.32	2001	ChevronTexaco	92.04
Texaco	35.55	2001		
Total	27.70		TotalFinaElf	96.94
PetroFina	n.a.	1999		
Elf Aquitaine	n.a.	2000		
Conoco	14.70		ConocoPhillips	58.38
Phillips Petroleum	13.37	2002		
Tosco	n.a.	2001		
Eni	35.92		Eni	46.33
Repsol	20.96		Repsol YPF	34.50
YPF	4.97	1999		

*Only includes acquisitions of companies with revenues exceeding $1 billion.

enough to afford the time, money, and risk required to play in this poker game can hope to thrive. Because the stakes are so high, finding that 'elephant' of an oilfield has become the industry's obsession."[30]

Evidence of significant economies of scale associated with being a "supermajor" rather than a "major" are hard to find. Downstream there are substantial cost and market power advantages associated with market share in individual national and regional markets, but few scale economies at the global level. Upstream, size increases bargaining power, especially in dealing with host governments, but the main scale economies relate mainly to the utilization of infrastructure, which is specific to particular regions and hydrocarbon basins. The principal advantages of size in exploration and production may relate mainly to risk and learning. The huge costs and risks of developing oil and gas fields mean that there are risk spreading advantages from holding a large portfolio of projects. In terms of learning, the more projects of a similar type that a company undertakes (e.g. deep sea drilling in the North Sea, Gulf of Mexico, and offshore West Africa), the greater the scope for learning, innovation, and sharing of best practices.

The Economics of Exploration and Production

Upstream provides the primary source of profit for the energy industry. Indeed, the primary rationale for vertical integration was the companies' desire for secure market outlets for their production. In oil, such vertical integration is no longer essential – the development of international spot and futures markets for crude oil has all but eliminated the need for vertical integration. In the natural gas industry, however, difficulties in transporting natural gas (it requires either pipelines or expensive liquefaction facilities) mean that deriving value from gas reserves depends critically upon the availability of a nearby market or transportation infrastructure.

The superior profitability of upstream activities over refining and marketing and chemicals is evident in the sectoral financial performance of the majors (see table 12.4). Although upstream activities accounted for only one-fifth of revenues for large oil firms, they contributed over two-thirds of overall profits in 2002. The reasons for the disparity between upstream and downstream profit rates are not immediately obvious. Oil and gas are commodities supplied by many competing companies and in a global industry where production capacity typically exceeds demand. For most primary raw materials, including metal ores, coal, building materials, or agricultural products, these conditions typically result in miserable rates of profit. The world oil market differs in the existence of an effective cartel. Although the Organization of Petroleum Exporting Countries (OPEC) accounted for only 46 percent of world oil production in 2001, OPEC's commitment to maintaining price stability through production quotas for its individual member countries has had an important influence on oil prices since the early 1970s. When OPEC's discipline over its members' oil production disintegrates, prices drop – sometimes catastrophically. In the summer of 1986 and at the end of 1998, crude oil prices fell below $10 a barrel. Since summer 1999, OPEC discipline together with disruptions to supplies in several key production areas has resulted in crude oil prices remaining, almost continuously, above $20 a barrel.

So long as crude oil prices remain at or above the mid-teens, most of the majors earn comfortable upstream profits. However, the extent of each company's profitability depends critically upon its costs. These vary between the companies (see table 12.5) and across geographical locations (see table 12.6). Eni's above average finding costs were primarily a result of the high cost of upstream activities in Italy.

Finding and development cost per barrel is the outcome of a chain of activities. Exploration begins with acquiring the legal rights to begin prospecting for reserves (typically allocated through a competitive bidding process). Geological and seismic analysis is then used to identify any "traps" (reservoirs of underground hydrocarbons). Drilling exploratory wells is extremely costly: hence, companies have invested heavily in new technologies to help identify potentially profitable traps prior to any drilling. However, until exploratory drilling confirms the presence of hydrocarbons, all prior analysis is scientifically informed guesswork. The main investment costs are incurred in bringing proven oil reserves into production through the construction and operation of drilling rigs, storage and loading facilities, and other infrastructure. As exploration has been forced into increasingly inhospitable locations – offshore locations in particular – the capital costs of exploration and production (E&P) have increased

Table 12.4 The majors' return on assets by business segment

	Exploration and production		Refining and marketing		Gas and power		Chemicals		Corporate and other	
	ROA 2000–2002	Share of total assets 2002	ROA 2000–2002	Share of total assets 2002	ROA 2000–2002	Share of total assets 2002	ROA 2000–2002	Share of total assets 2002	ROA 2000–2002	Share of total assets 2002
Exxon Mobil+	26.6%	48.8%	11.1%*	29.5%	n.a.	n.a.	5.8%	15.4%	(2.2%)	5.5%
RD/Shell	33.3%	36.1%	6.5%	37.8%	4.5%	12.1%	3.4%	11.6%	(5.0%)	3.3%
BP	19.8%	56.9%	10.7%	28.4%	32.2%	2.4%	1.8%	11.6%	(47.5%)	0.1%
ChevronTexaco	18.5%	66.6%	1.6%	28.6%	n.a.	n.a.	0.0%	1.7%	(146.8%)	3.3%
Eni	35.1%	58.9%	23.0%	9.2%	48.6%	21.3%	(15.4%)	4.9%	3.8%	0.4%
Total	25.0%	54.0%	16.3%	19.1%	n.a.	n.a.	7.3%	15.9%	16.4%	9.8%
Repsol	14.4%	41.0%	7.3%	32.3%	11.0%	6.8%	2.2%	7.4%	(1.8%)	12.5%

Notes: ROA is measured as segment operating earnings as a percentage of identifiable segment assets. Profit rates for Exxon Mobil and BP are Return on Capital Employed (in the case of BP, profit is measured on a replacement cost basis). ChevronTexaco's return is net income as a percentage of net fixed capital. Eni's returns are operating income as a percentage of net fixed assets.

n.a. = not available

* Includes gas and power

Source: Companies' annual reports.

Table 12.5 Finding and development costs by company, 1998–2002

	$/barrel of oil equivalent
TotalFinaElf	4.20
BP	4.20
Exxon Mobil	4.40
Repsol YPF	4.50
ChevronTexaco	4.80
Royal Dutch/Shell	5.60
Eni	6.30
Occidental	6.70
Burlington	6.90
ConocoPhillips	7.20
Unocal	8.70
Anadarko	9.60

Source: Eni, "Upstream Performance: Eni versus Benchmark Group", 2003.

Table 12.6 US energy companies finding costs by region, 1993–2000 (dollars/barrel of oil equivalent)

	US onshore	US offshore	Canada	OECD Europe	Africa	Middle East	Other, Eastern Hemisphere	Other, Western Hemisphere	World-wide
1993–1995	4.53	4.58	6.35	5.25	3.32	3.23	5.51	2.66	4.65
1998–2000	5.21	10.52	7.18	7.85	2.93	5.92	7.88	4.59	6.14

Source: Energy Information Agency, *Performance Profiles of Major Energy Producers, 2000*, US Department of Energy, Jan. 2000.

substantially. For natural gas fields, development costs are especially great due to the need for either pipelines or liquefaction plants. Yet, despite the industry's move to offshore locations, new technologies – 3D seismic analysis, directional drilling, light-weight platforms, semi-submersibles, enhanced recovery, reservoir modeling, to mention but a few – resulted in declining reserve replacement costs during the 1980s and 1990s.

New technology has not been the only source of upstream cost reduction in E&P. The oil and gas companies have outsourced more and more of their exploration and production activities. Drilling, seismic surveys, rig design, platform construction, and oilfield maintenance are increasingly undertaken by oilfield service companies. As these companies have developed proprietary technologies, deepened their experience, and grown through mergers and acquisitions, so sector leaders such as Schlumberger,

Baker Hughes, Halliburton, Diamond Offshore Drilling, Weatherford International, and Saipem have emerged as powerful players within the international petroleum industry. Increasingly they have emerged as risk-bearing partners with the oil and gas majors.

The political changes of the 1990s greatly expanded upstream opportunities for the petroleum majors. The collapse of the Soviet Union and the global trend to economic liberalization offered access to oil and gas reserves previously reserved for national oil companies. During the 1990s, China and the former Soviet Union were the main targets of attention. The immense, undeveloped, oil and gas reserves of the Caspian Sea have been especially attractive to western oil companies. Among the leading OPEC members, Saudi Arabia, Venezuela, and Iran have each opened their doors to investment. In May 2001 Saudi Arabia welcomed eight major petroleum companies led by Exxon Mobil to build a $25 billion natural gas infrastructure in an effort to free up more oil for export. Venezuela recently auctioned 35-year leases to explore, pump, and sell natural gas.

Over time, major discoveries create new oil producing nations (Norway, UK, Angola, and Colombia) while other countries gradually exhaust their reserves (USA, UK). In the future, the league table of leading producers will shift substantially. While Saudi Arabia, Iraq, Iran, Azerbaijan, Kazakhstan, and Venezuela have over 60 years of reserves at current rates of production, USA, Canada, Norway, UK, and Indonesia have 10 or less (see table 12.7).

The attractive rates of return earned in the upstream sector have meant that capital investment by the integrated majors has become increasingly focused upon E&P. During 1998–2001, the leading majors invested between three and four times as much upstream as downstream (see table 12.8).

Refining and Marketing

In oil, downstream businesses include refining and the wholesale and retail marketing and distribution of refined oil products. The most important refined product is gasoline; other important products include diesel fuel, aviation fuel, heating oil, liquefied petroleum gas (LPG), bitumen, and petrochemical feedstocks (e.g. naphtha). For almost all the majors, profitability of downstream activities has been dismal. Table 12.9 compares upstream and downstream profitability for US petroleum companies (see table 12.4 for the sectoral profitability of the individual majors). In both North America and Europe, the downstream sector has been subject to intense competitive pressure. Low demand growth (due mainly to increased energy efficiency and competition from natural gas), combined with heavy investment in catalytic cracking, and increased investment in refineries by the national oil companies, has resulted in serious excess capacity in refining. At the marketing level, the chief problem has been an excessive number of retail outlets. While the majors have sought to consolidate their market position through asset exchanges, joint ventures, and outright mergers, their attempts to reduce price competition in downstream markets have been thwarted by exit barriers and new entry. Downstream markets in Europe were particularly depressed – demand had been stag-

Table 12.7 Oil and gas production and reserves by country, 1991 and 2001

	Oil production (thousands of barrels/day)		Gas production (billions of cubic meters)		Oil reserves (billions of barrels)	Gas reserves (trillions cu. meters)
	2001	1991	2001	1991	2001	2001
Saudi Arabia	8,768	8,820	54	35	261.8	6.2
USA	7,717	9,076	555	510	30.4	5.0
Russia	7,056	9,326	542	600	48.6	47.6
Iran	3,688	3,500	61	26	89.7	23.0
Mexico	3,560	3,126	35	28	26.9	0.8
Venezuela	3,418	2,501	29	22	77.7	4.2
Norway	3,414	1,923	58	27	9.4	1.3
China	3,308	2,828	30	15	24.0	1.4
Canada	2,763	1,980	172	105	6.6	1.7
UK	2,503	1,919	106	51	4.9	0.7
UAE	2,422	2,639	41	24	97.8	6.0
Iraq	2,414	279	–	–	112.5	3.1
Kuwait	2,142	185	10	1	96.5	1.5
Nigeria	2,103	1,890	13	4	24.0	3.5
Algeria	1,563	1,351	78	53	9.2	4.5

Source: *BP Statistical Review of World Energy, 2001.*

Table 12.8 Capital investment by business sector among the majors, 1998–2002

	Av. annual capital expenditure ($, million)	Upstream (%)	Downstream (%)	Chemicals (%)	Other (%)
Exxon Mobil	13,255	66.1	19.8	11.5	1.4
Royal Dutch/Shell	15,690	62.1	25.0	8.8	3.5
BP	19,711	50.6	25.1	10.7	14.6*
TotalFinaElf	9,071	66.4	13.5	16.8	3.3
ChevronTexaco	11,645	66.5	15.5	2.9	15.2
Eni	7,179	63.1	25.3	5.0	6.5

* "Other" includes acquisition expenditures.
Source: Company annual reports.

nant for five years while excess capacity has remained stubbornly high. European refining margins fell below $2 a barrel in 2001, and continued to fall during 2002.

As refining capacity grew in the Middle East, European downstream markets came under increasing competitive pressure. At the retail level, the entry of supermarket chains into retail gasoline distribution was a key problem for the petroleum majors in several European countries (France and the UK especially). The majors responded by diversifying their retail activities. Increasingly, service stations have added restaurants and convenience stores to their dispensing of gasoline.

Table 12.9   Return on investment by line of business for US petroleum companies, 1980–99

	1980–4	1985–9	1990–4	1995–9
US oil and gas production	15.4%	4.0%	5.8%	10.1%
US refining and marketing	5.1%	8.0%	2.7%	5.7%
Foreign oil and gas production	19.3%	12.2%	9.1%	12.4%
Foreign refining and marketing	10.4%	6.8%	10.1%	7.0%
Coal	5.5%	4.7%	2.9%	6.1%

Source: Energy Information Administration, US Department of Energy.

Downstream Gas and Power

Among the petroleum majors, Eni was unusual in being established on natural gas rather than oil. For most of the majors, oil had been their dominant interest and, as a result, few had pursued the same strategy of vertical integration in gas that they had in oil. As the result, in most countries the gas chain was more fragmented than the oil chain with exploration and production undertaken by the petroleum companies, and distribution traditionally undertaken by state-owned or state-regulated utilities. As demand for natural gas increased during the 1980s and 1990s, the petroleum majors reoriented their upstream activities towards gas. However, gas reserves were valueless unless they could be brought to market. Hence all the majors developed interests in the transportation and downstream distribution of gas. Regulation of downstream gas markets and privatization of publicly owned gas utilities created the opportunities that the petroleum majors needed to increase their presence in gas marketing and distribution. Similar deregulation in electricity generation and marketing produced further opportunities for the majors – not only could they enter the electricity business directly, they could also seek to supply natural gas to independent power producers.

Although downstream gas and power offered growth opportunities for the petroleum majors, these activities typically did not offer rates of return comparable with their upstream businesses. The newly liberalized gas and electricity markets attracted entrants from a number of different sectors and were fiercely competitive. Moreover, the oil majors were relative newcomers to these markets compared with the traditional utilities. Fierce competition coupled with overinvestment could decimate profitability. During 2002, wholesale prices for electricity plunged in the US and UK forcing a number of power producers into acute financial difficulty.

Chemicals

The petrochemical sector displayed many of the same structural features as oil refining: capital-intensive processes producing commodity products, many competitors, and a continual tendency for excess capacity (much of it resulting from investments in the Far East and in the oil-producing countries) to drive down prices and margins. In their approach to chemicals, the petroleum majors fell into two groups. Some, like Eni, viewed chemicals as a fundamentally unattractive industry and believed that chemical plants were better run by chemical companies. Others (including Exxon, Shell, and Total) viewed chemicals as part of their core business and considered that vertical integration between refining and petrochemicals offered them a cost advantage.

During the 1990s, all the majors repositioned and restructured their chemical businesses. The two trends were: first, withdrawal from fertilizers, agricultural chemicals, and many specialty chemicals in order to concentrate on bulk petrochemicals; second, within bulk petrochemicals, the companies engaged in a series of asset swaps and joint ventures in order to build positions of leadership within specific product categories. Such leadership was founded upon two types of advantage: economies of scale and technological advantages through product or process innovations. By 2002, even the companies with the heaviest commitments to petrochemicals (Exxon, Shell, BP, and TotalFinaElf) were reducing their investments in chemicals as sluggish demand and continued new investment by Asian and Middle Eastern producers depressed profitability.

■ ENI IN 2003 ■

2003 was another year of sustained progress: operating income and net income were higher than 2002 and Eni comfortably exceeded its targets for oil and gas production and cost cutting.

Mincato was content that Eni had realized most of the goals that he had envisaged on becoming chief executive at the end of 1998. Eni was independent and financially and operationally robust. Its strong stock market performance would make it a difficult acquisition target, even without the protection of the Italian government's "golden share." Most important, Eni had a well-defined strategy and a clear identity as a company. Shorn of its various diversified businesses, Eni was purely an energy company. Within the industry, Eni had established a unique strategic position that fitted both its heritage and its capabilities. Through heavy capital investment in exploration and production and a series of acquisitions, Eni had greatly expanded its upstream position. Through its ambitious pipeline schemes and entry into the gas markets of Portugal, Spain, and Germany, Eni had built upon its dominant position in the Italian gas market to create one of the world's biggest vertically integrated natural gas businesses. By resisting the trend towards outsourcing engineering and oilfield service requirements, Eni had built a powerful set of technical capabilities.

Yet, for all Eni's solid achievement and increasing respect from both its energy industry peers and investment analysts, Mincato believed that the next four years would be critical for Eni. After spending its first half century playing catch up with leading oil majors, Eni had emerged as one of the most profitable and rapidly growing of the world's leading energy companies. (Appendix 4 shows financial performance of the leading majors.) However, increasing profits and creating value for shareholders was likely to be more difficult in the future than in the past. By 2003, Eni had divested most of its non-core businesses and eliminated most of the inefficiencies that it had inherited from its state-owned past. Increasing profits in the future would require pursuing profitable growth opportunities, more effective exploitation of existing competitive advantage, and building new sources of competitive advantage.

In many respects, Eni was well positioned with regard to the principal trends affecting the world's energy sector. Eni's traditional strength in gas had given it a vertically integrated presence that no other petroleum company could match. Italy's geographical position in terms of its proximity both to the huge gas reserves of North Africa, and to the markets of Europe, offered Eni a unique opportunity to link the two – particularly with its in-house engineering and construction capabilities.

But fulfilling Eni's potential would require developing the responsiveness and coordination that it needed to combine technology, physical assets, expertise, and human ingenuity to exploit the opportunities constantly emerging in the world's fast-changing energy markets. At the forefront of Mincato's mind were the internal challenges that Eni would have to overcome in order to successfully execute its strategy. Although major changes had taken place in organization (notably the creation of a divisionalized structure) and human resource management, further internal change was essential. The most obvious challenge was that of internationalization. Although Eni was internationally diversified upstream and in engineering and services, downstream – both in oil products and gas – Eni was heavily dependent on the Italian market. Overall, Italy accounted for almost half of Eni's sales and assets (see table 12.10). Internationalization was not just about increasing investment outside of Italy. The greatest challenges lay in internationalizing Eni's culture and personnel – including senior management ranks, where non-Italians and extensive overseas management experience were both scarce.

The second internal challenge was that of integration. Eni's large downstream gas business offered a market for its upstream gas production and its internal engineering and construction capabilities provided the means to link the two. Eni's ability to pursue vertical integration in gas represented a significant source of competitive advantage for the company. However, to realize this potential required effective collaboration between Eni's different divisions and subsidiaries. Although Mincato had created a more integrated divisional corporation, effective coordination required Eni's independently minded businesses breaking down organizational barriers and sharing information, know-how, and opportunities.

Other challenges were likely to emerge from the external environment. The most troubling of these was whether Eni could find sufficient investment opportunities to achieve its growth targets without undermining its profitability. Eni had achieved its growth by a combination of organic growth and selective acquisitions. Organic growth was inevitably incremental – the key to maintaining upstream profitability was to develop new E&P activities in locations where Eni had an existing infrastructure. More rapid growth could be achieved through acquisition, but here Mincato was aware that reckless acquisition would cause earnings dilution.

The second external challenge related to the investment community's apparent lack of appreciation for Eni's solid operational and financial performance. Mincato and Chief Financial Officer, Marco Mangiagalli, had cultivated sound relationships with shareholders and investment analysts. Yet, they were continually dismayed by the stock

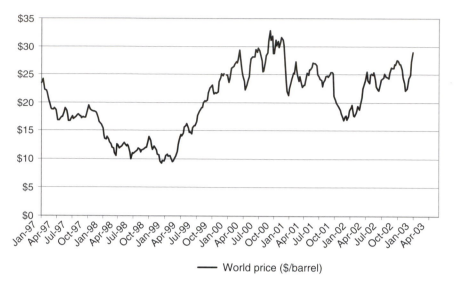

Figure 12.2 Average world spot price of crude oil, 1997–2003

APPENDIX 1

Table 12.A1 Eni SpA: selected financial data, 1997–2003

Income statement In millions of US$ except per share	1997	1998	1999	2000	2001	2002	2003*
Revenue	34,323	33,177	31,225	45,854	44,368	51,379	52,400
Cost of goods sold	21,854	21,730	20,247	29,518	28,330	33,440	34,566
Gross profit	12,469	11,447	10,978	16,336	16,038	17,939	17,834
Gross profit margin	36.3%	34.5%	35.2%	35.6%	36.1%	34.9%	34.0%
SG&A expense	3,339	3,415	2,801	2,615	2,538	3,253	3,166
Depreciation and amortization	3,955	4,423	3,617	3,608	4,247	5,771	5,151
Operating income	5,175	3,609	4,560	10,113	9,253	8,915	9,517
Operating margin	15.1%	10.9%	14.6%	22.1%	20.9%	17.4%	18.2%
Nonoperating income	739	1,634	1,561	91	1,635	45	17
Nonoperating expenses	250	48	502	481	423	206	154
Income before taxes	5,447	4,589	5,087	9,723	10,465	8,664	9,346
Income taxes	2,467	1,698	2,068	4,070	3,142	3,279	3,241
Net income after taxes	2,980	2,891	3,019	5,653	7,324	4,816	5,585
Net income from continuing operations	2,893	2,725	2,877	5,435	6,908	4,912	
Net profit margin	8.4%	8.2%	9.2%	11.9%	15.6%	9.6%	0.0%
ROACE	12.2%	10.7%	12.5%	21.5%	23.9%	13.7%	15.6%
Diluted EPS from total net income	3.62	3.41	3.59	6.80	8.83		
Dividends per share	n.a.	0.28	0.34	0.46	0.84	0.79	0.75

Table 12.A1 *continued*

Balance sheet	Dec 97	Dec 98	Dec 99	Dec 00	Dec 01	Dec-02	Dec-03*
Cash	1,736	912	1,220	1,168	1,162	3,423	3,265
Net receivables	11,067	10,733	10,838	12,566	12,219	14,186	13,530
Inventories	2,878	2,859	2,644	2,929	2,504	3,355	3,200
Other current assets	3,165	1,941	2,316	2,070	1,620	1,868	1,781
Total current assets	18,846	16,445	17,019	18,733	17,505	22,832	21,776
Net fixed assets	22,593	24,434	23,236	25,157	29,653	35,327	33,693
Other noncurrent assets	7,441	7,512	6,265	9,024	8,684	10,840	10,339
Total assets	48,880	48,391	46,520	52,914	55,842	69,000	65,808
Accounts payable	3,824	4,110	4,171	4,550	4,427	5,806	5,537
Short-term debt	8,673	5,793	4,797	5,015	4,656	8,273	7,890
Other current liabilities	6,413	6,294	6,292	9,440	7,341	8,560	8,165
Total current liabilities	18,910	16,197	15,260	19,005	16,424	22,639	21,592
Long-term debt	5,853	5,288	4,821	4,803	5,415	6,868	6,550
Other noncurrent liabilities	4,443	4,835	4,768	6,506	8,021	9,766	9,315
Total liabilities	32,107	29,478	27,993	30,314	29,860	39,274	37,457
Minority interest	809	1,107	1,117	1,570	1,519	2,196	2,094
Total shareholders' equity	16,773	18,913	18,527	22,600	25,982	27,530	28,351
Shares outstanding (mil.)	1,600	1,600	1,600	1,600	800	4,002	
Cash flow statement	1997	1998	1999	2000	2001	2002	2003*
Net operating cash flow	7,135	8,035	8,306	9,935	7,251	11,091	10,827

*2003 sales and net income are in millions of euros.

APPENDIX 2

Table 12.A2 Eni's operating performance, 1993–2003

	Units	1993	1994	1995	1996	1997	1998	1999	2000	2001	2002	2003
Exploration and production												
Hydrocarbon production	boe/d (×10³)	901	941	982	984	1.021	1.038	1.064	1.187	1.369	1.472	1.562
Hydrocarbon reserves	boe (×10⁶)	4.175	4.224	4.318	4.675	5.073	5.255	5.534	6.008	6.929	7.030	7.272
Reserve life index	years	12.8	12.4	11.9	13.1	13.6	13.4	14.0	14.0	13.7	13.2	12.7
Gas and power												
Primary distribution natural gas sales in Italy	cm (×10⁹)	48.65	47.43	52.55	53.23	53.10	55.64	60.19	59.92	58.89	52.56	52.80
Primary distribution natural gas sales in Europe destined to Italy	cm (×10⁹)					0.04	0.05	0.05	1.30	3.10	7.70	9.30
Sales of natural gas in secondary distribution outside Italy	cm (×10⁹)				2.80	2.79	2.73	2.67	3.48	3.91	3.79	4.44
Natural gas volumes transported on behalf of third parties	cm (×10⁹)	4.93	5.34	6.01	6.64	8.07	9.97	11.29	14.70	16.76		
Electricity production sold	GWh								4.766	4.987	5.004	5.550
Refining and marketing												
Production available from processing	ton (×10⁶)	33.7	40.5	38.1	37.8	36.4	40.1	38.3	38.9	37.8	35.6	33.5
Refining capacity utilization rate of owned refineries	%	90	89	86	87	94	103	96	99	97	99	100
Sales	ton (×10⁶)	53.1	52.3	51.9	51.4	51.6	54.2	51.8	53.5	53.2	52.0	49.9
Service stations	units	13.705	13.699	13.574	13.150	12.756	12.984	12.489	12.085	11.707	10.762	10.647
Average throughput per service station	l/year (×10⁶)	1.399	1.402	1.431	1.448	1.463	1.512	1.543	1.555	1.621	1.674	1.771
Oilfield services and engineering												
Orders acquired	mil euro	1.586	2.710	2.616	2.937	3.849	3.242	2.588	4.709	3.716	7.852	5.876
Orders backlog at 12/31	mil euro	2.598	3.471	4.035	4.350	5.163	4.931	4.438	6.638	6.937	10.065	9.405
Employees	units	108.556	91.544	86.422	83.424	80.178	78.906	72.023	69.969	72.405	80.655	76.521

Source: Eni Fact Books.

APPENDIX 3
Eni's Business Operations, 2003

Eni is an integrated energy company operating in the oil, natural gas, electricity generation, petrochemicals, engineering, and oilfield services through its divisions or affiliated companies. Figure 12.A3.1 shows the divisional structure.

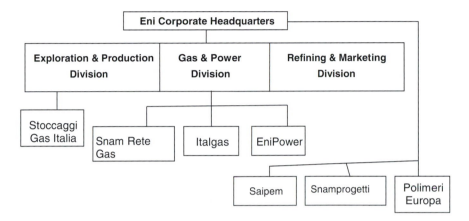

Figure 12.A1 Eni's organizational structure

Exploration and Production

Eni operates in exploration and production of oil and natural gas in Italy, North Africa, West Africa, the North Sea and the Gulf of Mexico. It also operates in areas with great development potential such as Latin America, Australia, the Middle and Far East and the Caspian Sea.

Eni intends to maintain a strong production growth in the near future leveraging on internal development and targeting over 1.8 million boe/day in 2006 (a yearly average increase of approximately 6 percent). Eni's proved reserves reached over 7 billion boe in 2003.

Eni is pursuing a program for the rationalization of its portfolio of assets aimed at concentrating its activities in areas with significant growth potential where Eni is operator: in 2002 Eni sold 16 interests in fields in the North Sea, Italy and Qatar, as well as exploration permits and other assets; Eni also acquired interests in operated or partially held assets in Kazakhstan, the United Kingdom, Norway and Australia.

The importance of the Kashagan oil field discovery in the Kazakh offshore of the Caspian Sea was confirmed by the appraisal activities performed and still underway in the area. The field's recoverable reserves, calculated according to the most recent estimates as 7–9 billion barrels, reaching 13 billion by employing the gas reinjection techniques, make Kashagan the most relevant discovery of the past thirty years.

E&P Strategies

Keep strong production growth rates
Rationalize and optimize asset portfolio
Select exploration areas
Intensify actions for efficiency improvement

Gas and Power

Gas Eni operates in natural gas supply, transmission, distribution, and sale. In 2002, sales of natural gas totaled 52.6 billion cubic meters in Italy, 8.2 billion cubic meters in Europe, and 3.8 billion cubic meters in secondary distribution outside Italy.

With the purchase in joint venture with German company EnBW of 97.81 percent of GVS, one of the largest regional operators in natural gas in Germany (where it transports and sells approximately 7 billion cubic meters of gas per year), Eni enters a large natural gas market and consolidates its European leadership in gas and power.

The agreement underway for the purchase of a 50 percent interest in Spanish natural gas company Unión Fenosa Gas, with an investment of euro 440 million, is an important step in Eni's strategy of international expansion of gas activities. . . .

Within its program of development of electricity generation capacity at Eni's industrial sites, work started for the construction of a new combined cycle power plant at Ferrera Erbognone (Pavia) . . . and for the upgrade of the Ravenna power plant.

Gas and Power Strategies

Develop natural gas sales in Europe
Maintain market shares in Italy at the levels set by new laws leveraging on the gas power
Implement significant marketing actions
Obtain a significant competitive positioning in electricity generation by building new power
    stations

Refining and Marketing

Eni operates in the refining and sale of refined products mainly in Italy, Europe, and Latin America. In distribution, with its Agip and IP brands, Eni is market leader in Italy. In 2002, Eni's sales of refined products amounted to 52 million tonnes, of which 33 million tonnes was in Italy.

Eni is implementing a rebalancing of its retail distribution activities in Italy and outside Italy and will continue the upgrading of its network in Italy by selling and closing marginal service stations and developing the stronger part of its network (service stations with high throughput and high non-oil potential) and its non-oil retail activities. Eni's objective is to reach European standards in terms of average throughput, services to customers, and automation. Outside Italy Eni intends to strengthen its position in selected areas in Europe where it can obtain logistical and operating synergies and exploit its well-known brand name. Eni also intends to increase the flexibility of its refining system [and] will intensify its efforts for efficiency improvements. . . .

Refining and Marketing Strategies
Continue the upgrading of the Italian distribution network and develop in selected areas outside
Increase refining complexity
Intensify actions for efficiency improvement

Oilfield Services and Engineering

Eni operates in oilfield services and engineering through Saipem and Snamprogetti. Saipem, a company listed on the Italian Stock Exchange (Eni's interest 43 percent), operates in oilfield services and is a world leader in the laying of underwater pipelines and the installation of offshore platforms, thanks to exclusive state-of-the-art technology and a world-class fleet of vessels, which has been upgraded with an investment plan amounting to over 1 billion euros, started in 1997. In the engineering and contracting area, Snamprogetti is one of the major international operators in the area of plants for hydrocarbon production, refining complexes, terminals for natural gas treatment, fertilizer and petrochemical plants, power stations, pipeline transport systems and infrastructure.

MAJOR PROJECTS

1. *Deep water*. Thanks to the experience gained in different areas of the world and the competence of its personnel, Eni has developed innovative technologies and methods for all phases of the activity: from exploration to drilling and production. Eni operates in several exploration projects in deep waters (more than 450 meters) and ultra-deep waters (more than 1,500 meters) including offshore Nigeria, Angola, Congo, and Gabon. Ultra-deep water offshore activities are also underway in the Gulf of Mexico and off the coast of Brazil.
2. *Transmed*. This 2,200 km gasline links Italy to one of the world's biggest natural gas reservoirs, located in the Algerian desert. Construction of the first pipeline was completed in 1983. In 1997, a second pipeline was laid.
3. *Blue Stream*. The Blue Stream is undoubtedly one of the most challenging projects of its type ever attempted because of the difficulties in terms of design, construction, organization, and logistics. The 1,250 km gasline links the gas distribution network of the Krasnodar region in southern Russia to the central Turkish grid at Ankara. Supplies of natural gas will start in 2003 and continue up to 2025, peaking at 16 billion cubic meters a year.
4. *Karachaganak project*. Eni works with British Gas to produce oil, gas, and condensates in Karachaganak field in the northwestern region of Kazakhstan. The project involves over 70 wells, collection and distribution networks, and constructing pipelines to connect Caspian Pipeline Consortium. Eni's production share will peak at around 72,000 barrels per day in 2009.

Source: "Eni SpA: Operations and Strategies" (www.eni.it).

APPENDIX 4

Table 12.A3 The world's top 20 petroleum companies, 2000

	PIW Index*	Company	Ownership	Reserves		Output		Refinery capacity (thous. B/D)	Product sales (thous. B/D)
				Liquids (mil. BBL)	Gas (BFC)	Liquids (mil. BBL)	Gas (BFC)		
1.	100.0	Saudi Aramco	State	259,200	213,300	8,044	3,302	1,992	2,650
2.	98.8	Exxon/Mobil	Public	11,260	56,796	2,444	11,378	6,400	8,887
2.	98.8	PDVSA	State	76,852	146,719	2,950	4,000	3,096	2,500
4.	98.0	NIOC	State	87,993	816,882	3,620	5,144	1,534	1,342
5.	97.4	Royal Dutch/Shell	Public	9,775	58,541	2,268	8,218	3,212	6,795
6.	92.1	British Petroleum	Public	7,572	35,526	2,061	6,067	2,801	5,002
7.	91.8	Pemex	State	28,400	30,005	3,343	4,791	1,528	1,650
8.	85.4	Pertamina	State	7,860	118,702	973	6,300	1,050	1,190
9.	84.5	TotalFinaElf	Public	6,869	13,385	1,468	3,175	2,586	3,168
10.	81.6	KPC	State	96,500	52,700	2,025	936	1,075	1,165
11.	80.2	Sonatrach	State	8,830	136,303	1,480	7,587	485	750
12.	79.9	PetroChina	State**	10,999	24,603	2,124	674	2,066	1,367
13.	77.8	Petrobras	State	8,100	10,663	1,191	1,235	1,953	1,818
14.	77.0	Chevron	Public	4,784	9,056	1,127	2,513	1,524	2,384
15.	73.2	Texaco	Public	3,480	8,108	885	1,999	1,417	3,221
16.	70.3	Adnoc	State	50,710	196,100	1,240	3,185	234	455
17.	67.1	ENI	Public	3,137	13,665	666	2,342	824	940
18.	63.0	Repsol YFP	Public	2,150	14,310	451	1,298	1,206	920
19.	62.7	INOC	State	112,500	109,800	2,528	320	348	520
20.	59.5	Libya INOC	State	23,600	46,243	1,211	600	380	400
20.	59.5	Petronas	State	2,952	64,469	636	5,097	290	425
		Totals		823,523	2,175,876	42,735	80,161	36,001	47,549

*Petroleum Intelligence Weekly's ranking based on reserves, output, capacity and sales; **IPO or ADR listed on NYSE April 2000; 89% of shares held by state-owned parent company; BBL = barrels; BCF = billion cubic feet; B/D = barrels per day.

Source: Standard and Poors. Oil and Gas: Production and Marketing Industry Survey.

NOTES

1.   After Exxon Mobil, Royal Dutch/Shell, BP, TotalFinaElf, and ChevronTexaco.
2.   Fred Kapner, "Chief keeps it 'orderly' at Eni," FT.com, 30 January 2003.
3.   We refer throughout the case to "Eni." For most of its history as a state-owned enterprise, the company's full name was Ente Nazionale Idrocarburi, but was known by its acronym, ENI. On becoming a joint stock company, its name was changed to ENI SpA. Under Mr Mincato's leadership the acronym ENI was replaced by the simple word Eni.
4.   In common with other European governments, Italy recognized the growing strategic importance of oil and wished to avoid dependence upon foreign-owned multinationals for its fuel supplies. The British government had purchased a controlling interest in BP in 1914 and France had established the Compagnie Française des Pétroles (Total) in 1924.
5.   Dow Votaw, *The Six-Legged Dog: Mattei and ENI – A Study in Power*, University of California Press, Berkeley, CA, 1964, p. 15.
6.   Daniel Yergin, *The Prize*, Simon & Schuster, New York, 1992, p. 502.
7.   www.Eni.it/english/panorama/storia/storia.html.
8.   Ibid., p. 23.
9.   Ibid., p. 23.
10. Section sourced from "L'Eni di Fronte a un Bivio," Eni SpA, 2002.
11. Dow Votaw, *The Six-Legged Dog: Mattei and ENI – A Study in Power*, University of California Press, Berkeley, CA, 1964, p. 71.
12. "L'Eni di Fronte a un Bivio," Eni SpA, 2002, p. 5.
13. *Franco Bernabè at Eni*, Harvard Business School Case No. 9-498-034, April 7, 1998.
14. Chairman Gabriele Cagliari later committed suicide in prison.
15. "L'Eni di Fronte a un Bivio," Eni SpA, 2002, p. 11.
16. "Eni savors the taste of freedom," *Financial Times*, June 9, 1994.
17. Securities and Exchange Commission, ENI SpA, Form 20-F, 1996.
18. "Eni savors the taste of freedom," *Financial Times*, June 9, 1994.
19. *Franco Bernabè at Eni*, Harvard Business School Case 9-498-034, April 7, 1998.
20. Securities and Exchange Commission, ENI SpA, Form 20-F, 1996, p. 3.
21. Ibid, p. 1.
22. "Interview Vittorio Mincato," *Financial Times*, October 12, 1999.
23. Ibid.
24. "Letter to shareholders," Eni Annual Report 1999, pp. 4–5.
25. "L'Eni di Fronte a un Bivio," Eni SpA, 2002, p. 14.
26. "The important thing is that the target company should be rightly sized to be integrated easily," observed Mincato ("Eni, Thinking Big," *Petroleum Economist*, February 11, 2002).
27. "A quiet baritone on Italy's oil and gas stage: Vittorio Mincato," *Financial Times*, May 28, 2001.
28. Interview with Vittorio Mincato, *ECOS*, Vol. 30, No. 6, 2001, p. 12.
29. In December 1998, crude prices fell below $10 per barrel.
30. Interview with Vittorio Mincato, *ECOS*, Vol. 30, No. 6, 2001, p. 12.

Birds Eye and the UK Frozen Food Industry

Robert M. Grant

On February 12, 1946, George Muddiman arrived in Liverpool from Canada to take up the job as first chairman of Birds Eye Foods Ltd. "It was raining," he recalled. "There were no lights on the streets; it was seven o'clock at night and dark. As I looked out of the cab window my heart went into my boots and I thought, 'What have I done? Why have I left Canada to come to this?'"

By the early 1950s, after a host of problems with production, raw materials, and distribution, Birds Eye was firmly established. In 1952, it opened the "Empire's largest quick-frozen food factory" in Great Yarmouth and was set to embark upon a period of continuous expansion. By 1964 the food sales for the previous year had grown to £75 million (from a mere £150,000 in 1946), with Birds Eye accounting for 70 percent of the market.

However, from the late 1960s both return on capital and market share declined as competition in the market intensified. By the retirement of Birds Eye's second chairman, James ("Mr Fish Fingers") Parratt in July 1972, the company's fortunes had passed their peak and by 1983, Birds Eye's share of retail frozen food sales had shrunk to 18.5 percent.

■ **BEGINNINGS**[1] ■

Quick-freezing arrests the process of decay in perishable foods and enables fresh foods to be distributed to the consumer, wherever located and at any season. However, the freezing process must be quick to prevent the formation of large ice crystals that damage the cell structure of the food. By the late 1920s General Foods Corporation was

This case is based upon an earlier case by Robert M. Grant, subsequently developed by David Collis and published by Harvard Business School (*Birds Eye and the Frozen Foods Industry [A]*, Case Number 9-792-074, 1994).

successfully manufacturing and marketing "Birds Eye" frozen foods in the United States using the multi-plate quick-freezers developed by Clarence Birdseye.

The establishment of Birds Eye frozen foods in the UK was the initiative of Robert Ducas, chairman of a Kent engineering company, Winget Ltd, who had tried frozen foods in the US and was impressed by their British potential. In August 1938 Birds Eye Foods Ltd was incorporated, owned by General Foods Corp., Robert Ducas, and Chivers and Sons Ltd (a British canner and jam-maker).

Birds Eye was not alone in pioneering frozen foods in Britain. Commercial quick-freezing had begun in Britain before 1939, initiated by Smedley's (National Canning). In the early years Smedley's was better established than Birds Eye. Among other leading firms striving to establish viable frozen food businesses were several distributors and marketers of fish, notably Smethurst Ltd, Mudd and Son, and Associated Fisheries Ltd (through Eskimo Foods Ltd). A cold storage company launched "Fropax" frozen foods and Manuel's, an importer and wholesaler of frozen foods, obtained the UK concession for importing and distributing Findus frozen foods.

By 1942, Unilever had become strongly interested in the Birds Eye business for its value to its subsidiaries Macfisheries (fish), Batchelors Peas (dried peas), and Poulton & Noel, Ltd (poultry). At a meeting of Unilever's management committee on February 4, 1942, the guidelines for a frozen food business were established.

> They expected to see the business develop in three main groups of produce – fruit and vegetables, fish, and meat. They hoped to see Birds Eye companies in operation all over the world, and they expected to get together a team of people who could go wherever they were needed to give help with setting up these new companies. They could see that some of their products were likely to be expensive, and they were not against running luxury lines, but in the true tradition of a business founded on the demand of the mass market for everyday products, they hoped that, in general, the business would be built on the large-scale development of certain main products.[2]

In March 1943, when World War II was at its height, Unilever acquired Birds Eye Foods. Its task of establishing a frozen food business in the UK was formidable:

> The costs of quick-freezing are high, and it does not pay to freeze any food except the best, that will sell for a price high enough to cover overhead and yield a profit worth having. . . . Next, food must be frozen at the top of its condition or most of the value of the process is lost. That means that something must be done to see that produce is gathered at precisely the right moment and processed, if possible, within hours. For fish, of course, and for some other foods there can be no control over production, but there must be a highly efficient buying organization.
>
> When the produce is frozen, there is the problem of keeping it frozen until it reaches the [consumer]. Since many of the products, such as peas, are seasonal, that means keeping them for months in cold storage. On the journey from factory to shop, there must be insulated vehicles. In the shops themselves, there must be cabinets; the shopkeepers must be persuaded to find room, and somebody must finance them – either the shopkeepers themselves or the freezing firms.[3]

Birds Eye's early history was directed towards establishing an organization that was fully integrated from controlling food production to stocking the retailer's frozen food cabinet. In the absence of a well-developed infrastructure for producing, storing, distributing, and retailing frozen foods, Birds Eye was forced to build its own system.

■ BUILDING MARKET LEADERSHIP ■

Production and Raw Material Supplies

In production, the chief problems arose from the concentration of processing into a short time space, the unreliability of machinery, and the lack of skilled labor. Much of the machinery had to be imported from the US and Canada, and capital costs were high. Over two-thirds of processing costs were fixed, although each plate freezer could be used to freeze almost any food depending on seasonal availability. The location of frozen food processing factories was determined primarily by the source of raw materials. Prepared foods, like desserts or entrees, could be located anywhere. However, for vegetables and fish, production needed to be located on the eastern side of Great Britain, near the vegetable growing areas and the big fishing ports. Peas, for example, needed to be processed within 90 minutes of picking so processing plants were concentrated in Humberside, Lincolnshire, and East Anglia. By 1960, Birds Eye operated six factories and associated cold stores at Great Yarmouth, Lowestoft, Kirkby, Grimsby, Hull, and Eastbourne. Each factory produced a number of different products in order to utilize manpower and equipment efficiently in the face of seasonal availability of raw materials.

Once production facilities had been planned, the next task was to secure supplies of high-quality raw materials. For vegetables, this was usually achieved through annual contracts with farmers who committed a certain acreage to Birds Eye, in return for a fixed price per ton according to quality. Birds Eye exercised close control over the crops, supplying the seed, determining the planting times, and approving the fertilizer and insecticide used. Technicians monitored the moisture level in the produce to determine the optimal harvesting time and radioed the processing plants, which coordinated the movement of harvesting equipment from farm to farm and the transportation of produce from farm to factory.

Initially, Birds Eye owned most of the harvesting equipment that growers used. Equipment took the place of manual labor because of the speed with which the crop needed to be harvested before freezing. Over the years, growers bought their own machines under long-term contracts with Birds Eye, which agreed to repurchase the equipment if the parties could not agree on an annual acreage contract. Because of the high cost of pea harvesting equipment, farmer cooperatives became the main source of vegetables. By 1974 they were supplying 70 percent of the peas and 60 percent of the beans used for freezing. Many had been supplying Birds Eye continuously for 20 years. As the demand for frozen vegetables grew, the frozen food industry became the single most important customer for green vegetables. In 1975, half of all the peas were grown for freezing, as were three-quarters of green beans.

The fish used for quick-freezing was whitefish, mainly cod, haddock, halibut, plaice, sole, and coley. Most of it was either bought fresh from dockside auctions, or imported from Scandinavia in frozen blocks of fillets for use in fish fingers and other heavily processed items. Some fish, however, was frozen at sea and bought on contract. A typical contract guaranteed to buy a proportion of the catch, provided the catch exceeded a certain size, at a price up to 5 percent below the previous month's auction price. By the late 1960s, one-third of the total whitefish catch went to frozen food companies; as a result, contracts were tending to replace open auction at fish markets. Birds Eye also purchased fish at dockside auctions – mainly at Grimsby.

In some instances, Birds Eye sought direct ownership of its sources of raw material. It entered the broiler chicken industry in 1958 and within a few years had built a capacity for producing 6.5 million birds a year at about twenty farms. It sold the farms to Ross Poultry in 1972 in the face of overproduction in the broiler chicken industry and a belief that it was of suboptimal size. In 1965, Birds Eye acquired a majority stake in a fishing company to secure a regular supply of cod. Operating problems coincided with a drop in world fish prices, and Birds Eye sold the assets of the fishing company in 1969.

As Birds Eye developed a number of innovations in food processing and freezing techniques and developments in quality management, it sought improvements in the production of its raw materials. In horticulture, Birds Eye was responsible for improvements in vegetable cultivation techniques, and harvesting equipment.

Distribution

Production problems were minor in comparison with those of establishing a national system of distribution. Distribution costs were estimated at between 15 and 25 percent of total costs for frozen food.[4] Only a limited capacity existed in public cold stores, which were used primarily for frozen meat, frozen fish, and ice cream. These were concentrated near big cities. Cold stores were also expensive. A minimum efficient scale cold store of 2.4 million cubic feet cost £0.6m in the mid-1960s. It was estimated that each doubling of capacity reduced operating expenses by 20 percent.

Birds Eye's investment in cold storage and refrigerated distribution was primarily through its sister company, SPD (Speedy Prompt Delivery) – also a wholly owned subsidiary of Unilever:

> SPD was increasingly drawn into the problem. They developed their cold storage capacity and added insulated vehicles to get the goods to shops. . . . Cold storage has increased steadily, with buildings that were more and more advanced in their design. Depots were run in close conjunction with SPD and increased to the point where Birds Eye could store about 50,000 tons of frozen food.[5]

By the end of the 1960s, SPD had built a national system of frozen food distribution for Birds Eye. It operated from 42 depots and enabled Birds Eye to directly serve some 93,000 outlets. Birds Eye treated it as an integral part of its own activities, paying for its services at cost and making an annual profit contribution to cover the capital employed by SPD on Birds Eye's behalf. In the few areas that it could not serve cost-effectively, Birds Eye franchised exclusive wholesalers to distribute its frozen foods to retailers. The coordination of investment between Birds Eye and SPD allowed Birds Eye's tonnage sales to increase at a remarkable 40 percent per annum during the 1950s.

Retailing

The biggest barrier to the development of the frozen foods industry was the state of retail distribution. During the 1940s and early 1950s retail distribution was highly fragmented, with many small shops and with counter service nearly universal. The structure of the retail trade virtually ossified in the early post-war period as a result of food rationing which continued until 1953 and almost eliminated competition among retailers. The chief short-term problem was persuading food retailers to install refrigerated cabinets:

> At an average cost of about £150, a QIF cabinet is a big enough outlay to cause the average retailer to think twice about installing one. However, it can be shown that an average-sized cabinet of 10 cu. ft. can be made – even without proper siting – to yield an annual turnover of anything between £500 and £1,500. On an average retail margin of 20%, a retailer with an annual turnover of, say, £1,000 can net a profit of £200 before servicing and maintenance charges are deducted. Over the 12–15-year life of the cabinet this represents a substantial return on investment.[6]

In the supply of ice cream, the major manufacturers lent cabinets to retailers. The problem of this approach was the enormous capital requirements (equivalent at least to the size of investment in production facilities). In 1953, Birds Eye decided that it would not rent cabinets to retailers. Instead, it persuaded two producers of industrial refrigerators and air-conditioning equipment, Prestcold and Frigidaire, to start the production of "open top" display cabinets suitable for frozen food storage and display. Birds Eye only sought new business with retailers that installed such cabinets.

Market Development and Product Innovation

With the infrastructure in place, demand for frozen foods expanded. In the beginning, frozen foods were regarded as a luxury preferred over canned or dried food for their retention of the appearance and flavor of the fresh product.

As the price of frozen foods fell, growth increased rapidly, though the price elasticity of demand remained very high and seasonal and annual fluctuations in the consumption of frozen foods were strongly influenced by the price and availability of fresh produce. Between 1956 and 1981, sales increased at an average annual rate of about 15 percent, although the rate of growth of tonnage sales tended to decline over time. From 1956 to 1961, average annual growth was 36 percent, falling to 10.5 percent per annum between 1962 and 1973, and 6.9 percent between 1974 and 1980. Table 13.1 shows the growth in UK spending on frozen food sales.

During the 1950s and 1960s, the number of retail outlets supplying frozen foods expanded rapidly. So too did the range of frozen foods available. Beginning with seasonal produce – green vegetables and fruit – a wide variety of processed foods and prepared meals soon appeared.

Once Birds Eye had established its integrated system of production and distribution during the 1950s, its strategy became more marketing oriented. With a national, inte-

Table 13.1 UK frozen food expenditure 1967–82

	Total constant 1975 prices (£ million)	Freezer owners (%)	Non-freezer owners (%)	Consumption	
				In-home (%)	Catering (%)
1967	322	–	–	84	16
1973	510	17	54	71	29
1974	527	20	50	70	30
1975	500	24	48	72	28
1976	515	30	46	76	24
1977	508	32	43	75	25
1978	514	37	40	77	23
1979	539	40	37	77	23
1980	570	47	32	79	21
1981	593	53	28	81	19
1982	621	59	24	84	16
1983	646	63	21	84	16
1984	692	67	18	85	15

Source: Birds Eye.

grated organization in place, the company's principal task was to expand sales by introducing new products, promoting consumer awareness of the convenience and value for money of frozen foods, and developing consumer recognition of the quality associated with the Birds Eye brand. The introduction of fish fingers in 1955 was followed by beefburgers in 1960 and by a stream of new fish, meat, and dessert products. The five biggest-selling products – peas, beans, chips, fish fingers, and beefburgers – accounted for nearly 40 percent of revenue. The introduction of commercial television in 1955 was vitally important for its marketing strategy by allowing it to engage in mass-market advertising of its brand and new products. The medium also gave Birds Eye a big advantage over smaller producers – until 1958, Birds Eye was the sole industry advertiser.

Birds Eye pioneered frozen foods with a product quality higher than people were used to in processed food and with a personality that combined efficiency, hygiene, confidence, and completeness. Bird Eye added values beyond the physical and functional ones that contributed to a clear and likeable personality for the brand.[7]

■ BIRDS EYE'S MARKET DOMINANCE ■

The result of Birds Eye's pioneering efforts backed by massive investment by the Unilever Group was Bird Eye's dominance of the fast-growing UK frozen food market. Throughout the 1950s and 1960s, Birds Eye accounted for over 60 percent of UK frozen food sales on a tonnage basis. In terms of the retail market, the company estimated its brand market share at over 70 percent by value and around two-thirds by tonnage for most of the period. Among the outlets served by Birds Eye, its share of

Table 13.2 Brand shares of the UK retail market for frozen foods (% of total volume)

	1966	1970	1974	1978	1982
Birds Eye	62	60	45	29	20
Ross	5	8	6	6	8
Findus	13	13	11	8	4
Own-label	–	6	14	21	28
Other	20	13	21	35	40

Table 13.3 Comparative profitability (pre-tax return on capital employed %)

	1964	1967	1971	1972	1973	1974
Birds Eye	16.2	22.2	19.1	18.4	18.7	15.9
Findus	n.a.	n.a.	7.2	5.9	7.2	8.9
Ross	n.a.	n.a.	n.a.	7.6	5.5	4.3
UK manufacturing industry	14.6	12.0	12.5	14.9	17.4	17.4

Source: Monopolies and Mergers Commission.

frozen food sales was 75 percent, and some 40,000 retail outlets were served exclusively by Birds Eye. Its top twenty retail customers accounted for nearly a third of total sales.

Birds Eye held a substantial competitive advantage over its closest competitors, Ross and Findus, and consistently achieved higher returns on capital employed (on an historic cost basis) than them. In 1974, for example, while Birds Eye's return on capital stood at 15.9 percent, Findus earned 8.9 percent (frozen food only) and Ross Foods earned 4.3 percent (all food businesses). Both Findus and Ross acted as followers to Birds Eye, while Birds Eye pioneered the development of the market. Findus and Ross followed with similar approaches to production, distribution, product development, and marketing. Because they imitated many of Birds Eye's product and marketing strategies, their advertising expenditures were limited. Ross Foods' parent company, Imperial Foods, told the Monopolies and Mergers Commission that it "considered massive brand support aimed at achieving dramatic increases in sales, to be far beyond the means of its frozen food companies and it never sought to answer Birds Eye's intensive advertising in kind. In 1973, Ross Foods virtually ceased advertising its retail packs since it was not making it more competitive."[8] Tables 13.2 and 13.3 show Birds Eye's brand leadership and superior profitability.

Neither of these leading competitors was prepared to undercut Birds Eye. Birds Eye's brand leadership was evident in the pattern of pricing behavior observed in the industry. Based on the evidence of published list prices, the Monopolies and Mergers Commission concluded: "The recommended retail prices of Birds Eye, Ross Foods, and Findus frozen food have until recently moved broadly in parallel, with Birds Eye more often than not, being the first to change its price."[9] The willingness of smaller producers to follow Birds Eye was explained by Imperial Foods:

In supplying frozen foods to retailers for sale under the Ross name, Ross Foods sets its prices generally at the same level as Birds Eye. Since Ross Foods only advertises and promotes its products on a very limited scale, it cannot hope to win space in retailers' cabinets and charge prices above those charged by Birds Eye. On the other hand it cannot afford to undercut Birds Eye's prices to any significant extent.[10]

Birds Eye's retail dominance was assisted by a system of discounts that encouraged larger retailers to give Birds Eye the major part of their frozen foods business. The company offered discounts to a number of retailers. The size of discounts from its published trade prices depended on the annual turnover of the retailer, the cabinet space allocated to Birds Eye products, and the frequency and size of deliveries. Overall discounts averaged 6 percent of the gross revenues of all retailers. Its "criterion in discount negotiation was to achieve a consistent level of gross profitability from various customers"[11] and the discounts were intended to capture differences in the costs of serving different customers. As a result, "large retailers achieved the highest discount – over 10% of the gross value of their purchases – although these were said to exceed the cost savings in supplying them."[12]

■ THE GROWTH OF COMPETITION ■

During the 1970s and into the 1980s, Birds Eye's market share, and its profitability, declined as competition grew in the frozen foods market.

Developments in Retailing

In the 1960s, developments in food retailing began to influence the frozen food industry. First was the move away from counter service towards self-service which increased vastly the marketing opportunities available to the frozen food processors, including introducing new and novel products and packaging. Second was the emergence of supermarkets and large supermarket chains. In 1960 there were only 367 supermarkets (self-service food shops with 2,000 square feet or more floor space). The ability of the supermarket chains to pass on their cost savings to consumers, together with consumers' demand for the wider variety of goods made available by supermarkets, were major factors behind increasing concentration in the grocery trade.

Many of the major supermarket chains operated central or regional warehouses from which they distributed grocery products to their individual supermarkets. They also began to supply their own brands of frozen foods. Following the introduction by Sainsbury of its own brand of frozen peas in 1967, retailers' brands took an increasing share of retail frozen food sales.

The impact of supermarkets in expanding the amount of retail cabinet space available was reinforced towards the end of the 1960s by the introduction of specialist frozen foods stores to serve the increasing number of home freezer owners. To serve this growing market, a new model of frozen food retailing emerged: home freezer centers that combined the sale of home freezers with the sale of large packs of frozen

Table 13.4 Shares of UK packaged grocery sales by type of retailer

	1970	1974	1978	1981
Multiples	49	53	64	70
Cooperatives	19	21	18	17
Voluntary groups	16	14	10	
Independents	18	13	8	6
Four-firm concentration ratio	0.26	0.27	0.34	0.42

Source: C. Baden Fuller, *Rising Concentration: The UK Grocery Trade 1970–82*, London Business School, 1984.

foods (packed for caterers). The retailing of frozen foods by these outlets was characterized by large pack sizes, wide product range, lack of brand consciousness, and low prices. Larger cabinet capacity, usually with backup storage, enabled freezer centers to require fewer deliveries with bigger drops. Their share of frozen food sales was 18 percent in 1978 and 23.5 percent in 1986. Table 13.4 shows the changing structure of UK grocery retailing.

New Entry

While the early development of the industry had seen a consolidation around three major, vertically integrated suppliers, there was a wave of new entries in the 1960s and 1970s. For companies already engaged in food processing, a new technology, blast freezers, could be purchased "off the shelf" for as little as a few thousand pounds for a small unit. These allowed freezing and packing to occur together and eliminated the need for two separate production processes. While large-scale processing and freezing offered opportunities for automation and greater division of labor, the cost savings from increased scale of production tended to be small.

New entrants to the industry were a diverse group. The Monopolies Commission observed in 1976 that:

> A number of new companies have entered the frozen food processing industry during the past twenty years. They include Jus-Roll Ltd and Primecut Foods Ltd (then W. B. Wright Provision Ltd) in 1954, Northray Foods Ltd in 1956, Kraft Foods Ltd in 1963, McCain International Ltd and Potato and Allied Services Ltd in 1968, Frozen Quality Ltd in 1969, Country Range Ltd and King Harry Foods in 1970, White House Foods Ltd and Fife Growers Ltd in 1971, and Wold Growers Ltd in 1974.
>
> Although some of the new entrants have been new enterprises, most have been either established companies or subsidiaries of established companies. In many cases companies already engaged in the production of food have extended production to include frozen foods. Many of the smaller processors of vegetables and fruit, for example, Northray Foods Ltd, Frozen Quality Ltd, Fife Growers Ltd and Wold Pea Growers Ltd originated as agricultural cooperatives. Among the meat companies which have entered frozen food processing are FMC Ltd, Dalgety Ltd (chiefly through Dalgety-Buswell Ltd and Dalgety Frozen

Foods Ltd) and Thos Borthwick & Sons Ltd (through Freshbake Foods Ltd). Several fishing and fish merchanting companies have developed the processing of frozen food, notably Associated Fisheries Ltd, J. Marr (Fish Merchants) Ltd and Chaldur Frozen Fish Co. Ltd.

[Most] companies specialize in one or other of the broad categories of frozen food products, namely vegetables, fish, meat products and fruit and confectionery. Some companies specialize in a single product only – McCain's output is exclusively potato chips and King Harry Foods produces mainly pizzas.[13]

In addition, marketing-only companies, such as W. B. Pellew-Harvey & Co. Ltd and J. Muirhead, emerged. These bought frozen food from other manufacturers and placed their own brand names, "Angelus," "Chef's Garden," and "4F," on the products. Independent companies such as Christian Salvesen handled their physical distribution needs.

Specialist storage, freezing, and transportation providers played a critical role in allowing the entry and viability of these smaller, specialist, frozen food suppliers. Public cold storage companies such as Christian Salvesen, Union Cold Storage, and Frigoscandia doubled their cold storage capacity between 1969 and 1973. These companies came to offer not only storage facilities but also a comprehensive range of processing, freezing, and distribution services. By 1974, Christian Salvesen's cold storage capacity was almost one-third of Birds Eye's. In 1978, Christian Salevesen processed three-quarters of the vegetables it stored, up from 20 percent in 1969. Services were made available on medium term, multi-year contracts. Salvesen's fleet of refrigerated trucks operating out of its national network of cold stores was also available for rent, either on long-term contracts or as needed. Sainsbury and Marks & Spencer, two of Britain's largest food retailers each with a wide range of own-brand frozen foods, used Christian Salvesen for some of their refrigerated distribution needs. Other firms specialized in the importing, broking, and distribution of frozen foods. For example, Frionor and Bonduelle began marketing products imported from their overseas parents while companies such as Anglo European foods, Snowking, Frozen Foods, and Flying Goose specialized in distribution (mainly to the catering trade).

The rapid growth of eating away from the home by the British, and the rapid shift of the catering industry from fresh and canned foods to frozen foods, provided a particularly attractive opportunity for new entrants into frozen foods. Catering establishments were served by a separate segment of the market that was more concerned with price than with brand name recognition and sophisticated product packaging. Smaller processors could easily market their products to the catering trade without the need for investing in brands and distribution. From serving the catering industry it was easy to expand into supplies to retail home freezer centers and to supermarkets' own-label products.

Decline and Strategic Reappraisal

The retirement of Birds Eye's chairman, James Parratt, in July 1972 marked the highpoint of the company's fortunes. Under his successor, Kenneth Webb, Birds Eye was to face a new era of competitive pressure that led to a fundamental reassessment of its strategy.

Although still far and away the UK market leader in frozen foods, Birds Eye's market dominance existed primarily in sales of small retail packs to independent grocers and to a lesser extent, supermarkets. Birds Eye was poorly represented in some areas: in home freezer centers its share was around 8 percent in 1974 and it had little involvement in retailers' own labels. In the catering sector Birds Eye's market share by value was about 10 percent in 1973. After the early 1970s, the company's share of tonnage sales fell continuously although the market as a whole continued to expand, albeit at a slower rate.

To respond to changes in the market – particularly the rise in bulk buying by consumers with home freezers – and to the competition of recent entrants in this sector, Birds Eye introduced bulk packs to the retail market in 1972 and followed this with the establishment in 1974 of a new business, County Fair Foods, to supply the home freezer centers and other purchasers willing to accept a minimum drop size. County Fair Foods shared production facilities with Birds Eye but had a separate distribution system using Christian Salvesen because of the different requirements of freezer centers with regard to quality, product types, distribution, prices, and promotion. In 1976, Birds Eye established Menumaster Ltd to supply frozen prepared meals to caterers. In the traditional retail market, Birds Eye's main aim was to maintain sales growth, primarily by extending its product range through new product introductions. During the 1970s the company's dependence upon its traditional products – vegetables, fish fingers, and beefburgers – was reduced by a constant flow of new product introductions – especially ready-to-eat meals, desserts, and ethnic dishes (e.g. Chinese, Indian, and Italian dishes).

The widening of Birds Eye's product range and increased range of market segments that it sought to serve posed major difficulties for Birds Eye's marketing strategy and the allocation of its advertising budget. The marketing effort necessary to promote Birds Eye's products in widely different sectors – promoting up-market prepared dishes while expanding into economy packs of commodity products – was difficult to orchestrate. "We will be walking a tightrope," explained marketing director Keith Jacobs, "the company's advertising will have two jobs to do: to maintain its image as a basic convenience foods company and to make it credible as a purveyor of, for example, pizzas." In relation to advertising, Birds Eye adopted a more targeted approach. It focused its national TV advertising on its lead lines, while new products were introduced with more regionally and segment-focused advertising. Advertising support was largely withdrawn from "support products."

In response to the growing power of large supermarket chains, Birds Eye redirected its marketing efforts. During the 1960s, marketing had been focused almost exclusively on the consumer. During the 1970s, Birds Eye shifted its focus from consumer marketing to trade marketing, with particular emphasis on developing relationships with major supermarket chains, including joint promotion efforts.

On the production side, the mid-1970s witnessed a program of heavy investment in modernization and rationalization that was designed to exploit efficiency from volume production. Between 1977 and 1980 expenditure on this program amounted to some £20 million. A key feature of the program was the focus of production resources for different product groups at specific factories – fish products at Hull and Grimsby, ready meals at Kirkby and Yarmouth, vegetables at Hull and Lowestoft, and cakes and desserts

Table 13.5 Birds Eye Foods Ltd: financial data for 1972–9 (£ 000s)

	1972	1973	1974	1975	1976	1977	1978	1979
Sales	91,838	113,997	132,636	157,142	187,415	212,322	226,308	266,018
Operating profit	2,110	2,875	3,445	4,414	3,453	2,477	6,310	9,352
After-tax profit	1,223	1,465	1,468	1,925	249	(679)	1,094	1,094
Group service charge	n.a.	n.a.	n.a.	n.a.	n.a.	5,305	5,527	8,145
Net current assets	15,164	24,717	31,034	32,069	44,792	53,337	59,141	59,141
Stocks (Inventories)	17,479	26,012	29,263	30,983	40,356	52,431	54,317	54,317
Debtors	5,928	10,677	12,124	13,739	17,483	13,523	21,102	28,522
Creditors	4,863	7,484	8,768	9,481	10,592	14,563	15,350	24,573
Capital employed	33,893	42,947	48,993	52,199	90,383	100,004	122,352	132,801

Source: Robert M. Grant, "Birds Eye and the UK Frozen Food Industry," case study, July 1985, p. 13a.

at Eastboume – since it was observed that some specialist producers achieved much higher levels of automation.

The quest for lower costs was instrumental in the decision to merge Unilever's two principal frozen product operations, Birds Eye Foods and Walls Ice Cream, into a single company, Birds Eye Walls Ltd. Although the potential for cooperation and the elimination of duplicated functions between Birds Eye and Walls had been identified in the 1960s, the two Unilever subsidiaries had been almost entirely independent prior to the merger. During 1979–81, Birds Eye Walls worked on merging and rationalizing the two companies' distribution networks. On January 1, 1982, the combined refrigerated distribution company, Unicold-Walls, was transferred to Birds Eye Walls with the intention of speeding the reorganization of distribution and improving coordination. The plan was to complete the reorganization of distribution by early 1985 with a streamlined national network of seven regional distribution centers in operation.

Despite Birds Eye's efforts to adjust to new market circumstances, its market and financial performance continued to deteriorate throughout the 1970s. Although, in its 1979 Annual Report, Birds Eye was still able to report that "few brands in the British grocery market can claim the sort of dominance which Birds Eye has in frozen foods," that leadership was no guarantee of growth and prosperity. In the face of rising competition, Birds Eye maintained its advertising budget during the mid-1970s while cutting prices on some major-selling products. Though this approach raised sales volume, in July 1975 Chairman Kenneth Webb complained that profit margins had been halved over the previous two years and were currently one-third of the level consistent with the company's heavy investment in manufacturing and distribution facilities. In 1976, the company barely broke even and in 1977 it registered a post-tax loss. Table 13.5 shows Birds Eye's financial performance.

The appointment of Mr Don Angel to the chairmanship of Birds Eye early in 1979 led to Birds Eye reappraising its strategy in the UK frozen foods market and considering a new phase of internal restructuring. Reflecting on the erosion of the company's dominant market position, Don Angel observed that the model that had served Birds Eye's development and growth during the 1950s and 1960s needed to be reconsidered and "choices must be made about what the company is best at." In particular, there was a widespread realization that the vertically integrated approach to the sourcing, processing, distribution, and marketing of frozen foods through which Birds Eye had developed the UK market for frozen foods may now be a weakness rather than a strength for Birds Eye.

NOTES

1. Birds Eye's history is outlined in W. J. Reader, *Birds Eye Foods Ltd: The Early Days*, Birds Eye Foods Ltd, 1963.
2. Ibid., p. 9.
3. Ibid., p. 3.
4. K. McClaren, "The effect of range size on distribution costs," *International Journal of Physical Distribution and Materials Management*, Vol. 10, 1980, pp. 445–56.
5. C. Wilson, *Unilever 1945–1965: Challenge and Response in the Post-War Industrial Revolution*, Cassell, London, 1968, pp. 172–3.
6. "Frozen Food: Market Prospects," *Retail Business*, Special Report No. 14, April 1959, p. 83.
7. S. King, *Developing New Brands*, London: Pitman, 1973, p. 13.
8. *Report on the Supply of Frozen Foodstuffs*, Monopolies and Mergers Commission, HMSO, 1976, p. 44.
9. Ibid., p. 53.
10. Ibid., p. 42.
11. Ibid., p. 32.
12. Ibid., p. 32.
13. Ibid., p. 9.

case fourteen

Euro Disney: From Dream to Nightmare, 1987–94

Robert M. Grant

At the press conference announcing Euro Disneyland SCA's financial results for the year ended September 30, 1994, CEO Philippe Bourguignon summed up the year in succinct terms: "The best thing about 1994 is that it's over."

In fact, the results for the year were better than many of Euro Disneyland's long-suffering shareholders had predicted. Although revenues were down 15 percent – the result of falling visitor numbers caused by widespread expectations that the park would be closed down – costs had been cut by 12 percent, resulting in a similar operating profit to that of the previous year. The bottom line still showed a substantial loss (net after-tax loss was FF1.8bn); however, this was a big improvement on the previous year (FF5.33bn loss). Tables 14.1 and 14.2 show details of the financial performance.

Regarding the future, Bourguignon was decidedly upbeat. Following the FF13bn restructuring agreed with creditor banks in June, Euro Disney was now on a much firmer financial footing. As a result of the restructuring, Euro Disneyland SCA was left with equity of about FF5.5bn and total borrowings of FF15.9bn – down by a quarter from the previous year. With the threat of closure lifted, Euro Disney was now in a much better position to attract visitors and corporate partners.

Efforts to boost attendance figures included a new advertising campaign, a new FF600m attraction (Space Mountain), which was due to open in June 1996, and changing the park's name from Euro Disneyland to Disneyland Paris.

In addition, Euro Disney had made large numbers of operational improvements. Mr Bourguignon reported that it had cut queuing times by 45 percent during the year through new attractions and the redesign of existing ones; hotel occupancy rates had risen from 55 percent in the previous year to 60 percent; and managers were to be given greater incentives. The net result, claimed Bourguignon, was that the company would reach break-even during 1996.

The stock market responded positively to the results. In London, the shares of Euro Disneyland SCA rose 13p to 96p. However, this did not take the shares much above their

Table 14.1 Euro Disneyland SCA: financial performance 1993–94. Operating revenue and expenditure (millions of French francs)

	1994	1993
Revenue:		
Theme park	2,212	2,594
Hotels	1,613	1,721
Other	322	559
Construction sales	114	851
Total revenue	4,261	5,725
Direct costs/expenses:		
Park & Hotels	(2,961)	(3,382)
Construction sales	(114)	(846)
Operating income	1,186	1,497
Depreciation	(291)	(227)
Lease rental expense	(889)	(1,712)
Royalties	–	(262)
General & Admin.	(854)	(1,113)
Financial income	538	719
Financial expenses	(972)	(615)
Loss	(1,282)	(1,713)
Exceptional loss, net	(515)	(3,624)
Net loss	(1,797)	(5,337)
Employees (cast members)		
Number	11,865	10,172
Annual Cost (FF, millions)	2,108	1,892

all-time low. On November 6, 1989, the first day of trading after the Euro Disneyland initial public offering, the shares had traded at 880p. Since then, Euro Disneyland stock had been on a near-continuous downward trend (see figure 14.1). The *Financial Times'* Lex column was also unenthusiastic:

> Still beset by high costs and low attendances, Euro Disney will find it hard to hit its target of break-even by the end of September 1996. Costs in the year were reduced by FF500m by introducing more flexible labor agreements (more part-timers, increased job sharing and the use of more students in the peak season) as well as outsourcing contracts in the hotel operation. But the company admits that the lion's share of cost reductions has now been realized. Now it hopes attendances are rising . . . Getting people to spend more once they are at the park might be more difficult. Euro Disney is pinning its hopes on economic recovery in Europe. It'll have to start paying interest, management fees and royalties again in five years' time. Management will not say whether it'll be able to cope then.[1]

Returning to his office at the end of the press conference, Bourguignon sighed. Since taking over from the previous chief executive, Robert Fitzpatrick, in 1993, the 46-year-old had been engaged in a continuing battle to ensure the survival of Euro Disney. Now

Table 14.2 Euro Disneyland SCA: financial statements 1992–4 (under US GAAP)

Balance sheet

	1994	1993	1992
Cash and investments	289	211	479
Receivables	227	268	459
Fixed assets, net	3,791	3,704	4,346
Other assets	137	214	873
Total assets	4,444	4,397	6,157
Accounts payable & other liabilities	560	647	797
Borrowings	3,051	3,683	3,960
Stockholders' equity	833	67	1,400
Total liabilities & stockholders' equity	4,444	4,397	6,157

Statement of operations

	1994	1993	1992
Revenues	751	873	738
Costs and expenses	1,198	1,114	808
Net interest expense	280	287	95
Loss before income taxes and cumulative effect of accounting change	(727)	(528)	(165)
Income tax benefit	–	–	30
Loss before cumulative effect of accounting change	(727)	(528)	(135)
Cumulative effect of change in accounting for pre-opening costs	–	(578)	–
Net loss	(727)	(1,106)	(135)

Source: Walt Disney Company, 10K report, 1994.

that survival was no longer an issue, Bourguignon now faced his next challenge: could Euro Disneyland ever become profitable?

■ DISNEY THEME PARKS ■

Walt Disney pioneered the theme park concept. His goal was to create a unique entertainment experience that combined fantasy and history, adventure, and learning in which the guest would be a participant, as well as a spectator. Current Disney-designed theme parks in California, Florida, Japan, and France are divided into distinct lands. All the parks include a number of similar lands with identical attractions. These include Main Street, Frontierland, Tomorrowland, Fantasyland, and Adventureland. The objective is to immerse the guest in the atmosphere of the particular land. The theme of each land is reflected in the types of rides and attractions, the costumes of employees, the architectural style of the buildings, and even the food and souvenirs sold within the boundaries of the particular land. Rather than presenting a random collection of roller

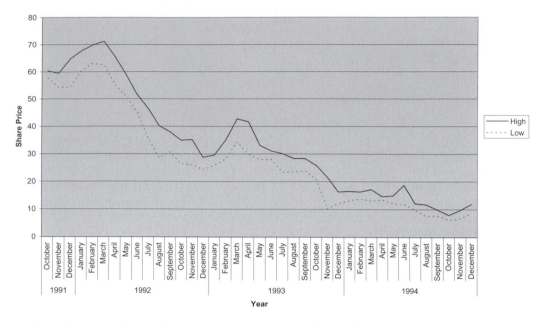

Figure 14.1 Euro Disneyland's share price in Paris, 1991–4 (in French francs)

coasters, merry-go-rounds, and other rides, the Disney parks create an all-embracing experience which envelops the guest in carefully designed, tightly managed fantasy experience such as space flight, a Caribbean pirate attack, a flying ride with Peter Pan, or a race down the Matterhorn in a bob-sleigh.

Disney theme parks benefit from the talent and expertise of the Walt Disney "family" of businesses. Parks are designed by the engineers and architects of a wholly owned subsidiary – WED Enterprises. The themes for the attractions and characters that are featured in them often have their origins in cartoons and live action movies produced by Disney's studios. The parks also benefit from management and merchandising techniques developed over many years at Disney. These techniques have led to tremendous successes. In merchandising, Disney retail stores achieved some of the highest sales per square foot in the United States.

Disney's success can be traced to the control of the environment to create a unique experience for the visitor. This control is achieved through highly systematized operations management and human resource management. Disney has sophisticated procedures for selecting and training employees to ensure the highest levels of service, safety, and maintenance in the industry. Disney's ability to reconcile a high level of occupancy with high levels of service and customer satisfaction is achieved through sophisticated methods of forecasting visitor levels on a daily basis, and careful design of parks to minimize the frustrations of crowds and waiting. Disney also emphasizes the continual renewal of its theme parks' appeal through investment in new attractions. It then supports these with heavy promotion.

Disney parks have historically had higher attendance levels than other theme and amusement parks throughout the world. During the late 1980s and early 1990s, Disney's theme parks in Anaheim, Orlando, and Tokyo together attracted over 50 million guest visits annually.

Los Angeles Disneyland

Shortly after developing the idea of a theme park, Walt Disney hired the Stanford Research Institute to conduct an economic feasibility study of his amusement park plan and then a follow-up study to analyze demographics and traffic patterns in order to come up with a recommendation for the site. Based on the results of this study, Disney acquired 160 acres of land in Anaheim, California in 1953, and later obtained financing from ABC Television to move forward with the plan. With the financing agreement, ABC owned 34.48 percent of the shares of the new "Disneyland" park, which was the equivalent of the proportion of shares owned by Walt Disney Productions. In order to finance construction, ABC put up half-a-million dollars and guaranteed loans for a further $4.5 million. The Los Angeles Disneyland theme park was finally opened in July of 1955.

Orlando Disney World

The success of Disneyland created a real estate boom in Anaheim, resulting in Disneyland being surrounded by a ring of hotels, motels, restaurants, and other businesses. For his next theme park project, Walt Disney aimed for undiluted control over the business and its revenue stream. Walt Disney World Resort opened in 1971 on a huge track of 29,000 acres that Walt acquired outside of Orlando, Florida. Walt Disney World eventually comprised three separate theme parks: the original Magic Kingdom, the Experimental Prototype Community of Tomorrow (EPCOT) Center that opened in 1982 which in itself hosted two themes: *Future World* and *World Showcase*, and Disney-MGM Studios which opened in 1989.

The experience of creating a theme park as a destination resort represented a major development in Disney's conception of a theme park and was influential in its expansion plans into Europe. The huge 27,000 acre site allowed Disney to broaden the scope of its theme park activities to create themed hotels, golf courses and other sports, convention facilities, night clubs, a range of retail stores, even residential housing. The complementary coupling of a theme park with resort facilities that could even host commercial activities (conferences, a technology park) became central to Disney's theme park strategy.

By 1990, Walt Disney World had become the largest center of hotel capacity in the United States with approximately 70,000 rooms, of which almost 10 percent were owned and operated by Disney. Even though the room rates charged by Disney were considerably higher than other hotels in the vicinity, they achieved a remarkable occupancy rate of 94 percent during the late 1980s.

Tokyo Disneyland

Tokyo Disneyland, which opened in 1983, was a major departure for Walt Disney Company. The Oriental Land Company Limited (OLCL), a Japanese development company, had approached Disney with a proposal to open a Disneyland in Japan. Disney's top management regarded a Disney theme park in another country with a different climate and a different culture as a risky venture. Disney insisted on a deal that would leave OLCL with all the risk: the park would be owned and operated by OLCL while Disney would receive royalties of 10 percent on the admissions revenues and 5 percent on receipts from food, beverages, and souvenirs. These royalties represented licensing fees for Disney's trademarks and intellectual property, engineering designs for rides, and ongoing technical assistance. Despite the challenges of limited space and cold winter weather, Tokyo Disneyland was a huge success. By the late 1980s it was drawing 15 million visits a year – more than any other Disney park.[2]

■ PLANNING AND DEVELOPMENT ■

Beginnings of Euro Disneyland

The success of Tokyo Disneyland was clear evidence to Disney's top management of the international potential for Disney's theme parks. Europe was considered the obvious location for the next Disney park. Europe had always been a strong market for Disney movies, and there was a strong European demand for toys, books, and comics that featured Disney characters – European consumers generated about one-quarter of revenues from Disney licensed consumer products. The popularity of Disney theme parks with Europeans was evident from the 2 million European visitors to Disneyland and Walt Disney World each year. Moreover, Western Europe possessed a population and affluence well capable of supporting a major Disney theme park.

In 1984, Disney management made the decision to commit to development of a European theme park and commenced feasibility planning and site selection. In assessing alternative locations, the following criteria were applied:

- proximity to a high-density population zone with a relatively high level of disposable income;
- ability to draw upon a substantial local tourist population, availability of qualified labor, and readily accessible transportation;
- availability of sufficient land to permit expansion of the project to meet increasing demand;
- provision of necessary infrastructure, such as water and electricity.

Two locations quickly emerged as front-runners: Barcelona and Paris. While Barcelona had the advantages of a better year-round climate, Paris offered key economic and infrastructure advantages, together with strong backing from the French government. Disney's interest in a European theme park corresponded with the French government's plans to develop the Marne-la-Vallée area east of Paris. The result was rapid progress of Disney's formal negotiations with the range of local government authorities and public bodies whose cooperation and agreement were essential for a project of this scale. The proposed site's demographic characteristics offered the right set of conditions for a successful theme park. The park rested on a 4,500-acre site 32 kilometers east of Paris, providing proximity to a metropolitan area and room for expansion; the high population of the greater Paris area (over 10 million) and Europe (over 330 million) provided a large consumer market; and existing and planned transportation equipped the park with access to vital infrastructure. Paris was already a major tourist destination with excellent air, road, and rail links with the rest of Europe.

On March 24, 1987, the Walt Disney Company entered into the Agreement on the Creation and the Operation of Euro Disneyland in France (the "Master Agreement") with the Republic of France, the Region of Ile-de-France, the Department of Seine-et-Marne, the Etablissement Public d'Aménagement de la Ville Nouvelle de Marne-la-Vallée, and the Régie Autonome des Transports Parisiens. This was followed by incorporation of Euro Disneyland SCA (the "Company") and the conclusion of an agreement with the SNCF (the French national railway company) to provide TGV (the French high-speed train) service to Euro Disneyland beginning in June 1994. The agreement involved commitments by Disney to establish Euro Disneyland as a French corporation, to develop a major international theme park, and to create 30,000 jobs in the process. The French authorities committed to provide land (at Marne-la-Vallée 32 km east of Paris) and infrastructure over the project's 30-year development period ending in 2017. The real estate deal involved Disney acquiring 1,700 hectares (approximately 4,300 acres[3]) of agricultural land at Marne-la-Vallée. In addition, a further 243 hectares were reserved for public facilities and infrastructure. The purchase price for the land included the raw land price (FF11.1 per square meter or approximately $8,360 per acre), direct and indirect secondary infrastructure costs, and certain financing and overhead expenses of the French authorities. The area of the total site was equivalent to one-fifth of the area of the city of Paris. The land for the first phase of the development was purchased outright by Euro Disneyland SCA, with purchase options on the remaining land. Euro Disneyland SCA also had the right to sell land to third parties, as long as the development plans of any purchasers were approved by the French planning authority.

The agreement provided for motorway links to Paris, Strasbourg, and the two international airports serving Paris – Charles de Gaulle and Orly, while the planned extension of the RER (the express commuter rail network) would allow visitors to reach the Magic Kingdom from the center of Paris within 40 minutes. Euro Disney[4] would also be linked to France's TGV system, with its own station serving the park. This would also give rail service from Britain through the Channel Tunnel. In addition to infrastructure, the French government's financial inducements included FF4.8 billion in loans and a favorable tax rate (34 percent). The total package of incentives added up to roughly FF6.0 billion.[5]

The Market: Demand and Competition

A key factor attracting Disney to Paris was market potential. The greater Paris metropolis has a population of over 10 million. Roughly 16 million people lived within

Table 14.3 Attendance at major theme parks

	Estimated attendance in 1988 (millions of guest visits)
Sea World – *Florida*	4.6
Tivoli Gardens – *Denmark*	4.5
Universal Studios Tour – *California*	4.2
Knott's Berry Farm – *California*	4.0
Busch Gardens – *Florida*	3.7
Sea World – *California*	3.4
Six Flags Magic Mountain – *California*	3.1
King's Island – *Ohio*	3.0
Liseberg – *Sweden*	2.8
Alton Towers – *United Kingdom*	2.3
De Efteling – *The Netherlands*	2.3
Phantasialand – *West Germany*	2.2

Source: Euro Disneyland SCA abridged offering circular.

a 160 km radius of the proposed site; within a 320 km radius were 41 million people; and within a 480 km radius were 109 million people. Paris' presence as a transportation hub facilitated access to this huge market. As a result, Euro Disneyland would be capable of achieving a high level of capacity utilization, even with much lower market penetration rates than those achieved by Disney's California and Florida theme parks. European vacation patterns were also seen as conducive to visits – Europeans received substantially more vacation time than US workers and in addition to their summer vacation, European families frequently took shorter vacations throughout the year. Projections of numbers of visitors to Euro Disney and their expenditures were made by consultants Arthur D. Little as part of their financial projections for Euro Disneyland SCA (see Appendix 1).

The ability of Euro Disney to achieve its visitor targets would depend not only on the size of the market but also upon the relative attractiveness and number of competing tourist destinations. Although Disney viewed its theme parks as unique in terms of the quality and intensity of the entertainment experience that it offered, the company also recognized that, ultimately, a wide range of family vacation and entertainment experiences compete for household disposable income. Although there were very few large-scale theme parks in Europe to directly compete with Euro Disneyland (most of the world's major theme parks were located in the US), there were a number of family-entertainment destinations within Europe that would be potential competitors (see table 14.3). In addition, European cities – such as London, Paris, Rome, Prague, Barcelona, and many others – offered a richness and variety of cultural and historical experiences that few US cities could match and represented an alternative to Euro Disney for short family vacations. In addition, there were a host of traditional forms of family entertainment in Europe, including fairs, carnivals, and festivals, some of which were small and local while others – such as the Munich Bierfest, the Pamplona bull-running festival, the Edinburgh cultural festival, and the Dutch tulip festivals – were major events attracting large numbers of international visitors.

Of particular concern was the tendency of Euro Disneyland to create its own competition. Within two years of Walt Disney Company's announcement that it planned to build Euro Disney, three French theme parks – Mirapolis, Futuroscope, and Zygofolis – had opened in an attempt to preempt Disney's entry into the market. By the summer of 1989, two more theme parks – Asterix and Big Bang Schtroumph – opened their gates. However, with aggregate annual losses of about $43 million on a total investment of over $600 million, these parks were considered financial disasters.[6]

The Development Plan

Euro Disney's Development Program provided for a theme park based closely upon the themes and concepts of Disney's US theme parks that would be the largest theme park and resort development in Europe. The plan established two stages for the project.

PHASE 1

Phase I, the major part of the overall project, was subdivided into two sections. Phase lA comprised the Magic Kingdom theme park, the Magic Kingdom Hotel (which would serve as the entrance area to the theme park), and a camping ground, which were to be completed at a budgeted cost of FF14.9 billion. Of the 570 acres allocated for Phase 1, Phase 1A would utilize 240 acres. The rest of the land would be developed in Phase 1B to accommodate five additional hotels; an entertainment, restaurant, and shopping complex; and sports facilities with an 18-hole championship golf course. Phase 1A also provided for the French government to construct two junctions with the nearby motor-way, main access roads to the park, a drinking-water supply and distribution system, storm drainage, sewers, solid waste treatment, and telecommunications networks. The cost of the additional infrastructure, including links with the RER and the TGV, was to be financed by Euro Disneyland SCA.

The Magic Kingdom theme park was to include five themed lands: Main Street USA, the gateway to the park; Frontierland, a reproduction of wooden streets typical of a mid-nineteenth-century frontier town; tropical Adventure Land, the most exotic of the park settings; Fantasyland, with attractions drawn from well-known Disney characters; and Discoveryland, which, through the sophisticated use of technology, illustrates the past and the future. Each offers appropriately themed restaurants and shopping facilities.

To permit year-round operation, Euro Disney included adaptations designed to make attendance less dependent on the weather, with more interconnected covered areas than at other Disney parks. Many modifications to the themes, architecture, and dining facilities were made to tailor the park to the European market. For example, while French is the first language of the park, universal signposting is used wherever possible to aid non-French-speaking visitors, and many attractions are identified by visual cues.

PHASE 2

Phase 2 of the Long Term Development Strategy extended to 2011. It envisioned a second theme park (Disney-MGM Studios) on a site adjacent to the Magic Kingdom; 15 additional hotels, which would increase the number of rooms available by 13,000; a water recreation area and second golf course; and residential and commercial development. This phase was left flexible to accommodate the policies of the French authorities, economic and market conditions, participant needs, and visitor preferences.

CONSTRUCTION

Disney exercised close control over design and construction of Phase 1A of Euro Disney. Lehrer McGovern Bovis Inc. (LMB), an independent construction management firm with international experience in the management of large-scale construction projects, was the main contractor. LMB reported to Euro Disneyland Imagineering SARL (EDLI), a French subsidiary of Disney that had overall responsibility for designing and constructing Phases 1 and 2 of the theme park. Also reporting to EDLI were separate Disney companies responsible for design, conceptual and otherwise; engineering; and the development and equipping of attractions.

PARTICIPANTS

As with other Disney theme parks, at Euro Disneyland Participants played an important role in financial and in marketing terms. Participants are companies or organizations that enter into long-term marketing agreements with the Company. Typically, these relationships represent a 10-year commitment and physically tie the Participant to the Magic Kingdom, where it hosts or presents one or more of the theme park's attractions, restaurants, or other facilities. Relationships with Participants may also involve marketing activities featuring the association between the Participant and the Company. Each Participant pays an individually negotiated annual fee, which may contribute to the financing of a particular attraction or facility. Initial participants at Euro Disneyland included Kodak, Banque Nationale de Paris, Renault, and Europcar.

■ FINANCIAL AND MANAGEMENT STRUCTURE ■

For Euro Disneyland, Disney chose a unique financial and management structure. Rather than a pure franchise operation similar to Tokyo Disneyland, Disney chose to retain management and operational control of the park while allowing European investors to take majority ownership and European banks to provide most of the debt financing. The relationship between Walt Disney Company and Euro Disneyland is depicted in figure 14.2.

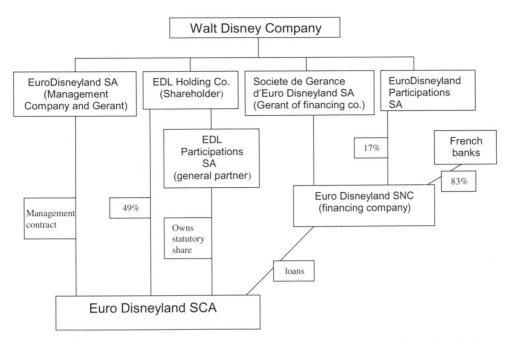

Figure 14.2 The financial and management relationship between Walt Disney and Euro Disneyland

Euro Disneyland SCA

Euro Disneyland SCA was formed to build and own Euro Disneyland. The company was a *société en commandite par actions* – the French equivalent of a limited partnership. The company was governed by a supervisory board elected by the shareholders and chaired by Jean Taittinger, the chairman and chief executive of Société du Louvre and Banque du Louvre. Disney took a 49 percent stake in Euro Disneyland SCA; the remaining 51 percent of equity was floated through an initial public offering underwritten by three investment banks. The shares were listed on the Paris and London stock markets. Although Disney held 49 percent of Euro Disneyland SCA equity it contributed only 13 percent of its equity book value (FF273 m net of incentives received). The difference was "granted" to the company, both as a goodwill "gesture" in recognition of Disney's reputation and credibility in the investment community and as compensation for Disney's assumed risk in the undertaking.

The Management Company

Euro Disneyland SCA was managed by a separate management company, Euro Disneyland SA (the "Management Company"), a wholly owned subsidiary of Disney. The Management Company, or *gerant*, was responsible under French law for managing

Euro Disneyland SCA and its affairs in the company's best interests. In turn, the Management Company agreed that the provision of management services to the Company would be its exclusive business. Under the Articles of Association, the Management Company was entitled to annual fees consisting of a base fee and management incentive fees. The base fee in any year was set at 3 percent of the Company's total revenues, and increased to 6 percent after five years of operation, or after the Company had satisfied certain financial targets. On top of the base fee, the Management Company was entitled to incentive fees based on Euro Disneyland SCA's pre-tax cash flow. These incentives increased in stages up to a possible maximum of 50 percent of Euro Disneyland SCA's net profit. The Management Company also received 35 percent of pre-tax gains on the sales of hotels. In addition, Euro Disneyland SCA was obligated to reimburse the Management Company for all its direct and indirect expenses incurred in its management role. The management contract was for five years.

The Shareholding Company and General Partner

Disney's shareholding in Euro Disneyland SCA was held by EDL Holding, a wholly owned subsidiary of Disney. This shareholding company also owned EDL Participations SA, which held the key role of "general partner" in Euro Disneyland SCA – it assumed unlimited liability for the debts and liabilities of Euro Disneyland SCA. As general partner, EDL Participations SA was entitled to a distribution each year equal to 0.5 percent of Euro Disneyland SCA's net after-tax profits.

The Financing Company

Euro Disneyland SNC was formed to buy the park facilities from Euro Disneyland SCA at book value plus development costs, then lease them back to Euro Disneyland SCA. Euro Disneyland SNC was owned 17 percent by Disney and 83 percent by French corporations. The rationale was to allow French corporations to take advantage of the tax benefits of Euro Disneyland's early years of projected losses. Once again, Euro Disneyland SNC was to be managed by a Disney subsidiary and Disney would act as its general partner with full debt default liability.

The License Agreement

Under the License Agreement, Walt Disney Company granted to Euro Disneyland SCA a license to use any present or future Disney intellectual and industrial property rights incorporated in Disney's attractions and facilities and made available to the Company for Euro Disney. These included the Walt Disney name, the Disney characters, and the proprietary technology in theme park attractions. Disney was to receive royalties as follows:

- 10 percent of gross revenues (net of TVA, the French value-added tax, and similar taxes) from rides and admissions and certain related fees (such as parking, tour guide, and similar services) at all theme parks and other attractions (including the Magic Kingdom and any future theme park);

- 5 percent of gross revenues (net of TVA and similar taxes) from merchandise, food, and beverage sales in or adjacent to any theme park or other attraction or in any other facility (other than the Magic Kingdom Hotel) whose overall design concept is based predominantly on a Disney theme;
- 10 percent of all fees due from Participants;
- 5 percent of all gross revenues (net of TVA and similar taxes) from room rates and related charges at Disney themed accommodations (excluding the Magic Kingdom Hotel).

■ CULTURAL ISSUES ■

Euro Disneyland presented huge challenges for Disney. Climate was a major problem. The long gray winter of Northern France created complex design problems that were absent from Disney's sun-drenched California and Florida parks. However, the challenges posed by adverse weather conditions were mainly technical and amenable to careful analysis. The issues of culture were much less tractable.

While the success of Tokyo Disneyland was a major factor behind the decision to create Euro Disney, the cultural challenges of France were very different from those of Japan. Tokyo Disneyland had been conceived, built, and operated on a wave of popular Japanese acclaim. As a result, Tokyo Disneyland had made very few concessions to Japanese culture. Although, at first, Disney wanted to adapt some of the attractions to the Japanese context (for example, Samurai-Land instead of Frontierland), their Japanese partners strongly resisted efforts to "localize" Disneyland, arguing that the park would attract more Japanese people if it were built as a perfect replica of US Disneyland. They emphasized that Disney's cartoon characters were very familiar to the Japanese people and that visitors would want "the real thing." As a result, only minor changes were made, such as the addition of Cinderella's Castle and the Mickey Mouse Theater.

After the enthusiasm with which the Japanese greeted Disney's entry, the response of the French could not have been more different. France presented a very different situation. French intellectuals had long shown antagonism towards American popular culture, and they were supported by widespread nationalistic sentiment that saw the French language and French culture as threatened by the global hegemony of the English language. At the political level too, France had been the most independent of the Western European powers in terms of its independent foreign policy and unwillingness to accept US leadership in world affairs. The announcement of the Euro Disneyland project was greeted by howls of outrage from the French media and from the intelligentsia who viewed the park as "a cultural Chernobyl," "a horrifying step towards world homogenization," "a horror made of cardboard, plastic, and appalling colors, a construction of hardened chewing gum and idiotic folklore taken straight out of the comic books written for obese Americans."[7] Euro Disney quickly became a focal point for anti-Americanism, fueled by multiple issues. For example, shortly after opening, Euro Disney was blockaded by farmers protesting US farm policies.

The design of the park incorporated many adaptations of French and European culture. Disney emphasized the European heritage of many of Disney's characters and storylines (referred to by chairman Michael Eisner as "European folklore with a Kansas twist"). Some attractions featured European adaptations: Cinderella lived in a French inn and Snow White's home was in a Bavarian village. Other attractions were unique to Euro Disney: Discoveryland (which substituted for Tomorrowland at other Disney parks) was based upon themes from Jules Verne and Leonardo da Vinci; "Visionarium" was a 360-degree movie theater showcasing French culture; an Alice-in-Wonderland attraction was surrounded by a 5,000 sq. ft. hedge maze. Designing and constructing these European-themed attractions added substantially to the cost of Euro Disneyland.

Some "American" themed attractions were adapted on the basis of market research findings. For example, the finding that European visitors to Disney's US parks responded positively to themes embodying the American West encouraged Disney to redesign several attractions around a Wild West theme – including a mining town setting for one ride, a "Davy Crockett" themed campground, and hotels named the "Cheyenne," "Santa Fe," and "Sequoia Lodge."

Other adaptations were made to cater to European social behavior and culinary tastes. Concern over European aversion to queuing resulted in the provision of video screens, movies, and other entertainment for guests waiting in line. Disney's no-alcohol policy was adjusted by allowing wine and beer to be served at Feastival Disney, an entertainment complex just outside the theme park. In the restaurant facilities, greater emphasis was placed on sit-down dining and much less on fast food. At a seminar at UCLA in 1990, Robert Fitzpatrick placed a major emphasis on the Company's determination to provide the highest standards of quality at Euro Disney. This was evident both in the cuisine and in the furnishings and service standards of the hotels. In both areas, Fitzpatrick argued, quality was well in excess of the standards at Disney's US parks.

Human relations management posed further cultural challenges. Central to the Disney theme park experience was the way in which "cast members" interacted with the guests. Disney was famous for its meticulous approach to recruitment, its commitment to employee training, and the maintenance of rigorous standards of employee conduct. For example, Disney's employee handbook spelled out a strict code with respect to dress and appearance, including:

- Above average height and below average weight
- Pleasant appearance (straight teeth, no facial blemishes)
- Conservative grooming standards (facial hair and long hair is banned).
- Very modest make-up, very limited jewelry (for example, no more than one ring on each hand)
- Employees were required to wear specific types and colors of underwear; only neutral colors of pantyhose were allowed.[8]

Training embraced both general principles and specific knowledge and behaviors. For example, employees were instructed that their behavior on the job should be governed by three major rules: "First, we practice a friendly smile; Second, we use only friendly phrases; Third, we are not stuffy."

To what extent could locally recruited employees provide the level and quality and consistency of service at Euro Disney that would match that of other Disney theme parks, and to what extent could Disney simply transplant its US HRM practices? Euro Disney's selection and training were closely modeled on Disney's US approach. A Euro Disney branch of Disney University was opened and recruitment of 10,000 employees began in September 1991. Selection criteria were "applicant friendliness, warmth, and liking of people." The rules for job applicants were spelled out in a video presentation and in the employee handbook, "The Euro Disney Look." The rules went far beyond weight and height requirements, describing the length of the men's hair, beard and mustache requirements, tattoo coverage requirements, and hair color specifications (for example, hair had to be of a natural-looking color, without frosting or streaking). Only moderate use of cosmetics was allowed. Women could wear one earring in each ear with the earrings' diameter not to exceed three-quarters of an inch.[9] The goal was a nationality mix that would match that of Euro Disney's customers, about 45 percent of whom were French. However, in response to local pressure and the greater availability of local applicants, some 70 percent of employees were French. At the management level, Disney relied on importing about 200 managers from other Disney parks and training 270 locally recruited managers (this involved training at Disney's other theme parks).

Disney's recruiting practices and employee policies produced a storm of protest. French labor unions started protesting right from the moment that Euro Disney started interviewing applicants. Representatives of the General Confederation of Labor handed out leaflets in front of Euro Disney's HQ warning applicants that the Disney hiring practices represented "an attack on individual freedom." Many of Disney's US hiring and employment practices contravened French law. Workforce flexibility was limited by the restrictions on terminating employees with more than two years with the company and the high severance payments involved. There were also legal limits over the recruitment and dismissal of seasonal workers. As for Disney's dress and personal grooming codes, French law prohibited an employer from restricting "individual and collective freedoms" unless the restrictions could be justified by the "nature of the objective to be accomplished and were proportional to that end." Since Disney estimated that no more than 700 employees would be involved in "theatrical actions," reasonable dress code limitations could only be imposed on those employees, not on those who would only be "back stage."

■ THE FIRST YEAR ■

Euro Disney's opening on April 12, 1992 combined both fanfare and protest. An extravagant opening ceremony involved some of the world's leading entertainers and was televised in 22 countries. Michael Eisner proclaimed Euro Disney to be "one of the greatest man-made attractions in the world" while the French Prime-Minister described the park as an "incredible achievement which transcends national frontiers . . . We are deeply attached to the links of friendship between our continent and yours. Euro Disney is one of the symbols of this transatlantic friendship." However, the opening was marred by a demonstration of local residents, a train strike affecting lines leading to the park, and a terrorist bomb that attempted to disrupt power to the park. By the end of the first day, park attendance had been way below capacity and only one-half of the anticipated number.

The park ran into early teething problems. Design problems ranged from insufficient breakfast facilities to an absence of toilet facilities for bus drivers and a shortage of employee accommodation. During the first nine weeks of operation, 1,000 employees left Euro Disney, about one-half voluntarily. Long hours and hectic work pace were the main reasons given for leaving. Nevertheless, visitor reactions were mainly highly positive. Negative comments related to frustration with long periods of waiting in line and the high cost of admission, food, and souvenirs. Some voiced concern over the multinational, multicultural flavor of Euro Disney: "They haven't yet figured out whether it's going to be an American park, a French park, or a European park . . . Differences in waiting line behavior is striking. For instance, Scandinavians appear quite content to wait for rides, whereas some of the southern Europeans seem to have made an Olympic event out of getting to the ticker tape first." Some visitors had difficulty envisaging Disney within a European context: "Disney is very much an American culture. Florida is the true Disney World, the true feeling of Disney, what Disney is trying to project. Americans are part of that, the French aren't."[10]

Start-up difficulties were normal in the theme park business – all major theme parks, including those of Disney, experienced some teething problems during the period of initial operation. Universal Studios in Florida had a disastrous first few months, but subsequently rebounded. With 30,000 visitors daily during the summer of 1992, it seemed that Euro Disney might reach its projected target of 11 million visitors annually. The concern was that visitor numbers would drop substantially during the winter months. However, it was soon clear that, despite good visitor numbers during the summer, Euro Disney's profitability would fall far below expectations. There were a larger number of day-visitors and fewer period-visits than had been anticipated. As a result, Euro Disney cut hotel rates by up to 25 percent. Moreover, average visitor expenditure on beverages, food, and gifts was about 12 percent of the $33 per day that had been anticipated. Part of the problem was the economic situation – during 1992, most of Western Europe was mired in one of the worst economic downturns since World War II. The depressed state of the French real estate market also prevented Euro Disney from boosting revenues through land sales.

By the end of Euro Disney's first full financial year, the extent of the financial underperformance was becoming clear. Even with exceptional items, the Company lost over FF1.7 billion. In terms of US GAAP, Euro Disneyland's pre-tax loss was over half a billion dollars. Top line performance was a key problem. Instead of the 11 million visitors forecast, Euro Disney attracted 9.8 m visitors during its first full year. Equally serious was the fact that average visitor spending was below target, and much lower than at Disney's US and Japanese parks. Fewer visitors than projected were staying in Disney theme hotels, deterred by room rates that were much higher than in comparable hotels in Paris. Hotel occupancy rates were below 50 percent in contrast to the 60 percent figure projected. On the cost side, Disney's emphasis on quality had boosted both construction and operating costs, while higher than anticipated debt together with rising interest rates caused interest charges to spiral upward. Labor costs amounted to a huge 24 percent of sales, rather than the forecasted level of 13 percent of sales. Much of the cost overruns could be attributed to Disney's belief that "Lacoste and Polo loving" Europeans would not tolerate anything unsophisticated or cheap. For example, in the US, "The Walt" restaurant had wallpaper but at Euro Disney the walls were covered in Moroccan leather. When it came to trading-off sophistication for lower prices, most Euro Disney customers opted for the latter.

For Walt Disney Company, the financial returns were better than they were for Euro Disneyland's other shareholders. During 1992 and 1993, Disney's 49 percent share of Euro Disneyland's losses was offset by royalties from its licensing agreement. These amounted to $36.3 million in 1993 and $32.9 million in 1992; however, Disney agreed to defer its base management fees for 1992 and 1993.

■ RESTRUCTURING ■

During the winter of 1993/94, Euro Disney visitor numbers plummeted. Despite a fall of the French franc against the US dollar, many Europeans found that Disneyland Florida was not only a more attractive destination during the winter months, it was also cheaper. "It's cheaper to go on a two-week holiday in Florida than to come to Euro Disney for five days," remarked one British traveler with a family of four. With low transatlantic fares, European visitors to Walt Disney World in Orlando increased sharply during 1992 and 1993. By early 1994, Euro Disney was in crisis. Faced with mounting losses, rising debt, and doubts about the Company's capacity to cover its interest payments, rumors were rife that the park would be forced to close.

The financial restructuring package agreed between Euro Disneyland and its creditors in June 1994 involved the following measures:

- A $1.1 billion rights offering of which Disney agreed to take up 41 percent
- The provision by Disney of $255 million in lease financing at an interest rate of 1 percent
- The cancellation by Disney of $210 million in receivables from Euro Disneyland
- The agreement by Disney to waive royalties and management fees for five years
- The agreement that Disney would receive warrants for the purchase of 28 million Euro Disneyland shares and would receive a development fee of $225 million once the second phase of the development project was launched. Euro Disneyland's lenders agreed to underwrite 51 percent of the Euro Disney rights offering, to forgive certain interest charges until September 2003, and to defer all principal payments for three years. In return, Euro Disneyland issued the lenders 10-year warrants for the purchase of up to 40 million shares of Euro Disneyland stock.

In a separate agreement, Disney agreed to sell 75 million shares, equivalent to 10 percent of Euro Disneyland's total shareholding, to Prince Alwaleed Bin Talal Bin Abdulaziz Al Saud. The sale reduced Disney's shareholding in Euro Disneyland to 39 percent.

■ LOOKING AHEAD ■

While the restructuring package had staved off disaster for the time being, the traumas of the past year made Bourguignon cautious about the future. Despite heavy advertising, the addition of new attractions, and the fine-tuning of Disney's image, customer service, and offering of food, drinks, and souvenirs, Euro Disney had yet to reach the initial forecast of 11 million visitors annually. Significant cost reductions had been achieved; however, the scope for further cost reductions was limited if Euro Disney was to maintain Disney's respectable standards and customer service excellence. While Bourguignon was convinced that the Company would be generating operating profits by 1995, such profits would have been the result of Disney's agreement to forgo its royalties and management fees. Once these were reinstated, Euro Disney's costs would increase by about $500 million annually.

Bourguignon believed that many of the problems that had dogged Euro Disney from the beginning had been resolved. In particular, the renaming of the park as Disneyland Paris had helped alleviate ambiguity and conflict over the park's identity. Euro Disney's top management avoided the early hyperbole about Euro Disney "meshing the cultural traditions of America and Europe." Disneyland Paris was to be a Disney theme park located close to Paris. Dropping the "Euro" prefix released the Company from the public's mistrust of all things Euro, and helped the park to avoid the debate over what European culture and European identity actually meant. Moreover, the new name firmly associated Euro Disney with the romantic connotations of the city of Paris. In terms of the need to differentiate Euro Disney from Disney's other theme parks, the experience of the past two years suggested that Euro Disney's expensive adaptations to meet European tastes and European culture were not greatly appreciated by customers. For the most part, visitors were delighted by the same rides as existed in Disney's US parks and generally preferred fast food over fine dining.

Over the next six months, Bourguignon recognized that key decisions needed to be taken:

- To what extent should Euro Disney cut admission prices in order to boost attendance? An internal study had estimated that a 20 percent reduction in admission prices would boost attendance by about 800,000 visitors; however, the net result would still be a reduction in total revenues of about 5 percent.
- The problems of insufficient demand related primarily to the winter months. In previous winters some senior managers had argued for the closure of the park. However, so long as most of Euro Disney's employees were permanent staff, such a closure would do little to reduce total costs.
- Bourguignon had already deferred Phase 2 of the development plan – construction of a Disney–MGM Studios theme park. The other members of his senior management team were urging him to go ahead with this phase of development. Only with a second theme park, they believed, would Euro Disney's goal of becoming a major destination resort become realized. However, Bourguignon was acutely aware of Euro Disney's still-precarious

financial situation. With net equity of about FF5.5bn and total borrowings of FF15.9bn, Euro Disney was not well-placed to begin the large-scale capital expenditures that phase 2 would involve.

As Bourguignon arranged the papers on his desk at the end of a long day, he reflected on his success at pulling off the rescue plan and the continuing uphill struggle to realize the ambitions that had driven the project in the early days. The wartime words of Winston Churchill summed up the situation well: "This is not the end. It is not the beginning of the end. It is the end of the beginning."

APPENDIX 1
Euro Disneyland SCA's Financial Model

The Company has prepared a financial model, based on the principal assumptions described below, which projects revenues, expenses, profits, cash flows, and dividends of the Company for 12-month periods beginning 1 April, 1992 and ending 31 March, 2017 as summarized in table 14.A1. Although the Company's accounting year-end is 30 September, years beginning 1 April have been used for the projections in order to represent whole operating years from the projected date of opening of the Magic Kingdom. The projections contained in the model do not constitute a forecast of the actual revenues, expenses, profits, cash flows or dividends of the Company. The model assumes that the Company will complete Phase 1 as described in this document and will develop the remaining elements of Euro Disneyland according to the Long Term Development Strategy. As discussed above, the Company retains the flexibility to change the Long Term Development Strategy and the designs for Phase IB in response to future conditions. Table 14.A2 summarizes the principal components of the development plan.

Table 14.A1 Euro Disneyland SCA: projected revenues and profits (FF, millions)

1992–6					
12 months commencing April 1	1992	1993	1994	1995	1996
Revenues					
Magic Kingdom	4,246	4,657	5,384	5,835	6,415
Second theme park	0	0	0	0	3,128
Resort and property development	1,236	2,144	3,520	5,077	6,386
Total revenues	5,482	6,801	8,904	10,930	15,929
Profit before taxation	351	620	870	1,676	1,941
Net profit	204	360	504	972	1,121
Dividends payable	275	425	625	900	1,100
Tax credit or payment	0	138	213	313	450
Total return	275	563	838	1,213	1,550
Per share (FF)	1.6	3.3	4.9	7.1	9.1

Table 14.A1   *continued*

Later years

12 months commencing April 1	2001	2006	2011	2016
Revenues				
Magic Kingdom	9,730	13,055	18,181	24,118
Second theme park	4,565	6,656	9,313	12,954
Resort and property development	8,133	9,498	8,979	5,923
Total revenues	22,428	29,209	36,473	42,995
Profit before taxation	3,034	4,375	6,539	9,951
Net profit	1,760	2,538	3,793	5,771
Dividends payable	1,750	2,524	3,379	5,719
Tax credit or payment	536	865	1,908	2,373
Total return	2,286	3,389	5,287	8,092
Per share (FF)	13.4	19.9	31.1	47.6

Source: Euro Disneyland SCA abridged offering circular.

Table 14.A2   Planned development of Euro Disneyland

	Phase 1A	Phase 1B	Long-Term Development	Total
Theme parks	1	–	1	2
Hotel capacity (rooms)	500	4,700	13,000	18,200
Camping ground (campsite plots)	595	–	1,505	2,100
Entertainment center (sq. meters)	–	22,000	38,000	60,000
Offices (sq. meters)	–	30,000	670,000	700,000
Corporate park (sq. meters)	–	50,000	700,000	750,000
Golf courses		1	1	2
Single-family homes	–	570	1,930	2,500
Retail shopping center (sq. meters)	–	–	95,000	95,000
Water recreation area	–	–	1	1
Multi-family residence	–	–	3,000	3,000
Time-share units	–	–	2,400	2,400

Source: Euro Disneyland SCA abridged offering circular.

In addition, the model is based on other assumptions developed by the Company in light of Disney's experience with existing theme parks and resorts, after taking into account analyses of local market conditions and an assessment of likely future economic, market and other factors. The major assumptions have been reviewed by Arthur D. Little International, Inc. ("ADL"), the independent consultancy firm retained by the Company to test and verify their reasonableness. Set out at the end of "The financial model" is a letter from ADL regarding its reports. While the

Company believes that the assumptions underlying the model are reasonable, there is no certainty that the projected performance of the Company outlined below will be achieved.

■ PRINCIPAL ASSUMPTIONS AND RATIONALE UNDERLYING THE FINANCIAL MODEL ■

Theme Park Attendance

In order to project the number of visitors expected to visit the Euro Disneyland theme parks, several internal and external studies were commissioned. The most recent of these studies was undertaken by ADL in 1989 to verify and confirm the methods and assumptions used in the previous studies, and to make its own estimates of attendance.

THE MAGIC KINGDOM

The model assumes that the Magic Kingdom will be constructed as described in this document, and that it will open and be fully operational by April 1992.

Summary figures for assumed attendance at the Magic Kingdom are shown in the table below. Attendance is measured in terms of the total numbers of daily guest visits per annum. For example, a visitor who enters a theme park on three separate days will count as three daily guest visits.

	1992	1996	2001	2011
Magic Kingdom (in millions of persons)	11.0	13.3	15.2	16.2

The assumed attendance of 11 million for the first full year of operation of the Magic Kingdom is in line with the average attendance achieved in the first year of operation of the Magic Kingdom theme parks in Florida and Japan, and is below the range of potential initial attendance estimated to be between 11.7 and 17.8 million in the attendance study conducted by ADL. Depending upon its seasonal distribution, the higher end of the range could require acceleration of the attraction investment program. ADL concluded that the attendance target of 11 million could be achieved if the development program envisaged for Phase 1A is accomplished and a well-conceived marketing campaign tailored to European patterns is carried out to support the opening of the Magic Kingdom.

Attendance at the Magic Kingdom is assumed to grow over the period covered by the financial model at an average compound rate of 2 percent per annum. This growth rate compares with an average growth rate of 3.8 percent per annum for the three Magic Kingdom theme parks in California, Florida and Japan.

The assumed growth rate, which is higher in early years, consists of a basic growth rate, adjusted for the effect of the addition of new attractions every two to three years and for the effect of the opening of a second theme park. The overall assumed growth rate is broken down as follows:

Years	2–5	6–10	11–20	20+
Annual growth (%)	4.9	2.7	0.6	0.0

The method used by ADL involved three steps: first, individual target markets were identified by distance and population; secondly, penetration rates (the percentage of the total population in a target market which visits the theme park) were estimated for each target market; and third, the average number of annual visits per guest from each target market was estimated.

ADL noted that a number of factors, including the following, contribute to the high attendance levels at Disney-designed theme parks:

- The design and scope of a Magic Kingdom theme park are such that a complete visit requires more than one full day. This means that visitors are likely either to extend their stay or to return at a future date.
- The quality and capacity available at Disney hotels allow the demand for longer stays to be satisfied.
- The level of recognition of the Disney name and the quality of the experience make Disney theme parks popular holiday destination resorts.

In the opinion of ADL these factors distinguish Disney-designed theme parks from existing theme parks and amusement parks in Europe, which are much smaller and are basically designed for single-day visits. Accordingly, in determining potential penetration rates and the number of annual visits per guest in order to derive projected attendance levels at Euro Disneyland, ADL relied largely on the experience at Disney-designed theme parks.

ADL concluded that because of the large number of people living within a convenient traveling distance of Euro Disneyland, the assumed attendance figures in the model could be achieved with market penetration rates at or below those experienced at other Disney-designed theme parks.

The Company believes that these factors will exist at Euro Disneyland and will support the assumed penetration rates and attendance levels, which are consistent with those experienced at Disney-designed theme parks. The Company also believes that the location of the site at the center of an area of high population density with well-developed transport links will enable Euro Disneyland to draw visitors from both local and more distant markets.

SECOND THEME PARK

The model assumes that a second theme park will be completed and will open to the public in the spring of 1996. Summary figures for assumed attendance at the second theme park are as follows:

	1992	1996	2001	2011
Second theme park (in millions)	–	8.0	8.8	10.1

Attendance at the second theme park is assumed to grow at an average compound rate of 2 percent per annum over the first ten years, and 1 percent per annum for the next ten years until 2016. These assumptions are primarily based on Disney's experience of opening a second theme park at Walt Disney World, where EPCOT Center drew attendance of over 11 million guest visits in its first year of operation.

Per Capita Spending

Theme parks derive their revenues principally from admission charges, sales of food and beverages consumed by visitors while at the park, and from sales of merchandise available at the park's shopping facilities. Revenues from these sources are measured in terms of *per capita* expenditure, which is the average sum spent per daily guest visit.

The Company has assumed *per capita* expenditure figures separately for the two theme parks under the four categories below:

	Magic Kingdom		Second theme park	
	Amount in 1988 FF[a]	Annual growth rate	Amount in 1988 FF[a]	Annual growth rate
Admissions	137.6	6.5%	137.6	6.5%
Food and beverage	56.7	5.0%	53.2	5.0%
Merchandise	74.9	5.0%	46.5	5.0%
Parking and other	5.2	5.0%	5.2	5.0%

[a] Excluding Value-Added Tax.

The assumed real growth rate of admission prices of 1.5 percent per annum is less than the average 2.6 percent experienced at the Disney theme parks since 1972.

The *per capita* spending assumptions are based upon experience in theme parks designed by Disney, adjusted for local conditions. A separate report on *per capita* spending was undertaken by ADL. In order to evaluate the reasonableness of the assumed admission prices, ADL reviewed the admission prices charged in Paris for major attractions which could be considered competitive in terms of entertainment value and also the prices charged by European theme and amusement parks. These reviews showed that the assumed admission prices for Euro Disneyland, although higher than those charged at other European theme and amusement parks, (i) could be considered low when related to prices charged in the Paris region for quality adult-oriented entertainment, and (ii) appeared in tune with prices charged for other family-oriented attractions. ADL concluded that the Company's assumed admission prices were justified, having regard for the destination resort features of Euro Disneyland and the high quality of its entertainment.

In order to evaluate the reasonableness of the assumed prices for food and beverage at Euro Disneyland, ADL analyzed the prices paid by residents of, and tourists to, Paris in those areas which were particularly attractive to visitors. ADL also examined food and beverage prices at other European theme and amusement parks and reviewed typical food and beverage expenditure patterns in France as compared with the United States. ADL concluded that Euro Disneyland's assumptions concerning food and beverage expenditure were reasonable.

ADL determined, in the case of assumed merchandise sales, that there was no comparable experience in the Paris region of small, high-intensity retail shops, exposed to a high volume of visitor traffic, as are found at Disney-designed theme parks. ADL accordingly concluded that it was reasonable to forecast Euro Disneyland's retail sales revenue on the basis of that at other Disney theme parks.

Revenues

Total revenues projected in the financial model for the two theme parks are summarized in the table below (in FF millions):

	1992	1996	2001	2011
Magic Kingdom				
Admissions and parking	1,909	2,981	4,664	9,314
Food, beverage and merchandise	1,759	2,692	4,065	7,401
Participant fees and other	229	303	417	421
Second theme park				
Admissions and parking	–	1,788	2,697	5,794
Food, beverage and merchandise	–	1,178	1,660	3,107
Participant fees and other	–	162	208	412

The first two categories of projected revenues are based on the attendance and *per capita* spending assumptions described above. Projected Participant fees are based on the assumption that approximately ten Participant contracts will have been signed by the opening of the Magic Kingdom. Four contracts have been signed, each with a term of at least ten years.

Operating Expenses

The principal operating expense assumptions are based on the following estimates:

Labor costs (including related taxes) have been estimated on the basis of experience at Disney parks, adjusted to the conditions of the French labor market. They include a premium on operating labor rates of approximately 10% over the market average, intended to attract high-quality personnel. On this basis, it has been assumed that gross operating labor costs will be FF424 million for the Magic Kingdom and FF 232 million for the second theme park (measured in 1988 French francs) in the respective opening years of these parks and that they will increase at the rate of inflation, taking into account increased employment associated with higher attendance levels. Cost of sales has been estimated on the basis of experience at Disney parks, adjusted to reflect factors specific to Euro Disneyland. The assumptions are:

	Cost of sales (% of revenue)
Magic Kingdom	
Merchandise	40–43[a]
Food and beverage	31
Second theme park	
Merchandise	41.5
Food and beverage	31

[a] Declining from 43% in 1992 to 40% in 1996 and thereafter.

Other operating expenses have similarly been based on Disney experience, adjusted to reflect local market conditions. Individually they are assumed to be as follows:

- maintenance expenses:
  - Magic Kingdom: 6 percent of revenues
  - Second theme park: 6.5 percent of revenues
- general and administrative expenses (which include marketing, legal, finance and data processing):

- Magic Kingdom: 14 percent of revenues
- Second theme park: 16 percent of revenues
- property and business taxes, which have been estimated according to the French tax regime
- the base management fee.

Operating Income

Operating income is the difference between revenues and operating expenses, but before royalties, financing costs and interest income, depreciation and amortization, lease expense, management incentive fees, and income taxes. The summary table below shows the operating income projected by the financial model for the two theme parks:

	1992	1996	2001	2011
Magic Kingdom (in FF millions)	1,603	2,773	4,226	8,006
Second theme park (in FF millions)	–	1,334	1,921	4,293
Total	1,603	4,107	6,147	12,299

Cost of Construction

The cost of construction of the Magic Kingdom is assumed to be FF9.5 billion and the total cost of Phase 1A is assumed to be FF14.9 billion, in accordance with the estimated cost for Phase 1A. The construction cost of the second theme park has been assumed to be FF5.9 billion, with construction and related expenditures being incurred equally in 1994 and 1995. The construction cost of the second theme park has been estimated on the basis of Disney's direct experience of recent theme park construction, notably in completing the Disney–MGM Studios Theme Park within Walt Disney World. The construction cost of that theme park was then adjusted for capacity considerations, inflation, and the construction cost differential between Florida and the Paris region.

Table 14.A3 summarizes Walt Disney Company's financial results during 1984–8.

Table 14.A3 Summary of Walt Disney Company financial results, 1984–8 (US$ millions)

	1984	1985	1986	1987	1988
Revenue					
Theme parks and resorts	1,097.4	1,257.5	1,523.9	1,834.2	2,042.0
Filmed entertainment	244.5	320.0	511.7	875.6	1,149.2
Consumer products	109.7	122.6	130.2	167.0	247.0
Operating income					
Theme parks and resorts	185.7	255.7	403.7	548.9	564.8
Filmed entertainment	2.2	33.7	51.6	130.6	186.3
Consumer products	53.9	56.3	72.4	97.3	133.7
Net income	97.8	173.5	247.3	444.7	522.0

Source: The Walt Disney Company annual reports.

APPENDIX 2

Excerpt from Walt Disney 1994 Annual Report

■ INVESTMENT IN EURO DISNEY ■

1994 vs. 1993

The Company's investment in Euro Disney resulted in a loss of $110.4 million in 1994. The loss consisted of a $52.8 million charge recognized in the third quarter as a result of the Company's participation in the Euro Disney financial restructuring, and the Company's equity share of fourth quarter operating results. The prior year's loss reflected the Company's equity share of Euro Disney's operating results and a $350.0 million charge to fully reserve receivables and a funding commitment to Euro Disney, partially offset by royalties and gain amortization related to the investment. The funding commitment was intended to help support Euro Disney for a limited period, while Euro Disney pursued a financial restructuring.

A proposed restructuring plan for Euro Disney was announced in March 1994. During the third quarter of 1994, the Company entered into agreements with Euro Disney and the Euro Disney lenders participating in the restructuring (the "Lenders") to provide certain debt, equity and lease financing to Euro Disney.

Under the restructuring agreements, which specify amounts denominated in French francs, the Company committed to increase its equity investment in Euro Disney by subscribing for 49% of a $1.1 billion rights offering of new shares; to provide long-term lease financing at a 1% interest rate for approximately $255 million of theme park assets; and to subscribe, in part through an offset against fully-reserved advances previously made to Euro Disney under the Company's funding commitment, for securities reimbursable in shares with a face value of approximately $180 million and a 1% coupon. In addition, the Company agreed to cancel fully-reserved receivables from Euro Disney of approximately $210 million, to waive royalties and base management fees for a period of five years and to reduce such amounts for specified periods thereafter, and to modify the method by which management incentive fees will be calculated. During the fourth quarter of 1994, the financial restructuring was completed and the Company funded its commitments.

In addition to the commitments described above, the Company agreed to arrange for the provision of a 10-year unsecured standby credit facility of approximately $210 million upon request, bearing interest at PIBOR. As of September 30th, 1994, Euro Disney had not requested that the Company establish this facility.

As part of the restructuring, the Company received 10-year warrants for the purchase of up to 27.8 million shares of Euro Disney at a price of FF40 per share. The terms of the restructuring also provide that, in the event that Euro Disney decides to launch the second phase of the development of its theme park and resort complex, and commitments for the necessary financing have been obtained, the Company will be entitled to a development fee of approximately $225 million. Upon receipt of the development fee, the Company's entitlement to purchase Euro Disney shares by exercise of the warrants described above will be reduced to 15 million shares.

In connection with the restructuring, Euro Disney Associes SNC ("Disney SNC"), an indirect wholly-owned affiliate of the Company, entered into a lease arrangement (the "Lease") with the entity (the "Park Financing Company") which financed substantially all of the Disneyland Paris theme park assets, and then entered into a sublease agreement (the "Sublease") with Euro Disney. Under the Lease, which replaced an existing lease between Euro Disney and the Park Financing

Company, Disney SNC leased the theme park assets of the Park Financing Company for a non-cancelable term of 12 years. Aggregate lease rentals of FF10.5 billion ($2.0 billion) receivable from Euro Disney under the Sublease, which has a 12-year term, will approximate the amounts payable by Disney SNC under the Lease.

At the conclusion of the Sublease term, Euro Disney will have the option to assume Disney SNC's rights and obligations under the Lease. If Euro Disney does not exercise its option, Disney SNC may continue to lease the assets, with an ongoing option to purchase them for an amount approximating the balance of the Park Financing Company's outstanding debt. Alternatively, Disney SNC may terminate the Lease, in which case Disney SNC would pay the Park Financing Company an amount equal to 75% of its then-outstanding debt, estimated to be $1.4 billion; Disney SNC could then sell or lease the assets on behalf of the Park Financing Company in order to satisfy the remaining debt, with any excess proceeds payable to Disney SNC.

As part of the overall restructuring, the Lenders agreed to underwrite 51% of the Euro Disney rights offering, to forgive certain interest charges for the period from April 1st 1994 to September 30th 2003, having a present value of approximately $300 million, and to defer all principal payments until three years later than originally scheduled. As consideration for their participation in the financial restructuring, Euro Disney issued to the Lenders 10-year warrants for the purchase of up to 40 million shares of Euro Disney stock at a price of FF40 per share.

Euro Disney has reported that it expects to incur a loss in 1995, which will have a negative impact on the Company's results. The impact on the Company's earnings, however, will be reduced as a result of the sale by the Company in October, 1994 of approximately 75 million shares, or 20% of its investment in Euro Disney, to Prince Alwaleed Bin Talal Bin Abdulaziz Al Saud. The sale will reduce the Company's ownership interest in Euro Disney to approximately 39%. Beginning in 1995, the Company will record its equity share of Euro Disney's operating results based upon its reduced ownership interest. The Company has agreed, so long as any obligations to the Lenders are outstanding, to maintain ownership of at least 34% of the outstanding common stock of Euro Disney until June 1999, at least 25% for the subsequent five years and at least 16.67% for an additional term thereafter.

1993 vs. 1992

The Company's investment in Euro Disney resulted in a loss of $514.7 million in 1993, including the charge referred to below, after being partially offset by royalties and gain amortization related to the investment. The operating results of Euro Disney were lower than expected, due in part to the European recession which affected Euro Disney's largest markets.

During 1993, Euro Disney, its principal lenders and the Company began exploring a financial restructuring for Euro Disney. The Company agreed to help fund Euro Disney for a limited period, to afford Euro Disney time to pursue the financial restructuring. The operating results for the fourth quarter and the year, and the need for a financial restructuring, created uncertainty regarding the Company's ability to collect its current receivables and to meet the funding commitment to Euro Disney. Consequently, the Company recorded a charge of $350.0 million in the fourth quarter to fully reserve its current receivables and funding commitment.

In 1992, the Company's investment in Euro Disney contributed income of $11.2 million. Although Euro Disney incurred a loss in 1992, the Company's 49% share of the net loss was offset by royalties and gain amortization related to the investment.

Source: Walt Disney Annual Report, 1994.

APPENDIX 3
Time Line: Major Events in the Development of Euro Disney

March 24, 1987	The Agreement of March 24, 1987, "for the creation and operation of Euro Disneyland in France," is signed by the French Government, the Walt Disney Company, the Ile-de-France Regional Counsel, the Seine-et-Marne Departmental Counsel, the Parisian public transport authority (RATP) and the Public Planning Board (EPA) for the new town of Marne-la-Vallée.
August 1988	Excavation work begins on-site
November 6, 1989	Stock market floatation (Paris, London and Brussels)
April 1990	The first facades of the Disneyland Hotel are constructed
September 1991	The Casting Center opens in Noisy-le-Grand
March 31, 1992	The Marne-la-Vallée–Chessy RER station is inaugurated
April 12, 1992	The Theme Park opens
June 1993	The "Indiana Jones™, the Temple of Peril" attraction is inaugurated
April 23, 1993	The Disneyland Paris Convention Center welcomes the first joint meeting of the two major international organizations in the tourism industry: the European Tourism Commission and the European Commission of the World Tourism Organization
February 1994	The first European Children's Summit is hosted: over 300 children representing 14 countries reflect on the world of tomorrow
March 1994	Inauguration of two new attractions: "Casey Jr., le Petit Train du Cirque" and "Le Pays des Contes de Fées"
May 19, 1994	Inauguration of the TGV station at the Park entrance
June 8, 1994	Extraordinary General Shareholders Meeting approves resolutions related to the financial restructuring
October 1, 1994	Euro Disneyland becomes Disneyland Paris. Euro Disney SCA remains the company owning and operating Disneyland Paris and its subsidiaries
May 31, 1995	The "Space Mountain – from the Earth to the Moon" Attraction is inaugurated

NOTES

1. "Euro Disney," *Financial Times*' Lex column, 30 October 1996.
2. "Disney Goes to Tokyo," in D. Ancona, T. Kochan, M. Scully, J. Van Maanen, and E. Westney, *Organizational Behavior and Processes*, Cincinnati, OH: Southwestern College Publishing, 1999, pp. M-10, 25.
3. The conversion factors used in the case are: 1 hectare = 2.47 acres, and 1 acre = 4,047 square meters. The US dollar/French franc exchange rates at the beginning of each year were: 1987 6.35, 1988 5.36, 1989 6.03, 1990 5.84, 1991 5.08, 1992 5.22, 1993 5.59, 1994 5.93.
4. "Euro Disney" is used to refer to the Euro Disneyland theme park; "Euro Disneyland SCA" or "the company" refers to the company that owns Euro Disney.
5. "The Euro Disneyland Project – Project Financing: Asset-Based Financial Engineering," Case Study: John D. Finnery, © 1996 by John D. Finnery, John Wiley & Sons.

6. "No magic in these kingdoms," *Los Angeles Times*, December 15, 1989.

7. "Disneyland goes to Europe," in Ancona, Kochan, Scully, Van Maanen, and Westney, *Organizational Behavior and Processes*, 1999, pp. 38–9.

8. Ancona, Kochan, Scully, Van Maanen, and Westney, *Organizational Behavior and Processes*, "Disneyland goes to Europe", op. cit., p. 15.

9. From Jacques Neher, "France amazed, amused by Disney dress code," *The New York Times*, October 5, 1995.

10. *Euro Disney: the First 100 Days*, Harvard Business School, Case No. 9-693-013, 1993, p. 14.

Richard Branson and the Virgin Group of Companies in 2004

Robert M. Grant

Although he would celebrate his 54th birthday later in the year, there was little evidence during the first few months of 2004 that age and maturity had sapped Richard Branson's energy or the entrepreneurial vigor of his Virgin group of companies. Many of his new ventures were outside of Britain. His Australian budget airline, Virgin Blue, completed its IPO in December 2003 (valuing Branson's remaining 25 percent stake at $800 million) and during 2004 was expanding rapidly. In the US, Branson was busy on several fronts. He was seeking a CEO for Virgin USA – a discount airline that would begin service in 2005. Branson's major US business venture – Virgin Mobile USA (a joint venture with Sprint) – signed up its millionth customer at the beginning of 2004. He was planning a reality TV show with Fox that would involve would-be entrepreneurs vying for Branson's support. Back in Britain, Branson was negotiating the floatation of Virgin Mobile – Britain's biggest wireless virtual network operator, he was setting up an online gambling company, and had agreed to acquire the remaining 50 percent of Virgin Money – an online supplier of personal financial services – for £90m.

Branson continued to court controversy and attract extensive press coverage. Virgin Atlantic's proposal to install bright-red urinals shaped as a woman's open lips at its JFK terminal was abandoned. However, he continued his project with Steve Fossett for a non-stop circumnavigation of the globe in a revolutionary plane, Virgin Atlantic Global Flyer.

While Virgin Blue and Virgin Mobile were huge financial successes, the same could not be said of all his new ventures. Several of the online retailing companies he set up at the peak of the dot.com boom – notably Virgin Car and Virgin Bike – had been failures. Several of his long-established businesses were also performing poorly. Virgin Express, the Brussels-based budget airline had lost money between 2001 and 2003; at Virgin Rail heavy investments in new trains dwarfed operating profits; Victory Corporation (clothing and toiletries) and Virgin Cola also continued to rack up losses. Meanwhile Virgin Megastores suffered from declining sales of recorded music.

While lauded by the British press for his entrepreneurship, eccentricity, consumer-orientation, and embodiment of "the friendly face of capitalism," questions were continually being asked about the financial health of his Virgin group. During the late 1990s, an inquiry into the fragmented and secretive structure of the Virgin group had painted a dismal picture:

> Virgin Travel is the only one of Mr. Branson's businesses to make a large profit . . . The rest of Mr. Branson's firms, in both groups, lost money in total. Those firms that he controls lost £28 million on a turnover of some £84 million. The firms that are jointly owned are mostly recent start ups and mostly loss-making. Together they lost £37.5 million.[1]

Further evidence of financial weaknesses in the Virgin group was supplied by the *Financial Times*, which pointed to negative cash flow and economic value added (EVA), and a deteriorating interest cover. The *Financial Times* suggested that Branson might have to resort to raising long-term capital through floating some of his larger companies on the stock market – an avenue that Branson was reluctant to go down because of the various irksome restrictions attached to running a publicly quoted company.[2]

London's *Independent* newspaper noted that performance problems of several Virgin companies were adversely affecting the reputation of Branson himself. In an article titled "Is Branson's honeymoon finally over?" the paper observed the slipping halo of a man "once ranked second only to Mother Teresa as a role model for the young."[3]

During 2002, the financial state of the Virgin group worsened as the group's cash cow, Virgin Atlantic, was incurring heavy losses in the aftermath of September 11, 2001. In response to financial pressures, Branson began to explore the opportunities for floating several Virgin companies on the stock market.[4]

As ever, Branson was dismissive of outside criticism, claiming analysts and financial journalists misunderstood his business empire. Each Virgin company, he argued, was financed on a stand-alone basis; hence attempts to consolidate the income and assets of the companies were irrelevant and misleading. Moreover, Branson had little regard for accounting profits, preferring cash flow and capital value as the critical performance indicators. Thus, most of the Virgin companies were growing businesses that were increasing in their real value and long-term cash-generating potential, even if accounting profits were negative. "The approach to running a group of private companies is fundamentally different to that of running public companies. Short-term taxable profits with good dividends are a prerequisite of public life. Avoiding short-term taxable profits and seeking long-term capital growth is the best approach to growing private companies."[5]

By early 2004, the financial situation of the Virgin group had stabilized – due mainly to the improving health of Virgin Atlantic and the proceeds from Virgin Blue's IPO. However, as Branson swung back into expansionary mode, questions once more arose over the strategic direction of this motley collection of over 200 separate companies. By 2004, the Virgin group had expanded from music and airlines into rail transport, soft drinks, radio broadcasting, clothing, bridal shops, hotels, insurance, mutual funds, Internet services, health clubs, and telecom services. In an era of corporate refocusing and the nurturing of core competences, what possible business rationale could explain

Strategy
Core
problem
Staff

the structure and composition of the Virgin group? Although attention had been directed at the adequacy of Virgin's financial resources, there were also concerns over the group's other key resources. Was there a risk that the Virgin brand would become overextended and that its appeal and integrity would be damaged? With regard to Branson himself, what should his role be in the management of his business empire? To what extent should he attempt to involve himself personally in guiding the various Virgin companies? As the group became bigger and more diverse and Branson became more of a strategic and charismatic leader rather than a hands-on manager, did the group need to establish a more systematic approach to control, exploiting synergies between businesses, and managing risk?

■ THE DEVELOPMENT OF VIRGIN ■

Style
core
values
rebellion
outsider
brash
independent

Richard Branson's business career began while he was a student at Stowe, a private boarding school. His start-up magazine, *Student*, was first published on January 26, 1968. The early success of the magazine encouraged Branson to leave school at 17 years old, before taking his final exams. Agreeing to the boy's request to leave, the headmaster offered the prophetic statement, "Richard, you will end up in prison or as a millionaire." Both predictions were to be fulfilled.[6]

This early publishing venture displayed features that would characterize many of Branson's subsequent entrepreneurial initiatives. The magazine was aimed at baby-boomers between 16 and 25 years old and was designed to appeal to the optimism, irreverence, antiauthoritarianism, and fashion consciousness of the new generation. It would also fill a "gaping hole in the market." *Student* was to be the "voice of youth" and would "put the world to rights." Its eclectic style reflected its founder's ability to commission articles by celebrities and to identify subjects not touched by many well-established magazines. Norman Mailer, Vanessa Redgrave, and Jean-Paul Sartre contributed pieces which appeared among articles on sex, rock music, interviews with terrorists, and proposals for educational reform.

The success of the magazine (Branson optimistically claimed a circulation of 100,000) promoted favorable notice in the national press. Branson was described in complimentary terms as "The editor, publisher and sole advertising manager . . . a teenage professional whose enthusiasm gets things done to an extent that would shame his elders." Certainly his energy and enthusiasm were needed to keep the organization going. The offices were transient, first in a friend's basement flat, later in a disused church. The staff – a closely organized cooperative of friends, acquaintances and hangers-on – distributed magazines, took copy and, frequently, avoided creditors. As Branson said at the time: "The staff all work for nothing. I supply them with somewhere to sleep and some food. It's not so much they are working for you as working with you."[7]

Virgin Records

Branson's next venture was mail order records. Beginning with a single advertisement in the last issue of *Student* magazine, Branson found that he was able to establish a thriving business with almost no up-front investment and no working capital, and could easily undercut the established retail chains. The name "Virgin" was suggested by one of his associates who saw the name as proclaiming their commercial innocence, while possessing some novelty and modest shock-value. Virgin Records brought together Branson and his childhood friend Nik Powell, who took a 40 percent share in the company and complemented Branson's erratic flamboyance with careful operational and financial management. In 1971 Branson opened his first retail store – on London's busy Oxford Street.

Expansion into record publishing was the idea of Simon Draper – one of Virgin's record buyers. Draper introduced Branson to Mike Oldfield, who was soon installed at Branson's Oxfordshire home with a fully equipped recording studio. *Tubular Bells*, launched in 1973, was an instant hit, eventually selling over 5 million copies worldwide. The result was the Virgin record label, which went on to sign up bands whose music or lifestyles did not appeal to the major record companies. Among the most successful signings were the Sex Pistols, who were contracted to Virgin until the band's breakup following the arrest and subsequent death of Sid Vicious.

The recession of 1979–82 was a struggle for Virgin. Several business ventures failed and several of Branson's close associates left, including Nik Powell, who sold his shareholding back to Branson for £1 million plus Virgin's cinema and video interests. Despite these setbacks, the 1980s saw rapid growth for Virgin Records with the signing of Phil Collins, Human League, Simple Minds, and Boy George's Culture Club. By 1983, the Virgin group was earning pre-tax profits of £2.0 million on total revenues of just under £50 million.

Virgin Atlantic Airways

Virgin Atlantic began with a phone call from Randolph Fields, a Californian lawyer who proposed founding a transatlantic, cut-price airline. To the horror of Branson's executives at Virgin Records, Branson was enthralled with the idea. On June 24, 1984, Branson appeared in a World War I flying outfit to celebrate the inaugural flight of Virgin Atlantic in a second-hand 747 bought from Aerolinas Argentina. With the launch of Virgin Atlantic, Branson had embarked upon a perilous path strewn with the wreckage of earlier entrepreneurs of aviation, including Laker, Braniff, and People's Express. Unlike Branson's other businesses, not only was the airline business highly capital intensive, it also required a completely new set of business skills, in particular the need to negotiate with governments, regulatory bodies, banks, and aircraft manufacturers.

Private to Public and Back

By 1985, a transatlantic airfares price war and the investment needs of Virgin Atlantic had created a cash squeeze for Virgin. Branson became convinced of the need to expand the equity base of the group. Don Cruikshank, a Scottish accountant with an MBA from Manchester and Branson's group managing director, was assigned the task of organizing an initial public offering for Virgin's music, retail, and vision businesses, which were combined into the Virgin Group plc, a public corporation with 35 percent of its equity listed on the London and NASDAQ stock markets.

Branson was not happy as chairman of a public corporation. He felt that investment analysts misunderstood his business and that the market undervalued his company. A clear conflict existed between the financial community's expectations of the chairman of a public corporation and Branson's personal style. With the October 1987 stock market crash, Branson took the opportunity to raise £200 million to buy out external shareholders.

As a private company, Virgin continued to expand, using both internal cash flows – mainly from Virgin Atlantic Airways – and external financing. The retailing group moved aggressively into new markets around the world. The Virgin Megastore concept provided the basis for new stores in Japan, the United States, Australia, the Netherlands, and Spain. This growth was facilitated by the formation of a joint venture with Blockbuster Corporation, the US video-store giant. New ventures launched during the early 1990s included Virgin Lightships, an airship advertiser; Vintage Airtours, an operator of restored DC-3 aircraft between Orlando and Key West; Virgin Games producing video games; West One Television, a TV production company; and Virgin Euromagnetics, a personal computer company. Meanwhile, Virgin Atlantic Airways continued to expand. It acquired gates and slots at London's Heathrow Airport and expanded its network to 20 cities – including Tokyo and Hong Kong. Its transatlantic market share grew and the airline won many awards for its customer service.

1990–2001: Continued Expansion, Selective Divestment

Expansion pressured cash flow and the Persian Gulf War of 1990–91 cut airline profits. Increasingly, Branson relied upon joint ventures to finance new business development. The period from 1990 to 1992 was one of major change for the Virgin group. During that time, Branson forged several important joint venture agreements with other companies. The partnering arrangements were primarily in retailing and included one with Marui, a leading Japanese retailer, and another with W. H. Smith, a prominent UK retail chain. Branson and his Virgin group have long relied on the joint venture as an important strategic tool for expanding into new businesses. In 1998, the company's various arrangements with partners continued to play a critical role in Virgin's overall strategy.

By now, the airline had come to dominate Branson's interests and imagination. As capital-hungry Virgin Atlantic needed more money, Branson would have to let go of other parts of his empire. In March 1992, Branson sold his most profitable and successful business, Virgin Music, the world's biggest independent record label, to Thorn EMI for £560 million (close to $1.0 billion). Virgin Music's tangible assets had a balance sheet value of only £3 million. The sale marked a dramatic shift in focus for Virgin away from its core entertainment business towards airlines and travel, and provided the capital to support new business ventures.

In the meantime, Branson's long-standing rivalry with British Airways took a nasty turn. Evidence emerged that British Airways had pursued a "dirty tricks" campaign against Virgin. This included breaking into Virgin's computer system, diverting Virgin customers to BA flights, and spreading rumors about Virgin's financial state. These allegations prompted furious denials from the BA chairman Lord King and criticism of both Branson and Virgin. The outcome was a UK court case which resulted in BA paying $1.5 million dollars in damages to Branson and Virgin. The hostility between Virgin and BA continued after Lord King's early retirement. During the late 1990s, Branson battled tirelessly against the proposed alliance between BA and American Airlines.

The second half of the 1990s saw acceleration in Virgin's business development activities with a host of new ventures in disparate markets. Virgin's new ventures were a response to three types of opportunity:

- *Privatization and deregulation.* The rolling back of the frontiers of state ownership and regulation in Britain (and elsewhere) created business opportunities that Richard Branson was only too eager to seize. Virgin's most important privatization initiative was its successful bids for two passenger rail franchises: the west coast and cross-country rail services. The resulting business – Virgin Rail – was a joint venture with transportation specialist, Stagecoach. Deregulation in the world's airline sector also created opportunities for Virgin. In 1996, Euro-Belgian Airlines was acquired and re-launched as Virgin Express, and in Australia, Virgin Blue began operations during 2000. Branson's bid to operate the British National Lottery was unsuccessful, but in 2001, Virgin Atlantic was part of the consortium that acquired a stake in the British air traffic control system.
- *Direct selling of goods and services to consumers.* Branson was continually on the lookout for business opportunities offering a "new deal" to consumers. Most of these ventures involved direct sales to consumers and passing on the cost savings from bypassing traditional distribution channels. Virgin Direct launched in 1995 as a joint venture with Norwich Union offered telephone-based financial services to consumers. Virgin Car and Virgin Bike challenged the existing dealership system of the automobile and motorcycle manufacturers by offering direct sales of cars and motorbikes at discounted prices. Virgin Wine was also launched.
- *TMT.* The "TMT" (Technology, Media, Telecom) boom of 1998–2000 created a tremendous buzz within Virgin. Virgin foundations were in media and the Internet offered a new channel for Virgin to reach consumers. In 1997 Virgin Net, an Internet service provider and portal, was launched as a joint venture between Virgin and cable operator NTL. The next year Virgin Mobile, a joint venture with Deutsche Telecom's One-to-One wireless telephone service, began business in Britain. The success of Virgin Mobile in Britain – half a million subscribers were signed up within the first year and four million by 2004 – encouraged Virgin to expand into the US, Australia, and southeast Asia. The ability of Virgin to communicate directly with customers through the telephone and the Internet was seen as offering important opportunities to the Virgin group as a whole. Text messaging allowed Virgin Atlantic to sell discounted airline seats to Virgin Mobile customers. *TheTrain.com* was set up as an online reservation service for train passengers. Virgin established a chat

room for Virgin Cola consumers. The Virgin.com portal became a shopfront for all of Virgin's consumer offerings.

The launching of so many new ventures provided the impetus for Branson to sell off equity stakes in some of his more established ventures. During this period, sales included: Virgin's stake in the ISP part of Virgin Net that was sold to partner NTL, the Virgin cinema chain (leaving only the Japanese cinemas owned by Virgin), Virgin Megastores in France, and 50 percent of Virgin Blue. However, by far the biggest deal was the sale of 49 percent of Virgin Atlantic to Singapore Airlines for £600 million. Over the next eight to ten years, several other companies within the Virgin empire are slated for floatation, including Virgin Atlantic, Virgin Rail, Virgin Mobile, Virgin Entertainment, Virgin Active, and Virgin Money.

Virgin's vision and a time line of the development of the Virgin group are given in Appendix 1 and Appendix 2, respectively.

■ THE VIRGIN GROUP OF COMPANIES IN 2004 ■

The Virgin group is not a single corporate entity. The Virgin companies comprise several holding companies and over 200 operating companies, most of which are based within Britain. The equity owned by Branson, both individually and through a series of family trusts, is held by Virgin Group Investments Ltd. The linkages between the companies include: the common use of the Virgin trademark, Branson's role as shareholder (both directly and indirectly through the trusts), Branson's role as chairman of the companies, and Branson's management role, which is primarily in publicity, public and government relations, and appointing senior executives. The Virgin empire comprises those companies which were wholly or majority owned by Branson and those in which Branson held a minority equity stake. Figure 15.1 shows the structure of the Virgin group of companies, including some major operating companies. Appendix 3 shows the main companies within the group.

Despite the remarkable diversity of the Virgin group, all of the Virgin companies possessed an entrepreneurial culture and a strategy that was based upon novel approaches to creating value for consumers (and, ultimately, for Branson). Consider, for example, some of the leading companies within the Virgin group.

Virgin Atlantic

The core of the Virgin empire was its travel business which was the major revenue generator and, until recently, the main source of profit for the group. The flagship, Virgin Atlantic, had launched as a cut-price airline, but its success was based upon targeting the lucrative business traveler segment of the North Atlantic market with superior and innovative customer service. The airline has offered business travelers amenities not even offered to first-class passengers on other airlines. Virgin had pioneered state-of-

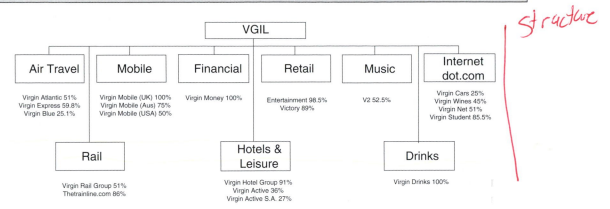

structure

Figure 15.1 The Virgin group of companies
Source: Virgin Management Ltd.

core values = fun

the-art reclining seats, in-flight massages, hair stylists, aromatherapists, and motor-cycle and limo home-pick-up service. In 1998 it began a luxury boat service up the Thames from Heathrow to the City of London allowing executives and bankers to dodge London traffic jams. In economy, Virgin was the first to provide passenger-controlled personal video screens in every seat-back. In-flight entertainment has included clowns, London buskers, even Richard Branson serving drinks while dressed as a female flight attendant. The inaugural transatlantic flight was still remembered fondly by travel writers who took the journey to New York. Bands played music in the aisles, Miss World danced with passengers, butlers handed out caviar, brandy, and cigars. Branson's father, who was along for the ride, commented, "When I die, I hope heaven is like this: 35,000 feet up, endless champagne and surrounded by pretty women."[8] What Virgin did was to re-create the mystique of air travel through mixing unique in-flight luxuries with circus side-show.

customer service

The airline won numerous awards for its customer service and became one of the most profitable of the world's smaller airlines. Its success in the North Atlantic market encouraged it to extend its routes to Asia (Tokyo, Hong Kong, Delhi), the Caribbean, and South Africa.

competition

A constant theme of Virgin Atlantic's development was its war against the major airlines and against British Airways in particular. This involved Branson in one of his favorite roles: casting his plucky Virgin upstart as David against the corporate Goliaths of big business. BA under Lord King was the ideal foil for Branson – big, stuffy, and establishment. Branson's fight, first against the BA "dirty tricks" campaign and then against the BA–American Airlines alliance, provided Branson and Virgin Atlantic with massive publicity and established them as virtuous underdogs representing entrepreneurship and the spirit of competition.

For all Virgin Atlantic's success, it was competing in a tough industry and defending a difficult strategic position. The international airline industry has been a financial disaster for most of the past decade – none of the major airlines had covered their cost of capital. Virgin Atlantic's dependence on business travelers was a major source of vulnerability when most companies were trimming their travel budgets. Virgin Atlantic's competitive advantage depended critically upon its superior service, yet almost all its service innovations were being imitated by the major airlines.

In 2000, Branson sold a 49 percent stake of Virgin Atlantic to Singapore Airlines for £600 million, using the proceeds to invest in growing divisions within the Virgin group, namely Virgin Mobile and Virgin Net. In the year to April 2001, Virgin Atlantic lost £82.7 million, compared with £42 million in the previous year. For the year to April 2003, the airline actually made a pre-tax profit of £15.7 million, and was forecasting a slight improvement for the year to April 2004. Buoyed by the recent performance, Branson boldly announced plans to double the size of Virgin Atlantic's fleet, hire 1,400 new workers, and, in the latest battle with BA, begin offering alternatives to BA's lucrative London–Sydney and London–Nassau routes.

Virgin Cargo

Air freight business was an important complement to Virgin Atlantic's passenger service. While planning the launch of Virgin Atlantic, Branson asked New York "Air Freight Godfather" Angelo Pusateri to join him on Branson's London houseboat to discuss the start-up of a Virgin Airlines cargo service. "It was sort of strange," remembered Pusateri. "He was a very relaxed guy, continually scribbling in this big notebook. He said he was putting together an airline and it was going to be fun. He told us, 'I don't know much about cargo, but I know it's important to our revenue package, and I'd like you guys to build an air freight operation for us. Go forth and develop.' Anyone who could lay out a plan of this size without a single typed piece of paper – I was impressed."[9] Based at the then-underutilized Newark airport, Virgin Cargo grew to handle close to 100,000 metric tons of cargo by 2000. The company managed freight operations for other carriers such as Lufthansa, America West, and Midwest Express. Pusateri was chief executive of Virgin Aviation Services, the parent company to Virgin Cargo and other smaller Virgin aviation companies. Under Pusateri's leadership, the Virgin management style based upon initiative, entrepreneurship, and a high level of autonomy worked well in the air cargo business. Managers were encouraged to tailor products to customer needs, price service aggressively, and take risks. When a federal regulation required US law enforcement agencies to discard outdated, but still effective bullet-proof vests, Pusateri had the vests collected and shipped free of charge to London's Metropolitan police force: "The bobbies get peace of mind, English taxpayers don't pay a quid, and Virgin gets some great PR."

Virgin Express

In April 1996, Branson purchased Euro-Belgian Airlines SA, a short-haul carrier based in Brussels servicing destinations throughout Europe. After changing the name to Virgin Express plc, 49 percent of its stock was floated on the Brussels and NASDAQ stock markets. Virgin Express took advantage of the liberalization of the European aviation market to expand its range of scheduled services. Virgin Express moved into profit in 1997, but in competing with low-cost airlines such as EasyJet and GO, was hampered by a high cost base resulting from its Belgium location. In July 1998, Virgin Express moved the company's registration to the Republic of Ireland to benefit from lower corporate and employment taxes. Its operational base remained in Brussels which meant that its routes did not link with those of Virgin Atlantic.

In 2003, Virgin Express recorded a £13.1 million loss, citing ongoing competition from budget airlines and a continued depressed market for air travel. The company also announced in March 2004 that it would be restating its 1999 to 2001 earnings to account for a €7.4 million hole caused by faulty reservation system software. Virgin Express is currently in talks with Belgian rival SN Brussels Airlines over a potential merger that would give SN shareholders a 70.1 percent stake in the new entity.

Virgin Blue

True to Virgin's modus operandi as an underdog challenging The Establishment, Virgin Blue was launched in August 2000 as a domestic Australian carrier to challenge the Qantas/Ansett duopoly. In contrast to Virgin Atlantic, Virgin Blue was a "no frills" airline with no meals, frequent flyer programs, or passenger lounges. Operating a single aircraft – the Boeing 737 – the airline initially offered flights between Sydney and Brisbane. Additional links to Adelaide, Melbourne, and Perth were soon added. When Ansett Airlines filed for bankruptcy in 2001, Branson seized the opportunity to expand Virgin's share of the Australian market. To raise capital, he sold off a 50 percent stake in the airline to the Patrick Corporation, an Australian freight company.

Virgin Blue has won several customer service awards since its launch, and has operated very profitably since launch. Despite the overall downturn in global airline industry, Virgin Blue managed to triple pre-tax profits from A$47 million in 2002 to A$158 million in 2003. The airline was floated on the Australian Stock Exchange in December 2003 at A$2.25 per share. As of April 2004, its stock had declined to A$1.75 per share.

Virgin Rail

Virgin's biggest, and potentially riskiest, diversification of the 1990s was its entry into rail travel. Early in 1996, Virgin Rail was formed to bid for operating franchises in the partitioned and privatized British Rail system. By 1997 Virgin Rail operated two rail companies: Virgin Cross-Country with train services between the South West, Midlands, and Wales, with Birmingham as a hub; and Virgin West Coast with services between London and Glasgow. In addition, Virgin was also one of the six investors in London and Continental Railway (LCR), which was responsible for running the Eurostar train service between London and Paris through the Channel Tunnel. To promote awareness of the Virgin brand, Branson had all of the trains painted in Virgin's cardinal red. Taking the period 1997–2003 as a whole, Virgin Rail was marginally profitable; however, these profits depended upon government operating subsidies of £56.5 million annually. In addition, the capital investment requirements of operating passenger rail services were substantial, though the sale of 49 percent of Virgin Rail to Stagecoach for £158 million had reduced Virgin's exposure. During 2001–04, Virgin Rail invested heavily in new trains and carriages with a view to upgrading both speed and the quality of customer service. Despite these investments, Virgin Rail suffered from the general woes of the UK's privatized rail network. Virgin Rail's record of poor punctuality (less than half of its trains arrived on time) was primarily a result of the poor state of Britain's rail infrastructure; however, these experiences did little to enhance the Virgin brand.

Virgin Entertainment Group

Virgin Entertainment Group comprises Virgin's retailing businesses together with Virgin's remaining cinema chains. The retailing companies include Virgin Megastores, with 122 locations around the world, and the UK Our Price chain. The Megastores sold music, music accessories, electronic equipment, clothing, and concert tickets. The Virgin Megastores did not form a single integrated business but were operated as separate businesses with different business partners in different countries. Thus, in Japan, Virgin Megastores were a joint venture with Marui, a Japanese department store, while in France Virgin no longer had an equity stake in the Megastore chain.

The other major retail business was the Virgin/Our Price music retailing chain, 75 percent of which had been sold to the book and newspaper retailer W. H. Smith in 1991 but was reacquired by Branson for £145 million in 1998.[10]

Despite the success of the Virgin stores as leading retailers of recorded music, the format failed to develop into a "category killer" in the same way as Home Depot in home improvement supplies, IKEA in home furnishings, or The Gap in casual clothing. Retailing revenues have totaled around half a billion pounds annually. However, profitability has been miserable. In April 2000, *The Economist* reported that Virgin Entertainment owed its banks £172 million and had run out of capital. The impact of Internet file sharing and illegal recording of CDs has been a major problem only partly ameliorated by Virgin's use of its retail network to sell mobile phones. Despite extensive refurbishment of the UK Megastores, the chain was still struggling in 2004.

Virgin Trading Group Limited

Virgin Trading Group, a wholly owned Virgin subsidiary, comprised Branson's beverage start-ups – the ventures had been widely viewed as pure follies by most outside marketing experts. Virgin Spirits, a joint venture with Scottish whisky distiller William Grant, was established to market and distribute Virgin Vodka. The brand failed to gain significant market presence outside of Virgin's own planes and hotels and the venture was wound up in March 1998. The Virgin Cola Company was a joint venture with the Canadian soft drink company Cott & Company, the world's largest supplier of retailer own-brand soda drinks. Virgin Cola was introduced in the UK in 1994 and achieved initial success in the pub and restaurant trade. The drink was packaged in a "Pammy" bottle based upon the body of Pamela Anderson. After gaining a peak of 8 percent share of the UK market, sales declined. In 1997, Virgin Cola lost about £5 million on revenues of £30 million. In 1998, Virgin acquired Cott's share of the business and launched Virgin Cola with a $25 million investment and the goal, according to Branson, of "driving Coke out of the States."[11] Despite gaining massive publicity, there was little evidence of Virgin being able to convert media coverage into sales. By 2002, Virgin Drinks Company was still marketing Virgin Cola in the UK, Continental Europe, and Asia, but no sales figures were available.

Financials

Virgin Money

The Virgin Direct (later renamed Virgin Money) financial services group was launched in the UK in March 1995. It was a joint venture between Virgin, which owned 49.9 percent, and Australian Mutual Provident (AMP). Virgin Direct offered retirement plans called "PEPs" (personal equity plans), life insurance, and other financial services. It was organized into several units, including: Virgin Direct Life, which offered life insurance and retirement plans; Virgin Unit Trusts Managers, which managed mutual funds; the Virgin One Bank, a joint venture with the Royal Bank of Scotland; and Virgin Credit Card, issued by MBNA. It direct-marketed several index-linked mutual funds ("unit trusts") that offered lower management costs and better average performance than most actively managed mutual funds. Within three years of the launch, Virgin Direct had some 250,000 customers and its mutual funds had £1.5 billion under management. By 2002, the financial services of Virgin Money were delivered primarily through the Internet. VirginMoney.com offered access to the full range of Virgin financial services, including bank accounts, credit cards, ISAs, home and car insurance, life insurance, mutual funds, and share dealing. Virgin's financial services were characterized by two features. First, they were low cost. Virgin's credit card interest rates, fund management charges, and other fees tended to be below those of the major financial institutions. Second, Virgin's product offered several ease-of-use features. For example, the Virgin One bank account allowed a number of products – home loans, savings account, checking account, credit card debt – to be pooled into a single account offering significant administrative and interest cost conveniences. Despite considerable market success, Virgin Money continued to lose money and, in July 2001, Virgin sold its 25 percent stake in Virgin One to the Royal Bank of Scotland for £45 million. Continuing losses prompted AMP to announce in 2003 that it was seeking a divestment of its 50 percent stake. In April 2004, Branson purchased AMP's 50 percent equity of Virgin Money for £90 million.

Victory Corporation

Victory Corporation – Virgin's clothing and cosmetics company – had also met with considerable criticism from outside commentators. The company was floated as a start-up on London's Alternative Investment Market in 1996. Its two parts were:

- Virgin Vie, a cosmetics and toiletries company which designed and marketed its own range of products (intended to expand to about 1,000 separate products) to be sold through 3,000 consultants and 100 UK stores, as well as an international launch. By mid-1998, the venture was going badly, with the planned store openings canceled after the pilot stores failed to achieve target sales.
- Virgin Clothing Company, a designer and marketer of men's clothing that sold through UK fashion retailers and through its Internet site, www.virgin-clothing.com. The company's advertisements showed a scruffy Richard Branson with the caption, "Giorgio designs. Ralph designs. Calvin designs. Don't worry, Richard doesn't." The clothing range did not sell well. Launches of new ranges were behind schedule because of the need to redesign.

Since floatation, Victory Corporation's share price declined from 55 pence to 3 pence in May 2002, reflecting the company's dismal sales and profit performance – the company turned in operating losses of £8 million for 1997. Finance director, Stephen Murphy, said that a key lesson for Virgin from the Victory Corporation experience was the danger of floating start-up companies: "Thrusting a start-up company into the public arena on day one is not a good thing to do. Because of the public company perspective, we did not grasp control in the way we should have done."[12]

Virgin Net

Virgin Net was both an Internet service provider and a portal offering a variety of content and retailing opportunities through partnership arrangements between Virgin Net and a range of partner suppliers. Virgin's monthly subscription rate undercut AOL, BT, and most other major ISPs. Virgin had attempted to dispose of its half share of the business to its partner, NTL; however, the sale ran into difficulties and the service continues as a joint venture.

Virgin Mobile

Virgin Mobile was the most successful of the UK's "mobile virtual network operators" – companies that partnered with major wireless operators to offer service over their partners' networks. Virgin's rapid market penetration may be attributed to its brand recognition; marketing through Virgin retail stores, Virgin.net, and Sainsbury's supermarkets; and Virgin's simple market approach – unlike other telecom companies, Virgin has no line rental, no monthly contract, and a simple tariff: 15p a minute for the first five minutes of each day and 5p a minute after that. This approach has made Virgin Mobile especially popular with the young, a group it has appealed to with piped-in music news from MTV and a "rescue ring" feature – a self-placed emergency call allowing the subscriber to bolt from an unwanted date. Virgin Mobile claims to be the fastest-growing mobile operator in the UK, with nearly 4 million subscribers. Virgin Mobile disclosed 2002 profits before tax of £5 million on sales of £300 million. It has scored a number of firsts, including being the first operator to scrap peak rate calls, introduce a daily discounting tariff, and was the first company in the world to introduce an integrated MP3 mobile phone. However, the relationship with partner T-Mobile was less than rosy, and Branson announced in 2004 that Virgin Mobile would repurchase T-Mobile's 50 percent stake, postponing the company's IPO until later in the year.

Virgin Mobile (Australia), a partnership with Cable and Wireless Optus, opened for business at the end of October 2000; Virgin Mobile (Asia), a joint venture with Singapore Telecom, was launched in summer 2001; and US entry in 2002 involved a joint venture with Sprint. Canadian entry is scheduled for 2004 under a joint venture with Bell Mobility.

Virgin Bride

Branson's Virgin Bride venture was a classic example of Branson's entrepreneurial opportunism in the face of an underserved consumer market. The idea had come from a Virgin Atlantic employee who was appalled at the inadequacies of bridal shops within the UK. The first Virgin Bride store was launched by Branson wearing a $10,000 bridal gown. The stores offered a full range of wedding goods and services, including apparel and wedding planning services.

■ FINANCIAL STRUCTURE AND PERFORMANCE ■

Financial reporting by the Virgin companies was fragmented, difficult to locate, and awkward to consolidate because of lack of public information and different financial years. As noted, the financial performance of the Virgin group as a whole was poor during the late 1990s. More recent evidence points to continuing poor performance of a number of the Virgin companies (see table 15.1).

The financial structure of the Virgin group has changed substantially over the years. In terms of financial structure, the primary feature of the group was the stand-alone financing of each company. At the beginning of the 1990s, the group had debts of more than $400 million, most of which were personally guaranteed by Branson or subject to cross-guarantees within the group. This left Virgin highly vulnerable to bad debts in one part of the group swiftly infecting the rest. Virgin's near collapse during the 1990–92 recession resulted in a more conservative approach to financing by Branson. Each company was separately financed, often with outside investors taking much of the risk. Lenders to Virgin companies have no recourse to Mr Branson's assets or those of any other part of the group.

However, the recurrent losses of several Virgin companies have forced Branson to shift finances between companies in order to prop up weaker businesses. While Virgin Atlantic was generating a strong positive cash flow, then the rest of the Virgin group was safe. Virgin Atlantic's transition from profit to loss during 2001–02 placed considerable added pressures on the group.

Table 15.1   The financial performance of major Virgin companies, 2002

Company	Revenue ($ million)	Profit (Loss) ($ million)	Ownership (%)
Virgin Atlantic	2,042	25	51
Virgin Mobile UK	480	8	50
Virgin Rail	442	12	51
Virgin Express Holdings	185	(21)	58
Victory Corporation	92	(13)	85
Virgin Travel*	2,028	73	51
Virgin Entertainment Group*	67	(21)	100
Virgin Money*	872	(62)	100
V2 Records*	72	(65)	66
Virgin Hotels*	38	(0.7)	100
Virgin Trading**	100	(6)	100
Virgin Bride**	30	(0.4)	100
Virgin Net**	20	(7)	51

Sources: Company press releases.

* 2000 data – ICC Information Ltd, 2001.

** 1999 data – *Fortune*, July 2, 2000.

The rapid diversification of the 1990s, together with the cash demands of the rail-road companies, retailing, and financial services, encouraged Branson to look increasingly to outside equity financing. This has resulted in Branson attracting investment by venture capital funds, joint venture partners, and initial public offerings. Of the 13 businesses that formed the bulk of Virgin's operations, only three were wholly owned by Branson and his interests: Virgin Money, Virgin Hotels, and the V Entertainment Group. The others all had substantial outside interests:

- Virgin Atlantic was 49 percent owned by Singapore Airlines.
- Virgin Rail was 49 percent owned by Stagecoach.
- Virgin Retail had different partners and investors. These included Blockbuster and Marui.
- Virgin Trading drinks ventures had been launched with investments from William Grant and Cotts.
- Victory Corporation, the fashion and toiletries companies, was pioneered by entrepreneur and investor Rory McCarthy. In addition, outside investors owned 25 percent of the equity. McCarthy also held one-third of V2 Music.
- Virgin Express was a publicly traded company, in which Virgin held a minority stake.
- Virgin Blue was a publicly traded company, of which Virgin held 25 percent.
- Apart from the joint venture partners and public stockholders, there were also a number of private investors – often major equity and venture capital funds.

A central role for Branson was his ability to attract outside investors through his high profile, personality, and network of connections. Typically, by offering the Virgin brand

and his own celebrity status to promote new ventures, Branson was able to acquire an equity stake in new ventures that was quite disproportionate to the size of Virgin's financial investment – which was typically small. For example, Branson put up only £2,000 initially for minority stakes in Virgin Clothing and Virgin Vie. The attractiveness of Virgin to The Royal Bank of Scotland and Australian Mutual was that it permitted these companies to develop a novel approach to marketing and distribution using one of the best-known and highly regarded personalities in Britain, without putting their own names at risk. The Virgin name together with the image and entrepreneurial drive of Branson were also major considerations in encouraging Stagecoach to acquire a major stake in Virgin Rail. In the case of Virgin Blue, Branson's initial investment was A$12 million. Following the IPO, Virgin Blue was valued at $2.5 billion. Branson's willingness to extend the Virgin brand to a wide range of new enterprises, many of them with minor equity stakes by Virgin, has stimulated the observation that Virgin was increasingly a brand-franchising operation.

■ ORGANIZATIONAL STRUCTURE AND CORPORATE CULTURE ■

As noted earlier, the Virgin group was an unusual organization. It comprised a loose alliance of companies linked primarily by the Virgin trademark and Branson's role as shareholder, chairman, and public relations supremo.[13] The group's financial and legal structure was partly a reflection of Branson's unconventional ideas about business and his wariness of the financial community. To some extent, the intricate structure of offshore-owned private companies was a deliberate attempt by Branson to cloak the Virgin empire in a thick veil of secrecy. This was apparent from the use of "bearer shares" by several of the Virgin holding companies through which minority shareholders (venture capitalists and other investors) could not be identified. However, there was more to the Virgin structure than opaqueness and tax efficiency. Branson viewed the loosely knit structure as consistent with his vision of people-oriented capitalism:

> We're structured as if we are 150 small companies. Each has to stand on its own two feet, as if they are their own companies. Employees have a stake in their success. They feel – and are – crucial to their company because they are one-in-fifty or one-in-a-hundred instead of one-in-tens-of-thousands. They indeed are all under the Virgin umbrella, but they are generally not subsidiaries. I'm over them to see if one company can't help another, but otherwise they are independent. Some people like the idea of growing fiefdoms – companies that brag about sales of over $5 billion a year – but there is no logical reason to think that there is anything good about huge companies. History in fact shows the opposite. Those huge corporations with tentacles and divisions and departments become unwieldy, slow growing, stagnant. Some chairmen want them like that so that one division's loss can make up for another's profit, but we'd rather have a lot of exciting companies that are all making profits – as are all of ours.[14]

The Virgin group has been likened both to a brand franchising operation and to Japanese *keiretsu* where member companies have financial and management links and share a common sense of identity. The reality, according to *Management Today*,[15] is somewhere between the two. Will Whitehorn, Branson's long-time strategist and business developer, describes Virgin as "a branded venture capital organization."

Although the formal linkages between the companies are limited to Branson's shareholdings, his presence or influence on the companies' board of directors, and the common use of the Virgin brand, there is also an informal corporate organization. Branson's London residence in Holland Park acted as an improvised corporate office where a small core of Branson advisors and senior executives spent time. These include:

- Will Whitehorn, originally Branson's press spokesman and head of PR, but widely regarded as Branson's second-in-command and sounding-board for issues of strategy and new business development.
- Rowan Gormley joined the Virgin group as Corporate Development Director after working as an accountant with Arthur Andersen & Co. He led Virgin's move into financial services in 1995 as chief executive of Virgin Direct. In January 2000, he became Chief Executive of Virgin Wine.
- Brad Rosser was Branson's head of new business development. An accounting and finance major from Australia with an MBA from Cornell, he was previously employed by Australian entrepreneur Alan Bond and by McKinsey & Company. He subjected new business proposals to rigorous criteria as to whether they fit the Virgin business model: "The products must be innovative, challenge authority, offer value for money, be of good quality, and the market must be growing."
- Michael Herriot, at 55, was one of the eldest of Branson's top management team. He was hired from Grand Metropolitan in 1989 to head up Virgin Hotels (a position he held throughout 2001).
- Rory McCarthy was business partner, friend, and soul mate of Branson. Having set the world hang-gliding altitude record as well as starting up a string of companies, he had similar drives to Branson. His McCarthy Corporation held 33 percent of V2 and 50 percent of Virgin Helicopters.
- Tom Alexander was recruited by Branson from BT Cellnet to head up Virgin Mobile.
- Gordon McCallum joined Virgin in 1997 as Group Strategy Director. He was formerly a McKinsey & Company consultant. In 2001 he was appointed to the board of Virgin Mobile USA.
- Frances Farrow joined Virgin Atlantic as Commercial Services Director from City law firm, Binder Hamlyn. She became chief executive of Virgin USA Inc. and a member of the board of Virgin Mobile USA.

A key feature of the Virgin group was the roles which senior executives played and the way in which they interacted. Although their formal positions were as executives of the individual operating companies, a number were long-time Branson associates who participated more widely in the management of the group. For instance, while heading up corporate services at Virgin Atlantic, Frances Farrow's legal background meant that she provided much wider legal advice within the Virgin group. Similarly, although Rowan Gormley's formal positions were with Virgin Direct and Virgin Wine, he was a source of new business leadership and strategy expertise for the group as a whole. Thus, although the Virgin group had no corporate structure, Branson and his senior executives and advisors did, in effect, form a team which exerted overall financial control, guided strategy, assessed new business ideas, and determined new appointments.

Staff

A key aspect of this informal integration and control was the Virgin culture. This was defined almost entirely by Branson's own values and management style. It reflected his eccentricity, sense of fun, disrespect for hierarchy and formal authority, commitment to employees and consumers, and belief in hard work and individual responsibility. The group provided an environment in which talented, ambitious people were motivated to do their best and strive for a higher level of performance. While the working environment was informal, anti-corporate, and defined by the pop culture of its era, expectations were high. Branson expected a high level of commitment, the acceptance of personal responsibility, and long hours of work when needed. Financial rewards for most employees were typically modest, but non-pecuniary benefits included social activities, company-sponsored weekend getaways, and impromptu parties.

The apparent chaos of the Virgin group, with its casual style and absence of formal structure and control systems, belied a sharp business acumen and forceful determination of the Virgin group. It was easy for more traditional business enterprises to underestimate Virgin – a key error of British Airways. Virgin possessed considerable financial and managerial talent, and what Virgin lacked in formal structure was made up for by a strong culture and close personal ties. The Virgin organizational structure involved very little hierarchy, offering short lines of communication and flexible response capability. Employees were given a great deal of responsibility and freedom in order to stimulate idea generation, initiative, commitment, and fun. The lack of a corporate headquarters and the small size of most of the Virgin operating companies were intended to foster teamwork and a strong entrepreneurial spirit.

■ BRANSON'S CHARACTER AND BUSINESS PHILOSOPHY ■

As the creator of Virgin and its unique corporate culture, and the primary promoter of its image and entrepreneurial spirit, Richard Branson was synonymous with Virgin. He has been referred to as the "hippie entrepreneur" of a "counter-cultural enterprise." To many of his generation he embodied the spirit of "New Britain." In a country where business leaders were members of "The Establishment" and upholders of the existing social structure, Branson was seen as a revolutionary. Despite a privileged family background (his father was a lawyer and Richard attended a private boarding school), Branson had the ability to transcend the social classes which traditionally divided British society and segmented consumer markets. As such, he was part of a movement in British culture and society that has sought to escape the Old Britain of fading empire, class antagonism, Victorian values, and stiff-upper-lip hypocrisy. In the remaking of British society in its post-imperial era, Richard Branson can be viewed – along with musicians such as the Beatles, politicians like Margaret Thatcher and Tony Blair, and other new-age entrepreneurs such as Anita Roddick of Body Shop – as an important change agent.

Style
Core
values

His informality and disrespect for convention were central to his way of business. Branson's woolly sweaters, beard, windswept hair, and toothy grin were practically a trademark of the Virgin companies. His dislike of office buildings and the usual symbols of corporate success was reflected in the absence of a corporate head office and his willingness to do business from his family homes – the Manor in Oxfordshire, a Maida Vale houseboat, and later his Holland Park house.

His lack of a clear distinction between work and his social and family life is reflected in the fact that his cousins, aunts, childhood friends, and dinner-party acquaintances were all drawn into business relationships with him. His approach to his business relationships was that work should be fun and his employees should gain both pleasure and a sense of fulfillment from their role in creating enterprises. Branson has experienced few problems in paying quite modest salaries to the great majority of Virgin employees. According to Robert Dick:

> Much of the operating style was established not so much by design but the exigencies of the time when Virgin was getting started. It has proved to be a successful model that Branson can replicate. His philosophy is to immerse himself in a new venture until he understands the ins and outs of the business, and then hand it over to a good managing director and financial controller, who are given a stake in it, and are then expected to make the company take off. He knows that expansion through the creation of additional discrete legal entities not only protects the Virgin group, but also gives people a sense of involvement and loyalty, particularly if he trusts them with full authority and offers minority share holdings to the managers of subsidiaries. He is proud of the fact that Virgin has produced a considerable number of millionaires. He has said that he does not want his best people to leave the company to start a venture outside. He prefers to make millionaires within.[16]

His use of joint ventures was an extension of this model reinforced by his dealings with the Japanese. Branson was impressed by the Japanese approach to business, admiring their commitment to the long term and the way they took time to build a business through organic growth rather than acquisition. His only major acquisition was the parts of British Rail that formed Virgin Rail. Prior to that Branson had made only two significant acquisitions: Rushes Video for £6 million and the forerunner to Virgin Express. He saw similarities in the Japanese *keiretsu* system (multiple companies interlocking through managerial and equity linkages in a collaborative network) and the structure he created at Virgin, with around 200 mostly small companies, which combined "small is beautiful" with "strength through unity." He explained this and other business maxims that he believed to be necessary for success in a speech to the Institute of Directors in 1993. "Staff first, then customers and shareholders" should be the chairman's priority if the goal is better performance. "Shape the business around the people," "Build don't buy," "Be best, not biggest," "Pioneer, don't follow the leader," "Capture every fleeting idea," and "Drive for change" were other guiding principles in the Branson philosophy.

Branson's values of innocence, innovation, and irreverence for authority were apparent in his choice of new ventures. He drew heavily on the ideas of others within his organization and was prepared to invest in new start-ups even in markets that were dominated by long-established incumbents. His business ventures, just like his sporting exploits, reflected a "just live life" attitude and a "bigger the challenge, greater the fun" belief. In identifying opportunity he was particularly keen to identify markets where the conservatism and lack of imagination of incumbent firms meant that they were failing to create value for customers. Branson entered markets with a "new" and "antiestablishment attitude" that sought to offer customers a better alternative. An example of this was Virgin's entry into financial services. Into a business that was long regarded as conservative and stuffy, Branson hoped to bring "a breath of fresh air."

What did these principles mean for the types of markets that Virgin entered and the kind of strategy that Virgin adopted? Will Whitehorn identified a number of common themes:

- "Challenging markets"
- "Taking competition to the next level"
- "Sticking it to the Big Boys"
- "Quality"
- "Value for money"
- "Challenge"[17]

At the same time, the affection of the British public towards Branson reflected the fact that Branson was a traditionalist as well as a radical. Branson's values and his sense of fair play were consistent with many traditional values that defined the British character. His competitive battles against huge corporations like British Airways and Coca-Cola link well with the English heroes who have battled against tyranny and evil: King Arthur, Robin Hood, and St George. His fights against British Airways' dirty-tricks campaign, and his resisting unethical practices in competing for the franchise to run the National Lottery, resonate well with the British sense of fair play. Even his willingness to appear in outlandish attire reflected a British propensity for ludicrous dressing-up whether at fancy-dress parties, morris dancing, or the House of Lords.

■ MARKETING ■

The Virgin brand was the group's greatest single asset. What the brand name communicated and how it enhanced the products to which it was applied was complex. It had connotations of value for money, but also linked with concepts of style and broader social values, too. Most importantly, the brand was not associated with any specific products or markets – it allowed Virgin to cross product and market boundaries more easily than almost any other brand name. While Marks & Spencer was successful in extending its St Michael brand from clothing to food, Ralph Lauren extended his brand from clothing to cosmetics, toiletries, and accessories, and Harley-Davidson applied its brand to clothing, toiletries, cigarettes, and cafés, no company had extended its brand to so diverse a range of products and services as airlines, railroads, cosmetics, financial services, music, and soft drinks.

The values and characteristics that the Virgin brand communicated were inseparable from Richard Branson the entrepreneur, joker, fair-playing Brit, and challenger of giants. The differentiation that the Virgin brand offered was linked to the innovation

Strategy – differentiation

and offbeat marketing approach that characterized the different Virgin start-ups. This differentiation was Virgin's positioning as a small, innovative customer-friendly alternative to big, established market players – BA in airlines, Coca-Cola in soft drinks, and the major banks in financial services. As Virgin moved increasingly into international markets, Branson had to consider how well this image could cross the boundaries of national culture. Although Branson was well known in Europe and North America, in many respects he was a quintessentially British character who was a product of time and place.

With the rapid diversification of the 1990s, there was also the risk that the Virgin brand had become overextended. The head of brand identity at consultant Landor Associates commented: "He's still way too unfocused. He should get out of businesses that don't fit the Virgin/Branson personality, such as beverages, cosmetics, certainly financial services, or come up with another brand name for them."[18] Other marketing experts suggested that Virgin's brand-stretching had damaged the goodwill associated with the Virgin name and compromised the core values it was founded on. Applying the Virgin name to rail services has been especially damaging – Virgin's vision of offering the traveling public new standards of speed and customer attentiveness had been swamped by the problems of Britain's privatized but poorly integrated rail network. The wisdom of applying a brand that had been identified with dynamic start-up business to the renaming of a former public sector monopoly was a source of much reflection within Virgin.

Despite his renown, Branson, too, might be waning in market appeal. Was there a risk that, having seen Branson as flight attendant, Branson in a wedding dress, Branson with successive prime ministers, and Branson attempting to fly around the world in a hot-air balloon, the public was beginning to tire of his exploits?

These concerns were not new. During 1996–7, a refocusing had begun within Virgin. The executive team identified a number of "core businesses" where it wanted to see growth: Virgin Atlantic, Virgin Express, Virgin Rail, and the international expansion of its retail and cinema businesses. "We are going to consolidate around these core areas," says Whitehorn, "because we have a lot to do with them."[19] The telecom and Internet revolution of the late 1990s changed all that. During 1997–2001, Virgin had embarked upon a number of new businesses mostly built upon the opportunities provided by wireless telecommunications and the Internet. By 2002, most commentators believed that a new phase of refocusing was inevitable.

■ LOOKING AHEAD ■

During early 2004, the Virgin group of companies was faced with two main issues. In the short term was the group's financial situation. A number of Virgin's businesses were experiencing substantial negative cash flows. Despite plans to generate funds through further IPOs – especially Virgin Mobile – this still left poorly performing companies such as Virgin Express, Virgin Megastores, and Virgin Money, where offloading Branson's equity stakes would prove more difficult.

Longer term, there were fundamental strategic questions about the future shape and rationale for the Virgin group. What kind of enterprise was Virgin? Was it a brand man-

Core Issue

agement and franchising company, an incubator of start-up businesses, a vehicle for Richard Branson's personal ambitions, or a novel form of conglomerate? Was Virgin a unified, if diversified, business or a loose confederation of many independent businesses?

Whatever the identity and rationale of the Virgin group, it was not apparent that the existing structure or organization fitted with any of these categories:

- If Virgin was a brand-franchising organization, then the critical role for the Virgin group was to develop and protect the brand and maximize the licensing revenues from its use by other companies. Clearly Branson would need to play a role in promoting the brand, but it was not necessary that he should have any strategic, operating, or ownership role in the companies using the brand.
- If Virgin is to be an incubator of new start-ups, then there needed to be a more systematic approach to evaluating new business opportunities and monitoring their progress and development.
- If Virgin was a conglomerate, then did this imply a stronger corporate role? What kind of strategic planning and financial controls were needed to ensure that value was not being dissipated? And could Virgin really perform across so wide a range of businesses?

Whichever path Virgin followed, it appeared that organizational changes would be needed in order to manage inter-company linkages. Although Branson liked to maintain that the different companies were independent and "stood on their own two feet," the reality was somewhat different. Some companies had been strong cash generators; others were heavy loss makers. At present, financial relationships between the companies were ad hoc, and Branson was proud of the fact that no consolidated financial statements were prepared, even for internal management purposes. Moreover, changes to Britain's capital-gains tax laws threatened to eliminate the advantages of multiple, offshore holding companies. Indeed, to obtain the tax benefits from Virgin's loss-making businesses, there were clear advantages in consolidation. Key questions also surrounded the management of the Virgin brand. To the extent that the brand was a common resource, how could it be best protected? The experiences of Virgin Rail had shown that adverse publicity from one company could negatively impact the overall status of the Virgin brand.

As always, the future of the Virgin group could not be considered without taking account of Branson himself. What kind of role did he anticipate now that he approached his 54th birthday? If Branson was to become less active as chief entrepreneur, public relations director, and strategic architect for the Virgin companies, who or what would take his place?

APPENDIX 1
Virgin's Vision

When we started Virgin as a mail order music business in 1970, we chose a brand name that could be applied to other businesses in the future. From that humble beginning a shop in Oxford Street followed in 1971 and a record company with its own recording studio in 1972. Thirty years later the dream of 1970 has become a reality and Virgin has evolved a unique business model as a branded venture capital organization. We invest, along with a range of different institutional and trade partners, in a wide range of businesses that either share or have the prospect of sharing common brand values.

Two important business developments helped create the Virgin brand of today. Firstly, the record company and the Virgin Megastore businesses created a youthful image for Virgin as it challenged the major record companies and was at the heart of the "Indy" revolution in the late 1970s. The Megastore business changed the face of music retailing and brought the concept of a home entertainment superstore to the marketplace for the first time. Secondly, through the launch of Virgin Atlantic, the brand took on the role of consumer champion and built up an enviable reputation by 1990 of quality, value for money, innovation and fun.

Following the sale of Virgin's original music business in 1992 to Thorn EMI Plc for £560 million, we began to build a business model based on the concept of developing discrete businesses with their own investors. These future businesses, if they were to use the Virgin brand, should fulfil or have the potential to fulfil both the emerging public perception of the brand and provide the shareholders with a good return on their equity investment.

The core developments of the last 8 years have been in the fields of travel, leisure, music, entertainment retailing, financial services and mobile telephony. As a result, the brand is now one of the most highly regarded in Europe with a world-wide presence that gives it the opportunity to become a global force in both consumer and business to business markets. We believe that Virgin can now build a number of truly global businesses from a strong consumer base in the UK. Virgin Atlantic has already established a presence in most of the world's major economies and is comfortably but also profitably providing service to the world's business community and independent travelers. We believe that a number of our brands can build on this success. In particular we are planning a global presence in travel, mobile communications, entertainment retailing and music. For example, plans are well under way to develop Virgin Mobile in all the world's major markets.

Virgin also intends to continue to develop the depth of its UK businesses and exploit the opportunities of "convergence marketing" which are emerging from the concurrent convergence of e-commerce and mobile telephony technologies. It is envisaged that these opportunities will provide significant consumer benefits whilst at the same time enhancing shareholder value. For example, it is likely that UK consumers will be able to use their mobile phone to bank, buy or book virtually any service. Travel (both rail and air), financial services and content businesses will be particular beneficiaries of these developments with more efficient yield management and lower transaction costs. The complementary UK business development will be the creation of a single branded retail chain, split between our large Megastores and smaller V.Shops coupled to a "clicks and mortar" strategy from Virgin's e-commerce and mobile activities.

During the past ten years, outstanding shareholder value has been created for investors through a number of transactions including the sale of Virgin Interactive Entertainment, Virgin Records, Virgin Radio, Virgin Cinemas and the partial sale of Virgin Atlantic and Virgin Rail. We would envisage continuing this policy of active venture capital over the next decade through growing our branded businesses and taking a number of them public.

The document you are reading comprehensively lays out our businesses and their prospects. We are in exciting markets which are set to benefit considerably from technological developments in distribution and fulfillment. I believe that Virgin has the opportunity to be in the top 20 of global brands by 2010.

Welcome to our world.

Source: Virgin.

APPENDIX 2
The History of Virgin

1968	First issue of *Student* magazine, January 26.
1970	Start of Virgin mail order operation.
1971	First Virgin record shop opens in Oxford Street, London.
1972	Virgin recording studio opens at The Manor near Oxford, England.
1973	Virgin record label launched with Mike Oldfield's *Tubular Bells*.
1977	Virgin Records signs the Sex Pistols.
1978	Virgin opens The Venue night club in London.
1980–2	Virgin Records expands overseas. Signs Phil Collins and Boy George/Culture Club.
1983	Virgin Vision (forerunner of Virgin Communications) formed to distribute films and videos and to operate in television and radio broadcasting.
	Vanson Developments formed as real-estate development company.
	Virgin Games (computer games software publisher) launched.
	Virgin Group's combined pre-tax profit climbs to £2.0 million on turnover of just under £50 million.
1984	Virgin Atlantic Airways and Virgin Cargo launched.
	First hotel investment (Deya, Mallorca).
	Virgin Vision launches The Music Channel, a 24-hour satellite-delivered music station and releases its first feature film *1984* with Richard Burton and John Hurt.
1985	Private placement of 7% Convertible Stock completed with 25 English and Scottish institutions.
	Virgin wins Business Enterprise Award for company of the year.
	Virgin Vision extends film and video distribution internationally.
	Virgin Holidays formed.
1986	Virgin Group, comprising the Music, Retail & Property, and Communications divisions, floated on London Stock Exchange. 35% of equity sold to 87,000 shareholders. Airline, clubs, holidays, and aviation services remain part of the privately owned Voyager Group.
1987	Virgin Records subsidiaries in US and Japan launched.
	British Satellite Broadcasting (Virgin a minority partner) awarded satellite broadcasting license. (Virgin sells its shareholding in 1988.)
	Virgin acquires Mastertronics Group, which distributed Sega video games in Europe.
	Virgin Airship & Balloon Company launched to provide aerial marketing services.
1988	Recording studios opened in Barnes, London.
	New international record label, Virgin, launched.
	Virgin Broadcasting formed to further develop Virgin's radio and TV interests.
	Virgin Hotels formed.
	Virgin Megastores opened in Sydney, Paris, and Glasgow.

Branson takes Virgin private with £248 million bid for outstanding shares.

1989   Virgin Music Group sells 25% stake to Fujisankei Communications for $150 million.

Virgin Vision (video distribution) sold to MCEG of Los Angeles for $83 million.

1990   Virgin Retail Group and Marui form joint venture company to operate Megastores in Japan.

Virgin Lightships formed to develop helium airships for advertising.

1991   W. H. Allen plc acquired. Merged with Virgin Books to form Virgin Publishing.

Sale of Virgin Mastertronic to Sega. Remaining part of the business becomes Virgin Games.

Virgin Retail Group forms 50:50 joint venture with W. H. Smith to develop UK retail business.

1992   Sale of Virgin Music Group to Thorn EMI plc.

Joint venture with Blockbuster to own and develop Megastores in Europe, Australia and US.

UK Radio Authority grants Virgin Communications and TV-AM plc the license for Britain's first national commercial rock station (Virgin 1215AM goes on the air in April 1993).

Virgin acquires Euro-Magnetic Products, a specialist in the personal computer consumable market.

Vintage Airtours established to fly Orlando–Florida Keys in vintage DC-3s.

1993   Virgin Games floated as Virgin Interactive Entertainment plc with Hasbro and Blockbuster taking minority equity stakes.

Virgin Euromagnetics launches a range of personal computers.

1994   Virgin Cola Company formed as joint venture with Cott Corp.

Agreement with W. Grant to launch Virgin Vodka.

Virgin acquires Our Price retail music chain, owned 75% by W. H. Smith, 25% by Virgin.

Virgin Retail Group forms joint ventures to develop Megastores in Hong Kong and S. Korea.

Virgin City Jet service launched between Dublin and London City Airport.

1995   Virgin Direct Personal Financial Service is launched as a joint venture with Norwich Union (whose stake is later acquired by Australian Mutual Provident).

Acquisition of MGM Cinemas, UK's biggest movie theater chain, to create Virgin Cinemas.

1996   Virgin Travel Group acquires Euro-Belgian Airlines to form Virgin Express.

V2 record label and music publishing company formed.

London & Continental Railways (in which Virgin is a major shareholder) wins a £3bn contract to build the Channel Tunnel Rail Link and operate Eurostar rail services.

1997   Virgin Rail wins bid to operate the InterCity West Coast and is awarded the 15-year rail franchise.

Virgin Net, an Internet Service Provider, formed with NTL.

Branson acquires a 15% stake in the London Broncos rugby league team.

Victory Corporation, a joint venture with Rory McCarthy, launches the Virgin Clothing and Virgin Vie toiletry products.

Majority share in Virgin Radio sold to Chris Evans' Ginger Media Group.

Virgin Bride, a chain of wedding retailers, formed.

Virgin One telephone bank account and "one-stop integrated financial service" launched in collaboration with Royal Bank of Scotland.

1998   Virgin Entertainment acquires W. H. Smith's 75% stake in Virgin/Our Price.

Virgin Cola launches in the US.

1999	Virgin sells its UK cinema chain to UGC for £215 million.
	Virgin launches mobile phone service in joint venture with Deutsche Telecom's One-to-One (November).
	49% of Virgin Atlantic sold to Singapore Airlines for £600 million.
	Restructuring and re-launch of loss-making Our Price record stores.
2000	Virgin Mobile launches US wireless phone service in joint venture with Sprint and announces plan to expand into Europe, Africa and South-East Asia. Virgin Mobile Australia (a joint venture with Cable & Wireless) begins service in October.
	Virgin Net, Virgin's portal and ISP venture, closes its content division.
	Virgin announces the closing of its clothing company (February).
	Virgin Cars, online sales of new cars, launched.
	Virgin and Bear Stearns set up Lynx New Media, a $130 million Internet-focused venture capital fund.
	Inaugural flight of Virgin Blue, Virgin's low-cost Australian airline (August).
	Branson knighted by the Queen.
	Virgin fails to win franchise to run Britain's government-owned National Lottery.
2001	50% of Virgin Blue sold to Patrick Corporation for A$138.
	Virgin expands into Singapore and SE Asia with joint ventures with local companies in radio stations, cosmetic retailing, and wireless phone services.
	Virgin.net merges its ISP and portal businesses.
	16 French Virgin Megastores sold to Lagardere Media for 150 million Euros.
2002	Virgin Bikes (UK) launched. Offers direct sale of new motorcycles at discount prices.
	Virgin Mobile offers wireless telecom services in the US.
2003	Virgin Blue initial public offering; Virgin retains 25% of equity.
2004	50% stake of Virgin Money repurchased from AMP for £90 million.
	Virgin Digital launched. Offers online music store and digital music download capabilities.
	Virgin Cars and Virgin Bikes sold to MotorSolutions, Ltd, of the UK for an undisclosed amount.

APPENDIX 3
Businesses within the Virgin Group, 2004

Virgin Active	Chain of health and leisure clubs in UK and South Africa.
Virgin Airship & Balloon Company	Commercial hot air balloons for advertising, brand building, and specialist film work.
Virgin Atlantic	London-based airline serving 20 destinations in the US, Caribbean, South Africa, and Asia.
Virgin Atlantic Cargo	Air freight using Virgin Atlantic's network.
Virgin Balloon Flights	Passenger balloon flights in the UK, Holland and Belgium.
Virgin Bikes	Direct motorcycle sales.
Virgin Blue	Low-fare airline flying in Australia.
Virgin Books	Publishes books on music, sport, TV, movies, and comedy.
Virgin Brides	Chain of bridal retail stores.
Virgin Business Solutions	Office supplies and services.
Virgin Cinemas	Chain of movie theaters in Japan.
Virgin Cosmetics	Direct sales of specially formulated cosmetics.
Virgin Credit Card	Credit card issued by Virgin Money.

Virgin Drinks	Distributes Virgin-branded soft drinks.
Virgin Enterprises	Owns the intellectual property of the Virgin group – primarily trademarks relating to the Virgin brand.
Virgin Experience	Offers innovative leisure experiences, from bungee jumping to Ferrari driving.
Virgin Express	Brussels-based airline offering scheduled flights to UK and other European destinations.
Virgin Holidays	UK based tour operator specializing in long-haul holidays to America, the Far East, Australia, and South Africa, using Virgin Atlantic flights.
Virgin Incentives	Corporate incentive vouchers exchangeable for Virgin goods and services.
The Lightship Group	Rents airships for advertising and promotional purposes.
Virgin Limobike	Motorcycle taxi service in London.
Virgin Limousines	Limos serving Northern California.
Virgin Megastores	80 Megastores in Europe, Japan, and N. America sell music, movies, computer games, and books.
Virgin Mobile	Wireless telephone resellers offering easy-tariff service with no line rental or fixed-term contract.
Virgin Money	Online financial services offering loans, mutual funds, and stock trading.
Virgin.net	UK-based Internet service provider.
Radio Free Virgin	UK digital radio broadcaster.
Virgin Space	Chain of Internet cafés.
Virgin Student	One-stop shop serving UK's student population.
Virgin Student.com	Student web site.
Virgin Trains	Major UK operator of passenger train services and facilities and allows booking of Virgin Train tickets online.
thetrainline.com	Online rail ticket sales and reservations.
Virgin Travelstore	UK-based online travel agency.
Virgin Wines	Direct seller of wines.
V.Shop	UK's High Street stores with off-the-shelf and online sales of music, movies, and wireless phones.
V2 Music	Independent record label (artists include the Stereophonics, Tom Jones, Moby, and Underworld).

NOTES

1. "Behind Branson," *The Economist*, February 21, 1998, pp. 63–6.
2. "The future for Virgin," *Financial Times*, August 13, 1998, pp. 24–5.
3. Michael Harrison, "Is Branson's honeymoon finally over?" *The Independent*, London, February 21, 1998, p. 3.
4. "Branson moots Virgin floats," Agence France-Presse, May 26, 2002.
5. Richard Branson, letter to *The Economist*, March 7, 1998, p. 6.
6. It is well known that Branson is one of Britain's richest individuals, with a net worth exceeding $1 billion. Branson also spent a night in Dover police cells when arrested for excise duty offenses after he sold through his Virgin store a batch of Virgin records intended for export to Belgium. The case was settled out of court.

7. Robert Dick, "The house that Branson built: Virgin's entry into the new millennium," INSEAD, Fontainebleau, France, 2000.
8. *Forbes*, February 24, 1997.
9. *Journal of Commerce*, January 26, 1998.
10. James Doran, "Branson plans 135m buyback of Virgin stores," *Scotland on Sunday*, March 22, 1998, p. 1.
11. Peter Robison, "Briton hopes beverage will conquer Coke's monopoly," *Bloomberg News*, December 14, 1997.
12. "The future for Virgin", *Financial Times*, August 13, 1998, pp. 24–5.
13. The only formal executive role that Branson holds is as CEO of Virgin Atlantic.
14. Robert Dick, "Branson's Virgin: the coming of age of a counter-cultural enterprise," INSEAD, Fontainebleau, 1995.
15. Chris Blackhurst, "At the court of King Richard," *Management Today*, May 1998, pp. 40–5.
16. Robert Dick, "The house that Branson built: Virgin's entry into the new millennium," INSEAD, Fontainebleau, France, 2000.
17. Will Whitehorn, Talk to Georgetown MBA students, London, March 16, 2000.
18. Melanie Wells, "Red Baron," *Fortune*, July 3, 2000.
19. Alan Mitchell, "Virgin in financing U-turn," *Marketing News*, April 17, 1997.

case sixteen

General Electric: Life After Jack

Robert M. Grant

When Jeff Immelt took over as Chairman and CEO of General Electric on September 1, 2001, he had no doubts that his predecessor, Jack Welch – "living legend," "best manager of the past half-century," would be a tough act to follow. But little did he realize just how tough it would be.

When Immelt addressed GE shareholders at the 2002 share owners' annual conference on April 24, 2002, GE's share price was below $33, compared with a peak of $60 in August 2000. GE was suffering from external events such as the global economic slowdown of 2001 and the fallout from the September 11 terrorist attacks in the US, but the primary problem was a rise of a tide of skepticism over GE's spectacular performance. In February 2002, GE announced record earnings for the previous year – net income was up 11 percent over the previous year – and return on equity was a robust 26 percent.

However, the post-Enron wave of cynicism over corporate financial reporting had drawn GE into its wake. After being lauded by analysts for its smooth earning growth, rumors of earnings manipulation by GE circulated among the investment community. More specific criticisms were directed at the way in which GE was able to disguise the true risks of its businesses by consolidating the financial statements of its industrial businesses within its financial services business, GE Capital. In March 2002, Bill Gross, of the IPCO fund management group, showed that GE was more a financial services company rather than an industrial enterprise. However, by supporting GE Capital with its industrial business, GE Capital had been able to operate on a narrow capital base while maintaining a triple-A credit rating. In addition, GE's famously reliable earnings estimates were also subject to doubt. Given the slowing demand affecting several of GE's industrial businesses, there was concern that the 2002 earnings forecast would be achieved only through manipulating the earnings data.

While investors held little hope that Immelt could ever match the incredible 50-fold increase in GE's market value that Welch had achieved, the management community was more interested in the changes in corporate strategy, organizational structure, and management systems that Immelt would initiate. Welch had been a revolutionary and an autocrat. He had swept away most of GE's carefully constructed structure and its greatly admired corporate planning system. He had relentlessly challenged GE managers for improved operational and financial performance; he had created a GE management style based upon his own personality, values, and beliefs. His management innovations at GE had exerted a huge impact upon management thinking and management practices throughout the whole corporate sector. Whole courses at business schools had been devoted to GE's approach to strategic planning, human resource management, knowledge management, international management, acquisition management, financial management, and quality management.

In the short term Immelt knew that his number one priority was to restore the confidence of the investment community in General Electric, particularly in relation to its financial structure and financial reporting. But looking further ahead, Immelt realized that his primary challenge was coming to terms with Welch's legacy at GE. Each of GE's CEOs had been associated with successfully adapting GE's strategy and management systems to the challenges of the particular era. Between 1950 and 1963, Ralph Cordiner had responded to the opportunities of post-war growth to diversify GE into a range of new markets and new technologies. His successor, Fred Borsch (1963–72), had reorganized GE around nine major growth sectors within which each business formed a strategic business unit. During 1972 to 1981, Reginald Jones established GE's highly regarded and widely imitated system of strategic and financial planning which reconciled strong central control with high levels of operational autonomy for divisions and business units. Jack Welch's contribution had been to adapt GE to a world of uncertainty, intense competition, and rapid competition. In building an organization and a management culture which reconciled the benefits of massive corporate size with flexibility and responsiveness, Welch undid much of Jones's management systems in favor of a system based upon personal accountability and high levels of performance expectations.

■ GENERAL ELECTRIC COMPANY ■

The General Electric (GE) that Jeffrey Immelt inherited in 2001 was widely regarded as one of the world's most successful companies of all time. It is the only company to have remained a member of the Dow Jones industrial index since the index was first created. Throughout its history, it has been associated with near-continuous growth and above average profitability. Table 16.1 shows profitability under successive CEOs.

GE was founded in 1892 from the merger of Thomas Edison's Electric Light Company with the Thomas Houston Company. Its business was based upon exploiting Edison's patents relating to electricity generation and distribution, light bulbs, and electric motors. During the twentieth century it became not only the biggest and most diversified industrial corporation in America, but "a model of management – a laboratory studied by business schools and raided by other companies seeking skilled executives."[1] Two decades under Jack Welch's leadership had only enhanced GE's reputation for effective management. In 2001, *Fortune* magazine named GE as America's "most admired company" for the fifth year in succession, and the *Financial Times* identified GE as the "world's most respected company" for the fourth consecutive year.

Table 16.1 GE's profitability under different chief executives

CEO	Av. annual pre-tax ROE
Charles A. Coffin, 1913–22	14.52%
Gerald Swope/Owen Young, 1922–39	12.63%
Charles E. Wilson, 1940–50	46.72%
Ralph J. Cordiner, 1950–63	40.49%
Fred J. Borch, 1964–72	27.52%
Reginald H. Jones, 1973–81	29.70%
John F. Welch, 1981–2001	25.81%
Jeffrey R. Immelt 2001–2	31.6%

[a] September 2001 to December 2002.
The dates given for each CEO are for the financial years that correspond most closely to each CEO's tenure.
Source: GE financial statements.

GE was not only one of the world's biggest companies, it was also one of the world's most diverse. While most of the conglomerates of the 1980s – Hanson, ITT, Seagram, Philips, General Mills, and United Technologies – had either undergone massive refocusing or broken themselves up entirely, GE had remained a broadly diversified company spanning a wide range of businesses from jet engines to mortgage banking. Figure 16.1 shows GE's major businesses.

GE's ability to thrive as a broadly diversified corporation was one of the wonders of the business world. Since the early 1990s, diversified firms had been handicapped by the "conglomerate discount" – the capital markets had capitalized their earnings at lower multiples than for single-business companies. The only solution was to refocus or break up. For GE this issue has never arisen; GE's remarkable financial performance was such that it had never been under pressure to spin off individual businesses or dismember itself completely. This superior performance is evident in GE's capacity to achieve both growth and profitability throughout the economic cycle (see table 16.2), and in its financial stability – GE had maintained its triple-A credit rating for 44 consecutive years.

As Immelt emphasized to shareholders, it was the combination of these different businesses with their different cyclical characteristics that allowed GE to sustain its earning growth:

> We have four strong, powerful long cycle businesses: Power, Medical, Engines, and Transportation. These businesses are strong, number one, with multiple levers to grow earnings through technology and services. Our Power business had led the way through the past few years of gas turbine growth and as that turbine market subsides, our Power business will thrive by servicing an installed base that has grown five-fold. Our Medical franchise has unlimited opportunities driven by world-class technology, favorable demographics, and global distribution. Our Aircraft Engines business gets even stronger every year as we continue to invest in new engine platforms and technology. The importance of these long cycle businesses is that they give you steady earnings growth over time, with stable product cycles and rapid service growth.

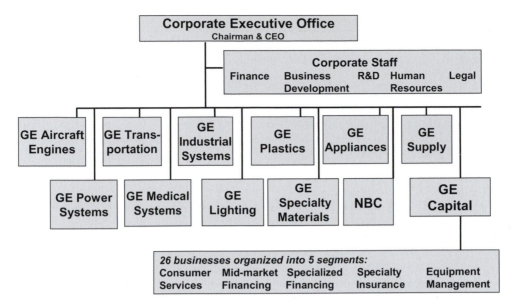

Figure 16.1 GE's organization structure, 2002
Source: Based on information in General Electric Annual Report, 2001.

We also have a leadership franchise in our short cycle businesses, like NBC, Plastics, Materials, Consumer, and Industrial businesses. These have been hardest hit by the downturn but so far in 2002 we are seeing encouraging signs of recovery . . .

We have the world's most diversified financial service business with consumer finance, mid-market financing, insurance, equipment management, and specialty segments. We're growing assets at GE Capital by 15 percent . . . The importance of GE Capital is that it can use GE's financial and industrial strength to generate superior returns over time . . .

The GE portfolio was put together for a purpose – to deliver earnings growth through every economic cycle. We're constantly managing these cycles in a business where the sum exceeds the parts.[2]

However, for all the emphasis on the complementary performance characteristics of GE's different businesses, it was also apparent that there were clear differences in terms of both growth and profitability between them (table 16.3).

■ THE WELCH HERITAGE ■

This ability of GE, not just to drive performance in the individual businesses, but also to create a corporation where the sum exceeds the parts, was the hallmark of Jack Welch's tenure as GE's chairman and CEO. Welch's contributions to the restructuring of GE's business portfolio, its organizational design, and its management systems will be described in subsequent sections, but underlying all these contributions was Welch's revolutionary impact on GE's culture and its management style.

Table 16.2 GE's performance 1991–2001

	2001	2000	1999	1997	1996	1995	1994	1993	1992	1991
Revenues ($bn)	125.9	129.9	111.6	90.8	79.2	70.0	60.1	55.7	53.0	51.3
Net earnings ($bn)	13.7	12.7	10.7	8.2	7.3	6.6	4.7	4.3	4.7	2.6
Return on av. shareholders' equity	26.0%	27.3%	26.4%	25.0%	24.0%	23.5%	18.1%	17.5%	20.9%	12.2%
Total assets ($bn)	495.0	437.0	387.4	304.0	272.4	228.0	194.5	251.5	192.9	166.5
Long-term borrowings ($bn)	79.8	82.1	73.5	46.6	49.2	51.0	37.0	28.2	25.3	22.6
Employees at year end ('000)										
United States	158	168	167	165	155	150	156	157	168	173
Other countries	152	145	143	111	84	72	60	59	58	62
Discontinued operations	n.a.	n.a.	n.a.	n.a.	n.a.	n.a.	5	6	42	49
Total employees	310	313	310	276	239	222	221	222	268	284

	1990	1989	1988	1987	1986	1985	1984	1983	1982	1981
Revenues ($bn)	49.7	54.6	50.1	48.2	42.0	28.3	27.3	26.8	26.5	27.2
Net earnings ($bn)	4.3	3.9	3.4	2.9	2.5	2.3	2.3	2.0	1.8	1.7
Return on av. shareholders' equity	20.2%	20.0%	19.4%	18.5%	17.3%	17.6%	19.1%	18.9%	18.8%	19.1%
Total assets ($bn)	152.0	128.3	110.9	95.4	84.8	26.4	24.7	23.3	21.6	20.9
Long-term borrowings ($bn)	20.9	16.1	15.1	12.5	10.0	0.8	0.8	0.9	1.0	1.1
Employees at year end ('000)										
United States	183	243	255	277	302	236	248	246	n.a.	n.a.
Other countries	62	49	43	45	71	68	82	94	n.a.	n.a.
Discontinued operations	53	n.a.	n.a.	n.a.	n.a.	n.a.	n.a.	n.a.	n.a.	n.a.
Total employees	298	292	298	322	373	304	330	340	367	404

n.a. = not available.

Source: General Electric Annual Reports.

During his 20-year tenure, Welch had remade GE in his own image. The culture and management style that he had fostered were reflections of his own personality and values. Welch attributes his management style to two formative influences: his mother and ice hockey. Welch credits his mother with nurturing self-confidence, determination, and strong values. He credits ice hockey with developing competitive spirit, confrontation, and camaraderie.

From the outset, Welch set lofty goals for GE: in 1981, as the newly appointed chairman and chief executive, he outlined his vision:

Table 16.3   GE's divisional performance, 1997–2001

	Revenue 2001 ($ billions)	Profit 2001 ($ billions)	Av. return on assets 1999–2001 (%)	Revenue growth 1997–2001 (%)	Profit growth 1997–2001 (%)
Aircraft Engines	11.4	2.6	24.2	46	91
Appliances	5.8	0.6	23.8	0	−17
Industrial Products & Systems	11.6	1.8	26.2	7	11
Materials	7.1	1.6	18.0	3	−2
NBC	5.8	1.6	31.6	12	31
Power Systems	20.2	5.2	28.3	153	305
Technical Products & Services	9.0	2.0	28.5	84	99
GE Capital	58.4	5.6	20.6	46	71

Source: GE Annual Report 2001.

> A decade from now I would like General Electric to be perceived as a unique, high-spirited, entrepreneurial enterprise . . . a company known around the world for its unmatched level of excellence. I want General Electric to be the most profitable, highly diversified company on earth, with world-quality leadership in every one of its product lines.

For 20 years, Welch continually pushed his subordinates for more. In the early days he continually reiterated his goal of creating a company that was "better than the best." This meant not just imposing "stretch goals" upon business-level managers, but encouraging GE's employees – at all levels – to embrace ambitious targets for themselves:

> Shun the incremental and go for the leap. Most bureaucracies – and ours is no exception – unfortunately think in incremental terms rather than in terms of fundamental change. They think incrementally primarily because they think internally. Changing the culture – opening it up to the quantum change – means constantly asking not how fast am I going, how well am I doing versus how well I did a year or two before, but rather, how fast and how well am I doing versus the world outside. Are we moving faster, are we doing better against that external standard?
>
> Stretch means using dreams to set business targets – with no real idea of how to get there . . . We certainly didn't have a clue how we were going to get to 10 inventory turns [a year] when we set that target. But we're getting there, and as soon as we become sure we can do it – it's time for another stretch.[3]

Welch's early years at GE were a war on bureaucracy. Formality, elaborate PowerPoint presentations, complex strategic plans, were ways in which managers avoided reality and avoided coming to grips with painful decisions. Welch favored confronting reality, acknowledging disagreement, and reconciling conflict through open argument. "Constructive conflict" was his key tool. Welch would force his managers to defend their views, even if that meant getting into shouting-match arguments. "Jack will chase you around the room, throwing arguments and objections at you," said one executive. "Then you fight back until he lets you do what you want, and it's clear you'll do everything you can to make it work."

He spelled out his management philosophy in an interview with *Harvard Business Review*:

> Good business leaders create a vision, articulate the vision, passionately own the vision, and relentlessly drive it to completion. Above all else, though, good leaders are open. They go up, down, and around their organization to reach people. They don't stick to the established channels. They're informal. They're straight with people. They make a religion out of being accessible. They never get bored telling their story.
>
> Real communication takes countless hours of eyeball to eyeball, back and forth. It means more listening than talking. It's not pronouncements on a videotape; it's not announcements in a newspaper. It is human beings coming to see and accept things through a constant interactive process aimed at consensus. And it must be absolutely relentless. That's a real challenge for us. There's still not enough candor in this company.
>
> I mean facing reality, seeing the world as it is rather than as you wish it were. We've seen over and over again that businesses facing market downturns, tougher competition, and more demanding customers inevitably make forecasts that are much too optimistic. This means they don't take advantage of the opportunities change usually offers. Change in the marketplace isn't something to fear; it's an enormous opportunity to shuffle the deck, to replay the game. Candid managers – leaders – don't get paralyzed about the "fragility" of the organization. They tell people the truth. That doesn't scare them because they realize their people know the truth anyway.
>
> We've had managers at GE who couldn't change, who kept telling us to leave them alone. They wanted to sit back, to keep things the way they were. And that's just what they did – until they and most of their staffs had to go. That's the lousy part of this job . . . The point is, what determines our destiny is not the hand you're dealt; it's how you play the hand. And the best way to play your hand is to face reality – see the world the way it is – and act accordingly.
>
> For a large organization to be effective, it must be simple. For a large organization to be simple, its people must have self-confidence and intellectual self-assurance. Insecure managers create complexity. Frightened, nervous managers use thick, convoluted planning books and busy slides filled with everything they've known since childhood. Real leaders don't need clutter. People must have the self-confidence to be clear, precise, to be sure that every person in their organization – highest to lowest – understands what the business is trying to achieve. But it's not easy. You can't believe how hard it is for people to be simple, how much they fear being simple. They worry that if they're simple, people will think they're simpleminded. In reality, of course, it's just the reverse. Clear, tough-minded people are the most simple.
>
> Simple doesn't mean easy, especially as you try to move this approach down through the organization. When you take out layers, you change the exposure of the managers who remain. They sit right in the sun. Some of them blotch immediately; they can't stand the exposure of leadership.[4]

By the end of the 1980s, Welch's ideas about management were summarized in the slogan "Speed, Simplicity, Self-Confidence":

> We found in the 1980s that becoming faster is tied to becoming simpler. Our businesses, with tens of thousands of employees, will not respond to visions that have sub-paragraphs

and footnotes. If we're not simple, we can't be fast . . . and if we're not fast, we can't win. Simplicity, to an engineer, means clean, functional, winning designs, no bells or whistles. In marketing, it might manifest itself as clear, unencumbered proposals. For manufacturing people, it would produce a logical process that makes sense to every individual on the line. And on an individual, interpersonal level, it would take the form of plain-speaking directness, honesty.

But just as surely as speed flows from simplicity, simplicity is grounded in self-confidence. Self-confidence does not grow in someone who is just another appendage on the bureaucracy; whose authority rests on little more than a title. People who are freed from the confines of their box on the organization chart, whose status rests on real-world achievement – those are the people who develop the self-confidence to be simple, to share every bit of information available to them, to listen to those above, below and around them and then move boldly.

But a company can't distribute self-confidence. What it can do – what we must do – is to give each of our people an opportunity to win, to contribute, and hence earn self-confidence themselves. They don't get that opportunity, they can't taste winning if they spend their days wandering in the muck of a self-absorbed bureaucracy.

Speed . . . simplicity . . . self-confidence. We have it in increasing measure. We know where it comes from . . . and we have plans to increase it in the 1990s.[5]

■ RECONFIGURING THE BUSINESS PORTFOLIO ■

Although Welch was resolutely determined to retain GE's identify as a broadly diversified corporation, he was clear that GE's business portfolio should, first, be focused around a limited number of sectors and, second, these sectors should be attractive in terms of their potential for profitability and growth. During the early part of his chairmanship, Welch announced his intention only to retain businesses that held number one or number two positions within their global markets. His intention was to focus GE's resources on its best opportunities: "My biggest challenge will be to put enough money on the right gambles and no money on the wrong ones. But I don't want to sprinkle money over everything." This involved increasing GE's emphasis upon technology-based businesses and service businesses. Welch sold off its consumer electronics business, mining interests (notably Utah International), small household appliances division, semiconductors, and radio stations.

GE's acquisitions included a few major ones such as RCA, NBC, Kidder Peabody, and CGR, and a host of smaller companies. During 1997–2001, GE made over a hundred acquisitions in each year. By far the largest sector for acquisition was financial services. During the 1990s, GE Capital's phenomenal growth was built upon continuous acquisition of businesses in leasing, consumer and commercial credit, insurance, and other areas of finance. The result was the emergence of GE Capital as one of the world's biggest financial services companies.

For all GE's expertise in identifying acquisition targets and then integrating them into GE's structure and systems, not all were successful. Kidder Peabody was a disaster for GE, and the acquisition of Montgomery Ward was viewed by some outsiders as a mistake. Most recently, GE's biggest takeover, Honeywell, was unconsummated because of opposition from the European Commission on antitrust grounds.

■ CHANGING THE STRUCTURE ■

The changes in the portfolio transformed the product-market face of GE and increased its growth potential. However, to realize this potential required revitalizing the management systems and management style in order to generate drive and ambition. Achieving this required changes to GE's structure. Under Welch, GE eliminated several layers of management and large numbers of administrative positions. In particular, Welch disbanded GE's sectors, requiring the leaders of GE's 13 businesses to report directly to the CEO. The office of the CEO was expanded, and a Corporate Executive Council (CEC) was created to provide a forum for GE's business-level chiefs and senior corporate officers. Further organizational layers were eliminated both at headquarters and within the businesses. Decision making was pushed down to the operating units.

> We are now down in some businesses to four layers from the top to the bottom. That's the ultimate objective. We used to have things like department managers, section managers, subsection managers, units managers, supervisors. We are driving those titles out . . . We used to go from the CEO to sectors to groups to businesses. We now go from the CEO . . . to businesses. Nothing else. There is nothing else there. Zero.
>
> When you take out layers, you change the exposure of the managers who remain. They sit right in the sun. Some of them blotch immediately – they can't stand the exposure of leadership. I firmly believe that an overburdened, overstretched executive is the best executive, because he or she doesn't have time to meddle, to deal in trivia, or to bother people. Remember the theory that a manager should have no more than six or seven direct reports? I say the right number is closer to 10 or 15. This way you have no choice but to let people flex their muscles, to let them grow and mature.[6]

Empowering line managers meant reducing the power – and number – of staff. Welch's goal was to "turn their role 180 degrees from checker, inquisitor and authority figure to facilitator, helper and supporter of the businesses . . . Ideas, initiatives and decisions could now move quickly. Often at the speed of sound – voices – where once they were muffled and garbled by the gauntlet of approvals and staff reviews."[7]

The result was massive reductions in numbers of employees. Between 1980 and 1990, GE's headcount fell from 402,000 to 298,000. The biggest cuts were at the upper levels of the organization: at corporate headquarters and within sectoral administration. In some areas employee numbers increased – particularly in overseas operations. Welch's ruthless attack on bureaucracy and administrative costs earned him the nickname "Neutron Jack" – the building remained, but the people had gone.

■ CHANGING MANAGEMENT SYSTEMS AND PROCESSES ■

Strategic Planning

The changes in GE's structure were aimed at creating a more flexible and responsive corporation. This goal also necessitated changes in GE's highly developed management systems. In particular, Welch led a major overhaul of GE's much celebrated and widely emulated strategic planning system. The framework of an annual planning cycle was retained, but the staff-led, document-driven process was replaced by a less formal, more personal process. Instead of the big planning reports, Welch asked each business head to prepare a slim "playbook" that summarized the key strategic issues that the business faced, and how it intended to address them. This document provided the basis for a half-day, shirtsleeves review in mid-summer when Welch and key corporate officers would engage in discussion and debate with the top management team of each business. On the 1986 meetings, Welch commented:

> We asked the 14 business leaders to present reports on the competitive dynamics in their businesses. How did we do it? We had them each prepare one-page answers to five questions: What are your market dynamics globally today, and where are they going over the next several years? What actions have your competitors taken in the last three years to upset those global dynamics? What have you done in the last three years to affect these dynamics? What are the most dangerous things your competitor could do in the next three days to upset those dynamics? What are the most effective things you could do to bring your desired impact on those dynamics?
>
> Five simple charts. After those initial reviews, which we update regularly, we could assume that everyone at the top knew the plays and had the same playbook. It doesn't take a genius. Fourteen businesses each with a playbook of five charts. So when Larry Bossidy is with a potential partner in Europe, or I'm with a company in the Far East, we're always there with a competitive understanding based upon our playbooks. We know exactly what makes sense, we don't need a big staff to do endless analysis. That means we should be able to act with speed.[8]

Financial Planning and Control

Supporting GE's strategic planning system was a sophisticated financial budgeting system which centered on the annual budget. Budget preparation began in July and involved extensive negotiation between the operating units, the intervening groups and sectors, and the corporate headquarters. Once the budget was set, managers were locked in to meet it "at all costs" regardless of changes in the marketplace. It was generally agreed that the system had undesirable consequences, such as gaming to set low targets, and cutting long-term development to meet short-term targets. Because managers were locked in to figures established 18 months before, the budgeting system often inhibited adjustment to external changes and gave little information on management performance.

Welch's commitment to a performance-driven organization meant that financial targets were of critical importance. However, the key was to create shareholder value rather than accounting profits per se. In addition, it was essential that the system should permit the performance of divisional and business unit managers to be assessed. Two changes were made. First, the controller's office prepared a set of financial objectives for each operating unit in order to reflect more realistically each unit's prospects and to reduce gamesmanship in target-setting. Second, the budgets (now called operating plans) were subject to revision as economic or competitive conditions changed. Thus, line managers could propose changes to the plans once the original assumptions on which they had been based could be shown to have changed. Performance evaluation was then made against the revised targets.

Central to the changes in financial control was the idea that performance was not about "making the budget." It was about raising performance expectations to be "as good as possible": The primary task of the businesses, emphasized Welch, was to produce earnings. As a guideline, Welch proposed that GE's earnings should grow at between one-and-a-half and two times the growth of GDP.

Human Resource Management

The key to GE's long-term development and performance was the development of its management talent. GE had a well-developed system of management appraisal and development which Welch retained. He believed that giving managers greater profit-and-loss responsibility earlier in their careers would be conducive to an even greater flourishing of managerial talent. But to encourage risk taking and higher levels of performance aspiration required more powerful incentives. Welch believed in giving more recognition to individual contributors and higher rewards to those who produced superior results:

> A flat reward system is a big anchor to incrementalism. We want to give big rewards to those who do things but without going for the scalps of those who reach for the big win but fail. Punishing failure assures that no one dares.[9]

Welch redesigned the bonus system to reach deep into middle management. The bonuses became much more discriminating. The typical 10 to 15 percent bonuses for senior managers were replaced by 30 to 40 percent bonuses for far fewer managers. In addition, stock options were extended from the top echelon of management to a much wider range of managerial and technical employees. By 1996, Welch was able to report that the number of employees receiving stock options had increased from 400 in the early 1980s to 22,000 by the end of 1995: "Today, stock option compensation, based on total GE performance, is far more significant than the salary or bonus growth associated with the performance of any individual unit or business. This aligns the interests of the individual, the Company, and the share owner behind powerful, on-company results."[10]

Welch believed that a performance-driven organization would not only encourage GE's managers to perform up to the limits of their capabilities, it would also nurture those capabilities. Welch firmly believed that GE's ability to outperform its peers ultimately depended upon having outstanding employees. GE could offer opportunities for career development and the acquisition of skills and expertise that no other company could match:

> Our true "core competency" today is not manufacturing or services, but the global recruiting and nurturing of the world's best people and the cultivation in them of an insatiable desire to learn, to stretch and to do things better every day. By finding, challenging and rewarding these people, by freeing them from bureaucracy, by giving them all the resources they need – and by simply getting out of their way – we have seen them make us better and better every year.

> We have a Company more agile than others a fraction of our size, a high-spirited company where people are free to dream and encouraged to act and to take risks. In a culture where people act this way, every day, "big" will never mean slow.
>
> This is all about people – "soft stuff." But values and behaviors are what produce those performance numbers, and they are the bedrock upon which we will build our future.[11]

Maintaining a vigorous, performance-driven culture required putting managers under continual pressure, including ongoing weeding-out of weaker performers. GE's system of evaluation was renowned for its thoroughness and its ruthlessness:

> In every evaluation and reward system, we break our population down into three categories: the top 20%, the high-performance middle 70% and the bottom 10%. The top 20% must be loved, nurtured and rewarded in the soul and wallet because they are the ones who make magic happen. Losing one of these people must be held up as a leadership sin – a real failing. The top 20% and middle 70% are not permanent labels. People move between them all the time. However, the bottom 10%, in our experience, tend to remain there. A Company that bets its future on its people must remove that lower 10%, and keep removing it every year – always raising the bar of performance and increasing the quality of its leadership. Not removing that bottom 10% early in their careers is not only a management failure, but false kindness as well – a form of cruelty – because inevitably a new leader will come into a business and take out that bottom 10% right away, leaving them – sometimes midway through a career – stranded and having to start over somewhere else. Removing marginal performers early in their careers is doing the right thing for them; leaving them in place to settle into a career that will inevitably be terminated is not. GE leaders must not only understand the necessity to encourage, inspire and reward that top 20%, and be sure that the high-performance 70% is always energized to improve and move upward; they must develop the determination to change out, always humanely, that bottom 10%, and do it every year. That is how real meritocracies are created and thrive.[12]

■ CORPORATE INITIATIVES ■

One of the distinctive characteristics of Welch's system of management was his use of periodic new corporate initiatives as mechanisms to drive particular aspects of company-wide performance. Thus, while strategic planning, financial control, and human resource management provided the basic systems for managing GE, about every two years, Welch would announce a major new initiative designed to energize the company and drive its performance in a particular direction. Over time these initiatives would become absorbed into the ongoing management systems of GE.

Work-Out

The idea for GE's "Work-Out" process began with the no-holds-barred discussion sessions that Welch held with different groups of managers at GE's Management Development Institute at Crotonville, New York. Impressed with the energy and impetus for change that these sessions generated, Welch initiated a company-wide process called "Work-Out."

The idea was to create a forum where employees could speak their minds about the management of their business without the fear of retribution by their superiors. Typically, the sessions assembled a cross-section of 50 to 100 of the business's employees for meetings that ran for two or three days. In an environment that Welch likened to an old New England town meeting, the group would be asked to openly and honestly review the management process and practices in their part of the operation. Initially they focused on unproductive or bureaucratic behaviors which had limited their personal effectiveness. At the end of each Work-Out, the group's manager returned to hear the findings and recommendations, and could either accept or reject them on the spot, or appoint a team to report back with more data by a given date. Welch believed that Work-Out could achieve fundamental changes in management:

> Work-Out has a practical and an intellectual goal. The practical objective is to get rid of thousands of bad habits accumulated since the creation of General Electric . . . The second thing we want to achieve, the intellectual part, begins by putting the leaders of each business in front of 100 or so of their people, eight to ten times a year, to let them hear what their people think. Work-Out will expose the leaders to the vibrations of their business – opinions, feelings, emotions, resentments, not abstract theories of organization and management. Ultimately, we're talking about redefining the relationship between boss and subordinate.
>
> These Work-Out sessions create all kinds of personal dynamics. Some people go and hide. Some emerge as forceful advocates. As people meet over and over, though, more of them will develop the courage to speak out. The norm will become the person who says, "Damn it, we're not doing it. Let's get on with doing it." This process will create more fulfilling and rewarding jobs. The quality of work life will improve dramatically.[13]

Initially, Work-Out focused on eliminating bureaucratic practices ("low-hanging fruit"). Over time, Work-Out sessions evolved to the evaluation and redesign of complex cross-functional processes – often involving suppliers and customers as well as GE employees.

The Boundary-less Organization

Welch reacted strongly to descriptions of GE as a conglomerate. But for GE to be greater than the sum of its parts required utilizing its product and geographical diversity to improve performance within each business. The key to transforming diversity into strength, believed Welch, was the frictionless transfer of best practices and other forms of learning within GE. But to achieve this required eliminating – or at least making permeable – GE's internal boundaries, as well as increasing openness to external learning. By 1990, Welch was developing the vision of a new GE organization that would be a truly "boundary-less" company. His boundary-less company was one in which both external barriers and internal barriers became blurred:

> In a boundary-less company, suppliers aren't outsiders. They are drawn closer and become trusted partners in the total business process. Customers' vision of their needs and the company's view become identical and every effort of every man and woman in the

company is focused on satisfying those needs. The boundary-less company blurs the divisions between internal functions; it recognizes no distinctions between "domestic" and "foreign" operations; and it ignores or erases group labels such as "management," "salaried," and "hourly" which get in the way of people working together.[14]

Unbounding GE required changes in structures, attitudes, and behaviors that would permit the "integrated diversity" that Welch envisaged. Examples of boundary-less behavior were widely publicized and praised:

> Two years ago, one of our people spotted a truly innovative method of compressing product cycle times in an appliance company in New Zealand. After testing it successfully in our Canadian affiliate, we transferred the methodology to our largest appliance complex in Louisville, KY. It has revolutionized processes, reduced cycle times, increased our customer responsiveness, and reduced our inventory levels by hundreds of millions of dollars. Teams from all of our manufacturing businesses are now living in Louisville so we can spread the New Zealand-to-Montreal-to-Louisville learning to every business in GE.[15]

Globalization

All of GE's businesses were given global responsibility, which meant exploiting international growth opportunities and exploiting the advantages of global reach in terms of exploiting global-level economies of scale and increased learning opportunities. Global diversity played an important role in allowing GE to cope with economic problems that affected particular countries or regions, and take advantage of the opportunities that such downturns offered. For example, as "financial contagion" affected much of Asia during 1997–8, GE was seeking acquisition opportunities:

> We've been down this road before. In the early 1980s, we experienced a United States mired in recession, hand-wringing from the pundits and dirges being sung over American manufacturing. We didn't buy this dismal scenario; instead, we invested in both a widespread restructuring and in new businesses . . . Europe looked a lot like the United States in the 1980s, and in need of the same remedies: restructuring, spin-offs, and the like. So, while many were "writing-off" Europe, we invested heavily, buying new companies and expanding our existing presence . . . "GE Europe" is now a $20.6 billion operation. Our revenues have more than doubled from 1994 to 1997; net income has tripled to more than $1.5 billion; and growth is accelerating as the European recovery progresses . . . Mexico in the mid-1990s was a similar story . . . GE moved, acquiring 10 companies and investing more than $1 billion in new and existing operations. The result was revenue growth of 60% and a doubling of earnings in the two years following the crisis. Today we are determined, and poised, to do the same thing in Asia we have done in the United States, Europe and Mexico: invest in the future.[16]

Six Sigma

From 1998 to 2000, Welch's Six Sigma program was its dominant corporate initiative and primary driver of organizational change and performance improvement. Welch described it as his next "soul-transforming cultural initiative." The methodology of defining, measuring, analyzing, improving, and then controlling every process that touches a company's customers until it reduces defects to 3.4 per million was borrowed from Motorola. However, at GE it was with unprecedented fervor across an unprecedentedly broad front. In four years some 100,000 people were trained in its science and methodology, and by 2001, GE was able to report: "Now Six Sigma is the way we work. We all speak a common language of CTQs (critical-to-quality), DPMOs (defects per million opportunities), FMEAs (failure mode effect analysis), and Needs Assessment Maps (to name just a few)." Across every one of GE's businesses major gains in performance ranking from reduced waste and lower operating costs to faster customer service and improved financial management were reported.

Digitization

Welch was a late convert to the electronic business. However, once converted, he became a raving evangelist, urging his line managers and launching his "destroy-your-business.com" initiative in 1999. Each organizational unit was encouraged to visualize how it might be crushed by the dot.com juggernaut. The result was widespread discovery of opportunities to use the Internet to improve internal processes and better serve customers. By spring 2001, Welch reported:

> As we said in our 1999 letter, digitization is transforming everything we do, energizing every corner of the Company and making us faster, leaner and smarter even as we become bigger. In 2000, these words began to turn into numbers, as we sold over $7 billion of goods and services over the net and conducted over $6 billion in online auctions. Digitization efforts across the Company will generate over $1.5 billion in operating margin improvements in 2001.[17]

GE's Operating System

By 2002, these different initiatives had been institutionalized to the point where GE referred to them as its "operating system." Thus, referring collectively to Work-Out, Boundarylessness, Globalization, Six Sigma, and Digitization, GE described an integrated system for performance improvement:

> The GE Operating System is GE's learning culture in action. It is a year-round series of intense learning sessions where Business CEOs, role models and initiative champions from GE as well as outside companies, meet and share intellectual capital.
>
> The central focus is always on sharing, and putting into action, the best ideas and practices from across the Company and around the world.
>
> Meetings take place year-round, in an endless process of enrichment. Learning builds from previous meetings, expanding the scope and increasing the momentum of our Company-wide initiatives.
>
> Driven by the Company's values – trust, informality, simplicity, boundary-less behavior and the love of change – the Operating System allows GE businesses to reach speeds and performance levels unachievable were they on their own.

The GE Operating System translates ideas into action across three dozen businesses so rapidly that all the initiatives have become operational across the Company within one month of launch, and have always produced positive financial results within their first cycle.[18]

■ JEFF IMMELT ■

Jeffrey R. Immelt was appointed CEO of GE at the age of 44. He had previously been head of GE's plastics business and, most recently, medical systems. He has an economics and applied math degree from Dartmouth and an MBA from Harvard. He claimed that his own experience of GE extended beyond his two decades with the firm – his father spent his entire career at GE. At GE Appliances, GE Plastics, and GE Medical Systems, Immelt acquired a reputation for turning around troubled units, driving customer service, and exploiting new technologies. He also demonstrated the ability to motivate others – an aptitude that he had revealed as an offensive tackler for Dartmouth's football team in the 1970s.[19]

As Welch's successor at GE, Immelt was broadly happy with most of the managerial and organizational innovations that his predecessor had introduced. At the same time he was acutely aware that the management system that Welch had created was closely linked with Welch's own personality. Immelt's personality and style were different from Welch's. *Business Week* observed: "Where Welch ruled through intimidation and thrived as something of a cult figure, Immelt opts for the friendlier, regular-guy approach. He prefers to tease where Welch would taunt. Immelt likes to cheer people on rather than chew them out. That style has given him a very different aura within GE. He may not be a demigod, but it's his man-of-the-people nature that draws praise from the top ranks to the factory floor."[20] Immelt knew that his different style of leadership would have important implications for his role as CEO and the ways in which he would influence GE's strategy, structure, and systems. However, Immelt believed that the major changes that he would initiate at GE would be a result of the changing environment that GE faced and the shifting priorities that it faced.

Between September 2001 and May 2002, Immelt had devoted himself primarily to shoring up confidence among customers and investors and within the company in the aftermath of the various shocks to the US and to business opinion. At the same time he was developing his strategic thinking about the future of GE. During the first four months of 2002, his speeches and interviews emphasized four main areas of development:

- *The business portfolio.* Like Welch, Immelt believed that GE needed to reposition itself to maximize growth opportunities and to achieve growth targets through sound acquisitions. Among the low-growth parts of GE's portfolio, many analysts believed that appliances and lighting would be early candidates for divestment. However, while acknowledging that their growth was low, Immelt confirmed that, "We'll stay in those businesses. They both return their cost of capital."[21] At the same time, further industrial acquisitions would be needed in order to keep GE balanced – if the rapidly growing GE Capital was to account for more than half of GE's earnings, then GE's risk status and earnings multiple might be adversely affected. Immelt committed to GE to continue to acquire high-margin, high-growth companies that expand GE's base: "We don't acquire companies just because we can. We don't go for unrelated fields. We acquire companies that give us new growth platforms where GE capability can improve financial performance and build shareholder value."[22]

- *Technology*. Immelt remarked on the fact that he represented a different generation from Jack Welch, and that his generation had a much closer affinity for technology. He identified technology as a major driver of GE's future growth and emphasized the need to speed the diffusion of new technologies within GE and turn the corporate R&D center into an intellectual hothouse.
- *Internationalization*. Like Welch, Immelt believed that GE's major opportunities for organic growth would be in its overseas operations – particularly in China, India, and Europe. However, to better exploit these opportunities Immelt believed that GE's upper management would need to become more international and more diverse.
- *Marketing and customer service*. A key feature of Immelt's career at GE was the extent of his customer orientation and the amount of time he spent with customers building relationships with them and working on their problems. Looking ahead, Immelt saw GE using IT and redesigned processes to become increasingly customer focused: "We're dramatically changing our resource base from providing support to creating value. Every business has functions that add high value by driving growth. These are the functions that deal with the customer, create new products, sell, manufacture, manage the money and drive controllership. Call that the front room. Every business has back room support functions that sometimes are so large and bureaucratic they create a drain on the system and keep us from meeting our customer needs and keep us from growing. So we're going to take more of the back room resources and put them in the front room – more sales people, more engineers, more product designers. We're changing the shape of this company and we're doing it during a recession."[23]

No one, either inside or outside GE, had any doubt that Immelt would not be a supremely effective leader for GE. The main questions concerned Immelt's ability to take GE to the next level – whatever that next level might entail. When Welch took over GE in 1981, it was certainly successful, but there was also tremendous scope for improvement within GE's sprawling, bureaucratic empire. For Immelt it was not so easy to identify opportunities either for improving existing opportunities, or to create new opportunities with the potential to lift GE to heights that Welch had never imagined.

NOTES

1. "Can Jack Welch reinvent GE?" *Business Week*, June 29, 1986, pp. 40–5.
2. Jeff Immelt's 2002 Annual Report to Share Owners, Waukesha, Wisconsin, April 24, 2002, pp. 4–5.

3. GE Annual Report, 1993, p. 5.
4. Noel Tichy and Ram Charan, "Speed, simplicity, and self confidence: an interview with Jack Welch," *Harvard Business Review*, September/October 1989.
5. Ibid.
6. *GE 1984*, Harvard Business School Case No. 385-315.
7. Tichy and Charan, Welch interview, *Harvard Business Review*, 1989.
8. Ibid.
9. Ibid.
10. Jack Welch, address to 1989 shareholders' meeting.
11. Chairman's letter, General Electric Annual Report, 2000.
12. Ibid.
13. Tichy and Charan, Welch interview, *Harvard Business Review*, 1989.
14. GE Annual Report, 1990.
15. Ibid.
16. Chairman's letter, General Electric Annual Report, 1997.
17. Chairman's letter, General Electric Annual Report, 2000.
18. The GE Operating System (www.ge.com).
19. "Running the house that Jack built," *Business Week*, October 2, 2000.
20. "The days of Welch and roses," *Business Week*, April 29, 2002.
21. "This is just about the best gig you can have," *Business Week*, September 5, 2001.
22. Jeff Immelt's 2002 Annual Report to Share Owners, Waukesha, Wisconsin, April 24, 2002, p. 8.
23. Ibid.

case seventeen

AES Corporation: Rewriting the Rules of Management

Robert M. Grant

God made us all a certain way. We're all creative, capable of making decisions, trustworthy, able to learn, and perhaps most important, fallible. We all want to be part of a community and to use our skills to make a difference in the world.

Dennis Bakke, CEO, AES

We broke all the rules. No overtime. No bosses. No time records. No shift schedules. No assigned responsibilities. No administration. And guess what? It worked!

Oscar Prieto, AES manager and director of Light Servicios de Electricidade, Brazil, October 1998

Spring 2002 presented AES Corporation, the world's largest independent power generator, with the most difficult business circumstances in its 21-year history. After almost uninterrupted growth and a steeply rising market valuation that had taken AES into the S&P 500 in 1998, AES's world had been shaken to its foundations by four major shocks. The first was the Californian power crisis of 2001. Although AES was only a minor player in electricity trading, as an independent power producer with plants in California it was caught up in the recriminations, lawsuits, and regulatory investigations that had followed California's electricity debacle. More generally, the California power crisis threatened continuing deregulation of the US electricity sector – it was this deregulation that had provided the rationale for AES's founding and the business opportunities for its continued growth. Second, AES had been caught up in the wake of Enron's collapse at the end of December 2001. Although AES's direct losses resulting from Enron's bankruptcy amounted to a mere $15 million, the sudden demise of this giant of the energy sector had a profound impact on investors' risk perception and upon the legitimacy of a range of previously accepted business practices, including off-balance-sheet financing. The third crisis impacting AES was Argentina. Argentina represented one of AES's largest overseas interests with over $1 billion invested. The meltdown of the Argentine economy had rendered these investments all but worthless and had had knock-on effects on AES's power interests in Brazil. The gloom affecting AES's Latin American operations was further increased by the mounting crisis in Venezuela. Finally, the aftermath of the September 11, 2001 terrorist attacks on the US had created further uncertainties for AES's global interests. With investments in several Muslim countries – in particular Pakistan and Kazakhstan – AES was again subject to greatly increased financial, political, and physical risk.

These factors had combined to ensure AES's entry into the infamous "90 percent club" – those companies (mainly technology, media, and telecommunication companies) that had lost more than 90 percent of their stock market value. After touching $70 a share in September 2000, AES's share price had fallen below $4 in February 2002, driven lower by sales by CEO and founder Dennis Bakke who was forced to liquidate a quarter of his 5.8 percent equity stake in order to meet margin calls. The sharp decline in AES's market value had placed considerable strain on AES's finances, making it increasingly difficult for AES to access the capital markets. In February, ratings on AES's unsecured debt were cut to below investment grade.

These combined pressures had forced an abrupt reversal of strategy at AES. After two decades of continuous and rapid expansion, the company was forced to retrench. In a series of measures announced in February 2002, AES began the desperate task of shoring up its finances and protecting itself against an increasingly hostile external environment. Capital expenditure was cut from $1,280 million to $790 million, over $1 billion in asset sales was announced, and AES was to begin withdrawing from some of its most risky areas of business – including Latin America and spot market sales.

For founder and CEO Dennis Bakke the most troubling aspect of the sudden strategic shift was not the abandonment of AES's ambitious growth targets. He believed that AES possessed the financial and management strengths needed to survive the current financial pressures. His concerns related much more to his personal mission to build AES as a different kind of company. Under the leadership of its two co-founders, Roger Sant and Dennis Bakke, AES had rejected profit and shareholder wealth as its raison d'être and committed itself to the pursuit of integrity, fairness, fun, and social responsibility. These principles were embedded in a management system which the *Wall Street Journal* referred to as "empowerment gone mad."[1] Its unique organization was referred to by board member Robert Waterman (of *In Search of Excellence* fame) as an "adhocracy." There were no staff functions or corporate departments; almost all traditional management functions were devolved to workers at the plant level.

So long as AES was a darling of Wall Street, investors and analysts were happy to accept AES's lofty values and its founders' disdain for profit. But the events of 2001 and early 2002 had changed all that. AES's values and unique management system which had been so effective in encouraging employees' loyalty and commitment, generating initiative and entrepreneurial drive, and promoting unmatched levels of operational efficiency was now having to come to terms with a very different environment.

The events of 2002 had cast a pall over the entire independent power production sector. At the same time, competition had greatly intensified within the sector. While AES had been a pioneer of independent power production, it was now a crowded sector. Competitors for electricity supply contracts included independent power producers (IPPs) such as AEP, Calpine, and Reliant Resources; traditional utilities such as Duke Power, Dominion Resources, Consolidated Edison, Electricité de France, and British Energy; gas companies such as Vectren, Centrica, and Gaz de France; and oil majors such as BP Amoco, Exxon Mobil, and Shell.

Moreover, AES was no longer a small, entrepreneurial start-up. By the end of 2001, AES had 179 plants in operation or under construction in 31 countries of the world, with a total employment of about 38,000. Growth had increased the complexity and diversity of the company: from a single plant in Texas, its operations now extended from the Ukraine to South Africa; it had gone from coal-fired plants to gas-fired and hydroelectric plants; from supplying power on long-term contracts to utilities, AES had expanded into power distribution and producing electricity for competitive markets on spot and short-term contracts. Growing scale and scope was placing increasing strains on AES's informal, ad hoc style of management, while AES's principles, with their basis in traditional American values of equality of opportunity, openness, and individualism, had to adapt to the diverse cultures where AES did business – traditional Islamic societies such as Pakistan, socialist systems such as China, and the oligarchic societies of Latin America.

■ AES'S ORIGINS AND DEVELOPMENT ■

In January 1982, Roger Sant and Dennis Bakke founded Applied Energy Systems based in Arlington, Virginia. Their purpose was to take advantage of a 1978 Public Utility Regulatory Policy Act (PURPA) that required utilities to purchase power from independent energy producers. Sant and Bakke believed they could build a business in a niche segment of the enormous power-generation industry.

At first glance, Sant and Bakke seemed a rather unlikely pair to start what has become a large international energy company. Although both held Harvard MBAs, their experience was primarily public sector. Sant headed the Ford Administration's energy conservation efforts and Bakke served as a chief aide. Following government service, they moved on to the Mellon Institute's Energy Productivity Center, where they spent several years researching various techniques for energy conservation. It was during this time that the pair came up with the idea of starting their own company.

Sant and Bakke had a very difficult time raising money at first, because nobody took them very seriously. According to Bakke, "[we] had the worst possible background for raising money . . . first government and then academic experience. It looked to investors like a combination of inefficiency and ivory tower."[2] However, Sant and Bakke had one key advantage: as a result of their involvement in drafting PURPA, they were among the first to recognize the opportunity for independent generators to produce power at much lower costs than the established utilities.

Sant and Bakke raised $1.3 million from private investors and began looking for deep-pocketed partners. From 1981 to 1985 Sant and Bakke sought alliances with Arco, IBM, and Bechtel to name but a few. In 1985, the founders decided to go it alone and built their first power plant adjacent to an oil refinery in Houston, Texas, using petroleum coke (essentially a waste product) for fuel. Because AES agreed to link the price of the electricity generated to the price of natural gas (which subsequently fell sharply), the plant was not profitable. However, the second and third plants that AES built "weren't disastrous, and four, five and six turned out to be superb. By 1989 it was clear that we had reached viability."[3]

In 1991, AES went public. With a stronger equity base it was ready to look at opportunities overseas. Because of the rapid growth in electricity demand in many emerging markets, inadequate generating capacity, and the trend towards privatization, Sant estimated that over 70 percent of AES's opportunities lay outside the US. The fast-growing Asian markets for electricity, especially the huge potential markets of India and China, were especially attractive. In the early 1990s AES inaugurated its international strategy by acquiring two plants in Northern Ireland and one in Argentina. International expansion involved participating in the auctioning of state-owned electricity companies by governments, and bidding for long-term power supply contracts from governments which were opening the generating end of their electricity industries to competition. During the mid-1990s, AES's biggest new investments in power generation were in Kazakhstan and China. The 1996 acquisition of Light Servicios de Electricidade, Brazil, was a major strategic departure for AES: this was its first entry into the distribution end of the power business. Overseas expansion was primarily through the acquisition of existing power-generating facilities rather than building new plants. A similar transition was occurring in the US. Changes in utility regulations at the state level resulted in some utilities selling off their generating facilities – AES was among the most prominent bidders for these facilities.

Between 1998 and 2001, AES continued to expand rapidly both at home and overseas.

- In 1998, AES acquired or built 34 plants, including major facilities in Bangladesh, India, Mexico, California, and New York, and bought electricity distribution companies in Buenos Aires, Georgia, and Sao Paulo.
- In 1999, AES acquired its first US utility, Cilcorp, hydroelectric generating facilities in Brazil, and DRAX, one of the world's largest coal-fired power plants, located in England.
- In 2000, AES acquired a major Venezuelan utility as well as plants in Chile and Colombia.
- In 2001, AES continued its expansion into large utilities with the acquisition of PALCO. In addition, AES expanded into the Ukraine and Cameroon.

Tables 17.1 and 17.2 show AES's plants and distribution facilities at the end of 2001.

The result of the years of expansion was not only a substantial growth in the size of AES between 1998 and 2001, but also increasing complexity of the business as AES

Table 17.1   AES's generating plants, December 2001

	Fuel	Year of acquisition or start-up	Location	Gross MW	AES equity interest (%)
Contract generation facilities					
North America					
Kingston	Gas	1997	Canada	110	50
Beaver Valley	Coal	1987	USA	125	100
Thames	Coal	1990	USA	181	100
Shady Point	Coal	1991	USA	320	100
Hawaii	Coal	1992	USA	180	100
Southland-Alamitos	Gas	1998	USA	2,083	100
Southland-Huntington Beach	Gas	1998	USA	563	100
Southland-Redondo Beach	Gas	1998	USA	1,310	100
Warrior Run	Coal	2000	USA	180	100
Ironwood	Gas	2001	USA	705	100
Red Oak	Gas	2002	USA	832	100
South America					
Tiete (10 plants)	Hydro	1999	Brazil	2,650	53
Gener-Termoandes	Gas	2000	Argentina	633	99
Uruguaiana	Gas	2000	Brazil	450	100
Uruguaiana	Gas	2000	Brazil	150	100
GENER-Norgener	Oil	2000	Chile	277	99
GENER-Centrogener (9 plants)	Hydro	2000	Chile	756	99
GENER-Electrica de Santiago	Gas	2000	Chile	379	89
GENER-Guacolda	Coal	2000	Chile	304	49
Europe/Africa					
Kilroot	Coal	1992	UK	520	92
Medway	Gas	1996	UK	688	25
Tisza II	Gas	1996	Hungary	860	100
Elsta	Gas	1998	Netherlands	405	50
Ebute	Gas	2001	Nigeria	290	95
Kelvin	Coal	2001	South Africa	600	100
Asia					
Khrami I	Hydro	2000	Georgia	113	0
Khrami II	Hydro	2000	Georgia	110	0
Mktvari	Gas	2000	Georgia	600	100
Wuhu	Coal	1996	China	250	25
Hefei	Oil	1997	China	115	70
Jiaozuo	Coal	1997	China	250	70
Yangcheng (3 plants)	Coal	2001	China	1,050	25
OPGC	Coal	1998	India	420	49
Lal Pir	Oil	1997	Pakistan	351	90
PakGen	Oil	1998	Pakistan	344	90
Meghnaghat	Gas	2002	Bangladesh	450	100
Barka	Gas	2003	Oman	427	85
Ras Laffan	Gas	2004	Qatar	750	55

Table 17.1 *continued*

	Fuel	Year of acquisition or start-up	Location	Gross MW	AES equity interest (%)
Kelanitissa	Gas	2002	Sri Lanka	165	100
Mt. Stuart	Oil	1999	Australia	288	100
Ecogen-Jeeralang	Gas	1999	Australia	449	100
Ecogen-Yarra	Gas	1999	Australia	510	100
Haripur	Gas	2001	Bangladesh	360	100
Caribbean					
Mirada III	Gas	2000	Mexico	484	55
Puerto Rico	Coal	2002	USA	454	100
Itabo	Gas	2000	Dominican Republic	587	24
Los Mina	Oil	1996	Dominican Republic	210	100
Andres	Gas	2003	Dominican Republic	310	100

Competitive supply facilities

North America

	Fuel	Year	Location	Gross MW	AES %
Deepwater	Coal	1986	USA	143	100
Placerita	Gas	1989	USA	120	100
NY-Cayuga	Coal	1999	USA	306	100
NY-Greenidge	Coal	1999	USA	161	100
NY-Somerset	Coal	1999	USA	675	100
NY-Westover	Coal	1999	USA	126	100
Mountainview Existing	Gas	2001	USA	126	100
Huntington Beach 3&4	Gas	2002	USA	450	100
Granite Ridge	Gas	2002	USA	720	100
Greystone	Gas	2002	USA	500	100
Wolf Hollow	Gas	2002	USA	720	100
Lake Worth	Gas	2003	USA	210	100
Mountainview Development	Gas	2003	USA		

South America

	Fuel	Year	Location	Gross MW	AES %
San Nicolás-CTSN	Coal	1993	Argentina	650	88
Rio Juramento-Cabra Corall	Hydro	1995	Argentina	102	98
Alicura	Hydro	2000	Argentina	1,000	100
Parana	Gas	2001	Argentina	845	100
Caracoles	Hydro	2004	Argentina	123	100

Europe/Africa

	Fuel	Year	Location	Gross MW	AES %
Borsod	Coal	1996	Hungary	171	100
Tiszapalkonya	Coal	1996	Hungary	250	100
Ottana	Oil	2001	Italy	140	100
Belfast West	Coal	1992	UK	120	98
Indian Queens	Gas	1996	UK	140	100
Barry	Gas	1998	UK	230	100
Drax	Coal	1999	UK	4,065	100

Table 17.1 *continued*

	Fuel	Year of acquisition or start-up	Location	Gross MW	AES equity interest (%)
Fifoots	Coal	2000	UK	360	100
Songo Songo	Gas	2003	Tanzania	112	49
SONEL	Hydro	2001	Cameroon	800	51
Asia					
Ekibastuz Gres	Coal	1996	Kazakhstan	4,000	100
Altai-Leninogorsk CHP	Coal	1997	Kazakhstan	418	100
Altai-Semipalatinsk CHP	Coal	1997	Kazakhstan	840	100
Altai-Shulbinsk Hydro	Hydro	1997	Kazakhstan	702	100
Altai-Sogrinsk CHP	Coal	1997	Kazakhstan	349	100
Altai-Ust Kamenogorsk Heat Nets	Coal	1997	Kazakhstan	310	0
Altai-Ust-Kamenogorsk CHP	Coal	1997	Kazakhstan	1,464	100
Altai-Ust-Kamenogorsk Hydro	Hydro	1997	Kazakhstan	331	100
Caribbean					
Bayano	Hydro	1999	Panama	150	49
Bayano	Hydro	2003	Panama	110	49
Esti	Hydro	2003	Panama	120	49
Chivor	Hydro	2000	Colombia	1,000	96
Colombia I	Gas	2000	Colombia	90	62
Large utilities					
North America					
CILCORP-Duck Creek	Coal	1999	USA	366	100
CILCORP-Edwards	Coal	1999	USA	772	100
CILCORP-Indian Trails	Gas	1999	USA	19	100
IPALCO-Georgetown	Oil	2001	USA	79	100
IPALCO-Eagle Valley	Coal	2001	USA	341	100
IPALCO-Petersburg	Coal	2001	USA	1,672	100
IPALCO-Stout	Coal	2001	USA	944	100
South America					
Light-Fontes Nova	Hydro	1996	Brazil	144	24
Light-Ilha dos Pombos	Hydro	1996	Brazil	169	24
Light-Nilo Pecanha	Hydro	1996	Brazil	380	24
Light-Pereira Passos	Hydro	1996	Brazil	100	24
CEMIG (35 plants)	Hydro	1997	Brazil	5,068	21
CEMIG-Miranda	Hydro	1997	Brazil	390	21
CEMIG-Igarapava	Hydro	1998	Brazil	210	21
Caribbean					
EDC-generation (4 plants)	Gas	2000	Venezuela	2,265	87

Source: AES, 10K report, 2001.

Table 17.2 AES's electricity distribution businesses, December 2001

Distribution facilities	Year acquired	Location	Number of customers served	Gigawatt hours	AES equity interest (%)
Asia					
Eastern Kazakhstan REC	1999	Kazakhstan	291,000	1,455	0
Semipalatensk REC	1999	Kazakhstan	178,513	1,117	0
Telasi	1998	Georgia	370,000	2,200	75
Kievoblenergo	2001	Ukraine	763,000	3,840	75
Rivnooblenergo	2001	Ukraine	383,000	1,700	75
Cesco	1999	India	600,000	2,102	48
North America					
IPALCO	2000	USA	433,010	16,256	100
Cilcorp-Electricity	1999	USA	193,000	6,743	100
South America					
Light	1996	Brazil	2,800,000	19,981	24
CEMIG	1997	Brazil	4,680,000	32,179	21
Eletropaulo	1998	Brazil	4,657,306	34,789	50
Sul	1997	Brazil	935,125	7,390	96
Eden	1997	Argentina	278,854	1,886	90
Edes	1997	Argentina	141,281	834	90
Edelap	1998	Argentina	279,568	2,102	90
Caribbean					
EDC-distribution	2000	Venezuela	1,131,552	9,724	87
CLESA	1998	El Salvador	226,000	669	64
EDE Este	1999	Dominican Republic	350,000	2,990	51
CAESS	2000	El Salvador	443,430	1,697	70
DEUSEM	2000	El Salvador	43,362	75	69
EEO	2000	El Salvador	162,496	339	83
Europe/Africa					
SONEL	2001	Cameroon	452,000	3,020	51

Source: AES, 10K report, 2001.

diversified its activities within the power sector. During 2001, AES recognized four lines of business activity:

- *Contract generation.* AES's traditional business was producing electricity supplied on long-term contracts (5 to 30 years) to distribution companies. By

Table 17.3 Revenues and gross profit by line of business, 2000 and 2001

	Revenue ($ billion)		Gross profit ($ billion)	
	2001	2000	2001	2000
Contract generation	2.5	1.7	0.83	0.77
Competitive supply	2.7	2.4	0.44	0.56
Large utilities	2.4	2.1	0.74	0.54
Growth distribution	1.7	1.3	0.30	0.13

Source: AES, 10K report, 2001.

matching the electricity supply contracts with long-term fuel purchase contracts, AES fixes its gross margin.

- *Competitive supply.* As electricity markets have become increasingly deregulated, so AES has expanded its involvement in such markets. AES's competitive supply line of business comprises generating facilities and retail supply businesses that sell electricity directly to wholesale and retail customers in competitive markets. These generating facilities sell a major part of their output into power pools, into daily spot markets, or on short-term contracts. The prices paid for these competitive supplies can be unpredictable and volatile.
- *Large utilities.* During the late 1990s, AES began acquiring large electrical utilities – regulated monopolies supplying electricity within specific geographical areas. At the end of 2001, AES owned five integrated utilities: two in the US, two in Brazil, and one in Venezuela. These utilities combine generation, transmission and distribution capabilities.
- *Growth distribution.* AES splits into a separate line of business distribution facilities that offer significant potential for growth because they are located in developing countries or regions where the demand for electricity is expected to grow at a higher rate than in more developed areas. As well as offering considerable opportunity, these businesses also present special challenges with regard to political risk, outdated equipment, non-technical losses (e.g. theft), safety, and non-payment. "Growth distribution" businesses include those in Argentina, Brazil, Cameroon, Dominican Republic, El Salvador, Georgia, Kazakhstan and Ukraine.

Table 17.3 shows revenues and gross profit earned by AES's four lines of business.

■ PERFORMANCE ■

AES's financial and operating performance during the 1990s placed the company among the top-performing firms of the decade, not only in its sector, but across the stock market as a whole. As a result, AES has been prominent among *Fortune* and

Washington Post lists of companies with fastest growing and best returns to share-holders. In the three years to April 1998, returns to shareholders averaged 80 percent a year.

This performance amazed many observers, since not only is electricity generation far from being a glamor industry, but profitability and shareholder returns are not the primary yardsticks through which AES monitors and assesses its own performance. AES's assessment of its progress over time focuses on four measures:

- *Shared values* – How did we do in having an organization that is fun, that is fair, that acts with integrity, and that is socially responsible?
- *Plant operations* – How safe, clean, reliable, and cost-effective were our facilities?
- *Assets* – What changes occurred in our assets, including AES people, during the year? This intends to measure the company's project development and construction progress as an indicator of future earnings potential.
- Sales backlog – What happened to our backlog of contract revenues during the year?

In terms of setting performance targets for the future, these tend to be a mixture of efficiency, employee satisfaction, community development, project development, and growth objectives. For example, AES's goals for 1998 were stated in "Our Wish List" published in the 1997 Annual Report. These included:

- Continuing progress in adapting to and living the AES principles and values
- Creating the most fun workplace since the beginning of the industrial revolution, and eliminating hourly payment systems
- Adding 10 to 15 new businesses to the AES portfolio
- Engineering a breakthrough in slow development businesses such as Ib Valley (India), Puerto Rico, and Nile Power (Uganda)
- Maintaining 100 new business ideas in the development pipeline
- Making our 1998 budgeted net income and cash flow

Operationally, AES plants have performed among the best in their industry. AES's US plants typically operate at around 95 percent capacity, compared to an industry average of 83 percent. Nor is operational excellence restricted to new plants. AES's West Belfast power station has achieved 95 percent availability in some years, remarkable for a 43-year-old facility.

Despite a history of growth, profitability, and operational excellence, AES is no stranger to crisis and its efforts have not always been successful. As already noted, its first power station was unprofitable from the start. In 1992, AES flirted with disaster when its Shady Point generating facility in Oklahoma was discovered to have been dis-charging polluted water and to have falsified the samples it provided to the Environ-mental Protection Agency. In the same year, AES was forced to abandon its rebuilding of a power plant at Cedar Bay, Florida following a dispute with state officials and the local community. These events caused AES's share price to fall by half.[4] Several of AES's acquisitions have proven disappointing: the 1997 acquisition of Destec's international

Table 17.4 AES's performance, 1991–2001

	2001	2000	1999	1998	1997	1996	1995	1994	1993	1992	1991
Revenue ($ million)	9,327	7,534	4,117	3,257	2,227	835	679	533	519	401	334
Sales backlog ($ billion)	n.a.	217	138	116	98	51	41	43	27	29	n.a.
Net income ($ million)	273	795	357	441	299	125	107	98	71	56	43
Earnings per share ($)	0.52	1.66	0.84	1.11	0.79	0.40	0.35	0.33	0.25	0.20	0.16
Total assets ($ billion)	36.7	33.0	23.2	12.9	11.1	3.6	2.3	1.9	1.7	1.6	1.4
Long-term debt:											
Non-recourse ($ billion)	14.7	12.7	9.5	4.5	4.5	1.6	1.1	1.0	1.1	1.1	n.a.
Recourse ($ billion)	4.9	3.5	2.2	1.6	1.1	0.5	0.1	0.1	0.1	0.1	n.a.
Stockholders' equity ($ billion)	5.5	5.5	3.3	2.4	2.0	0.7	0.6	0.4	0.3	0.2	n.a.
Equity generating capacity (thousands of MW)	50.8	n.a.	n.a.	n.a.	4.6	3.4	2.1	1.5	1.5	1.2	0.7
Return on average equity (%)	4.9	17.9	12.6	20.2	17.1	19.7	22.6	28.3	29.2	35.1	48.6

Sources: Annual Reports, UBS Securities Equity Research.

generation resulted in poor returns, while AES acknowledged that its venture in Ukraine had been an expensive error.

However, these problems had a limited impact on AES's financial performance; the problems that AES encountered during 2001 had a bigger impact. During 2001, revenues grew by a healthy 24 percent, mostly from acquiring new businesses and adding new plants. Revenue from existing operations grew by a more modest 5 percent. Net income fell sharply from $795 million in 2000 to $273 million in 2001 as a result of lower market prices in the UK, decline in the Brazilian Real resulting in currency transaction losses of $210 million, losses from closed telecom activities of $194 million, and higher sales, general and administrative expenses.

Table 17.4 summarizes some key indicators of AES's performance during 1991–2001.

■ STRATEGY ■

AES described itself as: "a global power company committed to serving the world's needs for electricity in a socially responsible way."[5] It describes its strategy as:

- Supplying energy to customers at the lowest cost possible, taking into account factors such as reliability and environmental performance;
- Constructing, acquiring, and operating projects of a relatively large size in geographically dispersed markets;
- To the extent available, maximizing the amount of non-recourse financing;
- When available, entering into longer term power sales contracts or other arrangements with electric utilities or other customers with significant credit strength;
- Where possible, participating in distribution markets that grant concessions with long-term pricing arrangements; and
- When available, entering into hedging, indexing, or other arrangements to protect against fluctuations in currency, fuel costs and electricity prices.

The Company also strives for operating excellence as a key element of its strategy, which it believes it accomplishes by minimizing organizational layers and maximizing company-wide participation in decision making. AES has attempted to create an operating environment that results in safe, clean and reliable electricity generation, distribution and supply. Because of this emphasis, the Company prefers to operate all facilities and businesses which it develops or acquires; however, there can be no assurance that the Company will have operating control of all of its facilities.

The Company attempts to finance each domestic and foreign project primarily under loan agreements and related documents which, except as noted below, require the loans to be repaid solely from the project's revenues and provide that the repayment of the loans (and interest thereon) is secured solely by the capital stock, physical assets, contracts and cash flow of that project subsidiary or affiliate. This type of financing is usually referred to as non-recourse debt or project financing . . .[6]

■ VALUES AND PRINCIPLES ■

AES's unique organization and management systems are the direct result of the values upon which the company was established and continue to define every aspect of its management. These values reflect the personal beliefs of the two founders, Sant and Bakke. Both men were brought up in strongly religious families: Bakke as a Baptist, Sant a Mormon. Bakke was raised on a farm in Washington State. From the age of five he had worked in the fields and by the time he was 18 he had built up a herd of 29 beef cattle. Bakke's attitude to enterprise and material possessions was strongly influenced by ideas of Christian stewardship, which emphasized responsibility, building for the future, and sharing good fortune with others. Sant attended Brigham Young University and spent two years as a missionary with Native Americans in Wisconsin. Over time, Sant became less committed to the church and increasingly active in the environmental movement.

From the outset, both men viewed AES as an opportunity for them to pursue their values and effect a fundamental change in business practices. In a section of its 10K report entitled "Principles, Values and Practices," AES states:

> A core part of AES's corporate culture is a commitment to "shared principles or values." These principles describe how AES people endeavor to commit themselves to the Company's mission of serving the world by providing safe, clean, reliable and low-cost electricity. The principles are:
>
> - *Integrity* – AES strives to act with integrity, or "wholeness." AES people seek to keep the same moral code at work as at home.
> - *Fairness* – AES wants to treat fairly its people, its customers, its suppliers, its stockholders, governments and the communities in which it operates.
> - *Fun* – AES desires that people employed by the Company and those people with whom the Company interacts have fun in their work. The Company believes that making decisions and being accountable is fun and has structured its organization to maximize the opportunity for fun for as many people as possible.
> - *Social Responsibility* – Primarily, the Company believes that doing a good job at fulfilling its mission is socially responsible. But the Company also believes that it has a responsibility to be involved in projects that provide other social benefits, and consequently has instituted programs such as corporate matching of individual charitable gifts in addition to various local programs conducted by AES businesses.
>
> AES recognizes that most companies have standards and ethics by which they operate and that business decisions are based, at least in part, on such principles. The Company believes that an explicit commitment to a particular set of standards is a useful way to encourage ownership of those values among its people. While the people at AES acknowledge that they won't always live up to these standards, they believe that being held accountable to these shared values will help them behave more consistently with such principles.
>
> AES makes an effort to support these principles in ways that acknowledge a strong corporate commitment and encourage people to act accordingly. For example, AES conducts annual surveys, both company-wide and at each business location, designed to measure how well its people are doing in supporting these principles through interactions within the Company and with people outside the Company. These surveys are perhaps most useful in revealing failures, and helping to deal with those failures. AES's principles are relevant because they help explain how AES people approach the Company's business. The Company seeks to adhere to these principles, not as a means to achieve economic success but because adherence is a worthwhile goal in and of itself.[7]

Sant and Bakke recognize that these values cannot easily be reconciled with the concept of a shareholder-focused, profit-maximizing corporation, and both leaders have made it very clear where their priorities lie:

> Where do profits fit? Profits . . . are not any corporation's main goal. Profits are to a corporation much like breathing is to life. Breathing is not the goal, but without breath, life ends. Similarly, without turning a profit, a corporation too, will cease to exist . . . At AES we strive not to make profits the ultimate driver of the corporation. My desire is that the principles to which we strive would take preeminence.[8]

AES's commitment to its values, at the expense of shareholder gain where necessary, is indicated by the proviso which AES inserts in all of its prospectuses for new security offers which identifies AES's values as a source of investor risk:

> The Company seeks to adhere to these principles, not as a means to achieve economic success, but because adherence is a worthwhile goal in and of itself. However, if the Company perceives a conflict between these principles and profits, the Company will try to adhere to its principles – even though doing so might result in dominated or forgone opportunities or financial benefits.[9]

The AES principles and the way they are implemented reflect a set of assumptions about human nature. Sant and Bakke believe in the ultimate goodness of people – "Man is made in the image of God," declared Bakke.[10] Hence, within organizations, people can and should be trusted to exercise responsibility, and at the same time should be held accountable. Critical to the ability to motivate people is the innate desire of people to make a contribution to society. This implies that, for an organization to be effective and to harness human effort and ingenuity, the organization must be committed to a wider social purpose. These views are at variance with many of the assumptions upon which many traditional management systems and techniques are based and imply a different approach: "[t]he people in AES are not principally economic resources. We are not tools of the corporation. Rather we hope the corporation is structured to help individuals make a difference in the world that they could not otherwise make."[11] AES's annual employee surveys are an indicator of the importance which is accorded to the company's principles and values. Dennis Bakke has commented that he devotes more attention to studying the annual employee surveys than the annual financial statements.

■ ORGANIZATIONAL STRUCTURE AND MANAGEMENT SYSTEMS ■

AES's organizational structure and management systems manifest the company's values and principles. AES describes the key features of its organization in its statement of values:

> In order to create a fun working environment for its people and implement its strategy of operational excellence, AES has adopted decentralized organizational principles and practices. For example, AES works to minimize the number of supervisory layers in its organization. Most of the Company's plants operate without shift supervisors.
>
> The project subsidiaries are responsible for all major facility-specific business functions, including financing and capital expenditures. Criteria for hiring new AES people include a person's willingness to accept responsibility and AES's principles as well as a person's experience and expertise. Every AES person has been encouraged to participate in strategic planning and new plant design for the Company. The Company has generally organized itself into multi-skilled teams to develop projects, rather than forming "staff" groups (such as a human resources department or an engineering staff) to carry out specialized functions.

Many people have asked us about our team structure and how it works. To begin with, there is no one person in charge of teams and there is no Human Resources department. Teams are the basis of our structure, and they encompass the four values of our company. They are fluid; many people are members of more than one team at one time. A team is somewhat autonomous; all decisions about a project are made within that team, with final say granted to that team. Decisions are made not from the top-down, but from the bottom-up. Furthermore, responsibility is pushed to the lowest level possible, encouraging everyone to be part of a decision. As a result, each team member views the project in terms of a whole. Colleagues and team members must trust each other to follow through to the best of their ability.

Because people are what make up AES, we have decided not to resort to an organizational model. Instead, we give you the following comments from AES people regarding teamwork. In general, AES teams work extremely well in both achieving a common goal and having fun while doing so. The following ideas provide insight on what makes teams work well and what can stimulate true and productive teamwork.

"Teams imply friendship; not only the ability but the desire to work together. Starting with the wonderful example set by the original AES team, Roger and Dennis, working together in small groups has been a natural way to get big things done while preserving the dignity of each person." *Tom Tribone.*

"There are two reasons why teams are successful at AES: the type of people we have here and the environment in which they work. People at AES tend to be independent and thrive in a loose environment where roles and responsibilities are not always clearly defined. The environment at AES is one where responsibility is pushed down to the lowest level possible, encouraging everyone to take ownership for not only their piece of the project, but for the project in its entirety." *Michael Cranna.*[12]

This is not to say that AES lacks formal structure altogether. The most striking feature of its organization is the few layers of hierarchy: until recently there were only three organizational layers between the front-line employees and the CEO. AES is divided into regional organizations or "groups." These groups comprise the different plants, each of which is headed by a plant manager. Within each plant there are typically seven areas or "families," each of which is headed by a superintendent.

Figure 17.1 shows AES's formal structure at the beginning of 2002.

No Functional Departments

The company does not have a legal, human resources, or any other department. Decisions in such matters are made by teams at the plant level, which oftentimes have little or no experience in those decision areas. A few years ago, CFO Barry Sharp estimated that the company had raised $3.5 billion to finance ten new power plants. But, he added, he was personally responsible for raising only $300 million of that sum. The rest was secured by decentralized, empowered teams. When AES raised 200 million pounds sterling (about $350 million) to finance a joint venture in Northern Ireland, two control room operators led the team that raised the funds.[13] The same goes for other areas of financial management. Treasury operations are decentralized to the individual plant level, where they are performed by teams of non-specialists:

```
┌─────────────────────────────┐
│      BOARD OF DIRECTORS      │
│          Chairman            │
│        (Roger Sant)          │
└─────────────────────────────┘
```

```
┌──────────────────────────────────────────────────────────────────────────────┐
│                          EXECUTIVE COMMITTEE                                    │
│                                 CEO                                             │
│                           (Dennis Bakke)                                        │
│ COO                COO                  COO                  COO                 │
│ Growth &           Contract Generation  Competitive Supply   Large Utilities    │
│ Distribution Business                                                           │
│ (Paul Hanrahan)    (John Ruggirello)    (Stuart Ryan)        (Barry Sharp)      │
└──────────────────────────────────────────────────────────────────────────────┘
```

```
┌──────────────────────────────────────────────────────────────────────────────┐
│                          CORPORATE OFFICERS                                     │
│ General Counsel  SVP & CFO    SVP, Investor Relations    SVP, Financial         │
│                               and Business Development    Forecasting and        │
│ (William Lurashi)  (Barry Sharp)                          Corporate Issues       │
│                               (Kenneth Woodcock)          (Roger Naill)          │
└──────────────────────────────────────────────────────────────────────────────┘
```

```
┌──────────────────────────────────────────────────────────────────────────────┐
│                          OPERATING DIVISIONS                                    │
│ AES Americas (Brazil, Venezuela)       AES Horizons (Ireland, Low Countries,    │
│ (Paul Hanrahan)                        Scandinavia, Baltic States) (Ann Murthow)│
│ AES Andes (Argentina, Chile)           AES Oasis (Middle East, South Asia)      │
│ (Joe Brandt)                           (Shahzad Qasim)                          │
│ AES Aurora (Mexico, Central America,   AES Orient (China)                       │
│ Caribbean) (Sarah Susser)              (Bill Rucius)                            │
│ AES Coral (Panama, El Salvador)        AES Pacific (Southern California)        │
│ (Ned Hall)                             (Mark Woodruff)                          │
│ AES Electric (England, Wales, France,  AES Sao Paulo (Brazil)                   │
│ Italy) (Michael Armstrong)             (Luiz Travesso)                          │
│ AES Endeavor (N.E. USA, E. Canada)     AES Sirocco (Balkans, Turkey, North      │
│ (Dan Rothaupt)                         Africa) (Mike Scholey)                   │
│ AES Enterprise (Mid-Atlantic USA)      AES Silk Road (former Soviet Union)      │
│ (Dan Rothaupt)                         (Garry Levesley)                         │
│ AES Great Plains (USA Midwest)         AES Transpower (Australia, N. Zealand,   │
│ (Lenny Lee)                            S.E. Asia) (Haresh Jaisinghani)          │
│                                        Think AES (retail and telecom)           │
│                                        (Tom Tribone)                            │
└──────────────────────────────────────────────────────────────────────────────┘
```

Figure 17.1 AES's company structure
Source: AES, 10K report, 2001.

His hands still blackened from coal he has just unloaded from a barge, Jeff Hatch picks up the phone and calls his favorite broker. "What kind of rate can you give me for $10 million at 30 days?" he asks the agent, who handles Treasury bills. "Only 6.09? But I just got a 6.13 quote from Chase."

In another room, Joe Oddo is working on J. P. Morgan & Co. "6.15 at 30 days?" confirms Oddo, a maintenance technician at AES Corp.'s power plant here. "I'll get right back to you."

Members of an ad hoc team that manage a $33 million plant investment fund, Messrs. Oddo and Hatch quickly confer with their associates, then close the deal. "It's like playing Monopoly," Mr. Oddo says as he heads off to fix a leaky valve in the boiler room, "Only the money's real."[14]

Similarly, there is no human resources department. At the corporate level there are no staff specialists dealing with salary ranges, or annual review procedures, or personnel policies, or contract negotiations with unions. There is a person whose responsibility is to track 401k retirement plan benefits and send out the necessary reports, but that's about it at the corporate level. Everything else is devolved to the individual divisions, and within these it is the teams within each plant that handle almost all the human resource functions.

The company operates without any written policies or procedures. Issues such as hiring practices, leave periods, and promotion criteria, which in more conventional companies would be spelled out in a "Policies and Procedures" handbook, are left at the employees' discretion. When trying to find out how much time she could take off after the birth of her daughter, a Project Director for AES Puerto Rico discovered that the company did not have a policy about maternity leave. After investigating what other "AES people" had done, she decided to do what made sense for both herself and the business requirements of the project. In the end she decided to take three months, but she made herself available at critical points in the project's execution.[15]

Virtually all human resource decisions are made at plant level, and, within the plant, decision-making authority is among the different teams. For example:

- *Recruiting.* The recruiting process is done at the plant level, without any support or guidelines from corporate headquarters. AES people at all levels are committed to the hiring process, and everyone can participate in it. The process generally involves an initial résumé review, and a phone interview followed by a group interview. Interviews usually do not include technical questions. Instead, they focus on characteristics that help determine how the candidate will fit with the company's culture and values. There is little importance given to the candidates' educational background or experience, as greater emphasis is placed on the candidates' desire to learn, contribute, and grow, as well as their personal values and self-motivation.
- *Training and development.* In line with corporate values, AES employees are empowered to make decisions about their own development. Training is mostly done on-the-job, through open communication channels and embedded advice-seeking practices. However, AES people are free to take outside classes and they are reimbursed for them, as long as the courses are work-related.
- *Career paths.* Regarding development, there are no established career paths. Rather, the company encourages flexibility, which is a necessary requirement in such a dynamic industry. Because one of the company's shared values is to "have fun," employees are encouraged to move within the company if they feel their current assignment is "boring." Job vacancies are always posted and promotion decisions are made at an area superintendent's meeting.
- *Compensation and benefits.* AES does not have a set salary schedule for any given job, and salaries are determined based on what others are being paid inside and outside the company. Raises are given every year and superintendents usually determine them in an annual meeting. Most AES people put their retirement savings in company stock, and the company matches up to 5 percent of the person's salary in the retirement plan.

This emphasis on multi-functionalism is central to AES's concept of making work fun. The key is to make people's work fulfilling by continually providing challenge and learning experiences. Moreover, argues Bakke, specialization does not promote efficiency or better decision making: "As soon as you have a specialist who's very good, then everyone else quits thinking," Bakke says. "The better that person is, the worse it is for the organization. The information goes through the specialist, so all the education is to the person who knows the most."[16]

Moreover, AES relies heavily on outside expertise. A key aspect of the system of empowerment is that individuals and teams are encouraged to seek out the best advice available, whether it is within the company or outside. In relation to finance, while AES's financial management and project management teams lack great depth in financial expertise, they draw upon the knowledge of bankers and financiers. In any event, Bakke's view is that most management expertise, whether functionally specialized or general management skill, is not inherently difficult. Motivation, attitude, and a willingness to learn are more important determinants of ultimate performance.

The "Honeycomb"

AES refers to its organizational structure as a "honeycomb." The idea is that each plant comprises a number of small, flexible, self-managed teams who are able to operate cooperatively and efficiently without any centralized direction. At the basis of this structure is the belief that organizations do not need to be managed. Thinking, motivated people can manage themselves and undertake the communication and mutual adjustment needed to coordinate complex tasks. According to Dennis Bakke, the key to effective decentralization is keeping the basic units of organization small:

> I think of AES as a conglomeration of small communities. And I don't think there's any company in the world that's so big that you can't organize this way. Even a plant with 400 people can be broken down into smaller groups. It's a small enough community that there is the ability to have an accountability structure within it, you know, a social structure as opposed to a military structure. We will break down the Kazakhstan plant into four units. How can we stay small and be big? By breaking the organization into groups with chief operating officers.[17]

The principle of self-organization imposes a very different role on managers from the conventional management model. Indeed, the term "manager" is seldom heard within AES; it is at odds with the principle of letting people decide for themselves. The example comes from the top. "The most difficult thing for me as CEO," confided Bakke, "is not to make decisions." If individuals are to develop, they must be given responsibility and allowed to learn:

> [T]he modern manager is supposed to ask his people for advice and then make a decision. But at AES, each decision is made by a person and a team. Their job is to get advice from me and from anybody else they think it's necessary to get advice from. And then they make the decision. We do that even with the budget. We make very few decisions here [indicating the headquarters office]. We affirm decisions.[18]

Sant has made similar observations:

> If Dennis and I had to lead everything, we couldn't have grown as much as we have. People would bring deals for us to approve, and we would have a huge bottleneck. We've shifted to giving advice rather than giving approval. And we've moved ahead much faster than we would have otherwise."[19]

One consequence of this approach is the small size of AES's corporate headquarters. At any point in time there may be between 40 and 70 AES employees at the Arlington office, but in terms of actual corporate staff, these number only about 35.

In terms of performance, one of the most important advantages of the AES system is that it permits speed in decision making, preparing bids, and completing projects. AES abounds with a folk history of teams and individuals given huge responsibilities or thrust into unique and unexpected situations. Consider the following:

- Oscar Prieto, a chemical engineer with two years' experience with AES, was visiting AES headquarters in May 1996 when he was asked by Thomas Tribone to join a meeting: "I've got 14 people from France and some guys from Houston coming to talk about buying a business in Rio de Janeiro. We've only got two AES people. Could one of you show up?" The meeting with Electricité de France and Houston Light & Power concerned a possible joint bid for one of Brazil's largest utilities, which was being privatized. Within a month, Tribone was on his way to Paris to negotiate an agreement with Electricité de France. The deal was concluded, and by 1997 Tribone had moved to Rio to become one of the utility's four directors and a key player in a succession of deals in which AES acquired a string of power plants and distribution facilities in Brazil and Argentina.

- The development of the $404 million Warrior Run power plant in Cumberland, Maryland was undertaken by an AES team of ten people who handled all the work necessary leading up to the plant's groundbreaking in October 1995. They secured 36 different permit approvals involving about 24 regulatory agencies and arranged financing that involved tax-exempt bonds and ten lenders. Within the industry, such a project would typically involve well over a hundred employees.

- Scott Gardner joined AES in 1992 right after graduating from Dartmouth College. Gardner joined a team developing a $200 million cogeneration plant in San Francisco. "It involved a lot of work and few people to do it," he says. "I took on tasks that ranged from designing a water system to negotiating with the community to buying and selling pollution credits." Gardner also helped lead a bid for a $225 million cogeneration plant in Vancouver, British Columbia. When a comparable deal emerged in Australia, Gardner volunteered for that assignment. Two weeks later, he was on his way to Brisbane. "My task was to understand an unfamiliar regional power system, develop a design for the plant, and prepare a financial and technical bid document – all in six weeks," he says. When Gardner's proposal made the final round of competition, his division manager had him negotiate the terms of the $75 million deal. "The stress was incredible, but I was having fun," he says. His bid won. "I held a press conference and was interviewed by local TV stations," says Gardner, who has since left AES to attend business school. "I had to pinch myself to be sure this was happening."[20]

- Paul Burdick, a mechanical engineer, had only been at AES briefly when he was asked to purchase $1 billion in coal. "I'd never negotiated anything before, save for a used car," he said. Burdick spent three weeks asking questions of people both within and outside of the company on how to accomplish the task. At AES, he says, "You're given a lot of leeway and a lot of rope. You can use it to climb or you can hang yourself."[21]

- Ann Murtlow, a chemical engineer with no experience in pollution abatement, was given the job of buying air-pollution credits. She had already purchased the option to buy $1 million in credits when she discovered that the option she had bought was for the wrong kind of credit and useless to AES.

The Relationship with Employees

The AES principles and its concept of the honeycomb organization imply a different type of relationship between those employed and the corporation than that which characterizes most companies. To begin with, the absence of functional specialists and the ideas about self-organization require a tremendous amount of information-sharing. According to the company, employees are given full access to the company's operating and financial information. Because of the extent of employee access to information that would normally be confidential at other companies, AES lists all its employees as "insiders" in its submissions to the SEC.

One of AES's current crusades is to eliminate the distinction between salaried and hourly paid employees and to put all employees on a salaried basis. The 1997 Annual Report stated the goal of eliminating hourly payment systems. By the end of 1998 considerable progress had been made with more than half of AES's US employees salaried – despite the restrictions imposed by Federal health and safety legislation which perpetuates staff/worker distinctions. The primacy that AES accords its "people," as the company refers to its employees, is emphasized by its practice of listing every employee's name in the back of the AES Annual Report. However, once AES's total employment passed the 6,000 mark, this was no longer feasible.

AES and the Environment

AES's deep commitment to the environment extends well beyond Chairman Sant's personal involvement in environmentalist issues and his active roles in the World Wide Fund for Nature and as a member of the Environmental Defense Fund. Because building and operating power plants is not one of the world's most environmentally friendly endeavors, AES tries to compensate for the emissions it generates. When the company constructed a coal-fired plant in Montville, Connecticut, it calculated that it would generate 15 million tons of carbon dioxide over its estimated life of 40 years. The company then captured national attention when it announced that it would plant 52 million trees in Guatemala to offset the Connecticut plant's carbon dioxide emissions. According to AES Executive Vice-President Robert F. Hemphill: "Making electric power historically has had a relatively high level of environmental assault. We are not planting trees as part of our strategy to make us a more valuable company, we're doing it because we think it's a responsible thing to do." AES's average company-wide emission levels are 40–60 percent of permitted rates. These actions are of course in line with one of the company's four core values: social responsibility.[22]

Emphasis on responsibility to the environment and to local communities is viewed as integral to the efficient running of power plants. Professor Jeff Pfeffer of Stanford Business School describes a visit to the Thames, Connecticut power plant:

> A visitor to the plant is immediately struck by its cleanliness, and the people who work in the plant are proud of its appearance. The walls of the plant exterior are very light colored (off-white), so that any dirt would be immediately visible. The color of the walls was intentionally chosen to encourage respect for the physical environment and cleanliness. The place where the coal is unloaded from the barges that bring it up the Connecticut River is also immaculate. The coal handling system is covered to avoid excess dust or debris getting into the surroundings and the loading dock and surrounding area is swept by a mechanical sweeper after the once a week delivery. There is no smell of sulfur in the air, and in fact, no odor at all. The attitude to cleanliness extends inside the plant as well. For example, there are two lunch rooms, both have stoves, microwave oven, cooktops, refrigerator, and dishwasher which makes them more than a typical plant eating area. Quite elaborate meals are cooked there. Both lunch rooms are clean with no dirty dishes sitting around. The cabinetry is of excellent quality and appearance as are the appliances. The turbine rooms are also immaculate.[23]

The Challenge of Multiculturalism

As more and more of AES's business becomes located outside the US, and non-US citizens far outnumber US citizens among AES's employees, an increasingly important challenge is to retain AES's culture as the company grows. The company acknowledges that even the stated value of having fun is difficult to accomplish with so many people with many different backgrounds. By the end of the 1990s, fewer than 8 percent of AES people were native English speakers. The principles of equality, teamwork, empowerment, and individual initiative are also likely to be more difficult to implement in traditional Islamic societies such as Pakistan, and countries with a socialist heritage such as China, Kazakhstan, Ukraine, and Georgia.

Nevertheless, AES remains committed to its principles not just for its US, but for its worldwide operations. Bakke firmly believes that the AES principles are universal and are not culturally specific either to the US or to the West in general. AES's experience so far is that its own corporate culture can be transplanted in many different national cultures. The challenges presented in running one of the world's biggest (and once one of the most dilapidated) coal-fired power stations in Kazakhstan, and turning around heavily bureaucratized, former state-owned utilities in South America have provided remarkable test-cases in AES's ability to export its company culture. The results have often been amazing. Even though AES has been unable to eliminate the distinction between salaried and hourly paid employees within the US, in England, Argentina, and Pakistan it has moved to an all-salary workforce.

Instilling the AES culture into the 100-year-old Light Servicios de Electricidade involved, first, a generous severance package to cut the workforce by half, second, the careful selection of young, motivated engineers and supervisors to take key positions as facility supervisors, and finally, the devolving of decision-making power to them. At Light's Santa Branca facility, Oscar Prieto chose Carlos Baldi, a 34-year-old engineer, to lead the plant. "I knew he was the right person," says Prieto, "He was young, eager to do more." After agreeing to shared goals and expectations – zero accidents, thrifty construction budgets – Prieto turned Santa Branca and a $35 million upgrading project over to Baldi. After a short while, Baldi was managing in the same way with his project and team leaders.[24]

■ 2002: RETRENCHMENT AND RESTRUCTURING ■

During the first quarter of 2002, CEO Dennis Bakke was forced to shift his attention from the issues that consumed his attention – AES's ability to maintain its values and live its principles – in order to address the fallout from Enron, Argentina, Venezuela, September 11, and the California power crisis that was increasingly dragging down AES. In a press statement released on February 20, AES announced a major shift of strategy. In the expectation that AES would be unable to access the capital markets in 2002 for additional parent capital, it would be forced to rely on its internally generated cash flows to fund operations and capital expenditures. The major retrenchment measures included:

- Reducing capital spending by $490 million in 2002 through eliminating or curtailing a number of construction projects.
- Selling existing businesses, including Cilcorp, its Illinois-based utility, a share of Ipalco, a utility in Indiana, and several overseas plants. Its biggest retrenchments were to be its withdrawal from its merchant generation businesses (under which AES sold electricity on to the spot markets in the UK, New York, and California) and a major pullback from Latin America.

However, several analysts were doubtful as to AES's ability to command a fair value for the assets it was putting up for sale. In a note to clients, Ronald Barone of UBS Warburg wrote: "The markets in which AES operates are depressed and there are a number of other companies that are already looking to dispose of similar assets."

Bakke recognized the extent of the company's strategic reorientation: he opened his conference call to analysts with the simple statement: "Our world has changed." In the accompanying press release he stated: "We are taking aggressive action to restructure and de-leverage AES. Given today's market climate we are going to rely on the cash flows of our solid operating businesses. We have taken additional steps to provide a more substantial liquidity cushion. We believe the actions we have announced will provide for a more conservative business model." His comments were echoed by

Chairman Sant: "The Board of Directors has unanimously approved this plan to de-leverage AES and position us for the future. The cutbacks in construction capital expenditures, the accelerated sale of businesses and selective project financings leave us stronger from a cash perspective with expected results in the short term. All of these steps are being taken in parallel with the cost-cutting efforts of AES businesses around the world. We believe these steps will leave us with a better-capitalized and stronger company with less earnings volatility. AES in the future will be less concentrated in Latin America and have greater emphasis on contract generation."[25]

To permit restructuring and cost reduction, organizational changes were also made. In addition to AES's regional organization through 17 groups that operated in different parts of the world, an executive office was created comprising Bakke as CEO together with four newly created chief operating officers – each with responsibility for one of AES's four lines of business. The reorganization was intended to: "enhance operating performance, including further reductions of operating costs and revenue enhancements . . . Each COO is directly responsible for managing a portion of the Company's geographically dispersed businesses as well as coordinating Company wide efforts associated with one of the Company's business segments. In addition, two special offices, the Cost Cutting Office and the Turnaround Office, have been created to bring improved focus and coordination to the management of expenses across the Company and to improve or dispose of businesses that AES believes to be under-performing businesses from a return on capital perspective, respectively. Each of these offices reports to the Executive Office."[26]

The Outlook

March 2002 was a hectic month for AES's senior managers. At home the Enron affair continued to drag in ever more companies from the US energy sector, while abroad troubles in Argentina, Venezuela, India, and Pakistan called for ongoing crisis management. As managers struggled to restore AES's financial strength and bolster confidence in the company's viability, some pondered the long-term implications of recent events for AES's longer term vision and identity.

Faced with threats to its very existence, AES's commitment to "integrity, fairness, fun, and social responsibility" had taken a back seat to the pressing needs for liquidity and investor confidence. Was this a temporary shift forced by temporary crisis, or was it part of the inevitable maturity of a young, idealistic company?

For those who, like Bakke and Sant, shared the vision of an alternative type of enterprise, the lessons of history were not encouraging. Many companies, from Kellogg & Company to Apple Computer, had been formed with a vision of redefining relationships between business and society, investors and employees, and workers and managers, yet almost all had evolved towards the dominant model of the shareholder-oriented capitalist corporation. Was it inevitable that growing organizational size and an increasingly competitive environment forced all organizations to renounce individuality and innovation in management ideas in favor of standard management principles?

Certainly, the business environment of 2002 was very different from that which had faced AES during the 1980s and 1990s. AES's ability to grow at so remarkable a rate was the result of specific circumstances: worldwide electricity generation was undergoing deregulation, privatization, and internationalization. By 2002, this process was largely completed. Indeed, in some countries (including the US) the momentum towards regulatory reform had halted – possibly even reversed. Meanwhile, competition was increasing on all sides and the business was becoming more complex. The simple model of producing electricity and selling it on long-term contracts to utilities and distributors was being superseded by more open competition involving competitive energy markets and more complex transactions (including spot and futures contracts, swaps, and an array of their energy derivative products). Among AES's competitors in these energy markets were major companies such as Shell, Exxon Mobil, Bechtel, and Eni who possessed not only massive financial resources, but an array of other resources and capabilities too, from political influence and hydrocarbon reserves to expertise in complex risk management techniques.

AES's unique organizational structure, management systems, and corporate culture had served it well. Although unorthodox, not only in the power industry, but in the corporate sector generally, the AES approach had shown itself to be highly effective both in the efficient operation of power stations and in supporting the entrepreneurial capabilities required for winning power supply contracts all over the world. Moreover, as an early mover in the international power business (it began operating plants overseas in 1992), AES has acquired a greater depth of experience in bidding for power contracts and operating power plants in more countries of the world than any other company. Moreover, because of its very low rate of employee turnover and open internal communication, it has been very effective in retaining this expertise and sharing it internally.

The long-term question facing Bakke and his senior management team was whether the combination of internal growth and external turbulence meant that the AES management philosophy had reached the limits of its effectiveness and henceforth AES would need to temper its enthusiasm for fun and social responsibility with more conventional management controls and greater responsiveness to Wall Street.

NOTES

1. "A power producer is intent on giving power to its people," *Wall Street Journal*, July 3, 1995, p. A1.
2. "Arlington's AES Corp. leads a battery of US energy companies overseas," *Washington Post*, May 22, 1995.
3. "The principles behind its power," *Washington Post*, November 2, 1998, p. F12.
4. An account of this period is found in *AES Honeycomb A* (Harvard Business School Case No. 9-395-132) and *AES Honeycomb B* (Harvard Business School Case No. 9-395-122).
5. AES Corporation, 10K submission to the Securities and Exchange Commission for 2001.
6. Ibid.
7. Ibid., p. 12.
8. Dennis W. Bakke, "Erecting a grid for ethical power," *The Marketplace*, May/June 1996, p. 5.
9. AES Corporation, 10K submission to the Securities and Exchange Commission for 2001.

10. Personal meeting, April 2000.
11. Dennis Bakke and Roger Sant, Annual Letter to Shareholders, *1997 AES Corporation Annual Report.*
12. AES Corporation, 10K submission to the Securities and Exchange Commission for 2001.
13. Alex Markels, "Power to people," *Fast Company*, 13 (March 1998), p. 155.
14. "A power producer is intent on giving power to its people," *Wall Street Journal*, July 3, 1995, p. A1.
15. Jeffrey Pfeffer, "Human resources at the AES Corporation: the case of the missing department," Graduate School of Business, Stanford University, 1997, p. 14.
16. "A power producer is intent on giving power to its people," *Wall Street Journal*, July 3, 1995, p. A1.
17. Jeffrey Pfeffer, "Human resources at the AES Corporation: the case of the missing department," Graduate School of Business, Stanford University, 1997, p. 14.
18. "The power of a team: Arlington's AES Corporation," *The Washington Post*, February 12, 1996, p. F12.
19. Alex Markels, "Power to people," *Fast Company*, 13 (March 1998), p. 160.
20. "The power of a team: Arlington's AES Corporation," *The Washington Post*, February 12, 1996, p. F12.
21. "A power producer is intent on giving power to its people," *Wall Street Journal*, July 3, 1995, p. A1.
22. "Power plant builder tries to reenergize environmental image," *The Washington Post*, July 6, 1992, p. F1.
23. Jeffrey Pfeffer, "Human resources at the AES Corporation: the case of the missing department," Graduate School of Business, Stanford University, 1997, pp. 6–7.
24. Alex Markels, "Power to people," *Fast Company*, 13 (March 1998), p. 164.
25. AES Corporation, Press Release February 19, 2002.
26. AES Corporation, 10K submission to the Securities and Exchange Commission for 2001, p. 3.